UNIVERSALISM NOT OF THE BIBLE:

BEING

AN EXAMINATION OF MORE THAN ONE HUNDRED AND TWENTY TEXTS OF SCRIPTURES, IN CONTROVERSY BETWEEN EVANGELICAL CHRISTIANS AND UNIVERSALISTS,

COMPRISING

A REFUTATION OF UNIVERSALIST THEOLOGY, AND AN EXPOSURE OF THE SOPHISTICAL ARGUMENTS AND OTHER MEANS BY WHICH IT IS PROPAGATED;

WITH A

GENERAL AND SCRIPTURE INDEX.

BY REV. N. D. GEORGE.

"Not walking in craftiness, nor handling the word of God deceitfully; but, by manifestation of the truth commending ourselves to every man's conscience in the sight of God."
PAUL.

NEW YORK:
FOR SALE BY CARLTON & PHILLIPS, 200 MULBERRY STREET.
BOSTON: JAMES P. MAGEE, 5 CORNHILL.
1856.

Geo. C. Rand & Avery, Printers, 3 Cornhill, Boston.

CONTENTS.

PART I.

PART II.

PREFACE.

THIS book is designed to expose the errors of Universalism and to aid the inquirer after truth. Does the reader desire to find a passage of scripture connected with this subject? let him turn to the "Scripture Index," and he is pointed to the page where the passage is explained. Does he wish to find an argument or a fact stated? he has only to turn to the "General Index," and he is directed to the place. It is not pretended, however, that every text or argument which may be used at times to teach Universalism, is examined in this work. But it will be admitted by Universalists themselves, that if their doctrine is not contained in these texts which are examined, it is not found in the Bible. I have endeavored to attend to all those upon which they rely with the greatest confidence, and conclude that but few, if any, of this class have escaped notice. Neither is it claimed that all the scriptures which go to establish future punishment are presented. The prominent texts are given, and the falsity and absurdity of Universalist interpretations shown.

A work upon this plan, where so many texts of like import are examined separately, must of necessity involve some repetition of thought and language. This, however, is obviated in part, by references from one section to another.

For twenty years past I have been a close observer of the modifications, tactics, and general operations of the order of Universalists, and having availed myself of their periodicals and books, by their principal men, am fully satisfied that, whatever a few of its advocates may profess in certain localities, *no future punishment* is the doctrine of the Universalist body in the United States, the exceptions being very few. There is but little regard among them for the future punishment views of the Restorationists. The force of their teachings for years, has been against them. See Sec. CXXXVI. This fact furnishes the reason why particular reference has been had to the no-future punishment sentiment and its concomitants in writing this book. Restoration views, however, are abundantly refuted in this examination.

I was a subscriber for, and constant reader of, the Universalist Trumpet more than two years before my conversion to God, and, as might be expected, imbibed its spirit and sentiments. Having known something of its blighting influence upon my own heart, and witnessing it extensively upon others, and believing that Universalism, as it exists among us, while it professes a regard for the Bible, contains within it all the elements of theoretical and practical infidelity, I have endeavored to tear off the mask, and present its true features; how successfully the reader will judge.

Acknowledgments are due Messrs. P. R. Russell, A. Royce, L. Lee, and C. Kingsley, for liberal extracts from their valuable books; also, to Rev. C. Munger, of the Maine Conference for two valuable articles contained in sections XX. and CX.

Although I have availed myself of all the helps at hand, yet it is believed that this production, for the most part, passes over ground heretofore unoccupied by any other writer. It has been prosecuted under a firm conviction of duty, and in accordance with the advice of judicious brethren in the ministry, whose opinions are worthy of respect. The book is submitted to a candid public, with the earnest prayer of the author, that it may be the means, under God, of saving some soul from death, and thereby hiding a multitude of sins.

N. D. GEORGE.

UNIVERSALISM NOT OF THE BIBLE.

PART I.

EXAMINATION OF SCRIPTURES IN CONTROVERSY BETWEEN UNIVERSALISTS AND BELIEVERS IN FUTURE AND ENDLESS PUNISHMENT.

I. "*And I will make of thee a great nation, and I will bless thee, and make thy name great; and thou shalt be a blessing: and I will bless them that bless thee, and curse him that curseth thee; and in thee shall all the families of the earth be blessed.*"—Gen. 12:2, 3. Repeated chapter 18:17, 18, also 22:13, with this variation, "*In thy seed shall all the nations of the earth be blessed.*" This is repeated to Isaac, chap. 26:4, and to Jacob, chap. 28:14. In Acts, 3:25, where Peter quotes it, the phrase "*all the kindreds of the earth,*" occurs.

This promise is often presented with great confidence, as teaching the salvation of all men; hence, Universalism has by its advocates, been denominated the "Abrahamic Faith." Before proceeding in our examination, it is proper to define Universalism, and show when, where, and by what means, it is contended that it will be accomplished. According to this theory, the whole race of Adam, i.e. all that ever have lived, now live, or may hereafter live, will be made holy and happy, not in this world, but in the future or resurrection state. Says

Mr. Skinner, "None, therefore, can be saved from all moral evil here. Add to this the fact, that salvation includes redemption from death, and you will see that the work will not be fully accomplished, till this corruptible puts on incorruption. In the morning of the resurrection we shall be complete in the Saviour, and join in the song of Moses and the Lamb."—*U. Ill. and Def.*, p. 261. Says Mr. Ballou, "the resurrection power, which brought again from the dead the Lord Jesus Christ, will finally, in him, make the whole human family gloriously immortal and incorruptible."—*Exp.* vol. 1, p. 78. Again says Mr. Skinner, "The resurrection introduces us into the kingdom of endless blessedness." "We shall all be equal in the resurrection," "all are alike, all equally honorable, glorious and happy. We shall be equal to the angels." "The resurrection is spoken of as a victory over death, the grave, and sin." "In the victory of the resurrection, there is no cause of regret. This is a victory in which a world is redeemed and saved. *U. Ill. and Def.*, pp. 289, 293. Mr. Whittemore, in an effort to show that dying in sin determines nothing relative to the future, says: "The question touching man's future condition is not, how did he die? but how will he be raised? What constitution will he put on in the future existence?—To the process of this change, (the resurrection) we are happy to leave not only the Jews, but all mankind.—The sting of death, which is sin, will (then) be destroyed; and all will be reconciled to the Father."—*Trumpet*, Oct. 6, 1855. See also a quotation from Williamson, in Sec. XCV. Quotations might be greatly multiplied from leading authors, but it is not demanded, as all who have any acquaintance with the system know what it attributes to the resurrection. Observe, it is not by faith in Christ, it is not by the atonement made by him, it is not by any conditions performed, but it is by "*the victory of the resurrection*, that a world is redeemed and saved." With this view, then, we are at liberty to construe the promise to Abraham as follows, "*In thy seed shall the whole race of man be made holy and happy in the future state by the resurrection*." We contend that Heaven never designed to convey such instruction in this promise and that there is no evidence whatever that Abraham, Isaac, Jacob, Moses, the Prophets, or our Lord and his apostles ever so understood it; but on the other hand there is an abundance in the Scriptures to show that it has direct reference to the spread of Christianity in the earth, and not to the unconditional holiness and happiness of all men after death. This evidence will now be presented. Mr. Whittemore in his *Guide*, p. 30, in what were once called his "One Hundred Arguments," manufactures at least six of them out of this promise. Now if we can show that his doctrine derives no support from it, we shall overthrow his six arguments at once. In one he gives a quotation from Dr. Clarke on Gen. 12:3, in which the Dr. states that the Messiah's "gospel shall be preached throughout the world, and innumerable blessings be derived on all mankind, through his death and intercessions." That all mankind have been graciously affected by the atonement is a truth to which we heartily subscribe, but it by no means follows that all will be saved in the future state; and Dr. Clarke, as Mr. Whittemore well knows, never intended to teach such a sentiment. That all the classes named, nations, families, and individuals, are said to be blessed, without being unconditionally saved in the future state, may be seen by referring to the following scriptures: Ps. 33:12; Num. 22:12; Gen. 9:1; 2 Sam. 6:11; Gen. 39:5; Judges, 13:24; Gen. 17:20.

In order to bring out the true import of this promise, let us inquire:

1. *What is meant by the seed of Abraham through whom the nations are to be blessed?*

In Gal. 3:16, we read as follows: "Now to Abraham and his seed were the promises made. He saith not, and to seeds, as of many; but as of one, and to thy seed, which is Christ." Here it is stated that Christ is the seed of Abraham. But it will be seen by examining the chapter, that the apostle states with equal clearness that believers are Abraham's seed. This matter is set in a very clear light in the following extract. "*He saith not and to seeds.* It was one particular kind of posterity which was intended: *but as of one — which is Christ;* i.e. to the spiritual head, and all believers in him, who are children of Abraham because they are *believers*, ver. 7. But why does the apostle say, *not of seeds, as of many?* To this it is answered that Abraham possessed in his family *two seeds*, one natural, viz., the members of his own household; and the other spiritual, those who were like himself because of their faith. The promises were not of a temporal nature; had they been so they would have belonged to his *natural* seed; but they did not, therefore they must have belonged to the *spiritual* posterity; and as we know the promises of justification, &c., could not properly be made to *Christ* himself, hence we must conclude his members to be here intended, and the word *Christ* is put here for *Christians.* It is from Christ that the grace flows which constitutes Christians. Christians are those who believe after the example of Abraham; they are therefore, the spiritual seed. Christ, working in and by these, makes them the light and salt of the world; and through them *under* and *by* Christ, are all the nations of the earth to be blessed. This appears to be the most consistent interpretation, though every thing must be understood of Christ in the first instance, and then of Christians only through him."— *Clarke in loco.*

That this view is correct, is evident from verses 7th and 29th of the same chapter which read thus: "Know ye therefore that they which are of faith, the same are the children of Abraham," i.e. they are the spiritual seed of Abraham. Again, "And if ye be Christ's, then are ye Abraham's seed and heirs according to promise." Now what truth do we arrive at by this view of the subject and these plain declarations of scripture? It is this: *All true Christians by virtue of their union with Christ, by faith constitute the spiritual seed of Abraham, and that it is through them that the nations of the earth are to be blessed.*

True Christians are Christ upon earth. They are his representatives; hence he said to his disciples when he sent them forth, "He that receiveth you receiveth me." Matt. 10:40. Having ascertained from the scriptures who are the seed of Abraham, we come to inquire:

2. *What is meant by the phrases all nations, all kindreds, &c.? Do they according to Scripture usage always mean a universal whole? What is their import in this promise?*

The phrase *all nations*, as used in the scriptures, does not always indicate a universal whole. By a universal whole we mean the whole posterity of Adam. This expression is sometimes used to denote a great number. The Saviour says, "Is it not written, my house shall be called of all nations the house of prayer?" Mark 11:17. Does the Saviour mean to convey the idea that the whole race of Adam should call the temple a house of prayer? Certainly not; for millions had died before the temple was known, and millions have died since without a knowledge of it. The Psalmist says, "All nations compassed me about, but in the name of the Lord will I destroy them." Ps. 118:10. The fact here brought out is, the great number of his enemies, and not that the whole of Adam's posterity had surrounded him, as all will see. Other instances, were it necessary, might be given where this phrase is used in a restricted sense; and although Universalist writers profess to see nothing but the whole human family made happy in the future state by the promise in question, because of the universal language employed, yet in considering Matt. 25:32, where the same phrase occurs, they can see with great clearness "all nations" gathered at Jerusalem's destruction! "*All kindreds.*" Great stress has been laid upon Peter's use of this in connection with the promise, Acts 3:25, as though Universalism must be the truth of God on account of it. In Rev. 1:7, we read, "Behold he cometh with clouds; and every eye shall see him, and they also which pierced him: and *all kindreds of the earth* shall wail because of him." Upon this the following is submitted:

1. Believers in the second personal advent of Christ do not consider this phrase to be here used in a universal sense. Wailing is expressive of distress, grief and sorrow. But they are warranted, by many other scriptures, to believe that the second coming of Christ will be a time of joy to saints; hence, they restrict the application to those who shall be unprepared to meet Christ as their judge.

2. But if, as Universalists will have it, the scene here described refers to some temporal calamity, then certainly the expression "all kindreds of the earth," is not used to designate the whole human race, as must be obvious to all.

The conclusion is, that these expressions are not always employed in the scriptures to convey the idea of a universal whole, but are sometimes used when a part only is intended, and the sense of such phraseology must be determined either by the connection in which it is found, or by other plain declarations of scripture respecting the same subject. The question now properly comes up, in what sense are these expressions used in the promise under consideration? Do they express a universal whole, or are they used in a restricted sense? We answer without hesitancy that they are used in a restricted sense, and not as meaning the whole race of man, but as expressive of the general spread of the gospel in the earth. This will be shown by indisputable scripture evidence under the next head.

3. *Our next inquiry is, what is the blessing promised, and where and how is it received?*

It has been already admitted that certain unconditional blessings are secured to the whole human race by virtue of the atonement, but we should never learn this fact, we think, from the Abrahamic promise. The gracious and universal effects of the atonement named, we conceive to be taught in other scriptures, while the promise in question assures us of the triumphs of Christ's kingdom in the earth. It is conceived, too, that the particular blessing to which reference is had, is that of justification by faith, as preparatory to a well grounded hope for the future. Gal. 3 : 8 ; Heb. 6 : 18, 19. We propose now to examine the prominent passages in the New Testament where this promise is quoted or referred to, and see to what results we are led. The first we present in proof of our position is found, Acts 3 : 21, 26. "For Moses truly said unto the fathers, a Prophet shall the Lord your God raise up unto you of your brethren, like unto me ; him shall ye hear in all things, whatsoever he shall say unto you. And it shall come to pass, that every soul which will not hear that Prophet, shall be destroyed from among the people. Yea, and all the Prophets from Samuel, and those that follow after, as many as have spoken, have likewise foretold these days. Ye are the children of the prophets, and of the covenant which God made with our fathers, saying unto Abraham, And in thy seed shall all the kindreds of the earth be blessed. Unto you first, God having raised up his Son Jesus, sent him to bless you, in turning away every one of you from his iniquities." (Sec. XXX.) The instruction imparted by the apostle in this passage is very plain. He states that Moses foretold the advent of Christ among the Jews as their prophet or lawgiver, and that they were to hear or obey him in all things whatsoever he should say, and declares to them that they should be punished for disobedience. He then states that all the prophets from Samuel, and those that follow after, had foretold these wonderful days of the Messiah's reign already commenced. They are then reminded of the fact that by natural descent they were the children of the prophets and of the covenant made with Abraham, and as such unto them *first*, God having raised up his Son in the flesh, sent him to *bless* them, in accordance with the promise made to Abraham, in turning every one of them from their iniquities. It must be obvious to every reader, we think, that Peter in this passage is speaking of the fact that the Jews were the first to have the gospel preached to them, and that gospel blessings in this world are the fulfilment of the promise made to Abraham. It is clear too, that he is speaking conditionally, when he says to the Jews that God sent his Son

Jesus "to bless you in turning away every one of you from his iniquities," for all the Jews were not turned from their iniquities, neither have they been to this day. Observe, God sent his Son *first* to bless them, i.e. the Jews. This blessing is the one promised to Abraham, (ver. 25.) But how shall we reconcile the Apostle's words with the assumption that the promise is to have its fulfilment in the resurrection state? Are the Jews to be blessed *first* in eternity? Are they to be turned from iniquity in the future state? Are the disobedient to be destroyed from among the people beyond the grave? Admit the fact that the promise secures the triumph of the gospel in this world, among "the nations of the *earth*," and all is plain. Christ "came into his own," (John 1 : 11,) i.e. the Jews, and in the commission given to his disciples they were to preach in "*all nations, beginning at Jerusalem*," (Luke 24 : 47,) and thus the offers of the gospel were first made to the Jews. In strict obedience to this command the apostles as they went forth preached first to the Jews. Thus did Paul and Barnabas. Acts 13 : 46. "Then Paul and Barnabas waxed bold, and said, it was necessary that the word of God should FIRST have been spoken to you: but seeing ye put it far from you, and judge yourselves unworthy of everlasting life, lo, we turn to the Gentiles." This was spoken to Jews who rejected gospel blessings. We learn then from the very passage in which the noted expression, "*all the kindreds* of the earth" is found, that the promise under consideration indicates the spread of the gospel in this world, and not the salvation of all men in eternity.

The following is from the inspired apostle to the Gentiles, who well understood the Abrahamic promise, and he conjoins the blessing promised with faith. Gal. 3 : 8 : "And the scripture foreseeing that God would justify the heathen through faith, preached before the gospel unto Abraham, saying, in thee shall all nations be blessed." Now how should this read to harmonize with Universalist views? Let the reader bear in mind that Universalism asserts,

1. That the Abrahamic promise pledges the unconditional salvation of all men.*

2. That "none can be saved from all moral evil here."

3. That the resurrection "is a victory in which a world is redeemed and saved."

To accord with these propositions, we are at liberty to paraphrase the apostle's words thus: "The scripture, foreseeing that God would make the whole human family holy and happy after death, by the resurrection, independent of their own agency, preached before the gospel unto Abraham, saying, in thee shall all mankind be blessed in eternity." Is this the mind of the Spirit? What a violent wresting of the Scriptures error demands! In the text quoted, we have the apostle's application of the promise, and learn,

1. That the blessing named is justification.

2. That the blessing is to be secured in this life, as it is "through faith." None expect to obtain salvation in the future state by an exercise of faith there; for "faith cometh by hearing" the preached word. Rom. 10 : 14–17.

3. That conditions are sometimes implied when not expressed. This is a prophetical promise, given in absolute language, without naming the conditions; but Paul, in applying this promise to personal salvation, explains it conditionally.

In Rom. 4 : 11, 22, 24, we read, "And he received the sign of circumcision, a seal of the righteousness of the faith which he had yet being uncircumcised, that he might be the father of all them that believe though they be not circumcised, that righteousness might be imputed to them also. And therefore it was imputed to him for righteousness. Now it was not

* When the expression "*unconditional salvation*" is used in these pages, it has reference to the future or final salvation of men. This, it is asserted, is accomplished independent of man's agency here. The death of Christ, even, has nothing to do with procuring it, (Sec. CV.,) and man's conduct here cannot procure, prevent, or modify it. See a quotation in point from Williamson, Sec. XCV. Universalists, with inconsistency, admit present salvation to be conditional.

written for his sake alone, that it was imputed to him. But for us also, to whom it shall be imputed, if we believe on him that raised up Jesus our Lord from the dead." Again, Gal. 3 : 26, 29 : "For ye are all the children of God by faith in Christ Jesus; and if ye be Christ's, then are ye Abraham's seed, and heirs according to the promise." Again, ver. 9 : "So then, they which be of faith, are blessed with faithful Abraham." In these passages the apostle makes a conditional application of this promise which need not be misunderstood, showing most conclusively that none can enjoy the blessing promised to Abraham but such as are imitators of his faith. Take the following from Acts 13 : 32, 33. "And we declare unto you glad tidings, how that the promise which was made unto the fathers, God hath fulfilled the same unto us their children, in that he hath raised up Jesus again." So far is the apostle from intimating that this promise is to have its fulfilment in eternity, that he explicitly declares that "God hath *fulfilled* the same unto us their children;" i. e. he has raised Christ from the dead, the gospel is preached, sinners believe, and thus the promise is fulfilled.

Take another passage, found in Rom, 15 : 8, 11. "Now I say that Jesus Christ was a minister of the circumcision for the truth of God, to confirm the promises made unto the fathers, and that the Gentiles might glorify God for his mercy; as it is written: For this cause will I confess thee among the Gentiles, and sing unto thy name. And again he saith, Rejoice ye Gentiles, with his people." Here we have the same view presented concerning the promise, namely, the spread of the gospel in the world, not only among the Jews, but Gentiles also. Zacharias, the priest and the father of John, refers to this promise, and states its design. Luke 1 : 68–75. "Blessed be the Lord God of Israel; for he hath visited and redeemed his people, and hath raised up an horn of salvation for us in the house of his servant David, as he spake by the mouth of his holy prophets, which have been since the world began, that we should be saved from our enemies, and from the hand of all that hate us.

To perform the mercy promised to our fathers, and to remember his holy covenant, the oath which he swore to our father Abraham, that he would grant unto us that we, being delivered out of the hands of our enemies, might serve him without fear, in holiness and righteousness before him all the days of our life." Does Zacharias even intimate that its fulfillment is to be accomplished by the salvation of all men after death? Nothing of the kind. He explains the design of the promise, which is of course spiritual in its nature, to be a deliverance in this world from the bondage of our spiritual enemies, that we may serve God without slavish fear "in holiness and righteousness before him *all the days of our life.*"

It has now been shown most convincingly, we think, from the word of God that that part of the covenant made with Abraham under examination, finds its fulfillment in this world by the spread of the gospel among the nations of the earth, that it is conditional, and that none can enjoy its blessings but the spiritual children of Abraham, or believers in Christ, such being Abraham's seed, and the only legitimate heirs according to promise.

At this point let us introduce the testimony of a Universalist minister. Mr. French delivered the Occasional Sermon before the Maine Convention of Universalists, at Thomaston, June 28, 1843, in which he rebukes his brethren for some of their gross perversions, and this promise among the rest; and says, "We would not with unholy hands tear down what has been so long in rearing, but you will permit us to query if the promise to Abraham, Gen. 22: 18, may have any reference to the future world? Is it consistent to quote it, especially if we deny that life and immortality are brought to view in the Old Testament? And do not Peter, Acts 3: 26, and Paul, Gal. chap. 3, both apply that promise to this life? Let our preachers be on good terms of consistency, if we would make advancement. Why should we furnish sticks for our enemies to beat us with?"—*Banner, Aug.* 5, 1843.

Whether or not all the ministers of this order understand the import of this promise, is not for us to determine; but we fear that all have not the candor of Mr. French in expressing their convictions.

There is one consideration more we gather from the subject which should forcibly impress us all as moral beings. It is this: that in order to possess a good hope of heaven, all should exert their moral agency to become heirs of promise. Hear the apostle Paul upon this, Heb. 6 : 17–20. "Wherein God, willing more abundantly to show unto the heirs of promise the immutability of his counsel, confirmed it by an oath; that by two immutable things, in which it was impossible for God to lie, we might have strong consolation, who have fled for refuge to lay hold upon the hope set before us; which hope we have as an anchor of the soul, both sure and steadfast, and which entereth into that within the veil, whither the forerunner is for us entered, even Jesus."

In view of this scripture let us inquire,

1. Who are the heirs of promise? Not all men, but only such as are Christ's. Gal. 3 : 29. All are not Christ's, for "if any man have not the spirit of Christ, he is none of his." Rom. 8 : 9. The heirs of promise are believers in Christ, but "all men have not faith." 2 Thess. 3 : 2.

2. Who have this strong consolation, and the hope which enters into heaven where Jesus is? Do all men have it? No: for "the wicked is driven away in his wickedness; but the RIGHTEOUS HATH HOPE in his death." Prov. 14 : 13. Some are "strangers from the covenant of promise, having NO HOPE, and without God in the world." Eph. 2 : 12.

A great play of words has been made upon the oath of God, named in this passage, as though this were something in favor of Universalism, and thus taking for granted what can never be proved, viz: that the promise which is confirmed by an oath, secures the unconditional salvation of all men in the future state. This we have shown again and again to be false, and it is refuted in this very connection; for to whom are these blessings named secured by the promise and oath of God, and who have the hope of heaven like an anchor to the soul? Not all men, surely, but such as "have FLED FOR REFUGE to lay hold upon the hope set before them." Has the neglecter, the swearer, the drunkard, the extortioner, the self-righteous man fled for refuge? To name this is to refute it. Universalism the "Abrahamic Faith!" What a gross perversion! The extension of Christ's kingdom in the earth is contemplated by it, and the blessing of justification is secured to all believers as preparatory for heaven.

II. Matt. 23 : 13. "*Woe unto you scribes*," &c.

Says Mr. Whittemore, "Jesus reproved the Pharisees for *shutting up the kingdom of heaven.* 'Woe unto you, scribes and Pharisees, hypocrites! for ye shut up the kingdom of heaven against men; for ye neither go in yourselves, neither suffer ye them that are entering to go in.' Matt. 23 : 13. These Pharisees were never charged with having shut up the kingdom of *hell*; that, they appear to have kept open. But they shut up the kingdom of heaven. Jesus desired to have all men enjoy his kingdom; and we are assured that at last all shall know the Lord, from the least unto the greatest. They will then all have entered the gospel kingdom." *Guide*, p. 44. Does Mr. W. admit that the "kingdom of heaven" here means salvation, or the place of it in the future world, or does he believe in a future hell? No: neither of them. Of the former he says, "the phrase 'kingdom of heaven,' in its common use in the New Testament, does not refer to the future world, but to the reign of the gospel in this world." *Guide*, p. 88. Would he allow that the Pharisees kept men from entering future heavenly bliss? If so, then Universalism is a fable. Yet he presents a contest between Christ and the Pharisees on these two states, confined as he will have them to this world, as evidence of the salvation of all men in eternity! Truly a man must be very ig-

3

norant or wicked to construct such an argument for such a purpose; for, remark, this is the whole of one of his "One Hundred Arguments," to prove Universalism, i. e. the salvation of all men in the resurrection state.

But it is not quite enough for his purpose that Jesus reproved the Pharisees thus; so it is added, that "we are assured that at last all shall know the Lord, from the least to the greatest." The passage to which Mr. W. refers, is found Jer. 31 : 33, 34. By turning to it, it will be seen that the covenant is not made with the whole human family, but with "the house of Israel." "For they shall all know me." Who? Not the whole race of man, but the "HOUSE OF ISRAEL;" v. 33. Now whatever the blessings herein contained, they are promised only to the house of Israel, and the application of these words to all men, to prove that they will all be saved in heaven, is but another instance of gross perversion. The prophet is speaking of a prosperous state of things in this world, and not of the salvation of all our race in eternity.

III. "*For ye are all one in Christ Jesus.*" Gal. 3 : 28.

"Paul saith to the Galatians, 'There is neither Jew nor Greek, there is neither bond nor free, there is neither male nor female; for ye are all one in Christ Jesus. And if ye be Christ's, then are ye Abraham's seed, and heirs according to promise.' According to what promise? Answer: According to the promise of God to Abraham, that in him, and his seed [Christ] all the nations, kindreds, and families of the earth shall be blessed. In Christ, therefore, none of the distinctions are known of which Paul there speaks. 'Ye are all one in Christ Jesus.' That point being settled, he adds, 'and if ye be Christ's, [as he had proved,] then are ye Abraham's seed, [that is, not by lineal descent, but spiritually,] and heirs according to promise.'" *Guide*, p. 49.

Here we have the argument with all its comeliness, built upon a gross perversion of the Scriptures. It is assumed that "*all*" in the text, means the whole human race. But is it so? Look at the context, and it will be seen who "are all one in Christ Jesus." "*Ye.*" Who? All men? No, but believers; for such he is addressing. They are those who had "put on Christ," v. 27, and such only. Taking those scriptures which are applied by the inspired penman to a particular class of men where the words *all* and *every* chance to occur, and applying them to the whole race of man, has been a very common work with writers of this school. This may deceive the ignorant, but it can never deceive the man who is acquainted with his Bible. The perversion of the Abrahamic promise, to make out the argument, is exposed in Sec. 1.

IV. "*Whosoever speaketh a word against the Son of Man, it shall be forgiven him; but whosoever speaketh against the Holy Ghost, it shall not be forgiven him, neither in this world, neither in the world to come.*" Matt. 12 : 32; Mark 3 : 29; Luke 12 : 10.

The course pursued by Universalist writers upon this text, is both evasive and sophistical. The author of the *Guide* labors first to contradict the Son of God by quoting Isa. 1 : 18, and 1 John 1 : 7–9, to show that all sins are pardonable, "the sin against the Holy Ghost not excepted;" then to show that the text is a Hebraism, and is not to be understood absolutely. To sustain this, a quotation is given, purporting to be from Grotius, the correctness of which we have not the means of ascertaining. He then brings to his aid the Doway, a Catholic translation. Now we suppose the Catholic priests are about as honest as Universalist expositors, and are equally anxious to promulgate the doctrine, in opposition to the Saviour, that sins of all kinds are pardonable, since they blasphemously assume the prerogative to pardon sin: and to admit that some are unpardonable, would curtail their revenues. After stating that a Catholic writer asserts that there is no sin which cannot be forgiven on repentance, Mr. Whittemore says, it is a "conclusion to which many of the very best orthodox writers have come, that all manner of sin and blasphemy is more easily forgiven than the sin against the Holy Ghost." Who these "*many of the very best orthodox writers*" are, we are not informed. This is probably a mere make-weight thrown in without any foundation in truth. And then if it is in accordance with the Divine government that all kinds of sins are pardonable, what folly to talk of some sins being more *easily* forgiven than others! Cannot Omnipotence pardon one sin as easily as another? For Mr. W. to labor to show that any sin "if duly and sincerely repented of" may be forgiven, is only to raise a false issue; for none, to our knowledge, ever disputed it. If there is evangelical repentance, God is bound by the principles of his own government, as revealed in his word, to forgive; while the same principles bind him not to forgive if men do not repent. The sin against the Holy Ghost places men where they will not and cannot repent as the gospel requires, and of course they will never be forgiven. Paul speaks of the same class of sinners (Heb. 6 : 4–6) when he says, "it is *impossible* . . . to renew them again unto repentance." (Sec. LXXXVIII.)

Nothing is gained to Universalism by limiting this sin to the Jews, who attributed the miracles of Christ to the power of the devil, as Dr. Clarke and some others are disposed to do; for if those Jews, and those only who were guilty of this died, unforgiven, and are to suffer eternal damnation, Universalism is just as false as though millions suffered it. Nearly two pages of the *Guide* are occupied by an effort well calculated to bewilder the superficial reader of the Bible. He is first carried to Heb. 9 : 26, and 1. Cor. 10 : 11, where the expressions "end of the world" and "ends of the world" occur; then to Eph. 2 : 7, where the phrase "ages to come" is found. It is then asserted that the passage in Matthew under consideration should read, "shall not be forgiven, neither in this world," or *age*, which ended when the gospel age began; "neither in the world," or age, "to come," that is, the age which succeeded it. The author of the *Guide* then adds; "Now, although the sin against the Holy Ghost was not to be forgiven neither in the then existing *age* or *world*, nor in the *age* or *world* which succeeded it, yet (mark, reader,) IN THE WORLDS TO COME, [for it is the same Greek word in Ephesians which you find in Matthew,] God will show the exceeding riches of his grace." The sentiment here put forth is this: the blasphemy against the Holy Ghost shall not be forgiven, neither in the Jewish age, neither in the Christian age, but in the ages to come: i. e., after the Jewish and Christian ages or dispensations have passed away, blasphemy against the Holy Ghost shall be forgiven. The Jewish dispensation is already past, and the Christian dispensation will continue till the end of time, till Christ shall deliver up the kingdom to the Father. 1 Cor. 15 : 24. It is in the future world, then, that blasphemers against the Holy Ghost are to be pardoned; so of course such sinners are found in eternity with guilt and condemnation upon them, or they would not need forgiveness after the Christian dispensation is past. Now if guilt is in the future world, there must be misery, and thus the no-future suffering doctrine so much insisted on by Mr. W. is destroyed by his own interpretations. Truth lies in a straight line, but error is crooked like the old serpent who is the father of it. Again, if this sin is not to be forgiven either in the Jewish or Christian age, then those who commit it must "*die in their sins*," and those who die thus must be excluded from heaven where Christ has gone. John 8 : 21; Acts 1 : 11. So nothing in reality is gained to Universalism, even by this interpretation. But the Lord from heaven has brushed away at a stroke all this web of sophistry which has been thrown around his truth; for as if he foresaw that men would rise up in these last days and attempt to prevent this truth of his, as given by one of his servants, he inspires another to present it to the world in language not to be quibbled away. Hear him: "He that shall blaspheme against the Holy Ghost HATH NEVER FORGIVENESS, but is in danger of ETERNAL DAMNATION."

Mark 3 : 29. If "hath never forgiveness" means that all shall be forgiven, and if eternal damnation means eternal bliss in heaven, then may Universalism be true. No man can be exposed to that which does not exist, and if no such thing as eternal damnation exists, then was Christ a deceiver. Mark, reader, this was addressed to Jews, who were believers in eternal damnation. That the Jews so believed, is fully admitted by Universalist writers. (Sec. CXXXII.) Such language could not fail to be understood by the Jews as teaching endless punishment; and as they understood it, so should we.

Since writing the above, a pamphlet has come to hand, by J. F. Witherell, in which the "most popular objections" to Universalism are "*fairly stated, candidly examined and fully answered.*" This is the profession. We take the following entire argument from the work. "Objection 4. "*The Bible teaches that some sin hath never forgiveness.*" Well, suppose it does, is that any proof that all mankind will not eventually be made holy and happy? Surely not. I say to the objector, that if he supposes the phrase, hath never forgiveness, is an objection to the doctrine of a world's salvation, he hath never properly understood it; but that is no proof that he never will. This little pamphlet hath never been burned, but that is no proof that some good brother, who cannot endure sound doctrine, will not commit it to the flames. Because a thing never has been, that of course is no reason why it never will be; and hence, because a certain sin committed eighteen hundred years ago, at that time had not been forgiven, that is no proof that it has not long since been forgiven; especially when the Saviour hath positively said that all manner of sin shall be forgiven." p. 25. Here we have the objection "fairly stated, candidly examined and fully answered"!! We see by this, also, what kind of coin passes current with the order; for in the author's note to the reader, in which he boasts of its ready sale and the wonders it has accomplished, he says, "It received complimentary notices from the Universalist presses throughout the country, and was cordially approbated by our minstering brethren generally." Such a flat contradiction of the Saviour's words carries its own antidote to all honest minds. The sense of the passage is this: all sins are pardonable on repentance, BUT the sin against the Holy Ghost. This sin formed an exception to the rule, hence, Luke reports the Saviour thus: "Whosoever shall speak a word against the Son of man, it shall be forgiven him; but unto him that blasphemeth against the Holy Ghost, it SHALL NOT be forgiven him." ch. 12, v. 10.

V. "*And so all Israel shall be saved: as it is written, There shall come out of Sion the Deliverer, and shall turn away ungodliness from Jacob.* Rom. 11 : 26.

The first clause of this text we often find either in blazing capitals or significant italics, to prove most positively that the whole of the Jewish nation are to be saved unconditionally in the future world, than which nothing can be more false, as we shall now show. Here let us inquire, what is the scope of the apostle's reasoning in this part of the Epistle? Is he laboring to prove that all the Jewish race will be unconditionally saved in eternity? Nothing like it. In the 9th, 10th and 11th chapters he is setting forth the equal privileges of Jews and Gentiles under the gospel, and shows that the Gentiles, if they believed, should share in its salvation; and that the Jews, if they disbelieved, should not be saved by its provisions. See chapter 11: 1–24. Without entering into detail, a few points will be fixed upon connected with the salvation of which the apostle is speaking, to show most clearly that it is conditional, and that he does not teach the absolute certainty of the salvation of the whole Jewish nation, and by parity of reason the whole human family, but a different sentiment. The course the apostle pursues lies with mighty weight against the Universalist notion. He says, in this same epistle, "Brethren, my heart's desire and prayer to God for Israel is, that they might be saved." Chap. 10 : 1. Why this intense emotion on the part of the apostle, if he was confident that all would be saved? What should we think of a Universalist minister in our day who should go about with the deep-toned feeling here expressed, praying that a particular class of men might be saved? We should think that his practice grossly conflicted with his theory. And who does not know that it is the boasted bliss of Universalism that it delivers its votaries from all such trouble about the salvation of men. Was Paul a Universalist? These remarks are based upon the assumption that the apostle is speaking of future salvation when he says, "And so all Israel shall be saved;" for this has not a single mark of future state reference which may not be found in chap. 10:1–10–13 and chap. 11:14. When the apostle says, "So all Israel shall be saved," he is speaking of the same salvation that he is all through chapters 10th and 11th; and this salvation is secured by confessing, believing, and calling upon the name of the Lord. Chap. 10: 9–13. As all must see, we think, this declaration of the apostle's has reference to that salvation which is the result of saving faith in Christ in this world, as preparatory to future bliss. Whether the time will come when in the progress of Christianity all the Jews who shall be then living will experience this salvation, or whether only a general reception of it, admitting of exceptions, is indicated, is a matter about which good men have differed. But one thing is clear: all God's true and persevering Israel shall be saved, whether Jews or Gentiles by birth, for Christ "has become the author of eternal salvation unto all them that OBEY him." Heb. 5 : 9. "All are not Israel that are of Israel," Rom. 9 : 6; but "we are the circumcision (that is, the true Israel) which worship God in the spirit and rejoice in Jesus Christ, and have no confidence in the flesh." Phil. 3 : 3. We shall obtain light upon this subject by examining the prophecy referred to and in part quoted by the apostle. He declares, "all Israel shall be saved;" and adds, "as it is written." Where is it written? In Isa. 59 : 20, as follows: "And the Redeemer shall come to Zion, and unto them that turn from transgression in Jacob, saith the Lord." Here we see who the Israel are to be saved and the conditionality of their salvation. They are those who "TURN FROM TRANSGRESSION." This salvation, then, is predicated of God's spiritual Israel, and not of the whole Jewish race. But should it be contended still that the apostle has virtually said that the Deliverer (Christ) promised he would turn away ungodliness from all the Jewish race, i. e. all of them who have ever lived, now live, or may hereafter live, we ask when this is to be accomplished? Is it to be accomplished upon the Jews before death? This will not be pretended, for tens of thousands of them have died in their iniquities, Universalists themselves being judges. Now this must be brought about either before or after death, for we cannot possibly conceive of the soul as existing neither in the body nor out of it. As it must be admitted that all the Jews are not turned from their sins in this life, it follows that, if ever, they must be turned from ungodliness after death; and if so, ungodliness or sin, and consequently misery, must exist after death, and thus the favorite doctrine of modern Universalists, that death puts an end to sin and misery, is all a fable. Truth never contradicts itself. All God's faithful Israel will be saved both in this world and that which is to come; and there is no authority, as we conceive, for denying that the time is coming when all the Jews then living upon the earth shall embrace the Messiah. But this idea furnishes no evidence that all men, or even the Jewish race, shall be saved in the future state. In view of the very common perversion of this text, how timely the rebuke of Mr. French, one of the ministers of the order, in a sermon before the Maine Convention of Universalists, as follows: "We as a denomination, have advocated the doctrine that all men shall be saved. But in our zeal to bring an abundance of evidence, have we not caused some of our proof texts to bear the marks of violent wresting? For instance, these words of Paul have been adduced as proof that all the Jews shall be happy after death: "and so all Israel shall be saved." Rom. 11 : 26. But does this passage have any more reference to their future state, than it does to the preservation of Noah and his family in the time of the flood? And yet, as if we had not enough of our own, we are at the expense of *importing* such arguments and such methods of proof."—*Banner, Aug.* 5, 1844.

VI. "*He that is dead is freed from sin.*"—Rom. 6 : 7.

If a man availing himself of his Universalist license, dies by drunkenness or suicide, this text is called into requisition on the funeral occasion, to prove most conclusively that he has been so wise as to rid himself of sin and all its consequences by his hasty departure. In an able work before us the perversion of this passage is exposed as follows: "Persons are said to be dead in several different senses. A person is dead when the connection between body and soul is dissolved; at other times a person is said, in Scripture language, to be dead when his soul has lost the favor of God; and at other times, a person is said to be dead who is crucified to the world and the world crucified to him. Now the question is, in which of these senses does the apostle use the word *dead* in this text? I answer without hesitation in the sense of being crucified to the world. Look at the context. See how the apostle introduces the *figure*: "How shall WE (Christians) that are dead to sin live any longer therein?" ver. 2. Here then you see that the persons who were dead were the living apostle and his Christian brethren at Rome, and the death which was upon them was a death to sin. So in the following context, the same idea is repeated: "Now if we (Christians) be dead with Christ, we believe that we shall also live with him." Here then you see that the apostle is not speaking of the death of the body, but on the contrary, of that death which is a crucifixion to the world."—*Russell.*

VII. "*For none of us liveth to himself, and no man dieth to himself. For whether we live, we live unto the Lord; and whether we die, we die unto the Lord; whether we live therefore, or die, we are the Lord's.*"—Rom. 14 : 7–8.

Mr. Whittemore builds one of his arguments upon this passage to prove the salvation of all men, and says: "The terms dead and living evidently signify all the race. Of course all the human race are Christ's forever."—*Guide*, p. 48. Here is another instance in which the children's bread is cast to the dogs. Now we say that these terms do not evidently signify all the human race. Suppose that after a battle an officer should receive orders to repair to the field and take charge of "the dead and living;" should we infer from that that he was to take charge of the whole human race? By no means. Paul is speaking of Christ's lordship over believers and none else, as we conceive. The context binds us to this. He is addressing Christians and not all men. He is cautioning them against uncharitably judging each other concerning things indifferent, and adds, "For none of US," Who? All men? No, but Christians, "liveth to himself," &c. "For whether *we* live, *we* live unto the Lord; and whether *we* die, *we* die unto the Lord." Do all men live and die unto the Lord? Does the drunkard, the swearer, the neglecter, the self-righteous live *unto* the Lord, and do such die *unto* the Lord? But suppose we admit that Christ's lordship over the whole human family is intended, what then? Does it follow as a conclusion that all will be holy and happy? Certainly not; for according to this assumption he is now Lord over the human race and has been for ages past, but the whole of mankind are not saved. This being the fact, we can see no reason why he may not exercise his lordship to all eternity, and still the sufferings of some of the race continue. For all men to be subjects of God's government is one thing, but for all men to be made holy and happy in the future world is quite another. So we see that take either view of it we please, Universalism cannot be possibly wrung out of the passage.

VIII. "*But the heavens and the earth which are now, by the same word are kept in store, reserved unto fire against the day of judgment and perdition of ungodly men.*"—2 Pet. 3:7.

Instead of an explanation, as the purchasers of his book had a right to expect from the statement in his preface, the author of the *Guide* has given this striking text the go-by as follows: "This passage has been frequently used to prove the destruction of the material earth, and a day of judgment in the future state. We have shown repeatedly in these pages that God's judgments are *in the earth.* But as this text is not generally adduced in support of strict endless misery, we pass it here." He then refers us to three or four works where he says the text is explained; works which not one in a hundred of his readers will ever see. "God's judgments are in the earth." The reader will turn to Sec. LI. where this idea is examined. He says, "But as this text is not generally adduced in support of strict endless misery, we pass it here." Observe, the apostle speaks not only of the day of judgment, but also of the "*perdition of ungodly men.*" Do not Christians generally believe the perdition of ungodly men to be endless misery? Most certainly they do, and Mr. Whittemore must have known it. We go to Balfour's Essays, one of the books referred to by Mr. W., and he says, "this passage refers to the day of God's temporal vengeance on the Jews."—p. 260. He also states with much confidence respecting ver. 13, that "it is universally allowed, that the new heavens and the new earth refer to the kingdom of the Messiah, which was to succeed the Jewish dispensation, and was predicted in the Old Testament."—p. 261. Mr. Balfour was either wanting in honesty, or ignorant of the subject upon which he wrote, for we find by consultation that instead of its being "*universally allowed,*" such commentators as Clarke, Scott, Chalmers, Dwight, Wesley, Storr, Rosenmüller, and Benson are directly against him, and yet this baseless assertion comprises the main force to be found in his evasion of this passage. Universalists profess to be full of wonder that the word hell occurs no oftener, if there is any future punishment taught in the Bible. But we ask, if the glowing descriptions of judgment and punishment found so often in the Bible had their fulfilment in the destruction of the Jews, is it not very strange that the expression Jerusalem, or Jerusalem's destruction, is NEVER found in connection with such descriptions in the New Testament? Yet such is the fact. Examine the context, and it will be seen that there is not the least evidence that the apostle is speaking of Jerusalem's destruction, or that those for whom he wrote once entertained the thought that that city would be spoiled by the Romans. The people addressed were Hebrew Christians, who had been educated in the belief of a future day of judgment and perdition of ungodly men. These doctrines were believed both among Jews and Gentiles. This is admitted by Universalist writers. Now can it be entertained for a moment that Peter would take this great event believed in by them, and use it as a figure to represent the destruction of *one* city? He brings up historical facts, viz: the creation and the deluge, and then institutes a comparison, not between those events and the destruction of the Jewish city, but between those events and the passing away of the heavens and the earth, and the appearance of a new material system in their place. The thoughts are majestic, but they are not the dress of fiction or poetry. The context, the comparison, the language used, the belief of the people addressed, the absence of every thing indicating the Jerusalem catastrophe, all bind us to believe the apostle is speaking of the day of judgment, as commonly understood, and of the eternal perdition of, not merely Jewish men, but, all ungodly men.

IX. *And the times of this ignorance God winked at, but now commandeth all men every where to repent; because he hath appointed a day in which he will judge the world in righteousness, by that man whom he hath ordained; whereof he hath given assurance unto all men, in that he hath raised him from the dead.*"—Acts 17 : 30, 31.

The perversion would be so glaring that but few Universalists, it is believed, have ventured to refer this text to Jerusalem's destruction, for all would at once see the absurdity of making the apostle urge the Jewish calamity as a reason why the Grecians should repent of their idolatry. But certain men are never at a loss for expedients, especially when a text of Scripture stands in their way, so they will have it that the day of judgment appointed is the gospel day. *Guide*, p. 176. But we are not quite ready to receive this forced and unnatural interpretation.

That Paul did not have reference to the gospel day is evident from the fact that he uses the future tense. "He (God) hath appointed a day in the which he *will* judge," &c. Now the gospel day had then come. Paul was *then* preaching the gospel, and the gospel had spread and was then spreading rapidly, as all know who are acquainted with the history of the church. Furthermore, Paul when speaking of the gospel day uses the present tense, and says, "Behold *now* is the day of salvation." 2 Cor. 6 : 2. Observe, St. Paul does not say to the Grecians, God hath appointed *this* day in which he *now* judges the world; but he speaks indefinitely and of the future : "He hath appointed *a* day in the which he *will* judge." By this it will be seen that it is a perversion to apply these words to the gospel day.

But why should the apostle speak of the world's being judged in righteousness at a set time or in the gospel day. According to Universalism, to talk of a day appointed in which God will judge the world in righteousness, is the height of folly. Are we not told that every man is judged, rewarded and punished according to his works as he passes along? If this be so, the world is no more judged in righteousness in the gospel day, than it was under any former dispensation. It is obvious too, that the apostle here presents the day of judgment as a motive of alarm, as a reason why "all men every where should repent."

But what had the Athenians or any other people to fear from the gospel day, especially if Universalism is the gospel, which proclaims bliss for all, and hell for none in the future, whether they repent in this life or not. Mr. Balfour enters into a labored Greek criticism, in his Essays, to make this passage mean that Christ is about to rule the Roman empire. But where do we find the fulfilment of this prediction? Did Christ ever rule the Roman empire? Are we pointed to the reign of Constantine? We deny that in the sense in which Christ governs, he governed the Roman empire then. His "kingdom is not of this world." But admitting that he did govern the Roman empire in the time of Constantine, his reign did not commence till A. D. 313, so that Mr. Balfour's *about to rule* did not take place till *about* three hundred years after the declaration was made! What influence could that day exert upon the Greeks at Athens to move them to repentance? And how absurd the thought that Paul took this blind method to teach the Grecian Philosophers that God had appointed a gospel day which was nearly three hundred years in the future in which Christ should rule the Roman empire! Admit the truth declared, namely: a future judgment, and all is clear. The Greeks admitted the doctrine of future retributions; they believed that Minos and Radamanthus would be the judges, while the apostles taught that Christ would judge the world; hence, when Paul spoke of the judgment of the world, they could but understand him as teaching a future judgment. We see by this how to account for the fact that they raise no opposition to the doctrine of a judgment, but when they heard of the resurrection, "some mocked." Ver. 32. The first named doctrine, so far as the idea of a future judgment is concerned, was received by them, while the resurrection was rejected. The apostle evidently speaks of the same judgment here that he does in Rom. 2:16; 14:11, 12; 2 Cor. 5:10, 11; Heb. 6:2–9, 27. See by the index where these scriptures are examined.

X. *And have hope towards God, which they themselves also allow, that there shall be a resurrection of the dead, both of the just and unjust.*" Acts 24 : 15.

Strange as it may seem to some, this text has been adduced in proof of Universalism. "Paul hoped for the resurrection of all men which he would not have done if a part were to be endlessly miserable ; therefore Paul was a Universalist." This in substance is the argument.

This argument is built upon the assumption that we believe that the resurrection procures and fixes the eternal doom of the sinner, whereas we entertain no such opinion. The wickedness of men in the present life is the cause of their suffering in the future state, and not the resurrection of the body. So we see upon our principles that Paul could hope for the resurrection, without hoping that some would be eternally miserable. He is however giving a statement of his belief rather than an expression of his desire. Dr. Clarke's exposition of this text is correct. "*And have hope towards God*, &c. I not only do not hold anything by which the general creed of this people might be altered, in reference to the *present state ;* but, also, I hold nothing different from their belief in reference to a *future* state ; for if I maintain the doctrine of the *resurrection of the dead* it is what *themselves allow*." *Clarke in loco.* We have most striking evidence from this very passage that Paul was not a Universalist. "And have hope towards God, which *they themselves allow*." What did the Jews *allow* concerning the resurrection ? Did they allow that all would be holy any happy in the resurrection ? Were the Jews who believed in a resurrection Universalists ? By no means ; for Universalists themselves assert that they believed in the endless punishment of a part of mankind. Now if Paul was a Universalist, he must have believed that all would be holy and happy in the resurrection, which was a very different thing from the Jewish belief. How then, we ask, could he in truth declare that he believed as they did concerning the resurrection ? Did Paul dissemble ? Or, rather, is it not rendered as clear as a sunbeam that he was not a Universalist; that it never entered his mind that all men were to be saved by the resurrection? We have another instance where the apostle declared himself a Pharisee, and a believer in the resurrection, and thus secured to himself the favor of the Pharisees. Acts 23 : 6–9. If Paul was a Universalist, he could not have failed of preaching the salvation of all men in connection with the resurrection, for no Universalist in our day would be guilty of such an omission. But were the Pharisees, those staunch believers in endless punishment, so friendly to a Universalist preacher, as to espouse his cause on the announcement of the very doctrine which Universalists in our time contend teaches the salvation of all men, and declare (v. 9) that "*we find no evil in this man?*" Reader, think of this.

XI. "*For whosoever will save his life, shall lose it; and whosoever will lose his life for my sake, shall find it.*" Matt. 16 : 25. Parallels, Matt. 10 : 39; Luke 17 : 33; John 12 : 25. On the last named text, see Sec. LXVIII.

We are told (*Guide*, p. 108) that the word rendered *soul* in the 26th verse, is the same as the one in the 25th verse rendered *life;* and that the *life* here spoken of is *natural life*. One doctrine cherished by Mr. Whittemore is, that the future existence "cannot in the nature of things, as it seems to us, be affected by the conduct of men in this life." *Notes on Par.* p. 354. If this be true, we ask how does the man who will lose his natural life for the sake of Christ, find it, or (John 12 : 25) "keep it unto life eternal," any more than he will save his natural life? Upon this principle the man's eternal life is just as secure who dies opposing Christ, as is his who dies for the sake of Christ. These words of the Saviour present a pyramid in argument against the notion that man's conduct here does not affect his condition in the future, which all the sophistry of its advocates cannot overturn. We have never seen an attempt to explain this text in any of their writings. It is found in the *Guide*, but all the author does with it is to show that the Greek word rendered *soul* in v. 26, is the same as the one rendered *life* in this, and contends that both mean natural life. The obvious sense of the text is this; "Whosoever will save his *natural life*, by neglecting, through fear or otherwise, to do his christian duty, shall lose it; that is, shall lose his eternal life: and whosoever will lose his natural life for my sake, shall find it; that is, shall find eternal life." That we are correct in understanding eternal life as used in antithesis with the life of the body, may be seen by the parallel passage, John 12 : 25. "He that loveth his life shall lose it, and he that hateth his life shall keep it unto eternal life." See Sections XII and LXVIII.

XII. "*What shall it profit a man if he gain the whole world, and lose his own soul.*" Matt. 16 : 26.

It is contended that the word *soul* in this text might be rendered *life*, to which we have no objection so far as our argument is concerned. But what life is meant? Not temporal life surely, for Christ is urging them to risk that in his cause: for he says, "Whosoever will save his life, shall lose it; and whosoever will lose his life for my sake, shall find it," v. 25. That there are two kinds of life named here is evident, for no man who saves his natural life will lose it, and none who lose their natural life for Christ will save their natural life. All must see that the life gained by losing our natural life for Christ, must be a life in the future state; that is, eternal life: and also that the life lost by an unwillingness to surrender natural life for Christ, must be eternal life. That we are to understand eternal life here as used in antithesis with natural life, is clear from the parallel text. John 12 : 25. (Sections XI and LXVIII.)

The Saviour is urging his disciples to take up their cross, and do their duty by following him through every danger; and as motives to stimulate to action, he assures them that if they were called to be martyrs for his sake, they should find eternal life after the death of the body; but if they should save or seek to save natural life at the expense of conscience and casting aside the cross, they should lose eternal life in the world to come. He then, to set it home with force, inquires, "What shall it profit a man if he gain the whole world and lose his own soul," (life,) i. e. his eternal life. It will require but little attention to the text and context to see that the loss of eternal life is indicated here. Indeed, no other construction can be given without reducing it to nonsense. But admitting, as Universalism contends, that the death of the body is intended, then the text lies with weight against that theory; for a question in this form is a strong negation. The sense is, that if a man in his avaricious pursuits were to gain the whole world and die in the effort, he would in reality gain nothing. Now all unite in the sentiment that heavenly bliss is inconceivably greater than everything enjoyed in the present life, even by the most holy; hence, the apostle says of himself "to die is gain." Universalism says, this gain is for all; even though some gain the whole world by their wicked and avaricious schemes, yet by death they shall gain as much as Paul, for it teaches heaven for all and hell for none,—that all shall be equal. (Sec. XC.) It goes farther. It teaches that the more wicked men are here, the more will they gain by death, inasmuch as the wicked suffer more in this life than the pious, therefore escape more by death, and enter into the same bliss with the most exalted saints. The Saviour speaks of a character which shall gain nothing by the death of the body; but Universalism says all, whether holy or unholy, shall be gainers by death. As Christ is to be considered a competent teacher in these matters, the conclusion is, Universalism must be false. The Saviour is speaking either of the loss of future and eternal life, or of the loss of natural life; either of which is fatal to Universalist views.

XIII. "*And it shall come to pass in the last days, that the mountain of the Lord's house shall be established in the top of the mountains, and shall be exalted above the hills; and all nations shall flow unto it.*" Isa. 2: 2.

We here give one of the "One Hundred Arguments," entire. "It is said that *all nations* shall flow unto the mountain of the Lord's house,—a figurative representation of the covenant of the gospel." *Guide*, p. 39. Well, suppose it is such a representation, does it prove the salvation of all in the future state? A man must be brought to a great strait to construct such an argument to prove Universalism. The connection, as all may see who will consult the chapter, shows that the glorious triumphs of Christianity over heathen nations in this world is prophesied here, and not the salvation of all men in eternity. But, then, the word *all* is in the passage, so it must mean Universalism!

XIV. "*I will also give thee for a light to the Gentiles, that thou mayest be my salvation unto the ends of the earth.*" Isa. 49 : 6.

This is brought in argument by Mr. Whittemore to prove his favorite doctrine; and he says of it, (*Guide*, p. 41,) "In this verse the prophet affirms that the blessings of the gospel should not be confined to the Jews. "I will give thee for a light to the Gentiles;" for what purpose? Answer: "That thou mayest be my salvation unto the ends of the earth." Mr. W. then asks, "Is this consistent with the supposed fact, that countless millions of the human race shall never hear of the blessings of the gospel?" To adopt the same method with another text, it can be proved that the whole human family were made holy and happy nearly three thousand years ago. The Psalmist says, (Ps. 98 : 3.) "All the ends of the earth HAVE SEEN the salvation of our God." Is this consistent with the supposed fact that millions of the human race are this moment sinning and suffering to an alarming extent? Now if by "salvation unto the *ends of the earth*," we are to understand the holiness of all in heaven, and if the Psalmist declared three thousand years ago that "all the ends of the earth *have seen* the salvation of our God," it is quite clear that the whole human race were saved in heaven at that time! The passage under consideration declares the general spread of the gospel in the earth, and giving it a future state reference to serve Universalism, is a gross perversion.

XV. "*Our Father which art in heaven.*" Matt. 6: 9.

As the question of divine paternity involves several texts, it will be considered somewhat at length in this section. It is worthy of remark that those our Saviour taught to pray were his disciples, which is destructive to the idea that this prayer teaches that all men are the children of God. But it may be replied that Christ said to the multitude, (Matt. 23: 1–9,) that "one is your father which is in heaven." Admitting that the Saviour meant to teach that God was the father of that multitude, then there is nothing gained to Universalism, unless it can be shown that this relation secures the salvation of all men in the future state. This, then, is the point at issue: is God the father of all men in such a sense as to secure their final holiness and happiness? We admit that there is a sense in which God is the father of all animate and inanimate creation, and of course the father of all men. He is the father of the rain, (Job 38: 28,) that is, he produces the rain. The prophet inquires, (Mal. 2: 10,) "Have we not all one father? Hath not one God created us?" Said a heathen poet, and Paul adopted it, (Acts 17: 28,) "For we also are his offspring." These passages teach us that God is a father in the sense of creator. Frequent appeals are made to human sympathy in connection with this subject.

The argument, brought into a small compass, stands thus: God is the father of all. No earthly parent would inflict endless punishment upon his children. God is better than earthly parents; therefore he will not inflict such punishment upon his creatures, but will make them all holy and happy. To make human sympathy the basis of such a conclusion, may deceive the unthinking; but those who reflect, will see that the originators of such arguments are obnoxious to the charge of making the

4*

Almighty altogether such an one as themselves. This mode of argument lies with all its weight against matter of fact, namely, the present sufferings of the human race. It will avail nothing to say that present suffering shall result in the good of all in the end, that it is only a disciplinary process, such as a kind father would adopt for the good of his children. A kind earthly parent may be under the painful necessity of inflicting discipline, because it is not in his power to reform his children by any other means; but, we ask, is the Almighty under such *necessity?* Reasoning from the attributes of God, as Universalists are in the habit of doing, and asserting that all will be saved because God has almighty power, infinite wisdom, and unbounded goodness, they cannot contend for a moment, with any consistency, that God is under the necessity of making the race of man suffer six thousand, or individuals scores of years, before he can make them holy and happy. Certainly it must have been as easy for the Almighty to have prevented evil, as it is to destroy it. He stood in the relation of father, the same before Adam fell as he now does; and if the paternal character of God is not pledged to save men from committing sin now, how can we view it as a pledge that all shall be saved from the results of sin? Again, if it is consistent with the paternal character of God that sin and misery should exist six thousand years, it may be equally consistent with his paternal character that some may suffer endlessly. (Sec. CXIV.) Making human sympathy, which is ever liable to lead us wrong, the test of the principles of the Divine government, and the true index of the future condition of man, is not only dangerous to man, but is highly dishonorable to God; for he is made by it as bad as the worst of men.

Let us illustrate this. The Lord rained fire and brimstone upon the Sodomites, and destroyed them. Would a kind earthly parent treat his children in this way? Certainly not. Then God is not a kind father! A parent has a family of children, all happy and in perfect health. If he is a kind parent, he will ardently desire to perpetuate their happiness. But what should we think of him, if, with a full knowledge of the consequences, he suffers a disease to come among them which mars their beauty, destroys their health, and renders them wretched all their days, when he could have prevented it as well as not? We should think him a fiend incarnate. Now if human action and sympathy are to govern our views of God, what character shall we give him? The first pair were holy and happy; but God not only failed to prevent sin, but, according to some leading Universalist writers, is the author of it (Sec. LXXXV); and millions are this moment groaning with untold agonies, as a consequence. To accord with Universalist notions, how are we to view him; as a kind father, or a fiend incarnate? The latter, most certainly; and thus God is dishonored. Again, what should we think of the parental character of a man who having the power to mould the will and affections of his son into perfect love and obedience to himself, and thus render all painful discipline unnecessary, but instead of so doing should suffer his son to remain in disobedience, and continue to inflict the stripes? We should think him a hard-hearted wretch. Universalists represent God, by their arguments upon his perfections, as able, not only to have prevented evil, but to destroy it now; yet instead of doing so, he has been inflicting stripes upon his children for thousands of years. Would a kind father do so? Never. So God is not a kind father!

In view of such reflections, as a result of the reasonings of this class of writers, might Jehovah not inquire concerning them as he did of certain wicked men anciently, "If I then be a father, where is mine honor?" Mal. 1:6. The sympathies of our nature can never be a just rule by which to determine what is right in the Divine government; for earthly parents are not always governed by true mercy nor strict justice. The son of a former governor of Kentucky was clearly convicted of murder, but was saved from the gallows by a pardon from his father, when it is evident he would have withheld pardon from another man under the same circumstances. Here paternal sympathy was not only arrayed against justice, but also against mercy; for this murderer was suffered to go at large, and, as we have been informed, took the life of another man. This teaches us the folly of making sympathy the rule to determine what God will do, who does not act from sympathy, but from his own immutable justice. Universalism would have God a father, and nothing else, led about by sympathy and caprice, just as earthly parents are. But the Bible not only represents him as a father to his children, but as a governor, lawgiver and judge, who will take vengeance and pour out wrath upon the ungodly.

In the time of our Saviour, the wicked Jews set up an argument in their favor from the Divine paternity, and said, "We have one Father, even God. (John 8 : 41, 42.) The difference between this and the claim set up by Universalists seems to be this: while both base their safety upon the Divine paternity, one confined the Divine favor in this respect to the Jews, and the other extend it to all men. The Jews counted themselves perfectly safe, notwithstanding their great wickedness, because God was their father. Universalists consider all men, no matter how vile and wicked, perfectly safe, because God is their father. But the Saviour denied this claim of the Jews, and said, "if God were your father, ye would love me;" and furthermore he told them, "Ye are of your father the devil;" and whether or not if he were now upon earth he would treat those with less severity who are wallowing in the mire of sin, yet basing their claims of heaven on the Divine paternity, the reader must determine. If all men are the children of God in such a sense as to secure their eternal salvation, then Elymas, the sorcerer, (Acts 13 : 10) was a child of God; for his wickedness, according to Universalism, could not destroy that relation. Paul then was wrong in calling him a child of the devil, and should have said, "O! full of all subtilty and mischief, thou *child of God*, thou enemy of all righteousness!" If the Bible teaches that all men, by virtue of the relation they stand in to God as Creator, are candidates for future bliss, then we are bound to believe it; but where is such instruction given? One thus saith the Lord upon this subject, would do more upon candid minds than all the arguments based upon the sand of human sympathy that have ever been constructed. Christ called the wicked Jews the children of the devil, and Paul called Elymas a child of the devil; and John says, "In this the children of God are manifest, and the children of the devil; whosoever doeth not righteousness is not of God." 1 John 3 : 10. Now according to Universalism, a man may be a child of God and a child of the devil at the same time! But let us view this subject more particularly in the light of the Scriptures. Gal. 4 : 4, 5. "But when the fulness of time was come, God sent forth his Son, made of a woman, made under the law, to redeem them that were under the law, that we might receive the adoption of sons." Now if all are the children of God by creation, in such a sense as to secure eternal bliss, they were so before the Saviour was given, for God was their Father in this sense prior to the gift of his Son.

Here is a thought, then. If all were sons, and their salvation sure as a consequence, where was the necessity of the great sacrifice of Heaven in giving his Son to suffer and die that they might receive the adoption of sons? This single text demolishes at once all the arguments that our opponents have ever built upon the paternal character of God. Take the idea of adoption. What is it? It is not making a son of a son, but it is making a son of one who is not. John 1 : 12. "But as many as received him, to them gave he power to become the sons of God, even to them that believe on his name." Here it will be seen, that they were not the children of God, but had power given them to become such. Rom. 8 : 14. "For as many as are led by the Spirit of God, they are the sons of God." Are all men led by the Spirit of God? But few will assert this. The passage clearly implies that all men are not led by the Spirit of God, and that those who are not led by the Spirit of God, are not the sons of God. Rom. 8 : 17. "And if children, then heirs;

heirs of God, and joint heirs with Christ; if so be that we suffer with him, that we may be glorified together." This supposes that some are not the children of God, and that such as are not children are not heirs of God, neither are they joint heirs with Christ. The apostle says, "if so be that we suffer with him, that we may be glorified together." Now according to Universalism, all men are sons in the sense to be heirs, and of course all will be glorified with Christ, which plainly contradicts the apostle's reasoning. Which shall we believe? That this has respect to future glory, is clearly established by the scripture following the last quoted text. (Sec. CII.) What folly to argue the salvation of men from a relation which does not constitute them heirs of heavenly bliss! How clear it is from these passages that salvation depends upon the relation saints sustain to God by adoption, and not by any relation we sustain to him by creation. Again, "For ye are all the children of God by faith in Christ Jesus." Gal. 3 : 26. This was not spoken of all men, but of Christians, as will be seen by the context; and shows that all are not the children of God in a true Christian sense. We might extend our remarks, and produce other scriptures against the assumptions of Universalism and to sustain our views, but deem it unnecessary, as we conceive what is presented to be a complete refutation. Remember, reader, that it is not even pretended that there is one text in the Bible that teaches directly the salvation of all men in the future state, as the result of the Divine paternity; but it is enforced by appeals to sympathy, and inferences drawn from a mode of reasoning most unsound and sophistical.

XVI. "*Therefore I endure all things for the elect's sake, that they may also obtain the salvation which is in Christ Jesus, with eternal glory.*" 2 Tim. 2 : 10.

What is the object of the apostle's intense anxiety and labor? It is that the elect, or Christians, may obtain the salvation which is in Christ, with eternal glory. It seems that Paul never once thought that all men were sure of eternal glory. In view of this plain declaration, how false is Universalism! How unlike is this to the teachings of its advocates, who boldly tell us that all are sure of Christ's salvation and eternal glory. Which will you receive, reader; the teachings of these men, or those of Paul, the Christian apostle, who received his instructions from heaven? Yet we are told, with great confidence, that Paul was a Universalist! The great labor of his professed successors in this faith is, to make the people believe that they cannot possibly fail of eternal glory; and let one of them express a doubt upon this point, and labor like Paul that men may obtain it, and he would at once be cast out of the Universalist synagogue.

XVII. "*For I will not contend forever, neither will I be always wroth; for the spirit should fail before me, and the souls which I have made.*" Isa. 57 : 16.

"Is this declaration consistent with the doctrine of endless misery? According to that doctrine, will not God contend forever? will he not be always wroth?" So inquires Mr. Whittemore, (*Guide*, p. 41); and this forms one of his "One Hundred Arguments." If the reader will turn to the passage in the Bible, he will find that this is not predicated of all men in eternity, but of those who put their trust in the Lord, v. 13, and of those who are of a "contrite and humble spirit," v. 15. It has respect to the gracious chastisements of God in this world, and on compliance with his requirements these chastisements were to cease, and they were to "possess the land and inherit his holy mountain," v. 13; "while the wicked are like the troubled sea when it cannot rest," v. 20. The subject upon which the prophet is speaking is not the salvation or damnation of all or any men in the future state; and to base an argument upon it to prove the salvation of all men in the next world, can hardly be called sophistical. It is another instance of glaring perversion.

XVIII. "*With whom is no variableness, neither shadow of turning.*" James 1 : 17.

"*Now faith is the substance of things hoped for.*" Heb. 11 : 1.

Before us is a tract by A. C. Thomas, containing a set of questions artfully constructed, designed to bewilder the minds of those who think but little, and in that state to plunge them into the quagmire of Universalism. The following is a sample.

"Is God 'without variableness or even the shadow of turning?'

"If God loves His enemies *now*, will He not *always* love them? If God will always love His enemies, will He not always seek their good?"

In reply we ask, Is God without variableness or even the shadow of turning? If God hates a certain class of persons, and is angry with them *now*, (Ps. 5 : 5; 7 : 11,) will he not *always* hate and be angry with them? If he always hates and is angry with them, will he not always seek their hurt; and if so, will they ever be holy and happy? See Sec. XCV. also XXXVII. Again Mr. T. inquires, "Is faith the substance of things hoped for?" Heb. 11 : 1. Do you hope for the truth of the doctrine of endless misery? If endless misery be not a thing hoped for, can it form any part of the Christian faith?"

In reply we ask, Is "faith the substance of things hoped for?" Do you hope for the truth of the doctrine of misery in the present world? If misery in this world is not a thing hoped for, can it form any part of the Christian's faith? Did primitive Christians hope for the dreadful calamities which befel the Jews, including innocent women and children, at the siege of Jerusalem? If it was not a thing hoped for, could it have formed any part of their faith? Yet Universalists will have it that the destruction of that city formed a very important part of their faith, so much so that almost every terrific thing they uttered referred to that event! The logic is this: If a man cannot hope that his friends or himself will suffer in the state prison, the existence of such a place where criminals are punished, must form no part of his belief! Such reasoning is well worthy the cause it is designed to support. Again he asks, "If God would save all mankind but *cannot*, is he infinite in power? If God can save all mankind but *will not*, is he infinite in goodness?" What of force there is here, lies with all its weight against matter of fact, namely, the present sufferings of our race? Is it said that present sufferings are disciplinary, and are the means God adopts to secure good to man in the end? We beg leave to ask, If God *would* save all men without present suffering, but *cannot*, is he infinite in power? If he *can* save all men without present suffering, but *will not*, is he infinite in goodness? With the license this writer takes, Universalism may be swept away at a stroke. We have seen a string of questions upon the same plan with Mr. T.'s tract, by a crafty atheist, concerning the being of God and Divine revelation; and we should think Mr. T. had taken that writer as his *beau ideal.* It were an easy matter to answer the whole tract, and turn its force upon his own theory, if space would admit. It presents a fine specimen of the priestcraft of Universalism.

XIX. "*Blessed are the dead which die in the Lord from henceforth: Yea, saith the Spirit, that they may rest from their labors; and their works do follow them.*" Rev. 14 : 13.

Here a class among the dead are named as enjoying exalted bliss. They are such as die in the Lord. But Universalism asserts that all are equally blest, and all rest from their labors, for beyond death there is no difference between the righteous and the wicked. We are aware that some of its advocates, in order to pare off a little of the absurdity, admit a difference in degrees of happiness growing out of a difference in capacity for enjoyment; but, nevertheless, all are holy and happy, for death puts an end to sin and all suffering. By the way, does not this idea border a little upon Partialism? Why did not God create and place men in circumstances perfectly equal all through their whole existence? But it is said "*their works do follow them.*" How can this be, if the present has nothing to do with the future? This text stands directly opposed to American Universalism.

XX. "*And as it is appointed unto men once to die, but after this the judgment; so Christ was once offered to bear the sins of many; and unto them that look for him shall he appear the second time without sin, unto salvation.*" Heb. 9: 27, 28.

Since the no-future punishment notion has come into vogue, this passage has become exceedingly troublesome to Universalists. That it taught a future judgment was never called in question till about 1818. Since that, various expedients have been resorted to in order to destroy its force. Mr. Balfour, in controversy with Mr. Hudson, says of it, "He (Mr. Hudson) will then ask me, what judgment comes after death? I answer, the judgment God pronounced on all mankind, (Gen. 3: 19,) 'dust thou art and unto dust shalt thou return.' Here is a judgment which comes after death, which is visible, universal, certain, and disputed by no man." *Essays*, p. 271. So when the unconscious body turns to dust, that is the judgment!! This needs no comment. To show the liberty taken with the Bible by these men of many inventions, we give the following upon this passage, found in a sermon by W. A. Stickney:

"As it is appointed unto men (human kind,) once to partake of flesh and blood, whereby the soul is subject to spiritual death, and after this the judgment of justification by a spiritual, immortal life, when the earthly tabernacle to which the spirit was first united is put off in natural death; so Christ once took on him flesh and blood, and when his body was thus put off, was once offered to bear (away) the sins of the many; that is, to make known, as the Mediator, or witness of the new covenant, the way in which full deliverance from moral death, and the power of sinful influence, is to be obtained." *Trumpet*, No. 723.

This, as all must see, is a theological curiosity. It is but justice, however, to say that these once *true* interpretations have become nearly obselete in the order. The most popular method to get rid of the troublesome text is the following: "As it is appointed unto men (the high priests), once to die, (in their sacrifices,) and after this the judgment, (which they bore upon their breast;) so Christ was once offered (that is, in a sacrificial manner), to bear the sins of many." *Guide*, p. 268.

It appears that the credit of this invention belongs to Mr. H. Ballou. See Section CXXXIII.

Our business now is to expose the sophistry of this stereotyped exposition, so often put forth with great confidence, by Universalist ministers, both great and small. In their criticisms, they tell us that the definite article should be placed before the noun *men*, so as to read, "As it is appointed unto *the men* once to die," &c. To this we do not object. But who are *the men* appointed to die? Not the Jewish high priest, as they affirm, for,

1. They were never appointed to die, either figuratively or literally, as such. We call upon Universalists to show us such an appointment from the Scriptures. They often refer us to Ex. 28: 29, 30, which reads thus:

"And Aaron shall bear the names of the children of Israel in the breast-plate of judgment upon his heart, when he goeth in unto the holy place, for a memorial before the Lord continually.

"And thou shalt put in the breast-plate of judgment the Urim and the Thummim; and they shall be upon Aaron's heart, when he goeth in before the Lord: and Aaron shall bear the judgment of the children of Israel upon his heart before the Lord continually."

Not a word is said here, or elsewhere in the Bible, about the appointment of high priests to die figuratively, in their sacrifices; and it is an unwarranted assumption to say that they were so appointed, or that they so died. The high priest typified Christ's priesthood, but did Christ die as PRIEST? Certainly not. He died as *sacrifice*, and was typified in this respect, not by the high priest but by the sacrificial lamb, offered by the high priest. Hence he is called "the Lamb of God." See, also, 1 Peter, 1: 18, 19; also Heb. 7: 22, 25, where the apostle shows that Christ, as priest, "*ever liveth* to make intercession" for his people.

2. The high priests were appointed to enter "into the holy place *every year*, with the blood of others." Ver. 25. But the men spoken of in the text were appointed *once* to die. It is said, "as it is appointed unto men once to die, so Christ was once offered." But if the men refer to the Jewish high priests, and the death to their sacrifices, then it must read thus, "As it is appointed unto the high priests once to die *every year* in their sacrifices, so Christ was offered once *every year*," and "then must he often have suffered since the foundation of the world," (ver. 25,) and thus is the apostle contradicted by this exposition. But who are the men appointed once to die? Ans. The many, (ver. 28,) for whom Christ died. "Christ was once offered to bear the sins of many." The adjective "many," is here put for the noun "men." Many men, or "*the many*," as it is in the original. Now, as the adjective "many" is here used for, or instead of, the noun "men," all that is necessary to express the exact sense, is to use the noun "men" instead of the adjective "many," i. e., *the men* instead of *the many*. The sense of the text, then, is fully expressed thus: as it is appointed unto *the men* once to die, so Christ was once offered to bear the sins of *the men*. Now who are the men for whom Christ died? Ans. "This is my blood of the New Testament, which is shed for many, (or *the many*, Gr.,) for the remission of sins." Matt. 26: 28. "He, by the grace of God, tasted death for every man." Heb. 2: 9. Thus we see, that *the many*, or *the men*, for whom Christ died are *all men*, *every man*.

We are now prepared to state the argument thus:

1. The men appointed to die, named verse 27, are the many for whom Christ died, named verse 28. As it is appointed unto *the men* once to die, so Christ was once offered to bear the sins of *the men*—that is, the men appointed to die.

2. The many, named verse 28, for whom Christ died, were all men, "every man."

3. Therefore, the men appointed to die are all men, and not the Jewish high priests, to die figuratively, as Universalists assert.

So we see that their own criticism, by which they add the definite article *the* to the common translation, goes to destroy the exposition they give of this passage. Here we state, without fear of successful contradiction, that the expression *the men* is never used in the Scriptures to designate the Jewish high priests, but on the contrary, they are called high priests, to distinguish them from *the men*, that is, the generality of men. Heb. 5 : 1.

This exposition contains the following false assertions :

1. It asserts that the high priests were appointed to die in their sacrifices, i. e., figuratively; which is false. It is mere assumption without a shadow of proof in the Bible.

2. It makes the text assert this: *as* the high priests died figuratively in their sacrifices, *so* Christ was offered figuratively in his; for it says, *as* the high priests, *so* Christ, thus making the death of Christ figurative instead of real!

3. It asserts that the high priests were appointed *once* to die, or offer sacrifices: that is, *only* once. This contradicts the apostle, for he says, ver. 25, that they entered "into the holy place *every year*, with the blood of others."

4. It asserts that the high priests died figuratively *themselves*, which is false, and again contradicts the apostle; for he says, ver 25, they offered "the blood of *others*."

5. It makes the text assert, that, as it is appointed unto the men, i. e., the high priests, once to die, so Christ was once offered to bear the sins of the *many*, or *the men*, who are the Jewish

high priests. Thus limiting Christ's atonement to the Jewish high priests!

6. It asserts that the phrase *the men* is used to designate the Jewish high priests, when it is never so used in the Bible.

To these thoughts, add the fact that this Epistle was addressed to those who had been educated in the belief of a future judgment and also, that among all the expositors of Scripture, for nearly eighteen hundred years, whose writings have come down to us, no one ever discovered this to be the meaning of the text: and that even Mr. Ballou, who it seems was so exceedingly anxious to get rid of the text, never made his discovery until he had been a constant student of the science of divinity for twenty-nine years, twenty-seven of which he was a Universalist preacher. (Sec. CXXXIII.) Take all these things into account, we say, and who does not see that the exposition given is unnatural, absurd and false.

The passage under consideration is too plain to need any comments, were it not that Universalists have so distorted its features. It will be seen, by the context, that the points connected with this passage are the two-fold appearing of Christ, which the Apostle was laboring to establish. Christ had once appeared as a sin offering, "to put away sin." He is to appear a "second time without sin," i. e., without a sin offering, "unto salvation," to those who look for him.

The substance of the Apostle's reasoning may be stated thus: all men are appointed to one temporal death, and only one; therefore, it was necessary for Christ to offer himself once, and only once, to redeem them; and as all men are accountable for the improvement they make of this grace, during their probation, and are to be judged after death, that is, after their probation has closed, so Christ will appear a second time to judge them, and to such as look for him, (not all men,) or believe in him, will he appear unto salvation. Christ came at the end of the Jewish dispensation as Redeemer. He will come at the end of the Gospel dispensation as judge.

The Apostle is speaking, doubtless, of the same event in this text that he is in Chap. 6 : 2 of the same Epistle, where, in the order of his arrangement, in giving a summary of Christian doctrines, he places "eternal judgment" after the "resurrection of the dead."

The passage teaches just what it seems to teach to an unsophisticated mind. It remains a truth, then, that men must die, and after this the judgment.

With the exception of a few thoughts, this refutation was furnished by Rev. Charles Munger.

XXI. "*After this I beheld, and lo, a great multitude, which no man could number, of all nations, and kindreds, and people,*" *&c.* *Rev.* 7 : 9, 10.

This passage has been pressed into the service of Universalism. *Pro and Con*, p. 105. But does it say one word about the salvation of all men? Does it say, "I beheld, and lo, *all men* stood before the throne, and before the Lamb, clothed in white robes, and palms in their hands," crying, Salvation to our God, &c.? Nothing like it. A particular class possessing peculiar qualifications is spoken of, and not the whole race of men. When it is shown that the whole of Adam's posterity will come up before the throne, having their robes washed and made white in the blood of the Lamb, Universalists will have done something to their purpose. What do Universalists believe concerning the efficacy of the blood of Christ to save in the future state? Just nothing. (Secs. XXIX and CV.)

XXII. "*If any man be in Christ Jesus, he is a new creature.*" 2 Cor. 5 : 17.

The author of the *Guide*, p. 48, constructs an argument to prove his theory as follows: "Paul saith, as in Adam all die, even so in Christ shall all be made alive." 1 Cor. 15 : 22. "If any man be in Christ Jesus, he is a new creature." 2 Cor. 5 : 17. Hence if all shall be made alive in Christ, they shall

all be new creatures in the resurrection of the dead. The text in 2 Cor. 5 : 17, refers to the state of the regenerated man in this world, and not to the resurrection, as may be seen by turning to the passage. The text from 1 Cor. 15 : 22, refers to the resurrection of the body, and not to the renewal of the heart. These scriptures referring to different subjects altogether, are brought together in good Universalist style, and are made to teach the salvation of all men in the future state. What cannot be proved in this way? In Gen. 4 : 8 we read, "Cain rose up against his brother Abel and slew him." In Luke 10: 37 it is said, "Go, and do thou likewise." Hence, to murder a brother as Cain did, is to obey the scriptures! Is not one argument as good as the other? Can a system of truth, given from heaven, require such work with the Bible to sustain it? Never. For an examination of 1 Cor. 15 : 22, see Sec XC.

XXXIII. "*And every creature which is in heaven and on the earth, and under the earth, and such as are in the sea, and all that are in them, heard I saying, blessing, and honor, and glory, and power be unto him that sitteth upon the throne, and unto the Lamb, for ever and ever.*" Rev. 5 : 13.

It is seldom that we see an effort to prove Universalism from the scriptures without the use of this text. But does it prove the doctrine? Let us see. We have been told for the hundredth time that Prof. Stuart said, in controversy with Dr. Channing, that spiritual worship is here intended, and also that here we have an instance of the common periphrasis of the Hebrew and New Testament writers for the universe, and the inference drawn by Universalists is, that if all the universe worship the Lamb then the whole human race will be saved. That the whole universe is here intended is doubtless correct; but with all deference to Prof. Stuart, with the Bible for our guide, we must dissent from his opinion that spiritual worship is intended. If spiritual worship is meant, then we have the whole universe, planets, angels, men, beasts, birds, fishes, creeping things, in a word, all animate and inanimate creation, engaged in it, speaking a language and ascribing blessing, honor, glory and power to God and the Lamb; and to carry out the Universalist idea, these are all to be holy and happy! The human race form but a small part of the universe. Christ sent his apostles to preach the gospel to every creature (Mark 16: 15); but the subject, the implied ability of those to whom it was sent, to receive or reject it, shows that by this moral agents are intended who are inhabitants of the earth; but in the case before us, not only is every creature which in heaven, earth, under the earth and in the sea, but also *all that are in them*, are giving these ascriptions. But should Universalists cease to quote Prof. Stuart and change their ground, as they sometimes do, and take the position that the human race, and not the whole universe, is intended, then they gain nothing. Observe, the assumption in the argument is, that the revelator had a view of all men saved in the future state. Now if human beings are intended by "*every creature*," and their so called spiritual worship is evidence of their salvation, a difficulty is at once encountered by the fact that these creatures, or human beings, doing this worship, are not only in heaven but *on the earth, and under the earth, and in the sea!* But when all shall be saved in heaven, will a part of them be on the earth, and under the earth, and in the sea? Yet to such a conclusion are we driven by such premises. The truth is, this figurative passage, from the most figurative book in all the Bible, was never designed to teach the salvation of all, or even any men in the future world. Its sole design is to give a luminous description of the glory of Him that sitteth upon the throne and of the Lamb; hence the whole universe is personified and represented as uniting in ascriptions of praise to them. The Psalmist calls upon all animate and inanimate creation to praise God, (Ps. 148,) but did he once think that this was equivalent to calling all the race of Adam to be holy and happy after death? Mr. Hosea Ballou, 2d, rebukes his brethren for their gross perversion of this text thus:

"Universalists have not wholly ceased to quote as proof of the final reconciliation of all men, this text, Rev. 5 : 13, a text which, if we mistake not their views concerning the general plan of this book, they can by no means suppose, on careful reflection, to refer to a period yet future." *U. Expositor*, v. 3., p. 196. Says Mr. Sawyer, a preacher in the order, "It has been, and may well be, doubted whether any part of the Apocalypse relates to the future and eternal world." *Pen. of Sin*, p. 16. Yet Universalist preachers continue to use this text to prove their doctrine, just because the phrase "*every creature*" is in it.

XXIV. "*And we know that this is indeed the Christ the Saviour of the world.*" John 4 : 42, also 1 John 4 : 14.

It is inquired, "How can he be the Saviour of the world without saving it?" *U. Ill. and Def.*, p. 268. This class of writers can see no possible way in which Christ can be the Saviour of the world, unless every human soul is saved. Let us help them a little upon this point. All are not saved now nor will they be, if Universalist views are correct, till the resurrection. Now observe, the text under consideration was spoken eighteen hundred years ago, and he was declared *then* to be the Saviour of the world. But millions have remained unsaved from that to the present, and if Christ has been the Saviour of the world for eighteen centuries and millions remain unsaved, we ask by what process in reasoning will it be made to appear that some may not remain unsaved forever, and yet Christ be the Saviour of the world. A man may by office be the surgeon of a whole regiment, but it does not follow that he must perform a surgical operation upon every one in the regiment. So Christ is the given or appointed Saviour of the world, but the effectual Saviour of those only who obey him. Heb. 5 : 9.

XXV. "*The wicked is driven away in his wickedness, but the righteous hath hope in his death.*" Prov. 14: 32, also Prov. 11: 7.

The twist given to this text to destroy its force is this: "In character, he (the wicked) is far away from Christ and God. He does not enjoy their companionship. He is in a peculiar sense without Christ and without God." *Banner*, March 23, 1850. So it does not refer to the dying hour but to the practice of wickedness in this life. He is driven away from Christ and God here. To be driven implies involuntary action, that is, force. But is not a departure from God, or sin, a voluntary act? Most surely, or it is not sin. And then who *drives* the wicked away from Christ and God in this world? The idea is repugnant to the whole gospel plan, which instead of driving the sinner from Christ and God, invites and welcomes him to them. Every unsophisticated mind will see that in this text the condition of the righteous and the wicked in death is contrasted. "The wicked is driven away," he goes reluctantly into the future world, is unwilling to die. He "is driven away *in*" not *out of* or *from* his wickedness, but carries the same moral character into eternity he bore when death found him. Of similar import is Prov. 11: 8. "When a wicked man dieth, his expectation shall perish; and the hope of unjust men perisheth." Now we ask, Universalism being true, what more the righteous man may hope for in death than the wicked man? Does the righteous man hope for heavenly bliss? May not the wicked do the same? Does he hope to escape the ills of this life? May not wicked men hope the same? Universalism says to all men, without respect to character, "you may hope in your death." But the Bible restricts it to the righteous only. The Bible *nowhere* says the wicked hath hope in his death. But this dogma says to the desperately wicked, "You may hope for a greater deliverance by death than the righteous, inasmuch as you are more wretched here and will fare just as well hereafter!" Which shall we follow, Universalism or the Bible?

XXVI. "*You that are troubled rest with us,*" &c. 2 Thess. 1 : 7–10, also 1 Thess. 4 : 15–17.

Universalist *truth* upon this passage used to be promulgated by Father Ballou as follows : "This fire is that in which *Christ* is revealed, and it comes from heaven. Is not this the fire with which he baptizes? Is not the fire revealed to destroy the hay, the wood, and the stubble? Undoubtedly ; and is the endless misery of the sinner to be proved from the action of that divine fire which alone is able to affect his salvation? But the objector says, the text reads for itself, 'Who shall be *punished* with *everlasting* destruction *from* the presence of the Lord, and from the glory of his power ;' and if the sinner is punished from the presence of the Lord he cannot be blessed *in* it, where there are joys forever more. Answer : There is not a place in the universe which is out of the presence of an omnipresent God ; therefore to put a sinner from the presence of the Lord he must be put out of the universe. But what means the text? says the reader. Answer : That divine light and heat, which destroys moral darkness, and purges man from all sin, is from the presence of the Lord as a production of the divine presence ; as it is written concerning the man of sin, whom the Lord shall consume with the breath of his mouth, and destroy with the brightness of his coming. If God were not able to punish the sinner in the manner described in the text, I should despair of his salvation ; but blessed be that divine spirit of light and love ; it truly takes such vengeance on the sinner as is worthy of a God." *T. on Atonement*, p. 183.

This *positive truth* has long since become obsolete, and now this class of writers, to which Mr. B. belongs, are just as positive that this passage had its fulfilment in the destruction of the Jewish polity by the Romans, as they once were that, "*punished with everlasting destruction*," "*flaming fire*," and "*taking vengeance*" meant, that divine light and heat which destroys moral darkness, and purges man from all sin !!

In order to give plausibility to his interpretation, the author of the Guide remarks as follows: "Who were those that troubled the Thessalonians? Answer: *The Jews.* See Acts 17 : 5–7. See also 1 Thess. 2 : 15, where Paul, speaking of the Jews who had persecuted the Thessalonians, says: 'Who both killed the Lord Jesus and their own prophets, and have persecuted us.'" Here a falsehood is presented by withholding a part of the truth. We turn to 1 Thess. 2 : 14, 15, and read as follows: "For ye brethren became followers of the churches of God which in Judea are in Christ Jesus; for ye also have suffered like things of your own countrymen, even as they have of the Jews: who both killed the Lord Jesus and their own prophets and have persecuted us." By this we learn that their "*own countrymen*" persecuted the Thessalonians as well as the Jews named, Acts 17 : 5–7. Did Mr. Whittemore know no better than to present the subject in this light, or did he do it to deceive? Judge ye. The Greeks then as well as the Jews troubled them.

"*When the Lord Jesus shall be revealed from heaven with his mighty angels,*" &c. This we are told was fulfilled when the Roman army destroyed Jerusalem. In reply we say, there is nothing in the history of that event which corresponds with the description given by the apostle. How was Christ "*revealed from heaven,*" the place to which he ascended after his resurrection? What is there connected with the Jerusalem catastrophe to answer to this? The Roman armies we are told were the angels that accompanied him. And were those fierce polluted heathens the *holy* (Matt. 25 : 31) angels of the immaculate Jesus? Did they come from heaven with him?

"*Taking vengeance on them that know not God and obey not the Gospel of our Lord Jesus Christ.*" Were the Jews at Jerusalem the only people who knew not God? The scriptures represent the Jews as distinguished from all other nations by their knowledge of the true God, and Paul in writing to this same church and giving them directions how to walk, says:

"Not in lust of concupiscence as the Gentiles which know not God." 1 Thess. 4 : 5. The Gentiles, then, "*know not God,*" which precludes the idea that the Apostle had exclusive reference to the Jews. This being the case he could not be teaching Jerusalem's destruction, for that was a punishment upon the Jews and not the Gentiles. At his coming, Christ is to take vengeance on them who "*obey not the Gospel.*" Were the Jews at Jerusalem the only people who disobeyed the gospel? Admitting that they were, it does not follow that this was spoken of Jerusalem's overthrow, for observe, this Epistle was written sixteen years before that event, and vast numbers of those in Judea who were living in disobedience to the gospel when Paul wrote, were dead long before the city was destroyed; and so far were they from suffering vengeance, that at that time they were enjoying heavenly bliss — i. e., if Universaliam be true. But Gentiles disobeyed the gospel as well as Jews, and persecuted Christians as we have seen. See also Acts, chapters 16 and 19. Now as vengeance was taken upon the Jews only in the destruction of Jerusalem, it follows that the Apostle does not refer to that event.

"*Who shall be punished with everlasting destruction from the presence of the Lord and the glory of his power.*"

"God permitted them (the Jews) to be driven away from their own land by the Romans under Titus." *Guide*, p. 192. This we are informed is the everlasting destruction from the presence of the Lord. Upon this we submit the following:

1. History informs us that at the taking of Jerusalem by Titus, one million one hundred thousand of the Jews perished in that city, and two hundred and fifty thousand elsewhere. These, then, instead of going "*from* the presence of the Lord," were brought immediately into his heavenly blissful presence — that is, if Universalism is true! The reader can see the sense attached to the expression, "*presence of the Lord,*" by the New Testament writers, and by Paul in particular, by turning to Heb. 9 : 24; 2 Cor. 5 : 8; also Jude 24.

2. As to the Jews being driven away from their place of worship, it is not in point at all. Of whom was the Apostle speaking? Not of the Jews as a nation or a class, as has been shown, but of a class of wicked persons who "know not God and obey not the gospel;" including Gentiles as well as Jews. Were Gentiles driven away from their place of worship and religious privileges at the time of Jerusalem's destruction? The Jews are not mentioned in the whole epistle. No more need be said.

"*Rest with us.*"

We are told that after the Jewish power was broken by the Romans, that Christians in all parts of the world had a glorious season of rest from persecution, and that this is the rest that Paul refers to here. But we look in vain to the history of that period for any such days of tranquility to the church as these writers assert. The Saviour, in Matt. 24 : 9–16, which Universalists apply to Jerusalem's destruction, represents that event as a time of great temporal calamity to Christians; and history informs us that "for two hundred and sixty years from the death of Christ, they had but short intervals of rest from persecution; for when the emperors themselves were not sanguinary, there were always inferior magistrates, who, under some pretence or other, harassed the poor, inoffensive Christians. It is supposed that three millions perished in three centuries." *Rel. Enc., Art. Persecution.* Was this the glorious rest that the faithful were promised? It is a "rest with *us*." It is not true that Christians at Thessalonica were to rest with Paul and others as a result of Jerusalem's destruction; for Paul suffered death under Nero at least four years before Titus sacked that city, and many others to whom and of whom he wrote were dead before that event. It is worthy of remark that Universalists, in order to fritter away the true sense of our Saviour's words, Matt. 10 : 28, (Sec. XCII.) contend that he is there giving instruction concerning the Jews and the Roman power; that the disciples need not much fear the Jews, as they were quite harmless, having not legal power to take life, but that they were to fear the Roman power. But in order to get rid of the passage under consideration, they will have it that the Jews are the terrible ones, and that when their power should be broken, Christians should enjoy great rest and peace under the Roman power! In the one case the Romans are the lion and the Jews the lamb, and in the other the Jews are the lion and the Romans the lamb. Any way to push forward Universalism. Of this revelation of Christ we read as follows: "Now we beseech you, brethren, by the coming of our Lord Jesus Christ, and by our gathering together unto him." Chap. 2, ver. 1.

Those to whom this was addressed were one thousand miles from Jerusalem, and there is no evidense whatever that these or any other Christians were gathered at that city at that time; but instead of gathering, it is a matter of history that Christians fled from Jerusalem "at the signs of approaching danger." Paul and others instead of being gathered at Jerusalem's destruction, were resting in the bosom of their God, having been put to death by that Roman power of which we hear so many fine things. Before Christ's coming, there was to be a great apostacy in religion. Paul cautions his brethren not to think that the day of recompense, of which he had been speaking, was near at hand; for, says he, "*that day* (the day when the Lord Jesus shall be revealed from heaven in flaming fire, taking vengeance on them who know not God), shall not come except there be a falling away first, and that man of sin be revealed, the son of perdition, who opposeth and exalteth himself against all that is called God." Chap. 2 : 4, 5. Observe, the coming of Christ spoken of in this epistle was to be subsequent to the fulfillment of this prediction. Ver. 1 and 8. Now we have no account whatever of an apostacy in the Christian church, prior to the destruction of Jerusalem, which in the least answers to this description. Furthermore, it would seem, that if the assumptions and abominations of popery are predicted anywhere in the Bible, they are here, which is an additional evidence against Universalist views, showing that the coming of Christ is yet future. Having exploded the absurdity of applying this passage to the destruction of the city of David, we now proceed to show that it does teach the final and personal coming of our Lord Jesus Christ to raise the dead and to judge the world. This will be seen,

1. Because the circumstances mentioned in the text meet not in any other coming of Christ. The reader has already seen the disposition once made of it by Mr. Ballou, and also the interpretation of more modern times, and that the latter is as truthful as the former, and no more so.

2. Because it is evident that the same advent of Christ is spoken of here that is spoken of 1 Thess. 4 : 15–17. "For this we say unto you by the word of the Lord, that we which are alive and remain unto the coming of the Lord shall not prevent them which are asleep. For the Lord himself shall descend from heaven with a shout, with the voice of the archangel, and with the trumpet of God; and the dead in Christ shall rise first. Then we which are alive and remain shall be caught up together in the clouds, to meet the Lord in the air, and so shall we be ever with the Lord." It would be an easy matter to show that if the coming of Christ here named refers to the destruction of Jerusalem, then his coming named in 1 Cor. 15, refers to the same event; and then truly the resurrection would be "past already," which would overthrow the faith of Universalists. We could easily prove that they both refer to the same event, but are saved the trouble by an admission of Mr. Whittemore. "Now when shall he (Christ) visit the earth bodily? Answer: At the resurrection of the dead. See Acts 1 : 10, 11, and 1 Thess 4 : 16." *Guide*, p. 36. The author of the Guide is right for once. He adduces the 16th verse of 1 Thess., 4th chapter, to prove that Christ will visit the earth bodily at the resurrection of the dead, which of course is taught in 1 Cor. 15, as no Universalist will deny. These events have never taken place. It would be fatal to the Universalist theory to admit

that they have. The bodily and personal coming, then, of our Lord Jesus is yet future. The question now comes up, is the Apostle treating upon the same advent of Christ in 2 Thess. 1 : 7–10 that he is in 1 Thess. 4 : 15–17 ? We answer, he most certainly is, for

1. The Epistles were both written by the same Apostle to the same church, and as in the first letter he speaks of Christ's coming to raise the dead, we safely conclude that the passage in the second letter relates to the same event, unless there is something in it to teach us a different application.

2. Instead of a different application being suggested, there are striking points of resemblance, too striking to admit of a doubt but they both relate to the same advent of Christ.

1. One says, "the Lord Jesus shall be revealed from heaven;" the other declares, "the Lord himself shall descend from heaven."

2. One says, he "shall be revealed from heaven with its mighty angels;" the other, that he shall descend "with the voice of the archangel."

3. One declares that he shall recompense rest to them that are troubled "when he shall come to be glorified in his saints;" the other says that the saints shall be caught up "to meet the Lord in the air; and so shall we ever be with the Lord."

Nothing can be plainer than that these both relate to the same great event. In the first Epistle the Apostle speaks more particularly of the righteous. In the second, both of the wicked and the righteous. In the first he asserts the resurrection of the dead; in the second, the punishment of the wicked. These facts teach us most conclusively that some men will be punished with everlasting destruction from the presence of the Lord and the glory of his power after they are raised from the dead. See Sec. XLI, where these passages are collated with Matt. 25 : 31 and 1 Cor. 15.

XXVII. "*For we must all appear before the judgment seat of Christ; that every one may receive the things* DONE *in* HIS *body, according to that he hath done, whether* IT BE *good or bad. Knowing therefore the terror of the Lord, we persuade men.*" 2 Cor. 5 : 10, 11.

This, too, refers to the judgment that came upon the Jewish nation when Jerusalem was destroyed! *Balfour's Essays*, p. 300; *Guide*, p. 187. The words in small capitals are supplied by the translators with which Mr. Whittemore is somewhat displeased, and will have it that the translators were under the influence of "long-nurtured prejudices." Were we to look no farther than Mr. W.'s Guide, we should conclude that this text stood perfectly independent of what preceded it, for he has very wisely, for his own cause, said nothing about the preceding verses. By turning to the chapter, it will be seen that the translators had the strongest of reasons from the context for adding the supplied words. The Apostle's theme is the separation of the soul from the body by death, and he very naturally cites his brethren to the event which should take place subsequent to this separation when the bodies of men should be raised and all should be judged. Without the supplied words it reads thus: "For we must all appear before the judgment seat of Christ; that every one may receive the things in body, according to that he hath done, whether good or bad." Now what is gained to Universalism by discarding the supplied words? Does it now say that we must all appear before the judgment seat of Christ at the destruction of Jerusalem? Does it now teach that all are rewarded and punished in this world? Will there not be a body of some kind after the resurrection of the *body?* and if so, may not men receive for their works "in body" in a future life? To say that the Apostle is calling the attention of his Corinthian brethren to the judgment to come upon the Jewish nation, is most false and absurd.

1. This Epistle was addressed to Christians, chiefly Gentiles. *Horne.*

2. Corinth was nine hundred miles from Jerusalem.

3. This Epistle was written at least twelve years before Jerusalem was destroyed.

4. Universalists have repeatedly told us that the destruction of Jerusalem was a judgment upon the Jewish nation for rejecting the Messiah, and of course was not a judgment on the Gentiles. It comes to this then: the Apostle sits down, twelve years before the destruction of Jerusalem, and writes to a Church composed chiefly of Gentiles, nine hundred miles from Jerusalem, as follows: For we (Paul, the Christians at Corinth, and others), must all appear before the destruction of Jerusalem by the Romans, that every one may receive the things in body according to that he hath done, whether good or bad! Did "*every one*" of the *church* at Corinth, mostly Gentiles, and nine hundred miles distant, appear at Jerusalem and there receive in body according to that they had done? Many of their bodies were mouldering in the dust long before that event. Was Paul there (he says, "*we* must all," &c.), to receive in his body? He died under Nero four years before. Again, if we may credit the authors Universalists quote, no Christian appeared before Jerusalem's destruction, but fled from the place at the "*signs* of the approaching danger." *Notes on Par.* p. 352. Mr. Whittemore usually manifests a remarkable confidence in the gullibility of his readers, but here he falters somewhat; as if he feared confining this to Jerusalem's destruction would be too large a dose even for his patrons, he adds, "at the destruction of the Jewish nation, there was a general judgment among the nations of the earth." *Guide*, p. 187. This is thrown in so that the judgment may extend off nine hundred miles to Corinth; but this helps not the matter at all, for how could those long since dead, like Paul, stand before that judgment seat? But where does Mr. W. find his authority for this bold assertion? He gives none, for the reason that he has none. This was doubtless manufactured by some one in the Trumpet office, Boston. History says nothing about such a general

judgment among the nations. That the Apostle teaches a judgment in a future state is evident from the language, the context, and the absurdity of any other construction.

XXVIII. "*All the ends of the earth shall remember and turn unto the Lord, and all the kindred of the natians shall worship before thee.*" Ps. 22 : 27.

"That all mankind will at last believe the gospel, the Bible does explicitly declare," *Guide*, p. 269 ; and then this text is quoted as proof. Now this has no more reference to the salvation of all men in the future world, than it has to the brimstone which fell upon the Sodomites. This remembering and turning unto the Lord must take place either in this world or the next. None will assert that universal salvation takes place in this world. It follows, then, that forgetfulness of God, and alienation from him, together with unbelief of the gospel, will exist in the future state ; and as these can be regarded in no other light than sins against God, it also follows that sin will exist in the future state, and consequently misery. How does this comport with the notion that death puts an end to sin and its consequences? How does it comport with the idea that all are to be ushered into bliss in a moment, in the twinkling of an eye, as some contend? This text indicates the progress and triumphs of Christianity in this world, and is perverted just because some men are willing to be deceived by a jingle of sounds. The word *all* is in the passage, hence it must mean universal salvation!

XXIX. "*Wherefore as by one man sin entered into the world, and death by sin,*" &c. Rom. 5: 12, 17–21. The reader will please turn to the passage.

As a portion of this passage is sometimes pressed into the service of Universalism, we shall examine it in reference to some of the prominent doctrines of the order, and see if they gain any support from it. The apostle says, v. 12, that sin and *death* entered the world by one man, and so *death* passed upon all men, &c.; and in v. 15, "For if through the offence of one many be *dead*," &c. Again, v. 17, "For by one man's offence *death* reigned by one." By the "*one man*," Adam is meant, v. 14. Well, what death do Universalists admit that Adam died, of which mention is here made? Do they admit that it was the death of the body? No: for they tell us that man was created mortal at first. Do they admit that it was eternal death or a death involving future and endless punishment? No: for they deny that Adam or any of his posterity were ever exposed to such a death; for if it were once admitted that all or any men were thus exposed, then all their arguments against such punishment from the attributes of God are destroyed at a blow; for if endless punishment was ever consistent with the attribute of God, it may be so to all eternity, as Universalists well know. But what death is meant? It is a moral death. Adam died to innocence the day he partook of the forbidden fruit. *U. Ill. & Def.*, p. 76.

Did this moral death extend beyond this present life? We hear Mr. Whittemore more than twenty years ago asserting that "Universalists now know of no condition for man, beyond the grave, but that in which he is as the angels of God in heaven." *Trumpet*, April 2, 1831. And who has not heard their perversion of Rom. 6 : 7 : "He that is dead is freed from sin," to prove that the most God-dishonoring, polluted rake in creation is freed from sin and all its consequences as soon as death does its work.

At this point let us inquire, do Universalists admit that Christ came into this world to save us in another? To answer this question, we will introduce Mr. Ballou, the father of modern Universalism, and Mr. Whittemore, his right hand supporter. These men have done more by way of originating and propagating Universalist doctrines than any other two men in the nation. Mr. Ballou says, "that Christ came into *this* world to save us in *another*, is contrary to all the representations found in the scriptures." *Lec.* p. 14. Mr. Whittemore says, "The truth is, we do not read one word in the Bible about saving men from punishment in the future state." The evils from which Jesus came to save men are in this world, and for this reason he came into this world to save them." *Guide*, p. 254. Now according to these teachers, all the blessings named in the passage under consideration, as a result of Christ's death and obedience, are confined to this world; so we are at liberty to paraphrase v. 18, as follows: "Therefore by the offence of Adam, judgment came upon all men to moral death in this world, even so by the righteousness of Christ, the free gift came upon all men unto moral life in this world!" This, as all must see, is a legitimate conclusion from the premises, and all that Universalism can derive from the text and its connection is, *that all men shall be made morally alive in this world*, which is just nothing; for neither moral life or death can fix the future condition of man, according to this dogma; and, furthermore, such a conclusion is contrary to matter of fact. Is it said that the blessings gained by Christ are more extensive than those lost by Adam? No matter how extensive the blessings, they are all confined to this world, inasmuch as they are *by* Christ, (v. 15, 17, 21;) and he came, as Universalist guides assert, not to save men in the future world, but in this. As it respects the reign of grace "through righteousness unto eternal life, by Jesus Christ our Lord," v. 21, that, according to Mr. Whittemore and others, cannot refer to the future state, for "This phrase (eternal life) is not used by the sacred writers to signify endless blessedness beyond the grave, but that state of spiritual life and peace which was the immediate effect of faith in the gospel of Jesus Christ." *Guide*, p. 140. Now if this phrase is not used by the sacred writers to signify bliss beyond the grave, of course it is not so used here, and accordingly the use of the phrase in v. 21, confines the blessings named to this life. Universal salvation is the holiness and happiness of all our race, not in this life, but in the future; so it will be seen at once that these men, by their own interpretations, deprive themselves of the right to bring any of the last eleven verses of this chapter to prove their doctrine. But as inconsistent as it is, as there is universal language employed, we find them weaving in a text now and then from this passage, to give plausibility to their arguments.

The design of the apostle is, to compare Adam's sin and Christ's obedience, in respect to their virtue and efficacy, and to show that the efficacy of Christ's obedience must needs be much more abundant than that of Adam's sin. He says, v. 18 and 19, "Therefore, as by the offence of one, judgment came upon all men to condemnation, even so by the righteousness of one, the free gift came upon all men unto justification of life. For as by one man's disobedience many were made sinners, so by the obedience of one shall many be made righteous." By this we learn that all men were passively condemned, in some sense, (not to endless misery,) by Adam's offence; EVEN SO, mark that, the free gift came positively upon all men to justification of life, or freedom from condemnation *here*, (not in heaven.) Thus as far as man was made a sinner in Adam, he is made righteous in Christ, and no farther. And as nothing which Adam did condemned the sinner to misery in the future state, independent of his own acts, so nothing that Christ has done can make him holy and happy without obedience to God; for he has become "the author of eternal salvation," not to all our race, but "UNTO ALL THEM THAT OBEY HIM" Heb. 5:9. Thus we see that through the benevolence of God, in the gift of his Son, all men are now saved from the condemnation of Adam's offence; and all moral agents may, by obedience to Christ, be saved eternally. But it is inquired, if any are doomed to endless punishment for their sins, how can it be reconciled with v. 20, where it is declared that "where sin abounded grace did much more abound?" Mr. Isaac, p. 68, answered this in his day; and it is as forcible now as then. He says, "Mr. Wright is mistaken as to the meaning of the word *sin* in this passage. He supposes it means all the sins of all men, in all ages. But if this were its meaning, the apostle's assertion in the next verses (chap. 6 : 1, 2) would not be true ; for if we continued in sin, grace would abound, and the more sin we committed there would be the more grace : but the apostle enters a caveat against putting any such sense upon his words, and says, '*God forbid.*' If sin in this place is to be understood in Mr. Wright's comprehensive sense, even then grace could only abound *as much* as sin ; for how it could abound *more than all sin*, I confess I have not penetration enough to discern ; but the apostle says '*much more.*' By sin, in this text, I understand the sin of Adam, which hath reigned unto death, v. 12. Grace abounds as much as this sin, by justifying us from it as soon as we are brought into existence, v. 18. And it abounds *much more* by taking away all the personal sins of believers, making them righteous, and conducting them to a glorious immortality. This interpretation is confirmed by v. 15, 16. Here the sin is called the '*offence of one,*' and the abounding of grace consists not only in the justification of many (all) persons from the sin of Adam, but also in the justification of all believers from their *many* personal *offences.* In this view, the words '*much more*' may be understood with strict propriety, if the pardon of all the offences committed by millions of believers may be considered as a matter of great importance."

It would be easy to show that the passage we are examining stands directly opposed to several points strongly insisted upon by Universalists. We have here clearly taught the vicarious character of Christ's death, and this based upon the fallen condition of our race as a consequence of Adam's sin,—doctrines which Universalists have no belief in generally. In the last verse we have the great design of the plan of redemption in these words, "That as sin hath reigned unto death, even so might grace reign through righteousness unto eternal life, by Jesus Christ our Lord." Let the Son of God himself decide the question whether or not he died to give this eternal life to all moral agents unconditionally. Hear him : "As Moses lifted up the serpent in the wilderness, even so must the Son of Man be lifted up ; that

WHOSOEVER BELIEVETH in him might not perish, but have eternal life." John 3 : 14, 15. Again, v. 36: "He that believeth not the Son, SHALL NOT SEE LIFE; but the wrath of God abideth on him." Does Paul teach that eternal life is secured to all unconditionally? No; but only those "who by patient continuance in well doing, seek for glory, and honor, and immortality," shall have "*eternal life.*" Rom. 2 : 7. Again, "I endure all things for the elect's sake, THAT THEY MAY OBTAIN the salvation which is in Christ Jesus, with eternal glory." 2 Tim. 2 : 10. What folly in the apostle, if eternal glory is secured to all! What should we think in our day to hear a Universalist minister expressing himself thus? It will be seen by the construction given by Universalists to the death by Adam, their denial of the future-state efficacy of Christ's death, and their rendering of the phrase "eternal life," that they utterly deprive themselves of any support to their theory from this passage. But should they change their ground, as some of them can with great ease, and admit that Christ came into this world to save men in the next, and that the expression "eternal life," means a life of bliss in the future, then they gain nothing for their cause here; for, as we have seen, the Son of God from heaven has declared against the unconditionality of his salvation, and says of some that they "*shall not see life;*" and the apostles reiterate the same in various ways.

XXX. "*And he shall send Jesus Christ, which before was preached unto you: whom the heaven must receive until the times of restitution of all things, which God hath spoken by the mouth of all his holy prophets, since the world began.*" Acts 3 : 20, 21.

Mr. Whittemore, (*Guide*, p. 36,) gives his testimony in full in favor of Christ's visit again to the earth bodily, at the resurrection of the dead (See. XXVI); a doctrine, by the way, which is scouted by Universalists generally; and even the same writer, on page 186 of the same book says, "The coming of the Lord took place, as we have said, during the apostolic age." And when Paul (2 Thess. 7) declares that "the Lord Jesus shall be revealed from heaven," the very sentiment Mr. W. favors, as above stated, we are told by the same writer that it took place when Jerusalem was destroyed! *Guide*, p. 189. The restitution of all things is to be consummated before the coming of Christ. Now if the coming of Christ, so often named in the Bible, occurred at the destruction of Jerusalem, then the restitution spoken of must have been closed up at that all-important event; and if the restitution indicates the holiness and happiness of all men, then all the human race were saved nearly eighteen hundred years ago! Seeing the consequences of such a reference, the author of the Guide was forced to the admission made concerning the bodily coming of Christ, in order, if possible, to press the text into the service of his cause. But in this he utterly fails. The very point in debate is assumed, viz: that this restitution of all things, is the salvation of all our race in eternity. By the restitution of all things, may be understood the restoration of all things which will ever be restored in this world, which is to be effected by the gospel. It is written, Matt. 17: 11, "Elias truly shall first come and restore all things." Did the Saviour mean to teach that before he could begin his work, John the Baptist must first save all men? No: but he was to restore all to be restored by his office and mission as the harbinger of the Messiah. (Sec. LXXIV.) In the case before us, the restoration or restitution of all things refers to the work of the gospel in this world; and when this shall be fully accomplished, according to all which God hath spoken by the mouth of all his holy prophets, then shall Christ come bodily from heaven to raise the dead. For observe, "the heaven must receive," or contain him, *until* this restitution; and so far is the apostle from teaching the salvation of all men by it, that he declares, respecting its progress, that "it shall come to pass that every soul which will not hear that Prophet, (Christ,) SHALL BE DESTROYED from among the people." See Sec. I., where this subject is further explained in connection with the Abrahamic Promise.

XXXI. "*And in this mountain shall the Lord of hosts make unto all people a feast,*" &c. Isa. 25 : 7–10.

"He will wipe away tears from off all faces." Does this include the whole human race? We answer, No. In reading the Bible, we should bear in mind that language expressive of a mathematical whole, is sometimes employed when a universal whole is not intended. In Matt. 3 : 5, 6, we learn that "all Judea and all the region round about Jordan" were baptised of John confessing their sins. But did every man, woman and child confess their sins and receive John's baptism? No sane mind will assert this. "All nations compassed me about, but in the name of the Lord will I destroy them." Ps. 118 : 10. The Psalmist's enemies were numerous, and he expected to overcome them, is the sense. And it is well understood that Universalists, when their case requires it, can readily make *all* mean a part of the race. (Sec. XLI.) As it respects the expression "*all faces*" it is said, (Joel 2 : 6,) "all faces shall gather blackness," and in Ez. 7 : 18, "Shame shall be upon all faces." But are these expressions predicated of all the race of man? By no means. We must learn the application of such language either by the connection in which it is found, or by other scriptures treating upon the same subject. If we go to the connection in which it is declared, "He will wipe away tears from off *all faces*," we shall find it is used in a restricted sense.

By the mountain, where the feast is provided, we understand the church of God in this world, and not the heavenly state; for the Prophet adds, (v. 10,) "For in this mountain shall the hand of the Lord rest, and Moab shall be trodden down under him, even as straw is trodden down for the dunghill." If we take this passage literally as it reads, it refers to the deliverance and prosperity of the Jews, and the destruction of the Moabites. But if we take a figurative view of it, then we shall see ushering in upon our benighted world, the light of the glorious gospel dispensation, providing a spiritual feast for all people, and removing the covering or the veil of idolatry and superstition from all nations. It teaches, too, the ultimate deliverance and salvation of God's people, and the destruction of his enemies. Any one who will pay attention to the whole passage, must see that what is said here is not spoken of all men in the future world; for always bear in mind that it is not in this world that universal salvation is alleged to take place, but in the future. Now we ask, are the Moabites to be destroyed, to be trodden down under the Lord, even as straw is trodden down for the dunghill, in the future state? This thought alone destroys the text for Universalism; for if men are trodden down or destroyed in the future world, then are they not saved. This conclusion is inevitable, if the prophet is speaking of the condition of men in the future state. This, however, is not the fact; and Universalists must admit that it is not, or give up their theory. The joy, sorrow and triumph of the church in this world, are taught here. We are then referred to the resurrection. "He will swallow up death in victory," v. 8, when the work of the church militant shall be closed up. But does this teach that God will put an end to all spiritual or moral death at that time. No: for we learn from the apostle that this refers to the resurrection of the body (1 Cor. 15 : 54); and as the scriptures nowhere teach that the soul is to be cleansed by the resurrection of the body, and thus produce holiness and happiness, this of course proves nothing in favor of Universalism, even though it were admitted that the resurrection of all men is intended. All men, doubtless, will be raised at the end of time, with the exception of those who shall experience a change equivalent to being raised. But the resurrection of the people of God is indicated here. This view harmonizes with the connection, and also with the apostle. 1 Cor. 15. See Sec. XC. It is worthy of remark, that the Saviour uses the same figure of a feast or supper (Luke 14 : 16–24) to represent the gospel provisions; and speaking of the treatment those provisions received when offered to some, the Son of God himself, who is represented by the lord of the feast, declares of such rejecters, that "THEY SHALL NOT TASTE OF MY SUPPER." This we conceive to be far from favorable to the idea that all men shall enjoy this feast forever.

XXXII. "*Now no chastening for the present seemeth to be joyous, but grievous; nevertheless, afterward it yieldeth the peaceable fruit of righteousness unto them which are exercised thereby.*" Heb. 12 : 11.

As may be seen by the context, this is addressed to Christians; and the subject upon which Paul is treating, is God's chastisments inflicted upon his children in this world, for their good; and to such they yield the peaceable fruits of righteousness. No one ever thought that endless punishment was taught in this text, yet the author of the Guide very gravely remarks, (p. 128,) "If this chastisement were strictly *endless*, how could it *afterwards* yield the peaceable fruits of righteousness? Is there any *afterwards* to eternity?" Thus a man of straw is made and torn in pieces, all for the good of Universalism!

XXXIII. "*Ask of me, and I will give thee the heathen for thine inheritance, and the uttermost parts of the earth for thy possessions.*" Ps. 2 : 8. Also the following texts are examined in this Section: John 3 : 35; 6 : 37; 17 : 2.

"God hath given all things to Christ, as the moral Ruler of the world. 'Ask of me, and I will give thee the heathen for thine inheritance, and the uttermost parts of the earth for thy possession.' Ps. 2 : 8. 'The Father loveth the Son, and hath given all things into his hand.' John 3 : 35. 'All things,' here, means all intelligent *beings*. So say the best commentators." *Guide*, p. 25. As this argument is made to prove Universalism, we must understand Ps. 2 : 8 as teaching the unconditional salvation of all Adam's race in the future state. To this we object, and appeal to the context. The king of Zion,

(v. 6, 7,) to whom the promise is given, is Christ, doubtless. But what is he promised? Is it that all shall be holy and happy in eternity? No, this is not it; but the heathen shall be his inheritance, and the *uttermost parts of the earth* for his possessions; and he is to break them with a rod of iron, and dash them in pieces like a potter's vessel (v. 9). Then an exhortation is given to kings and judges of the earth to "serve the Lord with fear, and rejoice with trembling," (v. 10, 11,) and that they "kiss the Son, lest he be angry, and they perish from the way when his wrath is kindled but a little (v. 12). Says Mr. Skinner, "None can be saved from all moral evil here." *U. Ill. & Def.*, p. 261. It is beyond death, then, that all are to be saved. But are the heathen to be given to Christ beyond death? Are the uttermost parts of the earth to be given to Christ beyond the grave; and is Christ to break the heathen in pieces with a rod of iron, &c., in eternity! How will such views comport with the idea that there is no condition for man beyond the grave, but that in which he is as the angels of God in heaven?

No more need be said to show the perversion of the text. Its evident teaching is the extension of Christ's kingdom in the earth, among the heathen nations. Let us now attend to the other text connected with this to make out the argument. "The Father loveth the Son, and hath given all things into his hand." Mr. French, who attempted to correct his brethren somewhat in a sermon before the Maine Convention of Universalists, says, "This is a favorite text with some, to prove our doctrine. But does it have the least, the faintest reference to it? Do not 'all things' here, denote the power which is given to Christ, or everything necessary for the accomplishment of his work? Does not the context require this explanation? And yet a certain book (*Guide*, p. 25) has it that 'all things' here, means intelligent *beings*. So say the best commentators.' These best commentators are beyond our knowledge; yet enough are at hand to bear a contrary testimony." *Banner*, Aug. 5, 1844. Thus discourseth Mr. French, concerning his brother Whittemore. He then names the commentators who are opposed to Mr. W.'s assertion, as follows: "Scott, Clarke, Campbell, Bloomfield, Livermore, and Tholuck." To these may be added at least three more: Henry, Benson, and Wesley. Among these are some of the *best* commentators, and they are opposed to Mr. W.'s view; yet Mr. W. says, "So say the best commentators!" We see that this argument is built upon perverted texts. Another argument is produced from the foregoing as follows: "God gave all beings to Christ that he might save them. 'Thou hast given him power over all flesh, that he should give eternal life to as many as thou hast given him.' John 17: 2. This plainly evinces that it was God's design, in giving Christ dominion over all flesh, that they should all enjoy eternal life." The phrase eternal life is, by this same author, confined to the spiritual life of the believer in this world. This being the case, what has Mr. W. proved by the argument? He has proved that as many as are given to Christ in the sense of the text, have *spiritual life in this world.* Yet this is presented as proof of the salvation of our race in the future state! Which shall we credit; Mr. W. on page 140 of his Guide, or Mr. W. on page 25 of the same book? The assumption is that all mankind are given to Christ, and that eternal life is bestowed upon all thus given. We are then told that the phrase eternal life "*is not used* by the sacred writers to signify endless blessedness beyond the grave; but that state of spiritual life and peace which was the immediate effect of faith in the gospel of Jesus Christ." *Guide*, p. 140. The inevitable conclusion is, as above stated, that all men have spiritual life and peace in this world. Hence, the jolliest Universalist, the ripest infidel, the most debased drunkard, the most polluted libertine, and the most humble and pious Christian, may all strike hands in joyful possession of that spiritual life and peace which faith in the Gospel of Christ imparts!! To such results do the crooked works of these expounders lead. But admitting that *eternal life* does mean a life of bliss in the future state, does not the text then teach the salvation of all men? No: for it has been shown most conclusively, that all are not given to Christ in the sense involved; and it can be shown by an abundance of scriptures, that eternal life is not bestowed unconditionally upon adult sinners. (Sec. XXIX.) We now come to another argument, built mainly upon the two we have considered. "It is certain that Christ will save all that the Father hath given him. 'All that the Father giveth me shall come to me, and him that cometh to me I will in nowise cast out.' John 6: 37. These three propositions are irrefragable evidence of the final happiness of all men." Now the whole of this work is built upon perverted texts and assumptions.

1. Christ is to have the heathen for his inheritance, &c. Ps. 2: 8. This is perverted to teach that all shall be holy and happy in the future state.

2. The Father loveth the Son, and hath given *all things*, &c. John 3: 35. This is perverted to mean all intelligent beings.

3. We are told that God gave all intelligent beings to Christ, that he might save them; i. e. save them in the future world: and then Mr. W. brings for proof an expression, the future-state reference of which he himself denies! He perverts this text, (John 17: 2,) however, not by referring it to the future, but by pressing it in to teach that *all* shall enjoy eternal life in the future state.

4. Then comes the text which is designed to top out the fabric so skilfully reared upon a rotten foundation. "All that the Father giveth me shall come to me; and him that cometh to me I will in nowise cast out." John 6: 37. "It is certain that Christ will save all that the Father hath given him. So says Mr. Whittemore. We have already seen the baseless character of his reasonings, built as they are upon perverted texts; and this is sufficient to show that nothing is proved for Universalism. But we have one more witness to introduce to show the falsity of this whole argument. We ask, then, has the Father given *all men* to Christ, to be saved in the sense of the text last quoted?

Let the faithful and true witness answer. "I pray not for the world, but for them which thou hast given me." "They are not of the world, even as I am not of the world." John 17 : 9, 16. Does the Saviour say that all men are given to him, and that he will save all men unconditionally in the future? Nothing like it; but those who are given to him, are distinguished from others who are called "*of the world*," and are not given to him. It is worthy of remark, too, that even those who are his, are not so given to him as to secure their unconditional salvation; for it appears that Judas was among those given, and yet he was lost (v. 12). See also Ps. 41 : 9, and John 13 : 18; also Matt. 26 : 24. That such as are given to Christ, or the elect, may be lost, is evident from the apostle, where he says, (2 Tim. 2 : 10,) "I endure all things for the elect's sake, that they may obtain the salvation which is in Christ Jesus, with eternal glory." All will see that the sufferings of Paul for these elect persons was wholly unnecessary if they were unconditionally safe and sure of heaven. In view of these facts, what becomes of Mr. Whittemore's boasted "irrefragable evidence of the final happiness of all men?"

XXXIV. "*For we which have believed do enter into rest.*" Heb. 4 : 3.

"Paul says, 'we which have believed do enter into rest;' which could never be true if they believed in the doctrine of endless misery." *Guide*, p. 51. To meet this foolish argument, it is only necessary to state that Paul says, "we which have believed do enter into rest;" which could never be true, if they believed in the doctrine of Jerusalem's destruction, where such awful calamities were to come upon their Jewish brethren. Can a system of truth from heaven require such an argument to sustain it?

XXXV. "*And the Lord said unto Cain, Where is Abel thy brother?*" &c. Gen. 4 : 9–15; also chap. 7 : 23, and 19 : 24, 25.

All we have to do with this passage is to expose the sophistry employed upon it, as Christians never supposed that either heaven or hell were taught here. Says one writer, "neither in the threatenings nor the fears of Cain, do we find anything of endless woe. He was to be a fugitive and vagabond in the earth." *U. Ill. & Def.*, p. 199.

The conclusion from this kind of argument is, that there is no future punishment. To show the unsoundness of this, it is only necessary for us to ask a few questions. Why did not God tell Cain something about the resurrection and heavenly bliss? When he complained that his punishment was greater than he could bear, why did not God inform Cain that he could not sin enough to bring upon himself any more punishment than should prove a blessing to him? Why was he not told that all punishment is disciplinary, and that "a remission of punishment would be a curse instead of a mercy; because a just punishment is as essential to our welfare as anything that love can do"? (*U. Ill. & Def.*, p. 250); or, in other words, why did not God tell Cain that he was about to bless him for murdering his brother? Again, when he expressed his fears, "every one that findeth me shall kill me," why did not the Lord comfort him by assuring him heavenly bliss in such a case? But all the comfort God administered to Cain in this trying hour, pertained to this life. Why was he not informed that all he could possibly have lost by dying in the very act of murdering his brother, would have been the *blessing* of punishment for that last sin? The reader will see that questions might be proposed and negatives asserted to almost any extent, which would amount to but little in argument. If the absence of the record that God told Cain about a future hell is proof that there is none, then for the same reason there is no resurrection, no world of bliss, and punishment is not disciplinary; for God told Cain nothing about these. This being the case, what becomes of Universalism? In a word, there is no future life whatever, and this is the result of such teachings.

The destruction of the old world, (Gen. 7 : 23,) and of Gomorrah, (chap. 19 : 24, 25,) they labor to turn to their account in the same way. It is asked: "If an infinite curse was to come on the antediluvians, why was God silent respecting it? Or if he preached it to the people, why have we no record of the fact?" Of Gomorrah it is said, "God said he would not hide from Abraham what he was about to do; but he gave no intimation of endless punishment." *U. Ill. & Def.*, p. 199. To meet this it is only necessary to ask, if Noah, a preacher of righteousness for a hundred and twenty years, was a Universalist, and conveyed the glad tidings to the wicked antediluvians that they all would go immediately to bliss when the flood should come, "why have we no record of the fact?" God would not hide from Abraham what he was about to do. Gen. 18 : 17. Now if Abraham understood the promise made to him (Gen. 18 : 12) to signify the salvation of all men in eternity, if he taught the filthy Sodomites that nought but bliss awaited them in the future world, or if he taught them anything relative to a future life, why are the scriptures silent about it? Why have we no record of the fact! It will be seen that the method adopted to render the case of Cain, the antediluvians, and the Sodomites, subservient to Universalism, can with equal propriety be turned against that system; and yet that dogma is dependent for its support upon just such work with the scriptures. Can it be the truth of God? Universalists have much to say concerning the absence of an explicit declaration in favor of future punishment among the Patriarchs or the Jews in the time of Moses, and consider this a strong argument in favor of their doctrine. But was it explicitly declared to them by God or any of his servants that there is no punishment beyond the grave, or that all shall be saved in the future world? Let the passage be produced, if it can be found. If it cannot be found, let Universalists be consistent, and deny a future life altogether.

XXXVI. "*And all bare him witness, and wondered at the gracious words which proceeded out of his mouth.*" Luke 4 : 22.

Upon this the author of the Guide makes an argument as follows: "Jesus when on earth preached in such a manner, that the people 'wondered at the gracious words which proceeded out of his mouth.' This could not have happened had he threatened the people with endless punishment." *Guide*, p. 43. Universalist authors not only admit that Christ foretold Jerusalem's destruction, but contend that no small portion of the New Testament is occupied with it. In view of their professions, one writer has advised them to label it, "THE DESTRUCTION OF JERUSALEM FORETOLD." Let us apply the argument. Jesus, when upon earth, preached in such a manner that the people (Jews) wondered at the gracious words which proceeded out of his mouth. This could not have happened had he threatened them with the horrid cruelties they suffered when the Romans came against them, together with the destruction of their city and temple, which they loved so well! Take the threatened destruction of Jerusalem out of the Bible, and one of the main pillars of Universalism is gone. All must see that the latter argument is as sound as the former, and that neither amount to anything. Was all Christ's language accounted "gracious words" by his hearers! He addressed some thus: "Ye serpents, ye generation of vipers, how can ye escape the damnation of hell?" See the whole of Matt. chap. 23.

XXXVII. "*God is love.*"—1 John 4 : 16.

By the manner this saying has been treated by Universalists, we should conclude that love was not an attribute of God, but constituted the divine substance, or essence, or in other words that love is God. But if we are to adopt this view because it is asserted that God is love, then we may with equal propriety affirm that light is God, and that spirit is God; for it is written, "God is a spirit," "God is light." By this method we might soon manufacture as many gods as the heathen have, with natures as opposite to each other. We are not to conclude because God is love, that therefore he is nothing else. The love of God is always displayed in harmony with his other perfections. We admit, as is contended, that God's love always did exist, now exists, and always will exist; but it by no means follows that all will be saved. For God to be love is one thing, and for men to love God is quite another. God's love exists independently of his creatures, but man's happiness depends upon his moral state. The unchangeableness of God's love has been urged as a reason why all are to be saved. But this very argument is fatal to the Universalist conclusion drawn from the love of God; for according this, God's love will be the same in all future ages that it is now, and was when sin and misery entered the world; and if his love did not prevent sin, and does not now save all men unconditionally, what evidence have we, merely from the fact that God is love, that it shall be done hereafter? Just none at all. It will amount to nothing in argument to say that the present untold misery of our race is only the result of a system of means adopted by love to secure to man a great good in the end; for such means are cruel and unnecessary if all men are to be saved unconditionally as the effect of love; for God's love can call to its aid almighty power and infinite wisdom to destroy sin and misery now, just as effectually as it can ages hence. Men may be under the necessity of adopting a severe and painful course to secure good to others, as the chastisement of a child, or the amputation of a limb to save life; but what man who loved his child or friend would do this if he could secure the same good without it? Now if it be a mere question of God's love, power, or any or all his attributes, irrespective of man's agency, he certainly can be under no such necessity as to introduce or permit sin and suffering for six thousand years in our world, for he can destroy these at once and spread peace and happiness throughout the universe. But sin and misery continue, which shows us the folly of reasoning from the love of God to prove the salvation of all men; for if present love does not save from present suffering, what presumption to suppose that future love will save from future suffering. The fact that God's love is unchangeable, lies with mighty weight against Universalism. If it could be proved that the love of God will change at a future time, so as to operate differently in his moral system from what it ever has before, then perhaps an argument might be raised from it to prove the salvation of all men as the result of such a change. But as God's love never changes, and as the wide-spread sufferings of our earth for thousands of years is not incompatible with it, so for aught that can be shown it may not be incompatible with it for impenitent men to suffer endlessly. For God to possess the attribute of love is one thing, but for him to so love all men as to save them unconditionally in the future world, is quite another thing, especially since he has said of certain characters, "I will love them no more." Hosea 9 : 15. On love as a passion in God, see Sec. CXX. On love consistent with eternal punishment, see Sec. CXXXIX. On the attributes of God, see Sections CIV. and CXIV.

XXXVIII. "*In the beginning God created the heaven and the earth.*" — Gen. 1 : 1.

Speaking of the Bible, Mr. Rogers says, "it informs me that 'in the beginning God created the heaven and the earth,' but no mention is made of his having created a HELL!" *Pro and Con*, p. 280. This argument is put forth by one who has been counted a Rabbi in the order. Such questions as where is hell? when was it created? are quite common with some; and not obtaining a satisfactory answer, it is quite evident to such that there is no future and endless punishment. It would be a severe reflection upon the understanding of their leaders to say that they know no better than to present such an *argument* for the reception of the ignorant. The truth is, we have no more history touching the creation of heaven, as a place of bliss, than we have of hell as a place of torments. The heaven named in the history is the firmament, as all may see by reading it. The argument stands thus: If there were any hell where men will suffer in the future world, there would be an account of its creation in the Bible. There is no such account in the Bible; therefore, there is no hell for men to suffer in the future world. Let us apply this in another direction. If there were any heaven where men will be happy in the future world, there would be an account of its creation in the Bible. There is no such account; therefore, there is no heaven for men to enjoy in the future world. There is then no endless suffering to be feared, and no endless bliss to be hoped for! To such results are we led in this warfare against the truth of God. If this is so, what becomes of Universalism?

XXXIX. "*Every valley shall be exalted, and every mountain and hill shall be made low: and the crooked shall be made straight, and the rough places plain. And the glory of the Lord shall be revealed, and all flesh shall see it together: for the mouth of the Lord hath spoken it.*" Isa. 40 : 4, 5.

As all men are not saved in this world, in the Universalist sense, the assumption upon this passage is, that all the progeny of Adam shall be made holy and happy in the future state. Any believer in a future retribution can admit that God's glory will be revealed in the future judgment, and that all men will see it together; and that too, without admitting that all will be saved. But we deny the future state reference of the passage. It is a highly poetical description of the achievements of the gospel in this world; and the leveling process preparatory to it had its fulfillment in the labors of John the Baptist. See Luke 3 : 35. But it is said, the expression "*all flesh,*" must mean the whole race of man. Not so, for Joel prophesied that God would pour out his "spirit upon *all flesh,*" (Joel 2 : 28,) and this, as the inspired Peter declared, had its fulfillment on the day of Pentecost. Acts 2 : 16, 17. All flesh here cannot mean the whole race of man, for millions had lived and died before that day. By the declaration that all flesh shall see the salvation of God, we may understand that there will be such a display of God's glory in the world through the gospel, that all men then living shall see it, or it may be enjoy it.

XL. "*The blood of Jesus Christ cleanseth us from all sin.*" 1 John 1 : 7.

"There is no sin that the blood of Christ will not wash away. Though our sins be as scarlet, they shall be white as snow; and, though they be red like crimson, they shall be as wool. Jesus can save the chief of sinners. 1 Tim. 1 : 15. He has the will, no less than the power; therefore, all men will be saved by his grace." *Guide*, p. 52. Here the entire argument of Mr. Whittemore is given to prove Universalism from this text, and we have seldom seen more perversion in so small a compass. As this argument is made to prove Universalism, it is of course assumed that the blood of Christ will cleanse unconditionally all the race of man from all sin. But the connection in which the text is found, clearly refutes this. The whole verse reads thus: "But if we walk in the light, as he is in the light, we have fellowship one with another, and the blood of Jesus Christ his Son cleanseth us from all sin." Cleanseth US. Who? All men? No; but such as "*walk in the light*," &c. Reference is made to Isa. 1 : 18. By turning to it, it will be seen that God is addressing the rebellious Jews and declaring to them, not his ability to save them independent of their moral agency, but that in case they gave up their rebellion and turned to him he would cleanse them. The whole of this silly argument is based upon the unwarranted assumption that Christ is willing and able to save all men irrespective of their agency, and having this ability and will, all men will be saved. But we are authorized from the Bible to say that there are some things that God himself cannot do. He cannot lie. He cannot deny himself; and as a moral governor he cannot save sinners without penitence. The almighty Saviour could not do many mighty works in one place because of their unbelief, (Matt. 13 : 5–8,) and although he is able to save to the uttermost, yet he only will save such as come unto him. Heb. 7 : 25. We deny the ability of Christ to save those who reject him. "Ye will not come unto me that ye might have life," said he to those who spurned his invitations.

XLI. "*When the Son of man shall come in his glory,*" &c. Matt. 25 : 31–46.

Universalists now seem to be quite astonished because we cannot see Jerusalem's destruction in this passage. But why should they be surprised at our dullness, since Mr. Ballou, with all his sagacity, preached for years before he thought of denying its future state reference, and even when he did deny it he never once thought of consigning the passage over to Jerusalem, but saw most clearly that it had its fulfillment on the day of Pentecost. In his "Treatise on the Atonement," p. 179, printed in 1828, ten years after he made the discovery that after death there is *no* judgment, the following exposition occurs: "The time of Christ's coming in his glory was the day of Pentecost. His holy angels with whom he came, were his chosen apostles. His glory is the gospel of eternal life. Sheep and goats signify believers and unbelievers. *Right* hand and *left* means gospel and law. The believer stands in the gospel of life. The unbeliever is condemned already, and the wrath of God, in the letter of the law, abideth upon him." This was given at the time with much positiveness, and doubtless many a sin-loving disciple was made joyful by such a handy method invented to get rid of a text so troublesome to wicked men. It was received as the pure bread of life, the truth, in opposition to the monstrosities of the purblind Partialists. Mr. Murray was quite sure that this passage referred to the future judgment, and that the sheep were all mankind, and the goats the fallen angels, or devils, (*Universalist Comp.* 1856, p. 20,) involving the absurd idea that the devils were condemned for not attending to their duty (v. 42–44,) in visiting Christ's followers in sickness and other calamities! It is but about thirty-eight years since Universalists began to deny that this scripture referred to the future world, and while some adopted the same quibbling that their modern brethren do, to show that the word everlasting does not mean endless, there were others among them who admitted that endless punishment is deserved and threatened in the Bible, but that all will be saved from it by the atonement, or that it will be remitted to all upon the same principle that the Ninevites were saved from their threatened punishment. Dr. Huntington (Sec. CXXVI.) was a man of learning, and wrote a book to prove Universalism. Mr. Whittemore says of him, that he "found fault with Universalists in general for *trifling* with the original word translated forever; and in reference to the question, "Does the Bible plainly say that sinners of mankind shall be damned to interminable punishment?' he answered, 'It certainly does, as plainly as language can express, or any man, or even God himself, can speak.' 'The endless duration of punishment,' said he, 'appears obviously just, no more than we deserve, and not in the least cruel for God to inflict.'" Mr. W. also says, "Huntington's system differed very little, if any, from Relly's." *Mod. Hist.*, pp. 384–5.

But the children have outgrown their fathers, and now it is denied that endless punishment was ever deserved or threatened, and it is boldly asserted that Christ never came into this world to save us in the next. Their once positive truth has become untruth, and they now as positively assert that the passage we are about to consider had its fulfillment in Jerusalem's destruction by the Romans. To assist us in coming at the truth in this examination, let us inquire into the current theology of the Jews in our Saviour's time. Did they believe in a general future judgment, and that a sentence consequent upon it of everlasting bliss and punishment should be passed by the judge upon men according to their works? Josephus, the Jewish historian of those times, treating upon Jewish belief, writes thus: "For all men, the just as well as the unjust, shall be brought before God the word; for to him hath the Father committed all judgment; and he, in order to fulfill the will of his Father, shall come as judge, whom we call Christ." "This person, exercising the righteous judgment of the Father towards all men, hath prepared a just sentence for every one, according to his works; at whose judgment seat, when all men, and angels, and demons shall stand, they will send forth one voice, and say, just is the judgment: the rejoinder to which will bring a just sentence upon both parties, by giving justly to those that have done well an everlasting fruition; but allotting to the lovers of wicked works eternal punishment." *Dis. to the Greeks concerning Hades.*

That the Saviour, Matt. 25:31–46, had this scene in view cannot be doubted for a moment by those who will compare the passage with the theology of the Jews. The question now is, did the Saviour take this tremendous scene, which the Jews firmly believe would take place in a future state, and use it as a figure to illustrate a temporal calamity about to come upon Jerusalem, and that, too, without the least intimation that he so used it? Are Universalist ministers of the present day in the habit of using the doctrine of future and eternal retributions to illustrate temporal evils, and that, too, without expressing the least dissent from it, or ever once informing their hearers that the figure they employ is a false notion and not a fact? All know that the great burden of their preaching in our day is to berate and disprove a future judgment and endless punishment; but for this work they have not a *single* precedent in all the labors of Christ and his apostles, as recorded in the Bible. (Sec. CXXXII.) How shall we reconcile the discrepancy between those claimed as ancient Universalists and modern receivers of the doctrine? On no principle other than that Universalism is FALSE.

While we admit that Christ speaks of the destruction of Jerusalem in Matt., 24th chapter, we do not admit that this is the only subject upon which he treats. The following thoughts may assist the reader in scattering the mist thrown upon the 24th and 25th chapters by Universalists. Christ said of the temple, chap. 24th, ver. 2, "There shall not be left here one stone upon another that shall not be thrown down." This led his disciples to inquire, ver. 3, "When shall these things be? and what shall be the sign of thy coming, and the end of the world?" In this we have a three-fold question relating to the destruction of Jerusalem, the coming of Christ, and the end of the world. Now in a reply from the Saviour we may expect an answer to each question, and in doing this he gives from verse 4th to 14th the general signs which have been taking place from the time of the Saviour to the present, the last of which is given as follows: "And this gospel shall be preached in all the world, for a witness unto all nations, then shall the end come." Now the *end* here cannot mean the end of the Jewish age or dispensation for that closed with the death of Christ. (Sec. LXXVII.) There is no authority from the scriptures for extending the Jewish dispensation to the destruction of Jerusalem, as Universalists are wont to do, for the Apostle clearly shows us, Heb. 9:16, 17, that the New Testament, or gospel dispensation, was introduced by the death of the Saviour. Now if the end here means the end of the Jewish age, then the gospel was preached in all the world, as a witness to all nations before the death of Christ! The truth is, the end here named means the end of the Christian dispensation, or the end of time, and this last general sign is being fulfilled now by the spread of the gospel among the nations. The reader can turn to the scriptures referred to, as we omit to copy the most of them on account of their length. We come now to his answer to their question, "*When shall these things be?*" This may be called the second division of Matt. 24, beginning with verse 15, and closing with verse 22. Here the Saviour imparts instruction concerning Jerusalem's destruction. Included here is the passage that has been used to disprove endless punishment. "For then shall there be great tribulation, such as was not since the beginning of the world to this time, no, nor ever shall be." Ver. 21. It has been affirmed, that as the Saviour asserts the destruction of Jerusalem to be the greatest tribulation, endless punishment must be false. Paul, years before the Romans came against that city, said of the Jews, 1 Thess, 2 : 16, "Wrath IS come upon them to the UTTERMOST." But are we to infer from this that our Saviour's prediction never had its fulfillment on the Jews? Such an idea would be considered the most paltry quibbling; but it is no more so than to attempt an argument from our Saviour's words against endless punishment. The text is a strong hyperbolic expression to show the dreadful calamity which should befall the Jewish nation in this world, irrespective of man's condition in the future, and to say that the Jews at that time were to suffer more than all, or any, men ever would after that event, well becomes the cause it is designed to support; but truth requires no such work. To confine, if possible, all our Lord's predictions in this (24th) chapter to Jerusalem's overthrow, his words in verse 34 are often quoted to show that all the things named were to take place during the natural lives of the then existing inhabitance, thus defining the term "*generation*" to mean the time from the birth of a man until he becomes a parent, or about thirty years. But in the Bible it is sometimes used to designate a *race* of men, or a *kind, sort,* or *species.* When the Saviour says, "This generation shall not pass away till all these things be fulfilled," he means, as we conceive, that the Jewish race should not become extinct until that which he had predicted should be fulfilled. In speaking upon the same subject, Luke 21 : 24, he says, "Jerusalem shall be trodden down of the Gentiles until the times of the Gentiles be fulfilled." This implies that Jerusalem should cease to be trodden down, and that too before that generation should pass away. Jerusalem is still trodden down of the Gentiles; but the Jewish race, though scattered and peeled in all parts of the world, as by miracle, still retain their national prejudices and forms of worship. Understanding, then, by this generation, the Jews as a distinct race, the prediction appears to be literally true, and in keeping with other prophecies relating to the same event. Paul says, (Rom. 11 : 51,) "For I would not, brethren, that ye should be ignorant of this mystery, that blindness in part is happened to Israel until the fullness of the Gentiles be come in." Thus will the Jews be preserved as a distinct people or generation. That the term in question is sometimes used in the Bible in the sense of species, breed, kind and race may be seen. Ps. 26 : 6; 22 : 30; 16 : 5; Prov. 33 : 12; 1 Peter 2 : 9. But admitting that the 24th chapter relates exclusively to the overthrow of the Jews, and by the phrase, *this generation*, we are to understand the people then living and them only, it does not follow that Matt. 25 : 31–46 relates to the same event. This forms at least a part of the answer to the question, "What shall be the sign of thy coming and the end of the world?" As Universalists are now just as positive that this had its fulfillment when Titus went against Jerusalem, as Mr. Ballou and others were once that it referred to the day of Pentecost, we will here notice some of the absurdities involved in such a reference.

1. "*When the Son of man shall come in his glory.*" Ver. 31. This, we are told, took place when Jerusalem was destroyed; that Christ came then not in person, but in *power*, to overthrow the Jews. See *Notes on Par.*, by T. Whittemore, p. 347. This *power* says to them on his right hand, "Come ye blessed," &c. For "I (the power) was an hungered and ye gave me no meat," &c. "Inasmuch as ye have done it unto one of the least of these my brethren," i. e., brethren to the power! All must see the absurdity of this.

2. "*And all the holy angels with him.*" Ver. 31. These, we are informed, were the Roman armies. *Guide*, p. 104. The Saviour calls the Roman armies "the abomination of desolation." Chap. 24, ver. 15. But Universalism requires that

the polluted idolatrous Romans be considered *holy* angels!! This is certainly worse than Mr. Ballou's invention, now obsolete, for there is more plausibility in asserting that the apostles were the holy angels than that heathen warriors were.

3. "*Before him shall be gathered all nations.*" Ver. 32. Says Mr. W., (*Notes on Par.*, p. 334,) "Such expressions as in *all the world*, and among *all nations*, are not to be understood strictly." But this same writer, and others like him, in considering the Abrahamic promise, assert that "*all nations*" means the whole of Adam's posterity! Since it is asserted that all nations, in the sense of the text, were gathered at Jerusalem, let us inquire who composed this gathering? To answer this we have only to learn who were separated, rewarded and punished at that time. Of this separation we are told that it was "between the faithful disciples and the persecutors of the church." *Notes on Par.*, p. 346. Speaking of the words in verse 46, this author asserts that they are not to be understood to teach endless punishment, assigning as a reason "the parable in which they occur was spoken of Jews," (p. 352,) and believers were those rewarded with eternal life. Ver. 46, p. 353. Jews and Christians, then, constitute the "all nations." Observe, those who were separated were *gathered* before the Son of man. Ver. 32. But was there any such gathering at Jerusalem's destruction? But few Christians, comparatively, were at Jerusalem when Titus marched against it, for they were scattered all over the Roman empire at great distances from that point. To some of the many places where Christian churches were located, the distances from Jerusalem were about as follows: To Rome 1,550 miles; Corinth, 900; Galatia, 600; Ephesus, 650; Philippi, 950; Colosse, 550; Thessalonica, 1,000. Now is there anything in history, have Universalists been able to produce anything, that bears the faintest resemblance to Christians being gathered, rewarded and punished at that time? Nothing of the kind can be found. Such a thought contradicts the Saviour, who instead of predicting that Christians would be gathered then, represents it as a time of flight from Judea

Matt. 24 : 16–20. And Universalists themselves, to serve another purpose, quote Eusebius to show that Christians fled from Jerusalem at the signs of approaching danger, and thus escaped "to Pella and other places beyond the river Jordan." *Notes on Par.*, p. 336. A strange gathering at Jerusalem that!

4. "*Then shall he sit upon the throne of his glory.*" Ver. 31. How the *power* sat upon the throne of *his* glory in Jerusalem's overthrow we are not informed; but it is evident that Christ was not enthroned there, either spiritually or literally.

5. "*And he shall separate them one from another, as a shepherd,*" &c. Ver. 32. Says Mr Rogers, who has been counted a tall man in the order, "Every grammarian knows that *nations* is the antecedent to the pronoun *them* in this place; *nations*, then, are what are to be judged and separated." "Are our opponents willing to abide a literal application of this text to a judgment in eternity? If so, we shall have the different nations of mankind severed from each other; and whilst some, *en masse*, are taken to heaven, others will be driven to hell." *Pro and Con*, p. 158. Now what of force there is here, lies with all its weight against a judgment at Jerusalem's destruction. Were *nations* judged there and severed and sent off *en masse?* Mr. Page, another great man in the order, presents an entire different view. He says, "*Shall separate them.*" Namely, the *people* of those nations. The pronoun in the original does not refer immediately to the word *nations*, it being of a different gender." *Page in loco.* Who shall decide when the doctors disagree?

6. "*The devil and his angels.*" Ver. 41. These, we are told, "were the leading Jews and their emissaries." *Notes on Par.*, p. 350. But Mr. Page passes it with this remark: "An allusion to the contemporary Jewish opinions, as in the parable of the wheat and tares." *Page in loco.* Comment is unnecessary.

7. "*These shall go away into everlasting punishment.*" Ver. 46. We are informed that everlasting in this passage

means limited duration, and that the Jews suffered everlasting punishment in the sense here intended in their destruction by the Romans. We are told, too, that all punishment is for the good of the punished. All punishment being corrective, "a remission of such punishment would be a curse instead of a mercy; but a just punishment is as essential to our welfare as anything that love can do." Again, "All the judgments of which the scriptures speak, are to destroy sin and reform the sinner." *U. Ill. and Def.*, pp. 248, 250. So it seems the Saviour (Luke 19 : 41) wept over the Jews in view of the punishment they were about to experience by which their sins would be destroyed and they reformed, a punishment which was as essential to their welfare as anything that love could do!! How unkind. Says Dr. A. Clarke, "But some are of the opinion that this punishment shall have *an end;* this is as likely as that the glory of the righteous shall have an end; for the same word is used to express the *duration* of the punishment, as is used to express the duration of the state of glory. I have seen the best things that have been written in favor of the final redemption of damned spirits; but I never saw an answer to an argument against that doctrine, drawn from this verse, but what sound learning and criticism should be ashamed to acknowledge." *Clarke in loco.* So much from Dr. Clarke, who, it is believed, had some knowledge of language. It is worthy of remark here, that those who have revived the long since exploded doctrine of annihilation, in order to sustain it, are driven to the same quibbles and sophistries to limit the word "*everlasting*" that Universalists employ: and, as might be expected, the effects upon religion and morality are the same.

8. "*But the righteous into life eternal.*" Ver. 46. "We consider that the life spoken of Matt. 25 : 46, is not confined to the immortal existence into which the human race are to be raised after natural death, but is that spiritual life which the believer enjoys in this state." So says Mr. Whittemore. *N. on Par.*, p. 353. Observe, it is of the *righteous* that the Saviour is speaking, and all must admit that such have spiritual

life. The interpretation, then, amounts to this: "The spiritually alive shall be made spiritually alive when Jerusalem shall be destroyed by the Romans!" Receive it who can.

Mr. Whittemore admits that Christ's bodily visit again to the earth is taught, 1 Thess. 4 : 16. *Guide*, p. 36. (Sec. XXVI.) That Mr. W. is right for once, is evident; for nothing can be more obvious than that the apostle is speaking of the same advent he treats so largely upon in 1 Cor., chap. 15. As Paul gives a description of Christ's coming in his Second Epistle to the Thess. 1 : 7–10, it cannot well be doubted but he refers to the same event spoken of in the First, as the epistles were both written by the same apostle, addressed to the same people, and both treat on the advent of Christ. All unite in referring 1 Cor. chap. 15 to the resurrection, and Mr. Whittemore admits that 1 Thess. 4 : 16 teaches that Christ will visit the earth bodily at that time. Let us now collate some of the prominent features as given by Christ, Matt. 25 : 31–46, and by Paul, 1 Thess. 4; 2 Thess. 1; 1 Cor. 15; and see if it is not strikingly clear that they all describe the same event.

MATT. 25:	1 COR. 15:	1 THESS. 4:	2 THESS. 1:
1. "The son of man shall come."	1. "At his coming."	1. "The Lord himself shall descend from heaven."	1. "The Lord Jesus shall be revealed from heaven."
2. "All the holy angels with him."		2. "With the voice of the archangel."	2. "With his mighty angels."
3. "Before him shall be gathered all nations."	3. "The dead shall be raised."	3. "The dead in Christ shall rise first."	
•	4. "The last trump; — for the trumpet shall sound."	4. "With the trump of God."	
5. "In his glory."			5. "To be glorified in his saints."
6. "These shall go away into everlasting punishment."			6. "Punished with everlasting destruction from the presence of the Lord."
7. "Come ye blessed of my Father inherit," &c. "The righteous into life eternal."		7. "And so shall we ever be with the Lord."	

The reader must see that these texts are co-relative, all teaching the same coming of our Lord Jesus Christ. The Saviour, in Matt. 25, refers to the same event Paul does in 1 Thess. 4, with this difference only. Christ speaks of the righteous and the wicked, while the apostle speaks of the righteous only. But the apostle in his second letter treats of both classes, as is seen by the comparison above. We learn from the words of Christ and the apostle,

1. That there will be a personal advent of Christ.
2. That holy angels shall accompany him.
3. That the trump of God, the last trump, shall sound.
4. That the dead shall be raised incorruptible, so that whatever be their doom, misery or bliss, their resurrection bodies will not be subject to decay, but will endure forever.
5. That all men, the wicked and the righteous, shall be brought before Christ the judge.
6. That the wicked shall be sentenced to everlasting punishment, but the righteous rewarded with life eternal.

Take into account the belief of those addressed by our Lord, the points of resemblance between his words and those in Paul's epistles, admitted by Universalists to refer to Christ's coming at the resurrection, together with the glaring absurdity of asserting the passage to be fulfilled at Jerusalem's destruction; take these into the account, we say, and who but those who are determined to support an opinion at all hazards, but will admit that our Lord here teaches a future judgment connected with, or subsequent to, the resurrection.

XLII. *And I, if I be lifted up from the earth, will draw all men unto me.*" John 12 : 32.

The importance attached to this text to prove Universalism, may be seen by the following: "Now were there no other argument in favor of universal salvation, this would be entirely sufficient to establish the doctrine." *U. Ill. and Def.*, p. 267. "This certainly assures us of the salvation of all men." *Guide,*

p. 266. Yes, reader, upon the strength of this somewhat equivocal text alone, these men assure us of the salvation of all men in eternity, while they can see no possible evidence of any future punishment whatever taught in the Bible! All are not drawn in the Universalist sense in this world, for wickedness and misery abound to an alarming extent, and Christ might say of many now, as anciently, "Ye will not come unto me, that ye might have life." John 5 : 40. Remark, the Saviour does not say, I will make all men holy and happy in the resurrection state; but simply, "I will draw all men unto me." Nothing is said in the text concerning the character or condition of those who shall be drawn. That all men will be drawn to Christ in a future state is admitted, yea, contended for by Christians, for they believe the apostle when he says, "For we shall all stand before the judgment seat of Christ." Rom. 14 : 10, 11, also 2 Cor. 5 : 10. But should it still be contended that this drawing indicates the salvation of all men, then we reply the Saviour presents a very different view when speaking of the same event, namely, his being "*lifted up*." Hear him. "And as Moses lifted up the serpent in the wilderness, even so must the Son of man be lifted up. That WHOSOEVER BELIEVETH IN HIM SHOULD NOT PERISH, BUT HAVE EVERLASTING LIFE." John 3 : 14, 15. As we consider the Saviour competent to give the true design of his being "*lifted up*," we conclude the Universalist construction to be false. It remains a fact, however, that all, whether holy or unholy, will be drawn to Christ in the judgment to receive their final sentence."

XLIII. "*For the Son of man shall come in the glory of his Father, with his angels; and then he shall reward every man according to his works. Verily I say unto you, there be some standing here, which shall not taste death, till they see the Son of man coming in his kingdom.*" Matt. 16 : 27, 28.

This passage, and especially the 28th verse, has been considered a kind of lever by which to overturn every argument brought in favor of the personal advent and of future judgment, and to tumble those scriptures urged in support of these doctrines into Jerusalem's destruction. Since some commentators have admitted it, and Universalists stoutly contend that that event is to be considered a coming of Christ, we have been somewhat careful in examining the scriptures to see if that is the fact, and have come to the conclusion that the coming of the Roman army against that city *is never called the coming of Christ.* Take the 27th verse, now under consideration, and is there anything in the overthrow of the Jews by the Romans, bearing the least resemblance to this description? Whoever saw, or imagined he saw, the Son of man or his angels at that time? Josephus was present, and has transmitted to us a number of prodigies which happened; but he says nothing about the coming of Christ. Then what in that event answers to the angels called (Matt. 25 : 31) holy angels? Were the fierce, polluted and idolatrous Roman soldiers these *holy* angels? Preposterous! It is false, too, that every man was rewarded according to his works, as the text asserts, when the Romans sacked Jerusalem and butchered and enslaved the Jews — for but a fraction of the human race were there — and those who were involved in the siege did not receive according to their works, for many of the women and infants were the greatest sufferers. So far from the t uth is it that Christ came at that time, that in predicting that event (Matt. 24 : 23) he faithfully warned his disciples against heeding such a doctrine. Hear him. "Then (at the destruction of Jerusalem), if any man shall say unto you, Lo! here is Christ, or there, BELIEVE IT NOT." What folly to talk of Christ's coming to destroy Jerusalem! The truth is, the 27th verse teaches the second personal advent of Christ, when he shall judge the world in righteousness; and the 28th refers to the model of that personal advent witnessed by Peter, James and John upon the mount, recorded in the following verses in the next chapter. The end of a chapter does not always end a subject; for it should be borne in mind, that dividing the Bible into chapters and verses was not the work of the inspired writers, but is comparatively a modern thing, for convenience sake. The last two verses of chap. 16, and the first five of chap. 17, when connected as they should be, read as follows: "For the Son of man shall come in the glory of his Father, with his angels; and then shall he reward every man according to his works. Verily I say unto you, there be some standing here which shall not taste of death till they see the Son of man coming in his kingdom. And after six days, Jesus taketh Peter James, and John his brother, and bringeth them up into an high mountain apart, and was transfigured before them: and his face did shine as the sun, and his raiment was as white as light. And behold, there appeared unto them Moses and Elias talking with him. Then answered Peter and said unto Jesus, Lord, it is good for us to be here: if thou wilt, let us make here three tabernacles; one for thee, and one for Moses, and one for Elias. While he yet spake, behold, a bright cloud overshadowed them: and behold, a voice out of the cloud, which said, This is my beloved Son, in whom I am well pleased: hear ye him."

Just examine in connection with this what Peter, who was an eye witness of this scene, says in the following: "For we have not followed cunningly devised fables, when we made known unto you the power and coming of our Lord Jesus Christ, but were eye witnesses of his majesty. For he received from God the Father honor and glory, when there came such a voice to him from the excellent glory, This is my beloved Son, in whom I am well pleased. And this voice which came from heaven we heard, when we were with him in the holy mount." (Sec. XLIV.)

Thus we have the prediction, its accomplishment, and remarks by one who witnessed the whole, and he calls the transfiguration, "The power and *coming* of our Lord Jesus Christ." This, then, and not the destruction of Jerusalem, is what the Saviour is speaking of when he says, "There be some standing here, which shall not taste death till they see the Son of man coming in his kingdom." Peter, James and John were present at that time, and after six days they were upon the mount and witnessed this presentation of Christ's final coming. There are five different comings of Christ named in the New Testament;

1. His personal advent in the flesh. John 1 : 11–14.

2. His spiritual coming to comfort and sustain his followers. John 14 : 18–23.

3. His transfiguration upon the mount, which, as we have seen, was a model of his second personal advent.

4. His providential coming, named Rev. 2 : 5, to punish apostate churches.

5. His final and personal advent to raise the dead and judge the world. This is usually called his second advent, because it is his second *personal* coming. Mr. Whittemore in his Guide, p. 36, bears testimony to this advent. (Sec. XXVI.)

We refer the reader to a few out of the many passages where this is taught: 1 Thess. 4 : 16; 2 Thess. 1 : 7–10; 1 Cor. 15 : 23; Phil. 3 : 20, 21; Matt. 25 : 31–46; Acts 17 : 31; 2 Cor. 5 : 10; Rom. 2 : 16. Collate John 14 : 3 with Acts 1 : 11. In this last named text it is declared that, "This same Jesus which is taken up from you into heaven, shall so come in like manner as ye have seen him go into heaven." With this text before him, to say nothing of many others, what man with honest purpose can deny that a second personal advent of Christ is taught in the Bible?

XLIV. "*For verily I say unto you, ye shall not have gone over the cities of Israel till the Son of man be come.*" Matt. 10 : 23.

"That this passage has no reference to the destruction of Jerusalem, is evident from the following considerations:

"1. This language was addressed to the apostles, according to Dr. Carpenter's *Gospel Harmony*, not more than six months before the crucifixion.

"2. The apostles finished their circuit among the cities of Israel, and returned to their Lord before the crucifixion.

"3. Before the ascension of Christ, they received an enlarged commission, and went out to preach the gospel to all *nations; to every creature.* As a matter of fact, then, in less than one year from the time when their Lord said, "*Ye shall not have gone over the cities of Israel till the Son of man be come,*" they had gone over the cities of Israel, and received a new commission — authority to preach to the Gentiles. The coming, then, here referred to, either took place within one year, or Christ must have uttered a false prediction. Take which horn of dilemma you please.

"4. Besides, Jerusalem was not destroyed till at least thirty-seven years after the apostles received their commission to preach in the cities of Israel. But long before this period had elapsed, the apostles had gone over the field which their first commission contemplated, returned and received authority to preach to the Gentiles; they had spread the gospel all over the eastern world, and with the exception of John, had all gone to the rewards of the faithful." *Russell.*

The coming of Christ, named 2 Peter 1:16–18, took place within a few weeks after the apostles were sent out, and before they had gone over the cities of Israel, and to that event he doubtless refers in the text. See Sec. XLIII.

XLV. "*I keep under my body, and bring it into subjection: lest that by any means, when I have preached to others, I myself should be a castaway.*" 1 Cor. 9:27.

Speaking of the competitors in the Grecian games, the apostle says: "Now they do it to obtain a corruptible crown; but we an incorruptible." That Paul has his eye on the immortal prize, and expresses a sense of danger, must be obvious to all candid minds. In the Olympic games, to which reference is made, the prize was at the end of the race, and in order to secure it, the race must be performed according to law, or the judge did not award the crown. So in the Christian race, the iucorrnptible crown of glory is at the end, and the race must be according to law; hence says the apostle, (ver. 24,) "So run, that ye may obtain." But if the Universalist theory be correct, all are sure of the immortal prize whether they run or not, and the man who blasphemes God with his latest breath, is as surely crowned as the apostle. Examine well the text and context and it will be seen that the apostle's course is strikingly at variance with Universalist teachings.

XLVI. "*Because sentence against an evil work is not executed speedily, therefore the heart of the sons of men is fully set in them to do evil.*" Eccl. 8 : 11.

Universalism declares that sentence against an evil work *is* executed speedily, that it is not delayed; while the Bible asserts that it "*is not* speedily executed." Which shall we believe, Universalism or the Bible? Notwithstanding this text stands directly opposed to a prominent feature of their theory, yet these men of many inventions attempt to turn it against evangelical truth, because of the abuse of the long-suffering named in the passage, and assert that our views are conducive to sin because we teach that its punishment is far off in the future. They are wont to discourse in this wise: "The sentiment which defers all punishment to another world is defective, because it provides a way of escape. It says: 'Go on in sin; live in it till the age of seventy, eighty or ninety; curse and blaspheme God; oppress and wrong the widow; ruin unprotected innocence; stain your hands in human blood; but repent before you die, and you escape all punishment; you go immediately to glory. Not only so,—it makes man a gainer by sin; for the same sentiment says—the wicked are happier in this world than the good.' Again: Suppose our laws were established on this principle, and that transgressors were not called to an account, till they arrive at the age of fifty or sixty; that all this time they are permitted to go on committing all manner of crimes; should we not call this ruinous policy?'" *U. Ill. and Def.*, p. 217.

Upon this we venture to say, that more misrepresentation

could not be crowded into so small a space. We are kindly informed what other sentiments say; now let us hear what Universalism says. It says, "Go on in sin; live in it till the age of seventy, eighty or ninety; curse and blaspheme God; oppress and wrong the widow; ruin unprotected innocence; stain your hands in human blood; never repent before you die; blaspheme God with your latest breath; fall either by your own hand, or in the act of destroying a fellow man, and at the next conscious existence you shall be equal unto the angels."

Surely this must be a powerful dyke raised against the floods of corruption flowing from depraved hearts! But we are complained of because we put punishment for sin far off into the future, and thus men are led to think they can commit sin with impunity. We answer, Christian ministers teach punishment beyond the grave for sin, because the Bible and reason so teach; but are they in the habit, as is represented, of assuring their hearers that this punishment is far off? Speak, ye hundreds of thousands who sit under their ministry. Do they not constantly proclaim the uncertainty of life, and the possibility of their hearers being cut down by death at any moment; that they may not boast themselves of the morrow, for they know not what a day may bring forth? Do they not announce to the wicked that an awful eternity awaits them every moment, and that in view of it they should *now* repent and lead a holy life? Do they not apprise them of the fact that probation may close with individuals even before death, by the dethronement of reason or the departure of the Holy Spirit? Most assuredly they, do as all know. And is this saying to men, go on in sin till the age of seventy, eighty or ninety years, and then repent and escape punishment? Never was there a charge more false than this. Another is, that it makes a man a gainer by sin; and that the wicked are happier in this world than the good. (Sec. LXIII.) But do not Christian pulpits thunder as loudly in proclaiming the evil consequences of sin in this life, as do the pulpits of Universalists? From them is heard constantly the declaration to sinners, that

> "In pain you travel all your days,
> To reap eternal woe."

Christian ministers, however, do not assure their hearers that there are absolutely no pleasures in sin, for that would not only be travelling beyond the scriptures, (Heb. 11:25; 2 Thess. 2:12; Prov. 4:16); but the experience of every sinner would contradict it. Hence a part of their labor is to point out their short-lived, delusive and ruinous character, that they may be avoided, and to show men that when compared with the pleasures of righteousnesss, they are as nothing, and that on the whole it is an evil and bitter thing to sin against God. Universalists claim that their system is pre-eminently reformatory, because it teaches that the penalty of sin visits the transgressor immediately. This is boasted of as its great moral power. That it is a perfect failure in this respect is known to all who have witnessed its operations. (Sec. CXXXVII.) It strikes us that the character of the penalty has something to do with detering men from crime. Suppose a law enacted against theft, fornication or drunkenness, the penalty of which is a soft loving rap upon the ear, to be inflicted immediately on the commission of the crime, and that, too, all for the good of the man who incurs the penalty; would such a penalty be likely to deter men from the commission of these crimes merely because there is no escaping it? Now this is an illustration of the Universalist doctrine of the penalty for sin. Says Mr. Skinner: "A just punishment is as essential for our welfare, as anything that love can do." *U. Ill. and Def.*, p. 250. So punishment is not a curse, but a blessing! Thus God is made to say to the wicked, "Refrain from sin, for as sure as you commit it I will bless you." Who can wonder that there is claimed for this system a great reformatory power! But it is said by the advocates of this system, that the punishment for which they contend is no light affair, but is much to be dreaded by the sinner. At this point it may be proper to inquire, in what does the punishment for a violation of God's moral law consist? While we are told with much assurance that men are punished all their sins deserve in this world, we are somewhat at a loss to learn from Universalist authors how this punishment is inflicted. There seems to be a strange confounding of things upon this subject. In the Trumpet, No. 1089, is the following question proposed. "If, as Universalists contend, a guilty conscience constitutes the only punishment for sin, how can those with a *seared* conscience be adequately punished in the present life?" Mr. Whittemore replies, "Our querist has based his question on a false view of the sentiments of Universalists. How did he learn that they believed that a guilty conscience constitutes the only punishment for sin in this life? Has he learned it from *them* or from their enemies? Suffer us to say, we do not believe that such an opinion is entertained by any them. A guilty conscience is no desirable companion on the journey of life, and it may be regarded as a punishment of guilt; but no one affirms that it is the *only* punishment. Are there not many other punishments? Poverty, degradation, disease brought on by sin, the loss of confidence and respect of our fellow creatures, imprisonments, &c., &c., &c., are not all these the punishments of sin in this life?" But Mr. Witherell, who, it seems, we must consider good authority in the order, (Sec. IV.) informs us that the hell Universalists believe in consists in mental sufferings, (p. 11,) and who has not heard from Universalists of the hell of conscience?

We purpose now to take a view of human suffering arising from different sources, and see if we can possibly conceive of the sinner as adequately punished in this life, for his actual sins against God. Let us consider men first, as physical beings. That men who violate the laws of their physical nature suffer, is true; but is this the method God takes to punish sin? Is physical suffering a sure indication of actual sin against God?

Wicked men may, and often do violate the laws of their physical and organic nature while sinning against God, and suffer as a consequence. The pious, too, often violate these laws, in doing good while influenced by the purest of motives, and of course incur no guilt. Other circumstances being equal, the man who breaks a limb in the act of taking life, experiences no more pain than the man who does the same thing in the act of saving life. A vast amount of physical disease comes upon the human family independent of their own agency. The wickedness and ignorance of parents often entails disease upon their innocent and virtuous offspring; and little children, incapable of moral action, are often subjects of extreme suffering for months together. Physical suffering is the result of a violation of physical laws, and these may be violated either with or without our own agency. Universalists very generally adopt a deceptive mode of reasoning upon this subject, by confounding the mere natural effects of sin with its punishment. (Sec. XLIX.) The Jews rejected Christ, the true light, and greater darkness came upon them. This was the natural effect, but not the punishment for this sin. Although they thus deceive the unthinking, by thus confounding things, yet to serve their purpose at times they are obliged to admit the distinction; for they tell us that the Jews were punished for rejecting Christ nearly forty years after, when Jerusalem was destroyed. If, as has been asserted, sin is its own punishment, then all other punishments, whether human or divine, are unjust and cruel; for if all have been punished, why should they be re-punished? Mankind, in practice, universally reject the idea that sin punishes itself. Every parent who applies the rod to a child for a fault, rejects it. Every civil magistrate, in passing sentence upon a criminal, rejects it. God himself, as often as he punishes transgressors, rejects it; and thus makes the distinction for which we contend. We observe, then, a wide difference between suffering *for* sin, and suffering from the *effects* of sin. The innocent may suffer from the effects of sin, or in consequence of it; while none but the guilty, or the one who takes the place of the guilty, as did the Saviour, (1 Pet. 3 : 18,) can suffer for sin. What folly, then, to account physical suffering the penalty of God's law against actual sin, since the innocent experience it as well as the guilty. Man is a social being. He possesses that nature and those feelings, which render him capable of society. Shall we look in this direction for God's penalties against sin? In the social relations are the righteous always exalted, and are the wicked always cast down? A competency of worldly substance is desirable in human society; but is this secured only to the good? Thousands of the purest spirits upon earth have been found in poverty's vale, suffering for the necessaries of life, while some of the wicked have prospered in the world, and have had more than a reasonable heart could wish. Ps. 73 : 7. Marriage forms an important relation in society; but do the good always derive comfort from this relation, and does it always prove an evil to the wicked? We see the pious and affectionate wife, suffering by the conduct of a perfidious, brutal, and drunken husband; while the faithful, indulgent, and pious husband, is tormented all his days with a faithless, brawling, and discontented wife; while, on the other hand, some of the irreligious find much comfort in the conjugal relation. Pious parents often suffer by the wickedness of their children, and pious children are often afflicted by the ungodliness of parents; while some of the wicked derive comfort from these relations.

We might name other things in the social state where the same inequality exists; but enough has been presented to show that not only the wicked, but the righteous suffer in their social relations, which establishes the point that these sufferings cannot be God's penalty against sin; for no innocent person will suffer that. As it regards the providences of God,— so dark and mysterious are many of them, that it is not always safe to judge of a man's moral condition by what we witness of God's dealings with him in this life. Job's friends ran into this error, and supposed he must have been a very wicked man, or he would not have suffered as he did; when, in fact, he was pre-eminently holy. The truth is, this is a state of probation, and not of strict recompense; hence the inequality apparent in the Divine administration in this world. God causes his sun to shine not merely upon the good, but upon the evil also, and his rain descends upon the unjust as well as the just. Matt. 5 : 45. It is not in man's social relations, then, that we are to look for the infliction of God's penalties against sin; for observation, experience, and the word of God unite in pressing upon us the fact that some wicked persons prosper in these relations, while others who are pious suffer in them. Furthermore, such has been the corrupt state of the world, as its history abundantly shows, that true piety has often called down upon its possessor all manner of cruel sufferings by imprisonment, rack, and otherwise, while many of the wicked have escaped such visitations.

Man possesses conscience, or, as it has been denominated, "moral sense." Does he suffer from this source all the penalty of the moral law in this life? Some assert that he does. This we deny, and submit the following, which might be greatly extended, to show the folly of such an assumption. It is a fundamental principle of modern Universalism, that no man escapes any just punishment for sin; and of course if the punishment for sin is confined to the conscience in this life, and if there be a just administration, every one must be punished in exact proportion to his crimes. To show that this is impossible, let us suppose two cases. A man becomes acquainted with the fact that a neighbor has a large sum of money, and resolves on murdering him to secure it. He follows him into a dark avenue, and in fifteen minutes from the time he formed the purpose, his neighbor is a dying man, and the murderer himself senseless by his side, in consequence of a death shot given in self-defence by his murdered victim. Now, according to the theory we oppose, that murderer could have suffered but fifteen minutes in his conscience, if we date his crime back to the time he formed the intention; and when we take into the account the excitement connected with such an act, we cannot conceive of very acute suffering during that short period.

Another case. A man has the same opportunity, forms the same purpose, and in the same space of time murders his neighbor, but secures the money, escapes himself, and survives his murdered victim twenty years; and not only suffers from conscience, but suspicion is fixed upon him as the murderer: he is arrested, examined, thrown into jail for six months or more to await the sitting of the court, has his trial, and undergoes all the fearful apprehensions of a death upon the gallows. Proof, however, fails, and he is cleared by the court, but is not cleared from the just suspicions of the entire community. In these two cases the crimes are equal, but are the punishments equal? Does the man who lives twenty years after the act of murder, suffer no more in his conscience than the one who dies in the act?

If we look this subject in the face, we shall see most clearly that either God's ways are not equal, or else that there is future punishment, and the Universalist notion is false. And then, as if to cap the climax of absurdity, this dogma teaches that the man who dies in the murderous act becomes as the angels of God in heaven; while the one who survives, yet no more guilty, suffers a Universalist hell in this world for twenty years! That the moral sensibilities become blunted by a continual course of sin, so that there is less suffering from conscience as the sinner advances in crime, is confirmed by experience, common observation, and the Bible. Indeed, all writers upon moral science have taken this view. The following is from Wayland: "The man who habitually violates his conscience, not only is more feebly impelled to do right, but he becomes less sensible to the pain of doing wrong. A child feels poignant remorse after the first act of pilfering. Let the habit of dishonesty be formed, and he will become so hackneyed in sin, that he will perpetrate robbery with no other feeling than that of mere fear of detection. The first oath almost palsies the tongue of the stripling. It requires but a few months, however, to transform him into the bold and thoughtless blasphemer. The murderer, after the death of his first victim, is agitated with all the horrors of guilt. He may, however, pursue his trade of blood until he have no more feeling for man, than the butcher for the animal which he slaughters. Burk, who was in the habit of murdering men, for the purpose of selling their bodies to the surgeons for dissection, confessed this of himself." *Moral Science*, p. 77.

Speaking of this influence of sin, Paul declares of some that their consciences were "seared with a hot iron." 1 Tim. 4:2. Conscience is not, as some assert, the unerring voice of God, but is right or wrong, according as the moral judgment and moral sense are right or wrong. As to mental suffering, we hazard nothing in saying that the man of tender sympathy, who by mistake or accident takes the life of a fellow being, suffers a hundred fold more, mentally, than the hardened wretch like Burk, who deliberately murders a man for a few paltry dollars. Since, then, it is an established fact that suffering from this source in this life is so far from increasing with crime that it actually diminishes, it cannot be the way in which a righteous moral governor punishes sin. The trouble experienced by the sinner from conscience, is caused by her remonstrance, under the Spirit of God, discovering to him his guilt, and pointing him to the law, with its fearful penalty. This conscience continues to do most faithfully until the Spirit is grieved, and she is hushed by repeated acts of sin and rebellion against God, and the sinner becomes past feeling, (Eph. 4:19,) and is left to believe a lie that he might be damned, because he believed not the truth, but "had pleasure in unrighteousness." 2 Thess. 2:12. The sufferings experienced here may be regarded as the consequences of sin, but not, strictly as its penalty. Let us illustrate. The penalty for highway robbery, we will say, is hard labor in the state prison for thirty years. A man commits this crime, is arrested, examined, and cast into the common jail to await his trial, which is to take place in six months. Satisfied that his guilt must appear, and that naught but the dread penalty awaits him, his mental sufferings are great. He is deprived, too, of his liberty, social enjoyments, and bodily health, by his incarceration. Now we ask, are these sufferings of the prisoner to be regarded as the penalty of the law against robbery? By no means. The court is not authorized to abate six months of the penalty, in consideration of his having been six months in the common jail. Suffering in the jail for six months is one of the consequences of the crime, but not the penalty, as all will see. So the sinner against God often suffers in this world physically, socially, and mentally, in consequence of his sins; but reason and scripture both unite in proclaiming the fact that there is punishment after death for the ungodly.

The doctrine of future punishment has been called, by way of reproach, a heathenish doctrine. That not only those nations who have been favored with the Scriptures, but those who have been destitute of them have believed in future retributions, in some form, is true; and this, so far from forming an objection to the doctrine, is but another evidence of its truthfulness. No candid mind acquainted with human affairs, can believe for a moment that the righteous and the wicked are adequately rewarded and punished in this life; and it is this common sense view which carries the mind of man to the future world, where this will take place. This furnishes a reason why this doctrine has obtained so generally, even where the Bible is not known. It will be seen by the candid reader, we think, from the few thoughts here presented, that men do not receive the penalty of God's law against sin in either their physical, social, or mental sufferings in this world, or in all of them put together. It remains a truth, then, that sentence against an evil work is not executed speedily, and that after death is the judgment. That God sends afflictions upon his children in this world for their good, we readily learn from the Scriptures; and that God punishes nations as such, here, is equally clear; and it is well known that when God showers his judgments down upon nations, the innocent often suffer with the guilty. This, however, only furnishes another argument in favor of a day in the future world when God shall judge in righteousness.

XLVII. "*Be thou faithful unto death, and I will give thee a crown of life.*" Rev. 2 : 10.

What means the conditionality of this promise, if Universalism is sound? It is perfect nonsense; for if all are to be saved, as Universalists assert, what matters it whether they are faithful or unfaithful? Are not the *un*faithful just as much heirs to the crown of life as the faithful? This short text is of itself sufficient to refute the infidel sentiment, that our conduct here has nothing to do with securing our future bliss.

XLVIII. "*Labor not for the meat which perisheth, but for that meat which endureth unto everlasting life.*" John 6 : 27.

Mr. Balfour, in his Reply to Stuart, (p. 74,) says: "You assume that 'everlasting life' refers to the future endless happiness of the righteous. This I deny. Everlasting life designates indeed the happiness of the righteous, but it is their happiness in this world." By this Christ is made to say, "Labor not for that meat which perisheth, but for that which endureth unto happiness in this world." And does not the happiness enjoyed in this world perish? This text, as all must see, lies directly against that form of error which denies the necessity of anxiety and labor in order to secure future bliss. "A company were following the Saviour for the loaves and fishes, and like many at the present time, were laboring exclusively for worldly good. Christ rebukes them, and exhorts them to labor for 'blessings which *endure* — *abide*, unto everlasting life.' How would such an exhortation sound from the lips of a Universalist preacher? Had Christ been a preacher of Universalism, the Jews might have turned upon him, and said: You acknowledge that our present business is to provide for our temporal wants, our eternal wants being above and beyond our reach. In seeking loaves and fishes, then, we are in our appropriate sphere!" *Russell.*

XLIX. "*And the angels which kept not their first estate, but left their own habitation, he hath reserved in everlasting chains under darkness, unto the judgment of the great day.*" Jude 6.

The author of the Guide asserts that there is nothing in this passage which renders it necessary to apply it to any order of beings above men. He makes a display of Greek criticism, to show that angel signifies a messenger; and asserts that the word *angel* is not a name of nature, but of *office*, which no one to our knowledge ever denied, and then states, respecting their not having kept their first estate and leaving their own habitation, that "all this has taken place among men on the earth." On the word everlasting, an opportunity is afforded to show that it is not always used to signify endless duration; hence we are reminded of the everlasting mountains, hills, priesthood, &c. And as it respects the judgment, he inquires, "But is there no judgment in this world? We read, 'Verily there is a God that judgeth [where ?] in the earth.'" (Sec. LI.) Concerning the phrase "*great day*," he finds somewhere in the Old Testament that "the day of the Lord is near," and somewhere in the New Testament that "the great day of his wrath is come;" and this of course is sufficient, with Mr. Whittemore, to deprive the text in Jude of its future-state reference. But while he does this, he leaves us staring about for its true interpretation. The absurdity of a reference to Jerusalem is so great, that even Mr. W. dares not hazard it. Observe, the author of the Guide denies that these angels are superhuman, insists that they are men, and that their retribution is in this world. Now how soon are men punished for their sins, according to this same Guide? Let Mr. W. answer. "One important truth embraced by Universalists is,—that the punishment of sin is not delayed until the future existence, but that it is swift, sure, and inevitable; that sin goes hand in hand with woe throughout its whole duration; that it is itself *hell*, into which the sinner cannot plunge, without feeling its flames and torments. In regard to retribution, such is the doctrine of Universalists." *Guide*, p. 262. Here it is given, as a denominational sentiment, that sin is not only punished as soon as committed, but that sinners are punished while committing it; that sin "is *itself* hell," i. e. sin and punishment for sin are one and the same thing!! But in the text under consideration, the angels, or men as Mr. W. will have it, are said to be "*reserved* in everlasting chains, under darkness, *unto* the judgment of the great day;" and we are also informed (2 Pet. 2:9) that "The Lord knoweth how to deliver the godly out of temptation, and to RESERVE the unjust unto the day of judgment to be punished." Now here is a particular, specified period, called the day of judgment, for which ungodly men are reserved, in which they are to be punished. Call this period Jerusalem's destruction or what we please, it is equally at war with the above quoted view of punishment. What folly to talk of sinners being *reserved* unto any particular period for punishment if they are punished without any remission as soon as they sin, or while sinning. According to this, every Jew had been punished all his individual sins deserved, up to the moment when the Romans besieged the city of David. To whom shall we attribute this folly? Not to the inspired apostle, surely, but to Universalist teachers who have perverted the word of God. No unsophisticated mind would ever see a mere temporal calamity in the words of Jude. He wrote for those who had been educated in the belief of future retributions, and they could but understand him as teaching the same doctrine. See Sec. L.

L. "*The Lord knoweth how to deliver the godly out of temptation, and to reserve the unjust unto the day of judgment, to be punished.*" 2 Pet. 2:9.

The author of the Guide has a very summary way of disposing of those knotty texts which teach most clearly a future judgment. It is to refer his readers to what he has said upon texts partly parallel, or perhaps referring to another subject altogether. For, to come right out and plainly say that Peter meant to say, "The Lord knoweth how to deliver the godly out of temptation, and to *reserve* the unjust unto the *destruction of Jerusalem*, to be punished," would present such an absurdity, that even his admirers would start back. He deemed it, doubtless, much more safe to withhold his explanation, and refer us to what he has said on Jude 6, where an opportunity is afforded for a display on the words angels, darkness, chains, everlasting, &c. Mr. Balfour, however, who never stands for trifles when writing upon the scriptures, hesitates not to throw this into the Jerusalem catastrophe. *Essays*, p. 257. So the wicked of the apostle's time were reserved four years, at least, to be punished in the siege of the Romans! But did none of the unjust of the apostle's time die before the Romans came against the holy city? Again, how does the idea of their being *reserved* unto that time, comport with the notion that "as quick as the thunder follows the lightning's flash, just so quick does punishment follow crime." *Witherell*, p. 31. Is the thunder unheard till four years after the lightning's flash? Peter's epistle bears date A. D. 66 — Jerusalem was overthrown A. D. 70, four years after. The text means just what it appears to mean. See Sec. XLIX, also Sec. VIII.

LI. "*For judgment I came into this world.*". John 9 : 39.
"*Verily he is a God that judgeth in the earth.*" Ps. 58 : 11.
"*Now is the judgment of this world.*" John 12 : 31.
"*I came not to judge the world.*" John 12 : 47.
"*I will raise him up at the last day.*" John 6 : 40.

In the Bible we find the words *judge* and *judgment* are frequently applied to events which have their fulfillment in this world, and none to our knowledge ever disputed it. But were we to derive our knowledge from Universalist authors only, we should conclude that those who oppose their views, either wickedly deny this, or else are grossly ignorant of the fact. The true question at issue between us is, Is there a *future* judgment? The negative of this is taken by their writers, and then they go on to prove most conclusively, from the scriptures, that God judges in this world; and this they offer as a sufficient reason why there shall be no future judgment! Take the following from Mr. Whittemore, as a specimen: "'For JUDGMENT I am come into THIS world.' John 9:39. It is absolutely disrespectful to the Son of God, who tells us that he came into THIS WORLD for judgment, to suppose that judgment is in *some other world!* Hear that, all ye Presbyterians, Methodists, Baptists, and so called Orthodox Christians, who oppose God by saying that Christ has gone into the future world for judgment." *Trumpet*, April 28, 1855.

With the same logical force do they frequently employ Ps. 58:11, "Verily he is a God that judgeth in the earth." The argument is this: God judgeth in the earth; therefore, there will be no future judgment. The sophistry of this will at once appear by adopting this method with other subjects. For instance, God is glorified in the earth; therefore God will not be glorified in the future state! "On earth peace, good will towards men;" therefore there can be neither peace, nor good will towards men in the future world!

"We which have believed DO enter into rest;" (Heb. 4:3;) therefore there can be no rest in heaven!

Take the words *saved* and *salvation*, which are often used to express temporal deliverance and the state of the justified soul in this world. Universalists talk much about salvation in the future world, as all know. Now what would be thought were we to rise up and deny future salvation, and make a great parade of texts in capitals, to prove that salvation pertained to this life — that men are said to be saved *now*, in a great number of instances? Suppose that, to meet all the texts Universalists could urge in support of future salvation, we were to insist upon it that they contain no evidence of future salvation for any of our race; and should contend, most stoutly, that God's salvation is in this world, and urge in proof of this, that the Israelites (Ex. 14:13) were commanded to "stand still and SEE THE SALVATION OF THE LORD," [which they could not have done if salvation is in the future state; and furthermore, to put the whole matter to rest, the words of Paul should be presented, (2 Cor. 6:2,) "NOW IS THE DAY OF SALVATION." And suppose, too, that we should demand of them such texts as the following, to establish the doctrine that men would be saved in the future state: "Men shall be holy and happy in *the future world*." "Men shall be saved in the *immortal state*." "Men shall be saved *beyond the grave*." Suppose, we say, that we should deny that there is any salvation in the future world, and bring such proofs, and make such a demand to sustain it, what would be thought of such a course? It would be judged the vilest quibbling, and a most egregious perversion of God's word. But as wicked as this would be, it is precisely the course pursued by Universalists respecting the judgment. If we speak of a future judgment, they reply with an air of triumph, (John 12:31,) "Now is the judgment of this world;" and the author of the Guide makes a similar demand with the one above named, respecting future punishment. (Sec. CXV.)

Since the last named text is so much in use, a few thoughts upon it will be given. Universalists seem to consider it of great importance, because the present tense is used, "*Now is*," &c. This was spoken nearly forty years before the destruction of Jerusalem. Well then, if, because the Saviour said, "*Now* is the judgment of this world," a future general judgment must be set aside, then for the same reason must a judgment at the destruction of Jerusalem be set aside. Take this out of their theory, what will they do with the texts they find it so convenient to refer to that event? There is another text in the same chapter with this, which this class of expositors see fit to let alone. It is this, (ver. 47,) "I came not to judge the world."

We have Mr. Balfour's Essay of 139 pages, in which he professes to examine all those places where the words judge and judgment occur in the New Testament, but no notice is taken of this text. There are five volumes of their books before us, each having a somewhat copious index of texts, yet none of them name this. So far as memory serves, we have never seen it named in any of their writings. Why they are thus silent upon ver. 47, while they so often quote a part of ver. 31 of the same chapter, the reader can easily judge. Ver. 47 *is not in the right shape for them.* The whole of ver. 31 reads thus: "Now is the judgment of this world: now shall the prince of this world be cast out." Mr. French, the Universalist minister named Sec. 1, while attempting to correct his brethren in a sermon before the Maine Convention, says:

"But do we not injure our cause by quoting the words of our Saviour, saying: "Now is the judgment of this world; now is the prince of this world cast out.' John 12:31. Is not Wakefield right, who applies this text to the decision which the Jews were about to make against Jesus; rejecting him, and declaring him worthy of death? But how different this from the judgment which God executes upon the world? Should we not make improvements by being more cautious, by selecting proof texts with more care and judgment?" *Banner*, August 5, 1843.

Their perversions are so numerous, that Mr. French has a task before him, if he thinks to reform the order in this respect; and furthermore, should he succeed, it would be the death of the system. This, the convention, it would seem, were aware of, and were so much displeased with his effort, that they did not vote the publication of his sermon. Christ says, (John 12:47, 48,) "If any man hear my words, and believe not, I judge him not: for I come not to judge the world, but to save the world; * * * the word that I have spoken, the same shall judge him in the last day." In this we are taught, that the design of Christ's first advent was not to judge men, but to save them, and are referred to a future judgment, when men shall be judged for their treatment of Christ's word or doctrine. This is to take place at the *last day*. While the author of the Guide fails to give us light upon ver. 47, he does favor us with an *exposition* of ver. 48. Upon this, as found Guide p. 166, we shall offer a few thoughts. The course pursued is, as usual with this class of writers, both evasive and sophistical, and discovers anything but a desire to bring out the true sense. He carries his readers away to the parable of the vineyard, (Matt. 21,) then to the parable of the marriage feast, (Matt. 22,) then to Matt. 24, where the phrase "*end of the world*" occurs, then to Heb. 10 : 25, where the apostle speaks of a "*day approaching*," then to 1 John 2 : 18, where the phrase "*last time*" is found, and he will have it, that all these texts relate to the destruction of Jerusalem, and assumes that John 12 : 48 refers to the same event. Now we ask, if truth only was the object of this man, why did he not refer his readers to the other passages, where our Saviour uses the expression "*last day?*" No one could learn from what he has said in the Guide on this text, that the phrase "last day" occurred anywhere else in the New Testament. Christ says, (John 6 : 40,) "And this is the will of him that sent me, that every one which seeth the Son, and believeth on him, may have everlasting life: and I will raise him up at the *last day*." See, also, verses 49, 44 and 54 of the same chapter, where the phrase is used in the same sense. How this expression was understood in our Saviour's time, we may learn from the conversation between him and Martha, on the death and resurrection of Lazarus. John 11 : 23, 24. "Jesus saith unto her, thy brother shall rise again. Martha saith unto him, I know that he shall rise again in the resurrection at the *last day*." (Sec. XC.)

It is obvious that the expression "*last day*," as used by our Lord and Martha, refers to the general resurrection. This being the case, can any be at a loss to know the meaning of the Saviour, in the passage under consideration? Christ says four times, (John 6,) that he will raise men up at the "*last day.*" Martha had confidence in the fact that Lazarus would rise in the resurrection in the *last day* (John 11 : 24); and Christ says, (John 12 : 48,) of him who rejects him and his truth, "The word that I have spoken, the same shall judge him in the *last day.*" It must be obvious to all, we think, that if one of these texts refers to Jerusalem's destruction, they all do, which represents Martha as believing in the resurrection of her brother from the dead, at the destruction of Jerusalem ! ! These texts, taken together, connect the judgment with the resurrection. They teach a resurrection and judgment at the end of time, or in the *last day*, which is fatal to modern Universalism. This, the author of the Guide probably saw, hence his labor to turn the eyes of his reader to some half dozen other texts, having no connection whatever with the one before us, while he would keep from their sight five passages in which the same expression is found. Thus the word of God is handled deceitfully, and Universalism propagated.

One thought more. Mr. Skinner asserts that, "All the judgments of which the scriptures speak are to destroy sin, and reform the sinner. *U. Ill. and Def.* p. 248. "I came not to judge the world," says the Saviour, or in other words, to harmonize with Mr. Skinner's doctrine, "I came not to destroy sin and reform the sinner" ! ! Did the Saviour mean to say that? Truth never thus belies the Saviour and his work.

LII. "*Ye shall seek me, and shall die in your sins; whither I go, ye cannot come,*" &c. John 8 : 21, 22, 23, 24.

"*Ye shall die in your sins.*" We are told (*Trumpet*, No. 577) that by this, "Jesus referred to the approaching destruction of the Jewish nation," and that "he spoke of a national and not a natural death." But what evidence is there that our Lord is discoursing about Jerusalem's overthrow here? Just none at all, either in the text or context. "*Ye shall seek me.*" Have not the Jews as a people continued to reject Christ to the present hour? How clear it is that the Saviour was speaking, not of the nation, but of individuals. Mr. Page in his notes disagrees with Mr. Whittemore, and says: "Some understand this to denote the national or political death which soon afterwards befell the Jews, on account of their sinfulness. To me it seems more probable that Jesus used the phrase *shall die* in its literal sense. I understand his argument thus: You are now sinful, and especially guilty of rejecting the Messiah, whose divine mission has been sufficiently authenticated: I shall soon depart from the earth; you will continue seeking for the Messiah, (for me, though ye know it not,) but cannot come to him or find him, for he will be in heaven. In this hopeless search you will persist, and will die without having found or recognized him,— guilty of having rejected him when he was manifested to you, in addition to all your other sins."

So we see that the Universalist commentator admits that it is not a national, but a literal death of the persons the Saviour addressed, who were to "die in their sins." But it is said that Christ expressed the same to his disciple (John 13 : 33) that he did to the Jews, viz.: "Whither I go ye cannot come." By a comparison of the passages, and the connection in which they are found, it will be seen that there is a very important difference.

1. Christ told the Jews that they should die in their sins. But he said nothing like this to his disciples.

2. Christ said to the Jews, "Ye are from beneath; I am from above: ye are of this world; I am not of this world;" and assigns it as a reason why he doomed them to die in their sins. This he never said to his disciples.

3. Christ explained to Peter what he meant by saying to his disciples, "Whither I go ye cannot come," as follows: "Whither I go thou canst not follow me now: *but thou shalt follow me afterwards.*" But he gave no such explanation and promise to the Jews: but on the contrary he declared to them most positively

that they should die in their sins, and that they should not go where he did.

The author of the Guide, p. 165, says: after quoting the words addressed to Peter, chap. 13 : 36, "The same word may be applied to the Jews. They could not follow Christ then, but they would at another time." Mr. Whittemore may so apply these words, but Christ himself gives them no such application. The oft perverted text, "So all Israel shall be saved," is lugged in by the author of the Guide to supply the Saviour's *omission*, and to prove that all the Jews will go to heaven where Christ has gone. See Sec. V, where this text is examined.

LIII. "*Blessed are ye when men shall revile you, and persecute you, and shall say all manner of evil against you falsely, for my sake. Rejoice and be exceeding glad; for great is your reward in heaven.*" Matt. 5 : 11, 12; also, Luke 6 : 22, 23.

There lies before us a work entitled "Scripture Doctrine," by S. R. Smith, designed for the instruction of children in Universalism, and has been used quite extensively in Universalist Sabbath schools. The following is the note upon this text entire, as found p. 28 : "Nothing is more common than for professing Christians to speak of heaven as a glorified state after death; and as being the place where believers will receive their reward. And yet it is believed there is no one place in which the word is used in the Bible, where it obviously means *life* or *happiness*, or the place of these, after death. Nor does any one seriously expect the felicity of immortality as the reward of his obedience — on the contrary, it is acknowledged to be the free gift of God. Why then encourage others to hope for that as a *reward*, which none can expect but as a gift? The truth is, the gospel is called heaven, and he who believes the gospel is in heaven. Eph. 2 : 6."

This is the instruction Universalists are imparting to the youth of our land, under the guise of Christianity, and this is the manner in which they dispose of this precious passage which has afforded support to Christians in all ages of the church under the most afflicting circumstances; which has enabled them to meet death in all its cruel forms, having respect to the recompense of reward. But now to support a rotten system, this must be given up; and we are told, by those who profess to be ministers of Christ, that it is folly to "*speak of heaven as a glorified state after death*," and that "*there is no one place in which the word is used in the Bible, where it obviously means the life or happiness of these after death!*" So we see a future heaven is denied as well as a future hell. Christians, then, are not to speak of heaven as a glorified state after death, and there is no reward for the righteous in the future world! This is Universalism. But let us turn from this to the Bible, and see if there is such a place as heaven after death. Where is the Saviour? "So then after the Lord had spoken unto them, he was received up into heaven and sat on the right hand of God." Mark 16:19. "Ye men of Galilee, why stand ye here gazing up into heaven? This same Jesus, which is taken up from you into heaven, shall so come in like manner as ye have seen him go into heaven." Acts 1:11. Peter speaking of Christ, says: "Who has gone into heaven and is on the right hand of God." 1 Peter 3:22. Paul says: "For Christ has not entered into the holy places made with hands, which are the figures of the true; but into heaven itself, to appear in the presence of God for us." Heb. 9:24.

Are any to be in heaven but Christ? The Saviour says, (John 14:2, 3,) when about to go to his Father: "In my Father's house are many mansions." "I go to prepare a PLACE for you, that where I am, there ye may be also." Speaking of this heavenly family, Paul says, (Eph. 3:15,) "For this cause I bow my knee unto the Father of our Lord Jesus Christ, of whom the whole family in heaven and earth is named;" and in view of the glories of heaven he says, (Rom. 8:17, 18,)

" And if children, then heirs; heirs of God and joint heirs with Christ; if so be that we suffer with him, that we may be glorified together. For I reckon that the sufferings of this present time are not worthy to be compared with the glory which shall be revealed in us." Christ prohibits laying up treasures on the earth, (Matt. 6 : 19, 20,) but enjoins laying up treasures in heaven. Peter in speaking to his brethren of an incorruptible inheritance, says of it, (1 Peter 1 : 4, 5,) " Reserved in heaven for you, who are kept by the power of God through faith unto salvation."

A host of other scriptures might be adduced equally plain. These teach that heaven is a place, and that Christians may expect a glorified state after death, too plainly to need comment. Again, it is said, " *The gospel is called heaven, and he who believes the gospel is in heaven;* " and in proof of this bold assertion we are referred to Eph. 2 : 6. Does this teach that the gospel is heaven, and that believers are in heaven? " And hath raised us up together, and made us sit together in heavenly places in Christ Jesus." What is there here to prove that the gospel is heaven, and that believers are in it? They sit together in *heavenly* places, i. e., places partaking of the nature of heaven, but not heaven itself." " He who believes the gospel is in heaven." But what is it to believe the gospel according to Universalist divines? It is to believe in Universalism, for with them nothing else is the gospel, as all know who hear them. So heaven is the inheritance of those, and those only, who believe in Universalism, and they are now in heaven!! Reader, did it ever occur to you before that those around you who clamor for Universalism are *now* the pure inhabitants of heaven? The doctrine of the Saviour, in the passage is this: The privations, persecutions and sufferings of every kind the Christian shall be called to endure in this world for his sake, will enhance his bliss and glory in the future world. The same thing is expressed 2 Cor. 4 : 16–18. A heart comforting and encouraging doctrine to afflicted faithful Christians;

and palsied be the hand that would deprive them of it by infidel perversions and sophistries. No Christian merits, or expects to merit, heaven; but God has *graciously* promised a reward in heaven in proportion to our sufferings and faithfulness here, for his sake. On salvation a *gift*, see Sec. XCIX.

LIV. "*For thou shalt be recompensed at the resurrection of the just.*" Luke 14 : 14.

This text connects human conduct with the eternal state, and of course it must be destroyed in some way: so Mr. Whittemore occupies nearly eight pages of his "Notes on the Parables," contending with common sense and the Bible to make it appear that the resurrection of the just took place when Jerusalem was destroyed. Speaking of Christ's coming to destroy the Jewish state, he says, (*N. on Par.*, p. 168): "At this time the Christians were to be exalted, raised from a low condition." Again: "This was the resurrection of the just; and at that time, those who had done them favors were to be recompensed." The Saviour was at the table of a Pharisee, whose creed included the doctrine of a resurrection, both of the just and unjust, (Sec. X.) and he addressed him thus: "When thou makest a dinner or a supper, call not thy friends nor thy brethren, neither thy kinsmen nor thy rich neighbors; lest they also bid thee again, and a recompense be made thee; but when thou makest a feast, call the poor, the maimed, the lame, the blind, and thou shalt be blessed; for they cannot recompense thee, for thou shalt be recompensed at the resurrection of the just." Did the Saviour mean to say to this Pharisee, you may look to the destruction of Jerusalem for your reward for entertaining the poor, maimed, lame and blind, for they shall all be raised to eminence and wealth then? The thought forms the very climax of absurdity. To attempt a serious refutation of such burlesque on the words of the guileless Redeemer, would be useless. "It is sufficient to say that this explanation makes the divine Saviour contradict himself in the same sentence. To reduce it to plain English it would read thus: Give not to the rich. Why? Because they can and will repay. But give to the poor. Why? Because they will soon become rich and then they will return the whole!" *Whitman.*

LV. "*The Lord will not cast off forever.*" Lam. 3:31.
"*Who will have all men to be saved.*" 1 Tim. 2:4.
We take the following from a number of the Trumpet:

"NEGATIVE AND AFFIRMATIVE.

"'The Lord WILL NOT cast off forever,' Lam. 3:31.
"'God WILL HAVE all men to be saved.' 1 Tim. 2:4.
"It is necessary to reverse both these, if the doctine of endless misery be true, and say God WILL cast off forever—God WILL NOT have all men to be saved, and come to the knowledge of the truth."

This doubtless is considered a potent argument in favor of their doctrine, by the readers of the Trumpet, while the whole of it is built upon the perversion of two texts. The text in Lam. 3:31, is made to teach as follows: "*The Lord will not cast off endlessly in the future state.*' When a stubborn text presents itself teaching endless punishment, it must be destroyed in some way; then come the quibbles, and quirks, and twists, and sophistries, and negatives, and bold assertions, and orthodox authorities, and garbled extracts, and scripture references, and Greek criticisms; and, while the "poor blind candidate" of a reader is groping about amid all this smoke, the question is fully settled, and he is brought out into the glorious light of Universalism by, "The Lord will not cast off forever," significantly put in italics or blazing capitals. For a specimen, see Whittemore's Guide, pp. 124–128. Now this text has no more reference to a future state, than it has to Jehu's furious driving. Did it read, "The Lord *will* cast off forever," and were we to bring it to prove our doctrine, we should be met with criticisms showing that the word forever, as used here, does not mean endless; that the subject, over which the prophet was lamenting, was not a casting off in a future state, but of the Jewish nation, in this world. That this was spoken of the Jews, "the daughter of Zion," "the daughter of Judah," all will see, who will examine. The Jews were then cast off. They were in captivity, at Babylon, and the prophet received encouragement from God that their captivity should have an end,— that he would not cast off forever, but that the nation should be restored to their native land. This perversion is so glaring, that some of the ministers of that order begin to see that it is no benefit to their cause. In the Banner, for August 5, 1843, is a sermon by W. R. French, delivered before the Maine Convention of Universalists, in which is the following:

"We contend that future punishment is not taught in the Old Testament; that all its inducements to reformation are drawn from the fear of punishment and hope of reward, as suffered or enjoyed in this life. Taking this ground, do we act consistently in quoting texts from that book to prove that all men will be happy in the future life? Does it look like going on to perfection? To specify texts: Who has not heard the declaration of Jeremiah: 'The Lord will not cast off forever,' Lam. 3:31, adduced in proof of our doctrine? Yet it has, probably, no more reference to the future life, than to the temporal state of the aborigines of America. Nor is this the sole text that might be mentioned; in a certain class of publications *such* evidence abounds."

True, Mr. French, this is not the only perverted text, and Universalist publications do abound with such evidence; and it is also true that Universalism can be sustained in no other way. The text connected with this to make out the *argument* is equally a perversion. Rev. Sidney Turner, who renounced this error in 1842, says, that while a Universalist preacher, he once took this text, and so conscious was he that it did not teach the salvation of all men, that he announced it to his congregation, and told them that he thought it expressed a will of desire, and not a will of purpose. This of course was not very grateful to his audience. We quote from memory. Hear Mr. French upon this text, in the sermon just named. He says:

"And would it not subject one to certain condemnation, a query might be raised respecting the language of Paul, saying: 'Who will have all men to be saved, and come unto the knowledge of the truth.' 1 Tim. 2:4. For saith Paul, 'I exhort therefore, that first of all, supplications, prayers, intercessions, and giving of thanks, be made for all men; for kings, and for all that are in authority: that we may lead a quiet and peaceable life in all godliness and honesty. For this is good and acceptable in the sight of God our Saviour; who will have all men to be saved, and come unto the knowledge of the truth.' If we let the context explain, will it appear that salvation, here, means anything more than leading a quiet and peaceable life in all godliness and honesty, which all those will possess who come to the knowledge of the truth."

Truly, if Mr. French keeps on throwing aside all the perverted texts, he will rip up the whole foundation, and the crazy and baseless fabric of Universalism will come tumbling down about his ears shortly. Mr. F. is still a Universalist preacher. We see, then, that Mr. Whittemore perverts two texts to make his argument. There are no two scriptures more frequently quoted by Universalists, than these. They seem to rely upon them with the greatest confidence, to prove their doctrine. On the will of God, see Sec. LXXXV.

LVI. "*Therefore leaving the principles of the doctrine of Christ, let us go on unto perfection; not laying again the foundation of repentance from dead works, and of faith towards God, of the doctrine of baptisms, and of laying on of hands, and of resurrection of the dead, and of eternal judgment.*" Heb. 6:1, 2.

Mr. Bulkely, a Universalist, in discussion with Rev. E. Hutchins, is of the opinion that "the several doctrines enumerated were certain tenets of the Judaising Christians, that were not essential to Christianity." But the apostle explicitly tells us they were "*the principles of the doctrine of Christ.*" Which shall we follow? If Mr. B. is correct, then the "resurrection of the dead" is not essential to Christianity, and if this is so, what becomes of Universalism? In his zeal against eternal judgment he has discharged a gun which has mortally wounded himself. But says Mr. B., "There is only one place in the scriptures where an *eternal judgment* is spoken of." Well, what of that? How many plain testimonies to a point are necessary before we are to believe what God says? As an offset to this, we state that the expression, "all shall be holy and happy," does not occur even once in the Bible, and the phrase "destruction of Jerusalem" is not found in the New Testament. Dr. Clarke has doubtless given the true sense of the expression, "*eternal judgment.*" "It is so called because the decisions of the judge will be irreversible and ever during, and not that he will be forever making that decision." Observe, the apostle in the order of his arrangement, places the judgment after the resurrection, which was in keeping with Jewish doctrines upon this subject. He wrote to the Hebrews, and as they would understand him so should we. These Christians are exhorted to leave these principles as the scholar leaves the elementary principles; not to abandon them as useless, but to go on to higher attainments, for so far are the elementary principles from being worthless, that, though he leaves them, they are of constant use to the scholar in making proficiency in the higher branches of knowledge.

LVII. "*For I am now ready to be offered, and the time of my departure is at hand. I have fought a good fight, I have finished my course, I have kept the faith: Henceforth there is laid up for me a crown of righteousness which the Lord, the righteous Judge, shall give me in that day,*" &c. 2 Tim. 4 : 6–8.

Of this striking passage the author of the Guide takes no

notice. It is not found in his index. But Mr. Balfour has occupied no less than *eleven* pages of his Essay, in which he has made his usual display of Greek criticism and scripture references, to prove that Paul had his eye upon the destruction of Jerusalem when he addressed the above words to Timothy! To mention this to the honest reader of the Bible is to refute it. Paul did not live to see Jerusalem's destruction, for he died under Nero at least four years before; neither did he expect to, for he says: "The time of my departure is *at hand.*" He stands, as it were, between two worlds, and takes a pleasing retrospect of his Christian and ministerial fidelity. He then looks forward with eagerness to the judgment after death, where his fidelity would be rewarded with a crown of righteousness. Thus he connects the present with his future state, for it is death that he anticipates, and he is ready to be offered. How false the notion that our conduct here affects not our future condition. (Sec. XXVI.)

Since writing the foregoing, a book has come to hand entitled "The Future Life," by. J. Harris, containing the last edition of the Universalist perversion of this text. Speaking of the crown upon which the apostle had his eye, he says: "We need not wonder that St. Paul should expect, after having fought his battles in the cause of Christ, to have his name written high on the records of the church." Page 191.

Posthumous honors, a great name in this world after death, then, was what the apostle aspired to. His ambition "*to have his name written high on the records of the church,*" was what prompted him to sacrifice and suffer so much; this was the crown of glory he had in view! But this crown was not only for him, but for all those who "love his appearing." Hundreds of his fellow Christians loved the appearing of Christ too, and of course were all entitled to a crown. But do all of their names appear high on the records of the church? But very few of them appear at all on the record. What an abominable perversion!

LVIII. "*And as he reasoned of righteousness, temperance, and judgment to come, Felix trembled.*" Acts 24 : 25.

Upon this text Mr. Whittemore inquires, "Does the passage say this judgment was to come in *the future state?* No." What paltry quibbling this, well befitting the cause it is designed to support. So a future judgment is not meant in the text because the exact expression, "*future state*" is not appended. Can Mr. W. cite us to a passage in the scriptures where it says in so many words, that all, or even any, men shall be saved in *the future state?* No. Is there therefore no future salvation taught in the Bible? Mr. W. fails to inform us what judgment is meant, but turns us over to Mr. Balfour. We take up Mr. B.'s Essays and find eight pages filled with his learned parade to show that Paul reasoned of the judgment about to come upon the Jewish nation. A sad announcement that to a Roman governor. No wonder that he trembled to hear that the enemies of Rome should be conquered, and their proud city destroyed! We leave the text with the common sense of the reader without further remark.

LIX. "*Or despisest thou the riches of his goodness,*" &c. "*For as many as have sinned without law, shall also perish without law; and as many as have sinned in the law, shall be judged by the law,— in the day when God shall judge the secrets of men by Jesus Christ, according to my gospel.*" Rom 2 : 4–16.

The falsity of refering this to the overthrow of the Jews, as Mr. Whittemore has done, (*Guide*, p. 179,) is apparent from the fact that this was addressed to converted Jews and Gentiles more than fifteen hundred miles from Jerusalem; and of course Christians so remote could have but little to fear from its destruction. Paul speaks of a day of wrath and revelation of the righteous judgment of God," (ver. 5,) which is not only general but particular. "To *every man* according to his deeds," to those Christians who continued in well doing, "eternal life."

But to those who should apostatize, "who are contentious and obey not the truth, but obey unrighteousness, indignation and wrath, tribulation and anguish." Ver. 8 and 9. But what had Christians at Rome to fear from the destruction of Jerusalem, even though they should apostatize and obey not the truth? Or had they anything to fear from the Roman government in case they renounced their Christian faith? It would have been the most ready way to have secured its favor, as all know who are acquainted with the history of those times. The destruction of Jerusalem was a judgment upon the Jews, as Universalists assert. Now as if the apostle foresaw that some might pervert his words by applying them to the Jewish calamity, he declares that the rendering of which he speaks should be made not only to the Jews, but "ALSO TO THE GENTILES." Ver. 9 and 10. This thought itself shows the glaring perversion of the passage by Universalists. In this day of judgment, those who had not the written law, heathens, are to be judged. Ver. 12–16. But heathens, as we have seen, were not judged at Jerusalem. The apostle is treating upon the same day of judgment he is in chap. 14 : 10–12. (Sec. LXI.)

LX. "*Some men's sins are open beforehand, going before to judgment; and some men they follow after.*" 1 Tim. 5 : 24.

Taking the position that no sinner is punished beyond this life, (Sec. XLIX.) Universalists have never been able to meet the argument against that view, drawn from the fact that some die in the act of sinning. (Sec. XLVI.) To escape the difficulty, a flippant use is occasionally made of this text to give the impression that God can and does punish sin, sometimes, at least, before it is committed. We shall now show the unsoundness of this position. If God punishes sin before it is committed, then the divine administration becomes indebted to the sinner, and he has the *right*, and can demand the privilege, of sinning as much as he has been punished for. There is no evaiding this, if justice is connected with the divine administration. Now as this involves an absurdity not to be conceived of in the administration of a wise and holy God, the doctrine which produces such a conclusion must be false. Every discerning mind must see that such a view is contrary to all just conceptions of human or divine law, and that none but those who are hard pushed with truth will have recource to so miserable a subterfuge.

Again : We are frequently told that there is no future punishment, because punishment is consequential and is inseparable from sin. But if sin is prepunished, then is the punishment seperate from the sin, which contradicts a very essential doctrine of American Universalism. We are told of the hell of conscience. But how can men suffer in their consciences for sins not committed, and of which they can have no conceptions? The passage at the head of this has no reference whatever to the infliction of God's penalties upon sinners. Paul is giving direction respecting appointing men to the sacred office of the ministry, and says, ver. 22 : "Lay hands suddenly on no man, neither be partaker of other men's sins," i. e., by inducting improper men into the sacred office. He then says, ver. 24 : "Some men's sins are open beforehand," &c. Upon this, Dr. Clarke gives the following : "In appointing men to sacred offices in the church, among the candidates Timothy would find,—

"1. Some of whom he knew nothing, but only that they professed Christianity. Let such be tried before they are appointed.

"2. Some, of whose faith and piety he had the fullest knowledge ; and whose usefulness in the church was well known.

"3. Some, whose lives were not all, or but partially reformed ; who were still unchanged in their hearts, and unholy in their lives.

"The sins of these latter were known to all ; *they go before to judgment ;* with them he could have no difficulty ; there might have been hypocrites among them, whose sins could not be known till *after* they were brought into the sacred office. The characters of all should be fully investigated. The sins of some, before this investigation, might be so manifest as to lead at once to condemnation. The sins of others might be found out *after*, or in consequence of, this investigation: and those that were otherwise could not be long hid from his knowledge, or the knowledge of the church. On all these accounts the exhortation is necessary, '*Lay hands suddenly on no man.*'" *Clarke in loco.*

LXI. "*Wherefore God hath highly exalted him, and given him a name which is above every name: that at the name of Jesus every knee should bow, of things in heaven, and things in earth, and things under the earth; and that every tongue should confess that Jesus Christ is Lord, to the glory of God the Father.*" Phil. 2:9–11; Rom. 14:10–12; Isa. 45: 23–25.

This text seems to be relied on with the greatest confidence to prove Universalism. But why do those who use it give us no light on its parallel, found Rom. 14:10–12? It reads thus: "But why dost thou judge thy brother? or why dost thou set at nought thy brother? for we shall all stand before the judgment seat of Christ. For it is written, as I live, saith the Lord, every knee shall bow to me and every tongue shall confess to God. So then every one of us shall give an account of himself to God." These texts are quotations of Isa. 45:23–25. "I have sworn by myself, the word is gone out of my mouth in righteousness, and shall not return, That unto me every knee shall bow, every tongue shall swear. Surely shall *one* say, in the Lord have I righteousness and strength; *even* to him shall *men* come; and all that are incensed against him shall be ashamed. In the Lord shall all the seed of Israel be justified, and shall glory." The passage in Romans is a more full quotation of the prophet than the one in Philippians as the following comparison will show :

ISAIAH.	ROMANS.	PHILIPPIANS.
"I have sworn by myself."	"As I live saith the Lord."	
"Every knee shall bow."	"Every knee shall bow."	"Every knee shall bow."
"Every tongue shall swear."	"Every tongue shall confess."	"Every tongue shall confess."
"Even to him shall men come."	"For we must all appear before the judgment seat of Christ."	

We examine four volumes of Universalist books, each with a copious index of texts ; but they furnish no light upon the passage in Romans, while the passage in Philippians is never omitted. We take up the Guide, look at the index, and are referred to p. 186 ; turn to it, and are put off with the author's sophistry on 2 Cor. 5 : 10. Now, why this concealment of the passage in Romans ? It is doubtless seen by these men that if it is brought out in connection with its parallel in Philippians it will destroy all their capital, by teaching a future judgment. Universalist writers unhesitatingly refer the passage in Philippians to the future state, for it is in the resurrection state that all, as they say, are to be saved. We also admit its future state reference. But it bears no mark of a future reference that the text in Romans does not. Universalist reader, be honest with yourself in this business. Remember that there is a reason why the leaders in your order maintain a dead silence respecting the last named text. They have labored to make you believe in no future judgment; and then that Isa. 45 : 23–25, and Phil. 2 : 9, 11 teach the salvation of all in the future world. But the truth is, Isa. 45 : 23–25, Rom. 14 : 10–12, and Phil. 2 : 9–10 *are co-relative passages, and if one is referable to a future state, all are, and then the judgment seat of Christ is in the future state ; while on the other hand if the judgment named is referable to Jerusalem's destruction, or any calamity in this world, the bowing and confessing named is confined to this world, and the passages in Isa. and Phil. can no longer be pressed into the service of Universalism.* Paul says in Romans : "We shall

all stand before the judgement seat of Christ." Question: How do you know this, Paul? Answer: "It is written, (Isa. 45 : 23,) as I live, saith the Lord, every knee shall bow to me, and every tongue shall confess to God. So, then, every one of us shall give an account of himself to God." Thus the apostle quotes Isaiah in proof of a future judgment. As this may meet the eye of one of the few, who, like Murray, admit of a future judgment, but conclude that universal salvation is indicated at that time, a few thoughts will now be offered upon some points relied upon. Stress has been laid upon the universality of the language, "every knee shall bow," &c. That all shall bow to Christ's authority in the judgment, we believe, whether willing or not; but it by no means follows that all shall be saved. But it is said, Isa. 45 : 24, "Every tongue shall swear." Some have concluded from this that all will swear allegiance to Christ and yield him a willing obedience; but this is all assumption. It is worthy of remark, that for the word *swear*, Paul substitutes the word *confess* in both of his quotations. All in the day of judgment will confess Christ's Lordship and the justice of his decisions to the glory of God the Father, who hath submitted to him this judgment. They will also confess their course of life to him. "So then every one of us shall give an account of himself to God." The devil once confessed Christ, (Mark 1 : 24); but this was no evidence of his holiness and happiness. "All that are incensed against him shall be ashamed." May not wicked persons be ashamed of conduct they still persist in. "In the Lord shall all the seed of Israel be justified, and shall glory." Universalism says, "In the Lord shall *all the human race* be justified, and shall glory." The prophet contradicts this by confining the blessings to "THE SEED OF ISRAEL." If reference is had to the natural descendants of Israel, then all men are not included; and if to his spiritual seed, which is doubtless the fact, then all are not embraced, but only believers in Christ. Rom. 9 : 6; Gal. 3 : 7, 29. Instead of universal-salvation, a universal judgment is taught, when all shall be obliged to confess the justness of its decisions to the glory of God the Father. But how can it be for the glory of the Father if all are not saved? We answer: In the same way that an earthly government is glorified by the righteous decision of its courts, and the just execution of its penalties.

One thought more. Universalists sometimes tell us that the change by which all are to be saved, will take place "in a moment, in the twinkling of an eye," that "there will be no condition for man in the future state, but that in which he will be as the angels of God in heaven." *Balfour's Essay*, p. 192. *Trumpet*, No. 679. Yet by the use they make of two of the foregoing passages they teach us that men in the future state will bow the knee, swear allegiance, be incensed, be ashamed, &c., &c. The reader must reconcile these as he best can. On confessing at the judgment, see a quotation from Josephus, in Sec. XLI.

LXII. "*For all shall know me from the least of them unto the greatest of them, saith the Lord.*" Jer. 31 : 33, 34.

In this chapter the Prophet is speaking of the superior advantages of the Christian dispensation over the Jewish, and of the spiritual blessings secured by the new covenant. See context, also Hebrews, 8th chapter. It will be perceived that the word *all* occurs in the text, and this is enough for Universalist expounders to seize it, and declare that it teaches the salvation of all men in eternity! "In regard to the future condition of mankind, the Bible declares explicitly, that all shall ultimately know God, 'from the least to the greatest.' Jer. 31: 34." *Guide*, p. 270. This is a perversion. The covenant is not made with *all men* but with "*the house of Israel*," v. 33, and the prosperous state of things named is not predicated of all men in eternity, but of the seed of Israel in this world, where it is possible for them to "cease to be a nation before the Lord," v. 36. The triumphs of Christianity are predicted here in the world, and God's true Israel will enjoy the blessings named. Rom. 2: 29; John 1; 47; Rom. 9: 6.

LXIII. "*But the way of transgressors is hard.*" Prov. 13:15.

Often has it been proclaimed that the teachings of Christian ministers tend to immorality, because they instruct the people that sin is pleasurable, and thus lead men to seek pleasure in sin; while Universalist ministers are the only true reformers, because they teach that the way of transgressors is hard. The manner in which this is often done, amounts to a gross libel on Christian ministers, as their constant hearers know full well. (Sec. XLVI.) The gospel minister has at his command all the motives a Universalist can possibly urge drawn from the effects of sin in this life; and in addition to these he has the powerful motive to urge of the fearful retributions of eternity. But while he shows the effects of sin upon the sinner here, and that on a comparative view there is no true and lasting peace to the wicked, he feels not at liberty to proclaim that there is absolutely no pleasure in sin,—for this would not only contradict the Bible, but the experience of every sinner; hence, he points out sinful pleasures, exposes their delusive character and ruinous effects, and labors to dissuade all, and especially the young, from following them. The man of observation, acquainted with his Bible and capable of reflection, knows that in man's depraved state, there are many sins committed for the sake of the sensual pleasure derived from the act. If Universalists choose to take the position that there is *no* pleasure in sin, why, then they are only at their own business—arraying themselves against common sense and the Bible. See Heb. 11:25; 2 Thess. 2:12; Prov. 4:16.

We subjoin the following, from the pen of another. "Those who believe in future and eternal judgment, regard the ways of the transgressor as hard indeed, involved as those ways are in darkness here, and terminating as they do in 'everlasting destruction from the presence of the Lord, and the glory of his power.' But if Universalism be true, the ways of the transgressor are not so very hard; they are quite tolerable. A Universalist conscience, benumbed with fatality and seared with guilt, and case-hardened by an almost total absence of a sense of accountability, cannot be supposed to give the transgressor a very serious annoyance in his ways, especially if he be strong in the faith that a life of pleasure, infamy and guilt, will inevitably terminate in glory. It will be a hard task to persuade such an one that 'all is (*not*) well that ends well.'" *Russell.*

LXIV. "*Concerning this sect, we know that every where it is spoken against.*" Acts 28 : 22.

The primitive church, in its purity, met with general opposition from *wicked* men; and Universalists, because their system is extensively opposed by *good* men, labor to make the impression that they are the only true successors of the apostolic church! To effect this, they avail themselves of this text. Universalism is extensively opposed, not by the wicked, for it meets their desires, and administers to them an opiate; but by Christians generally. And is the opposition of the mass of enlightened Christians, many of them possessing the best heads and hearts the world has ever seen, to be taken as evidence of the purity and truthfulness of that which they oppose? While it is true, as a general thing, that the wicked do oppose that which is religiously good, it is also true that we are not safe in considering a thing good merely because it is extensively opposed, even by wicked men. Look at the Mormon delusion. Sure we are that no sect in our country, in the nineteenth century at least, has suffered more by persecution from wicked men than the Mormons. But is this to be taken as evidence of the purity of their lives, and the truthfulness of their system? Universalists have never suffered a tithe of persecution compared with the followers of Joe Smith; neither have they suffered anything compared with the Baptists, Puritans, and Methodists. These have all seen the time when each could say, "*we* are the sect everywhere spoken against." Indeed, so far are Universalists from being the persecuted, that they have persecuted others. (Sec. CXIX.)

Reader, when you hear a zealous disciple claiming apostolic succession for Universalism from this text, just ask him if the Mormons have not a claim equally good.

LXV. "*And being made perfect, he became the author of eternal salvation unto all them that obey him.*" Heb. 5 : 9.

Does this text sound like Universalism? That declares that all shall have eternal salvation, whether they obey Christ or not. But the apostle, speaking of moral agents under the gospel, confines this salvation to such as OBEY Christ. Which shall we follow, Universalism or the Bible? And then, again, Universalists deny that Christ is the author of future salvation. He came not to provide it, but to proclaim it, is the doctrine. See Sec. XXIX.

LXVI. "*For if we sin wilfully, after that we have received the knowledge of the truth,*" &c. Heb. 10 : 26–31.

This passage evidently teaches the doctrine of future retribution. Death without mercy can be considered in no other light than the severest of temporal punishments. But the text threatens a *sorer* punishment even than "death without mercy." What will Universalists do with this? Do with it? Why, throw it into Jerusalem's destruction, the common receptacle of all stubborn texts. *Guide*, p. 104. How absurd! What evidence had the apostle that all or any of the Christians who might apostatize then, should live and be present to suffer by the Romans at Jerusalem? Just none at all. This epistle bears date A.D. 64, six years before Titus came against the Jews, and was addressed to Hebrew Christians who were scattered all over the Roman Empire. And then he does that which is a great abomination in the eyes of Universalist divines, for he appeals to the fears of Christians, to save them from apostasy. Hear him. "For we know him that hath said, Vengeance belongeth unto me, I will recompense, saith the Lord." So there is something in the Divine administration called VEN-

GEANCE. How unlike Universalist teachings is this! What would be thought of a preacher of that order who should urge the vengeance of God as a motive to move his hearers? (Sec. LXIX.) And how long would his people employ him as their teacher? Again, "It is a fearful thing to fall into the hands of the living God," v. 31. But why a *fearful* thing, if "a just punishment is as essential for our welfare as anything that love can do?" Why should the most vile apostate of our race fear to fall into the hands of the living God, if all are to be taken to heaven, irrespective of character here? Paul, in the passage, shows the possibility and awful consequences of apostasy, and solemnly appeals to their fears respecting the future; after which he appeals to their hopes and consciousness concerning the faithful Christian's reward in heaven. He reminds them of their former sufferings and sacrifices, and says; "For ye had compassion of me in my bonds, and took joyfully of the spoiling of your goods, knowing in yourselves that ye have in heaven a better and enduring substance. Cast not away, therefore, your confidence, which hath great recompense of reward. For ye have need of patience; that, after ye have done the will of God, ye might receive the promise," v. 34, 35, 36. Here it will be seen that *heaven, with its better and enduring substance*, is presented as the result of their Christian fidelity. Read the chapter from v. 24 to v. 36, and it will be seen that it lies with mighty weight against more points than one of modern Universalism.

LXVII. "*For as the rain cometh down, and the snow from heaven, and returneth not thither,*" &c. Isa. 55:10, 11.

In their very frequent use of this passage, Universalists always assume the very point in debate, namely, that it is the pleasure or purpose of God to save all men unconditionally in the future state. This we deny, for whatever the work to be accomplished by this "word," or wherever done, one thing is evident, which is, that its benefits are only to be received upon conditions. This is clear, not only from the context, (verses 6 and 7,) but from the figure employed in the passage. Observe, it is "*as* the rain," "*so* shall my word be." Is it the purpose of God, in sending the rain, to give the fruits of the earth to all men, whether they till it or not? By no means. But it is to "give seed to the *sower*," &c. There is no need of enlargement here. But what is God's word here spoken of, and is it to accomplish the salvation of all men in the future state, according to Universalist expositions of scripture? God's word mentioned in this passage, says Mr. Whittemore, is the gospel. *Guide*, p. 40. Well, what is the gospel? It is not the salvation of all men in the future state, but is simply the good news or glad tidings which announces the fact that all will be saved. So say Universalists. The gospel, according to their notions, is perfectly independent of the salvation of men in the future state, just as much so, as announcing the fact that there is such a place as London, is independent of that fact. It is contended that gospel salvation is the effects experienced in this life of believing the doctrine, that all will be saved hereafter, and that preaching, receiving, or rejecting the gospel, will not affect our future salvation in the least. Mr. Whittemore ridicules the idea of man's conduct being recompensed in a future state, and says, it "is alike reasonable with saying, that a man who sows a field of grain in Massachusetts, shall reap the harvest from it in the State of Ohio." *Trumpet*, No. 635. By the way, we suppose it is very reasonable to him for a man to sow a field of grain and reap the crop just as quick as he has sown it! In other words, it is quite clear to him, that men are punished for their sins as soon as they commit them. (Sec. XLIX.)

From the preceding we learn as follows:

1. The word that goeth forth, and is to accomplish that which the Almighty pleases, is the gospel, i.e., the good news of the salvation of all men in the future state.

2. This gospel, or good news, is independent of what it declares, and does not in the least affect the future condition of any man, as all will be saved in the future state, whether they hear

the good news in this life or not. It is seen, then, that according to Mr. Whittemore's own showing, the declared prosperity of the word or gospel named in the passage, does not secure the salvation of all or any men in the future state. Yet, when it will serve his purpose, he can give it a future-state reference, and use it to prove Universalism, as he has done on pp. 29 and 40 of his Guide. And thus the Scriptures are perverted, and the people deceived. If there is a jingle of words, if perchance, there is universal language in a passage, no matter what it was designed to teach, or what its connection, no matter whether it is spoken of the Jewish nation, or of the spread of the gospel in this world, or of Christians only — it is taken and connected, perhaps, with one or two other texts equally perverted, and thus a Universalist *argument* is made. In proof of this, see Mr. Whittemore's "One Hundred Arguments," which are wholly made up of mangled and perverted texts.

The design to be accomplished by this word is seen in the commission given by Christ himself to preach it, which is as follows: "Go ye into all the world, and preach the gospel to every creature. He that believeth, and is baptized, shall be saved; but he that believeth not, shall be damned." Mark 16: 15, 16.

LXVIII. "*What shall I do to inherit eternal life.*" Luke 18: 18.

The phrase in our translation rendered *eternal life*, occurs twenty-seven times in the New Testament; and the phrase rendered *everlasting life* occurs thirteen times; making in all forty times, all of which, according to Universalist writers, mean something experienced in this world. Mr. Whittemore says:

"Notwithstanding the 'everlasting life' spoken of in the New Testament is applied in these pages to that state of rest, purity and joy, into which believers of the gospel entered whenever they embraced it, the author takes this opportunity to say, that he undoubtingly believes that a future state of immortality and incorruption is revealed in the New Testament. This, like the present existence, will be the gift of God, and cannot, in the nature of things, as seems to us, be affected by the conduct of men in this life." *Notes on Par.*, p. 354.

Here it would seem that Mr. Whittemore is almost startled at his own sentiments, and lest he should be thought an infidel downright, he is under the necessity at the close of his book, of informing his readers that he believes that a future state is taught in the New Testament! Again he says:

"What is meant by eternal life? This phrase is not used by the sacred writers to signify endless blessedness beyond the grave, but that state of spiritual life and peace which was the immediate effects of faith in the gospel of Jesus Christ." *Guide*, p. 140.

The question may arise in the reader's mind, why it is that Universalists should desire to destroy the future-state reference of this phrase? It is because it stands in such connections in the Bible, that if it is admitted to mean a state of bliss, it confirms, by parity of reason, the doctrine of future punishment.

Notwithstanding Mr. Whittemore, in the Guide, denies the future-state reference of the expression "eternal life," yet such is the *twistical* character of the man upon this subject, that he can, in this same Guide, use this same phrase, "eternal life," four times, to teach the salvation of all men in the *future state!* See *Guide*, pp. 25, 45, 46, 52. How long would these men be troubled with the Bible at all, were they left to themselves, and the world sufficiently prepared for them to destroy it, and substitute one of their own inventing?

All true believers possess the seminal principles of a future blissful life in this world; and in view of it the inspired penmen use the phrase "everlasting life" in a few instances, in this sense, as in John 5 : 24, "He that heareth my words, and believeth on him that sent me, *hath* everlasting life;" also John 6 : 47, and a few other places. Universalists seize hold of these, and claim the right to interpret all the rest of the passages where the expression occurs by them, and thus deceive the people.

The truth is, the phrase, primarily and properly, means a life of bliss beyond this. This is evident,

1. *From Jewish belief.* In 2 Macc. 7 : 9, a Jew who was put to death for refusing to eat swine's flesh, says to his murderer, "Thou, like a fury, takest us out of this present life, but the King of the world shall *raise us up, who have died for his laws, unto everlasting life.*" We bring this simply as historical evidence of what the Jews believed respecting everlasting or eternal life. It bears date B.C. 167. Again, Josephus in his Discourse on Hades, speaking of the intermediate state, gives the following as the belief of the Jews: "But the countenance of the fathers and of the just which they see, always smiles upon them, while they wait for that rest, and *eternal new life in heaven,* which is to succeed this region." Now in the light of this belief of the Jews, let us look at the case of the young ruler. He being an educated Jew, well understood Jewish theology. His question is, "What shall I do to inherit eternal life?" The Saviour answers, and adds, "and thou shalt have *treasure in heaven.*" This answer shows most conclusively that the Saviour understood him to be anxious about his future state, and that "treasure in heaven" is synonymous with "eternal life."

That eternal life properly means a life beyond this, is evident,

2. *From the absurdities involved by the Universalist interpretation of the phrase.* Let us take two or three of these illustrations. Matt. 25 : 46, "But the righteous into life eternal." This, we are told, "is that spiritual life which the believer enjoys in this state." *Notes on Par.*, p. 353. Now the righteous must be already spiritually alive, or else they are not righteous. This interpretation, then represents the judge as sending *the spiritually alive into spiritual life,* which is manifestly absurd; therefore, cannot be the true interpretation. John 12 : 25, "He that loveth his life shall lose it, and he that hateth his life in this world, shall keep it unto life eternal." Life eternal, in this text, is contrasted with life in this world. Just confine the meaning of "life eternal" to this world, and

the passage is reduced to this absurdity: He that hateth his life in this world shall keep it, by gaining, by the loss of his life, that eternal life which is enjoyed in this world. Or, in other words, after he is dead he shall come back and enjoy spiritual life in this world! Is it said that the expression "this world" means "this age," before the destruction of Jerusalem? Then we may read it thus: He that dies before the destruction of Jerusalem, shall have eternal life by living through that destruction! But the word rendered *world* here, is not *aion*, which in some instances means "age," but *kosmos*, the most appropriate word for world. (Sec. XI.)

The more the reader thinks upon this passage, the more will he see the violent wresting and absurdity of those who confine the phrase "eternal life," to the spiritual life the believer enjoys in this world. Take one text more. Titus 1:2, "In hope of eternal life, which God that cannot lie," &c. Here Paul represents himself as hoping for eternal life. Hope respects the future. Paul was a holy Christian, and of course already spiritually alive. Now if eternal life means spiritual life in this world, then the hope of Paul implies that he was destitute of spiritual life, for what a man has in his possession he does not hope for. Was Paul destitute of spiritual life at this time? Was he a wicked man?

We here present the reader with an entire argument from Mr. Whittemore, in which he gives the expression "*eternal life*," a future-state reference, the very thing he denies on page 140 of the same book. He says, "The record which God hath given of his Son, is this: 'That God hath given to us eternal life; and this life is in his Son.' 1 John 5:11. Is this record true? It surely is. Who are called on to believe it? All mankind. If any man believes it not, he makes God a liar, by saying that God's record is not true. God, then, hath certainly given eternal life to all men, in his divine purpose." *Guide*, p. 52. This is one of Mr. W.'s One Hundred Arguments to prove Universalism, i. e., the salvation of all men in the future state; and thus he gives the phrase eternal life a future reference. Which is to be believed, Mr. W. on page 52, or Mr. W. on page 140 of the same book? If he is correct on page 140, and has proved anything by the argument, it is this: That God hath certainly given in his divine purpose, to all mankind, that spiritual life and peace which faith in the gospel imparts in this world? As matter of fact shows that this has not been accomplished, neither can it be, it is hoped we shall hear no more from the author of the Guide about the absolute character of the divine purposes. But, suppose that all the race of Adam were in possession of the spiritual life and peace the Gospel imparts in this world, would that secure them bliss in eternity? By no means, according to this author; for, as we have seen, in speaking of the eternal state he says, it "cannot in the nature of things, as seems to us, be affected by the conduct of men in this life." Beware, reader, how you follow such a crooked Guide. In the text pressed into this argument, the apostle says, "God hath given to us eternal life." This is spoken of believers, and not of all men, as may be seen by v. 13. See also John 3 : 15.

LXIX. "*Fear not, little flock; for it is your Father's good pleasure to give you the kingdom.*" Luke 12 : 32.

Mr. A. B. Grosh, a great man, an editor and minister in the Universalist order, uses this text, in connection with several others where the expression "*fear not*" is found, to show that men are not to be moved by fear "to repent and obey the commands of God." Of the Gospel, he says, "It makes its first advances to the world of sinners, by exhorting them to "*fear not.*" To substantiate this, and to show that none have anything to fear, he quotes the expression as found in the address to the shepherds, Luke 2 : 10; to Mary, Luke 1 : 30; to Zacharias, Luke 1 : 13; to Simon, Luke 5 : 10; to the disciples, Luke 12 : 32, also v. 7; to the women who sought the Lord at the sepulchre, Matt. 28 : 5; and also what the Saviour says to

John, (Rev. 1 : 17,) "Fear not; I am the first and the last," &c. He will have it that those who teach that wicked men ought to fear in view of God's penalties, are opposed to Christ, who said, "fear not;" and says, "but the wisdom of this world has mingled its own inventions with the wisdom from on high, and fear, *fear*, FEAR, is the grand instrument of convicting sinners, of converting them to the church, of confirming them in the faith, and of keeping them steadfast unto the end of their professions. Fear of an endless hell — fear of an almost almighty fiend —fear of the censures of the world and of the anathemas of the church — these are the motives principally appealed to in our days, to make and keep people religious." p. 52. With this kind of cant do the advocates of Universalism labor to bring into contempt the faithful teachings of Christian ministers.

Taking into the account the obvious design of the writer, it stands thus: The scriptures enjoin upon certain persons, respecting some particular subjects, the duty to "fear not;" therefore all wicked and ungodly men have nothing to fear, and no appeal should be made to their fears to deter them from sin! But where, we ask, is it to be found in the Bible that wicked men, while continuing in their sins, have nothing to fear? Has God ever said to such, "fear not?" Christians are complained of because they would have men fear "an endless hell." To this we plead guilty, but find ourselves in honorable company. Christ said to the wicked, "Ye serpents, ye generation of vipers, how can ye escape the damnation of hell." Matt. 23 : 33. Here is an appeal direct to the fears upon this point, by the Son of God himself. Hear him again; "He that blasphemeth against the Holy Ghost hath never forgiveness, but is in danger of eternal damnation." Mark 3 : 29. Is there nothing to be feared from eternal damnation? This, being addressed to Jews, must have been understood by them to mean just what it seems to mean, for they believed in eternal damnation. But men are made to fear "an almost almighty fiend." That gospel ministers strive to impress men with a sense of their danger from the temptations of the devil, is true; and that there is such a being, with subordinates, may be seen by turning to Sec. XCVIII. They are made to fear "the censures of the world." This is false, as all know who sit under the Christian ministry. With great unanimity they urge their hearers to embrace Christ, regardless alike of the frowns and flatteries of the world. Fear of "the anathemas of the Church." That Christians are instructed by their teachers to fear to violate their voluntary obligations to the church, we admit. Since Universalists now form some associations they call churches, what do they teach concerning such obligations? Do they teach their members to "fear not" to violate? It is complained that fear is the grand instrument in "keeping them steadfast unto the end." That the fears of Christians are appealed to frequently in the Bible, is most obvious. When the sinner embraces the gospel, he is not freed from the law as a rule of life, but strength is imparted by the gospel, to assist the better to keep the law. Every law for the regulation of human conduct has a penalty; for, to talk of law without a penalty, is a solecism. Every penalty is an appeal to the fears of those who are bound to obey; and although the Christian is delivered from the fear of the penalty for sins that are past, by his justification, yet he is to fear to violate the law in future, lest the apostate's hell be his doom. Hence the propriety of appealing to the fears, not only of unrenewed persons, but of Christians. Says Paul, "Let us therefore fear, lest, a promise being left us of entering into his rest, any of you should seem to come short of it." Heb. 4 : 1. This was addressed to Christians.* The Saviour enjoins fear upon his disciples. "Fear not them which kill the body, but are not able to kill the soul; but rather fear him which is able to destroy both soul and body in hell. Matt. 10 : 28. See also Heb. 10 : 26–31. We should be obliged to transcribe no small portion of the Bible, were we to present all the passages where the fears of the wicked are appealed to, and where fear is enjoined as a Christian duty. Yet Universalism stands up in the face of all this, and cries, "FEAR NOT!" We must admit, however, that at least in this, it is consistent with itself; for if "all the judgments of which the scriptures speak, are to destroy sin, and reform the sinner," and if "no more punishment will be inflicted than the good of the sinner requires," (*U. Ill. & Def.*, pp. 248, 195,) why should any, enlightened by the luminous rays of Universalism, ever fear the penalty of God's law? What should we think of a dying man who should fear to take a medicine he *knew* would cure him even though it were somewhat disagreeable? We say, then, that Universalism is consistent with itself upon this point; but this very consistency deprives it of the character of a Christian system, inasmuch as it is directly at war with the clear and evident teachings of the Bible. The faithful minister uses fear as a motive, because the Bible presents it as such; but it is not the only motive with him. He urges the love of God as developed in the gift of his Son, and the gospel provisions. He urges the goodness of God as seen in his mercy towards sinners, and in his long suffering—bearing with sinners long when they deserve punishment. But he appeals to the fears of men concerning the neglect and abuse of these blessings, and the danger consequent upon such a course. Noah was moved by fear to build the ark (Heb. 11:7); and Christ, as we have seen, inculcates the same principle upon his disciples. The love or goodness of God, it is admitted, is the most noble principle; yet, when we consider the fallen nature of man, and the circumstances in which he is placed, fear will be seen to be equally necessary. The truth is, God's government is a reign of terror to the finally impenitent, and this by Paul is urged as a motive against sin. "Knowing, therefore, the terrors of the Lord, we persuade men." 2 Cor. 5:11.

"It is a question of vast importance, and which I fear ministers in general do not sufficiently attend to, whether the *love* or the *terror* of God operates most powerfully *at first* on the minds of sinners. If they were governed by their reason, there would be no necessity to preach the terror of the Lord to them; because, as soon as they perceived that their interest and duty are united, they would begin to promote the one by the practice of the other: but he must have a superficial acquaintance with men, who does not know that, in general, they are governed by their corrupt passions and appetites, in opposition to the dictates of reason and religion. The privileges of religion will never operate as a motive on corrupt minds to practice its duties. Tell them about the comforts of the Spirit; the sweet communion with God in religious exercises; and the happiness of heaven, as consisting in the vision of God, and the society of saints, angels, and Jesus Christ; in investigating the works and ways of God; singing his praises; in loving and serving him forevermore; — I say, tell them of these things; but, since they have no disposition to enjoy them, they will express no desire after them. You might as well cast pearls before swine. The temper of their minds must be changed before such motives will have any influence upon them. Should a minister neglect to address the passion of fear, by leaving out the terror of the Lord, he may preach the love of God, the joys of heaven, moral virtue, or what he pleases, till his tongue cleave to the roof of his mouth, without converting one sinner from the error of his ways." *Isaac.*

LXX. "*Also unto thee, O Lord, belongeth mercy; for thou renderest unto every man according to his work.*" Ps. 62 : 12.

In view of the connection, the sense of the text is this: Mercy is attributed to God, because he would deliver his people and destroy their enemies (v. 3–8); while the obstinately wicked, who delight in lies, (v. 4,) trust in oppression, and become vain in robbery, (v. 10,) shall be rewarded according to their works. This scripture is often perverted to show that all punishment is for the good of the sinner, and that men shall be punished all their sins deserve, whether they repent or not. That every man suffers the full penalty for all the sins he commits, may be considered a cardinal doctrine with American Universalists. "Every man shall suffer to the full extent of his deserts. There is no remission of punishment, either on account of the Saviour's death, or the sinner's penitence." *U. Ill. & Def.*, p. 249. Quotations might be given harmonizing with this, from most of their leading writers. In order to sustain this false position, they are driven to another, viz., that the sinner may be fully punished and still forgiven. Says Skinner, "The common opinion that forgiveness is a remission of punishment, is altogether incorrect. We can be justly punished and still forgiven." *U. Ill. & Def.*, pp. 250, 254. Says Fernald, speaking of the Bible, "It never teaches the forgiveness or remission of *punishment* for sins committed. It is the forgiveness of *sins;* by which is understood, the blotting out, or cleansing from, *after due justice is administered.*" *U. against Part.*, p. 259. Says Sawyer: "Christ came to save men from *deserving* punishment, rather than from punishment deserved." *Letter to Remington*, p. 49. Another doctrine which Mr. Whittemore asserts to be denominational, is, that the punishment of sin is executed as soon as it is committed, or that sin punishes itself immediately. (Sec. XLIX.)

Now just compare these sentiments with the language of Paul. "And be ye kind, one to another, tender hearted, forgiving one another, even as God for Christ's sake hath forgiven you." Eph. 4:32. Again: "Forbearing one another, and forgiving one another; if any man have a quarrel against any, even as Christ forgave you, so also do ye." Col. 3:13. In these scriptures is taught most clearly that we are to forgive injuries in the same sense that God forgives sinners. Now if all sin is punished without delay, and if by gospel forgiveness none are saved from deserved punishment, then we are taught to show no mercy to those who have injured us; for observe, we are to forgive those we have a quarrel against, even AS God for Christ's sake hath forgiven us. Thus, to be in accordance with Universalist theology, the law of quick retaliation should universally prevail in human society! The injunction contained in these texts, when properly considered, entirely overthrows the doctrine of no escape from punishment. A display of texts is made by Mr. Skinner to show "that the scriptures never speak of forgiving punishment," and that "forgiveness of sin only is taught." *U. Ill. and Def.*, p. 250. This is not only weak, but wicked, for the design is deceptive. Nothing is said of forgiving punishment, for the good reason that the sinner does not commit *punishment*, but *sin*; and when this sinful act is forgiven, the sinner is saved from the punishment which would otherwise follow. "What is pardon but a revocation of the sentence of condemnation, and thereby a remission of the penalty of the law? We can form no other idea of pardon than this; and the reason is because sin — we speak of the transgression of the law — is an *action*, not a substance, and therefore untangible, and you cannot treat with it, either to forgive it, or to punish it, apart from the agent which commits it. A sinner is pardoned just so far as his punishment is remitted to him, and no farther." *Merritt.*

Great importance is attached to forgiveness, as every reader of the Bible knows. But according to the hypothesis that none are saved from deserved punishment by it, we think it would puzzle a philosopher, as well as a divine, to show what advantage a forgiven sinner possesses over one that is not forgiven. The forgiven is punished all his sins deserve, and the unforgiven is punished no more. Such forgiveness is of equal value with a pardon from his holiness the Pope. Having manufactured a new theology, the leaders in the sect have found it necessary to form a new language to suit it. What linguist has ever informed us that forgiveness or pardon means to save from sin by preventing it in the future, and that too without conveying the idea of deliverance from the punishment due sins that are past? These words are never so understood when employed in reference to the common affairs of life. A number of persons unite in petitioning the Executive of the State for the pardon of a certain criminal in the state prison. The bearer of it appears before the governor and explains as follows : May it please your Honor : your petitioners do not wish to be understood as asking that the criminal should be released from any punishment he is doomed to suffer ; but on the other hand we desire he should suffer the whole penalty. We mean by asking a pardon that you should take away his love of crime and prevent his committing it in future. The Executive would either count the man insane, or consider it an unmitigated insult. Some years ago, President Jackson pardoned a leader of a piratical crew who was under sentence of death in Boston. The pardon was granted, not because he was innocent of the charge of piracy, for none doubted his guilt, but in consideration of the pleadings of his wife, and of a heroic and humane deed in which at one time he had risked his own life to save others. On the reception of the communication the officer in charge, with the Universalist idea, would have reasoned thus : Pardon saves from the punishment of no sins already committed ; I will therefore proceed to hang the man at the time appointed ! All must see that such an act would be carrying out the Universalist idea of pardon, for in such a case he would suffer the whole penalty and be most effectually prevented from committing piracy in the future. But what would the world think of that officer's idea of pardon? The truth is, this notion that forgiveness implies no remission of punishment for sins committed, is at war with common sense, the common and established use of language, and the word of God. That penitents have been saved from deserved punishment, and that such salvation is established in the economy of God's grace, we purpose now to show most clearly from the scriptures. So numerous are the texts where this doctrine is taught, either directly or indirectly, that we shall present but a few compared with the number which might be adduced, Take the case of the woman in the house of Simon the Pharisee. The Saviour said of her, (Luke 7 : 47,) "Her sins, which are many, are forgiven." That this had respect to sins already committed, the language most explicitly declares. Remark :

"*Her* sins, which *are many*," &c. Now sins could not be *her* sins till she had committed them, hence she was, by her forgiveness, saved from the punishment she deserved. This is clear also from the illustration of the Saviour, as follows: "There was a certain creditor, which had two debtors: the one owed him five hundred pence and the other fifty. And when they had nothing to pay, he frankly forgave them both." Ver. 41, 42. Christ used this illustration to show Simon that the reason why this woman loved so ardently was that she had been forgiven much; hence, he proposed the question respecting the forgiven debtors, "which of them will love most?" Ver. 42. Simon answered: "He to whom he forgave most." Ver. 43. The Saviour replied: "Thou hast judged rightly." Ver. 43. But according to the newfangled notions of Universalists, the forgiveness of the woman relieved her from no punishment for past sins, and the Saviour should have illustrated the case as follows: "There was a certain creditor, which had two debtors: the one owed him five hundred pence and the other fifty, and he exacted the whole sum of them without remitting a single farthing, and then frankly forgave them both!" Such an act must have produced *great* love for the creditor, and especially on the part of the one that was forced to pay most!! So plain is this case, that every honest mind must admit that the Universalist doctrine of forgiveness is contradicted by the Son of God himself. If we are not taught in this case, salvation from punishment for past sins, by forgiveness, then, we can learn nothing from the Bible. That forgiveness saves from punishment for past sins is evident from these passages which speak of remission of sins. Take the declaration of Paul, where, speaking of Christ, he says: "Whom God hath set forth to be a propitiation through faith in his blood; to declare his righteousness for the *remission of sins that are past.*" Rom. 3:25.

Here the apostle asserts that Christ's righteousness was declared for the remission of sins that are PAST. To remit sin that is past cannot mean to prevent the act, for to talk of saving men from committing sin already committed, is to utter nonsense. Sin, after it is committed, admits of no salvation except from its guilt and punishment. What can be remitted of a sin past, but the punishment? Just nothing. Universalism opposes this view, and in this it conflicts again, not only with the word of God and Christian experience, but also with the most eminent linguists of the age. Webster, in defining "remission," refers to the scriptures, and says its meaning is, "Forgiveness; pardon; that is, the giving up of a punishment due to a crime; as, the *remission* of sins. Matt. 26; Heb. 9." God's declaration to sinners is, "When I say unto the wicked, thou shalt surely die; if he turn from his sin, and do that which is lawful and right; if the wicked restore the pledge, give again that he had robbed, walk in the statutes of life without committing iniquity; he shall surely live, he shall not die. None of his sins that he hath committed shall be mentioned unto him." Ez. 33 : 14–16. This has respect to past sins. Observe: "If the wicked restore the pledge, give again that he *had robbed*— none of his sins that *he hath committed*," &c. A righteous God never threatens a punishment which is not deserved, nor promises that which is false or inconsistent. It will be seen at a glance that salvation from deserved punishment for repentant sinners is here promised by the God of truth, and thus is the Universalist assumption again contradicted. (Sec. CIII.) Look at the parable of the barren fig-tree: "A certain man," &c. Luke 13 : 6–9. We suppose it will be readily admitted, that by the owner of this vineyard God is meant; and by the fig-tree we are to understand accountable beings. Those represented by the fig-tree deserve punishment. "Cut it down, why cumbereth it the ground?" The intercession of the dresser of the vineyard, saying: "If it bear fruit, well; if not, then after that thou shalt cut it down," clearly indicates that, on condition of its bearing fruit in future it should be saved from deserved punishment for its previous barrenness. As this was spoken to illustrate the dealings of God with men, salvation from deserved punishment is clearly taught.

The man of Christian experience needs no argument to convince him that forgiveness includes the idea of salvation from deserved punishment; neither does the man who is truly penitent for his sins ever once imagine he has been fully punished for them up to the present time, but enters deeply into sympathy with the Psalmist and prays, "For thy name's sake, O Lord, pardon mine iniquity, for it is great." Ps. 25 : 11. This supplication stands directly opposed to the notion of no salvation from punishment. Remark: Pardon *mine* iniquity or sin. No sin is *ours* till it is committed. For it *is* great; not *will be* great after it is committed. It was pardon for past sin that the Psalmist sought, as all must see.

Now we can form no conception of a blessing, called pardon for past sin, save that of salvation from its consequences. Said Ezra, that learned and pious scribe: "After all that has come upon us for our evil deeds, and for our great trespass, seeing that thou, our God, hast punished us LESS than our iniquities deserve, and hast given us such deliverance as this." Ezra 9 : 13. What language could be framed to more positively contradict Universalism than this? That says none suffer less than their iniquities deserve, which is directly opposed to the Bible, and of course must be false. The same fact is asserted by the Psalmist: "He hath not dealt with us after our sins; nor rewarded us according to our iniquities." Ps. 103 : 10. The reader will please turn to Ex. 32 : 8–14: "And the Lord said unto Moses," &c.

The following is from the pen of another upon this passage, and also upon the threatening of God against the Ninevites:

"Here God is represented as threatening his people with an overthrow, and as turning away from the evil which he thought to do, at the intercession of Moses. The evil with which God threatened them, was a punishment for the sin of idolatry, in making and worshiping a golden calf. Now, this threatened punishment was just, or it was not; if it was just, then God saved the rebellious Isralites from a just punishment; for he turned away from the evil which he thought to do unto them, and did it not; and if the threatened punishment was not just, then God once thought to do an unjust evil to his people; therefore, it must be admitted that God did save the people from a just punishment, in this case, since it cannot be admitted that he threatened and thought to do that which was unjust. The divine clemency exercised towards condemned and devoted Nineveh, is another instance of salvation from just punishment. God threatened Nineveh with an overthrow in forty days, and yet, on their repentance, it is said, (Jonah 3 : 10,) 'And God saw their work; that they turned from their evil ways; and God repented of the evil that he had said he would do unto them; and he did it not.'

"The remarks which have been just made, on the case of the idolatrous Israelites, will apply with equal force to the preservation of Nineveh. God either saved the people of Nineveh from a *just* punishment, or else he threatened them with an *unjust* punishment. It will not be a sufficient reply to this, to say that the punishment, with which they were threatened, would have been just had they not repented; but in view of the change which took place in their moral character, it was not just, and therefore was not inflicted; for this would be to suppose that the threatened overthrow was intended as a punishment for their sins which they had not committed, but which they would have committed in future time, which is false.

"1. They were threatened directly for what they had already done. The Lord said unto Jonah, (chap. 1 : 2,) 'Arise, go to Nineveh, that great city, and cry against it; for their wickedness *is come up before me.*' God here speaks of their wickedness in the present time, *is come up*, and not in the future, *will*, or *will have come up*. God did not command Jonah to cry against them because they were about to be very wicked, but because their wickedness had already come up before him.

"2. Jonah attributes the preservation of Nineveh to the grace, mercy and great kindness of God. (Chap. 4 : 2.) 'I knew that thou art a gracious God, merciful, slow to anger, and of great kindness, and repenteth thee of the evil.' Now, on the supposition that the Ninevites did not deserve the threatened overthrow, in view of their reform, wherein do the grace, mercy, and great kindness of God appear in their preservation? This view represents God as being gracious, merciful, and great in kindness, merely because he did not inflict an unjust punishment, which is too absurd to be indulged in for a moment. It is clear, then, that the punishment with which Nineveh was threatened, was just, in view of what they had already done; and if so, it is conclusive that God saved them from a just punishment." *Rev. L. Lee.*

In the light of these scriptures we see the meaning of the passage which Universalists drag into their service, found Ex. 34:6, 7: "And the Lord passed by before him, and proclaimed, the Lord, the Lord God, merciful and gracious, long-suffering, and abundant in goodness and truth, keeping mercy for thousands, forgiving iniquity, and transgression, and sin, and that will by no means clear the guilty." The sense of this text in obviously this: "God bears long with sinners when they deserve punishment, and if they repent he forgives them, but will by no means clear the guilty if impenitent." Many of the threatenings, as well as the promises of the Bible, have conditions implied, though not expressed. Take, as an illustration of this, God's message to Nineveh: "Forty days and Nineveh *shall be overthrown.*" Remark: It is not said it shall be overthrown, except the inhabitants repent; but the language is positive in its character, "*shall be overthrown.*" But there was a condition implied though not expressed, for by their penitence the evil was averted; or, in other words, God cleared the guilty as has been shown. Just so in the case before us; if penitent, God will clear the guilty, but he will by no means clear such if not penitent. The Lord in this passage declares himself to be long-suffering. Peter gives him the same character, (2 Peter, 3:9): and Paul speaks of his forbearance and long-suffering.

Rom. 2 : 4. By long-suffering is meant patience, clemency. By forbearance, omitting to punish, lenity; i. e., sinners are borne with when they deserved to be punished. But Universalist views drive long-suffering and forbearance completely out of the divine administration. If God punishes men to the full extent as soon as sin is committed, where, we ask, is his forbearance and long-suffering? A father punishes a child in every instance just as soon as his commands are violated. What would be thought of the man who should extol him for his long-suffering and forbearance? A child of eight years would know better. The falsity of the Universalist theory discovers itself in contradicting the Bible in this as well as many other things. The text at the head of this section is often used to prove that God is merciful to the ungodly in punishing them, therefore none will be punished more than shall be for their good. "We admit that punishment is often connected with mercy, but not that the mercy always extends to the individual sufferer. "God 'divided the Red Sea into parts — and made Israel to pass through the midst of it — but overthrew Pharaoh and his host in the Red Sea; for his mercy endureth forever.' Ps. 136 : 13–15. Mercy is here connected with the overthrow of Pharaoh and his host; but no man in his senses supposes the mercy extended to the Egyptians. It was a mercy to the Israelites to be delivered in this way out of the hands of their enemies." *Isaac.* So in Ps. 62 : 12, God is considered merciful because he would protect his people and destroy their enemies.

One text more, and we leave the subject with the reader: "He that blasphemeth against the Holy Ghost hath never forgiveness, but is in danger of eternal damnation." Mark 3 : 29. By this we see that forgiveness and damnation stand opposed to each other. He who is forgiven is not damned, and he who is damned is not forgiven. These words of Christ stand directly opposed to the Universalist doctrine, that forgiveness saves from no deserved punishment. To show that penitent believing sinners are saved from merited punishment, we might call to our aid the doctrine of atonement, so fully established in the Jewish economy and consummated by the death of Christ, and taught all through the New Testament, but especially in the epistle to the Hebrews. But a sufficiency has already been presented to establish the point with the candid. Universalist views of forgiveness are also refuted, Matt. 18 : 23–35.

LXXI. "*For God shall bring every work into judgment, with every secret thing, whether it be good, or whether it be evil.*" Eccl. 12 : 14.

It is inquired, "Is it said, 'God shall bring every work into judgment' in the future, immortal existence? No such statement is made. The Saviour said when on earth, 'Now is the judgment of this world.' John 12 : 31; 'for judgment I came into this world.' John 9 : 39; 'verily he is a God that *judgeth in the earth.*' Ps. 58 : 11." *Guide*, p. 73. (On the scriptures quoted see Sec. LI.)

Let us apply Mr. Whittemore's rule to his own doctrine. "Is it anywhere said in the Bible that all men shall be saved 'in the future, immortal existence? No such statement is made. The Saviour said when on earth,' '*This day is* salvation come.' Luke 19 : 9. Simeon said, 'Mine eyes *have seen* thy salvation.' Luke 2 : 30. Paul said, '*Now is* the day of salvation.' 2 Cor. 6 : 2."

Now, if the argument of the Guide sets aside a future judgment, then is future salvation set aside by the same method, and Universalism is proved a fable. So the man has discharged a gun which blows his own brains out! A kind of gun in very common use among the class of writers to which he belongs. The whole connection in which the text is found shows that a judgment beyond the grave is intended. The inspired writer brings it in as the winding up of the drama of human life. He is giving a description of the scenes of old age and death, and in a very impressive manner, adds: "Let us hear the conclusion of the whole matter: fear God and keep his commandments, for this is the whole duty of man. For God will bring every work into judgment," &c. By judgment is here meant an examination of conduct, a bringing to light of secret things, and deciding whether they be good or evil. But where in all the history of this world is there anything which suits this language? Some die in the very act of murdering others. Such must be judged in the future world if anywhere. See Sec. XLVI; also LX.

LXXII. "*Behold, I bring you good tidings of great joy, which shall be to all people.*" Luke 2 : 10.

What is meant by the good tidings named? "The word *evangelizomai*, here rendered, I bring you good tidings, is translated, preach the gospel. Luke 4 : 18; 20 : 1; Acts 16 : 10. The precise signification is expressed in the common translation." So says Page, the Universalist commentator. The preaching of the gospel, then, is what is meant by glad tidings. Well, what is it to preach the gospel according to Universalists? It is to proclaim the salvation of all men. It is assumed, too, that all our race are to be made joyful by these tidings. "The blessing was designed for all; hence the annunciation of it would be good news, tidings of great joy, to all." *Page in loco.* The tidings then are to produce the universal joy. But when is this universal joy to take place by the preaching of Universalism. Not in this world, surely, Universalists themselves being witnesses; for they tell us that the blind Partialists are enshrouded in gloom and sadness because they do not believe in their doctrine; and furthermore, millions have died who have never heard of universal salvation. Now as it is affirmed that all will be made joyful by the preaching of this gospel; and as it is an admitted fact that all are not made so in this world, it follows that to produce this universal joy, this gospel must be preached in the future state. But if this be so, then all are not joyful in the future world; for if they are, then they need no gospel preached to make them so, and thus the idea so fondly cherished, that "there is no condition for man beyond death, but that in which he is as the angels of God in heaven," is blown to fragments at once. In view of this conclusion, growing out of premises furnished by themselves, we see no other way for them but, after having made so much proficiency in the science of divinity, to go back to the old obsolete doctrine of their fathers, by which they taught that devils and damned spirits would have the gospel preached to them in hell, and thus be recovered. It cannot be well doubted but the commission given by Christ to preach the gospel would harmonize with the announcement of the angels respecting the same subject. If the angels, by their message, taught Universalism, the divine Saviour knew it; and if he was a Universalist, and came into the world to establish that doctrine, we might reasonably expect to see great prominence given to it in the gospel commission that he gave to his apostles, especially as they were to go out to preach among believers in endless punishment. (Sec. CXXXII.) We should expect to find in it something like the following: Go ye into all the world and preach to all classes of sinners, saying, fear not in your unbelief and wickedness, but rejoice and be exceeding glad, for heavenly bliss is yours, irrespective of your conduct here, as soon as death does its work, or at the next conscious existence. Fearlessly expose and rebuke, before every creature, the great errors of a future judgment and endless punishment, showing them that hell is a fable, that their conduct here takes no hold on the future, and that they cannot commit sin enough to incur any more punishment than shall be for their good. This, in substance, is a Universalist commission. But the one our Saviour gave is very unlike this, and reads thus: "Go ye into all the world and preach the gospel to every creature. He that believeth and is baptized shall be saved; and he that believeth not shall be damned." Mark 16:15.

Suppose Mr. Ballou had commissioned a class of men to have preached *his* gospel, would he have failed to have inserted future bliss for all, and hell for none. No Universalist of the modern school would be guilty of such an omission. But the Saviour not only omits this, but says of those to whom the gospel is sent, "he that believeth not shall be *damned.*" How deficient the Saviour was in commissioning men; or rather, how false is Universalism!

It is assumed that the phrase "*all people,*" must mean the whole of the posterity of Adam. That this is incorrect, is evident from the fact before stated, viz.: that millions have died who have never heard the gospel preached; neither will they, unless it is preached to them in the future world; and this will not be contended for by Universalists themselves, as it is destructive to other fond notions of theirs. God threatened the Jews, that if they worshiped other Gods he would make them "a proverb and by-word among *all people.*" 1 Kings 9:7. Were the Jews to be a proverb and by-word among the whole human race? Certainly not; but only among them who should know them after they had worshiped other gods. So the good tidings are designed for all people to whom they are sent; but the history of Christianity shows that they have failed to make all who have heard them joyful. That Christ died for all, and that God, as a moral governor, wills the salvation of all moral agents, is equally true; and it is true, too, that all do not yield obedience to his will. The Saviour preached his own gospel, but all who heard it did not become joyful, but many were exceedingly enraged, and despised him and his message; and his complaint was, "Ye will not come unto me that ye might have life."

He sent out apostles, and how did they succeed? Paul, although he was enabled to preach the gospel extensively, yet his labors proved a savor of death unto death to some, (2 Cor. 2:16); and he threatened those who were disobedient to the gospel with everlasting destruction. 2 Thess. 1:8, 9. Now if the good tidings preached by the Son of God himself, and by his inspired apostles, failed to produce joy in great numbers of those who heard them; what folly to argue universal joy or salvation as a result of the preaching of the gospel. It should be observed that the text under consideration does not say that the good tidings *shall make all people joyful*, but they were to be "*to all people*," that is, they were to be proclaimed, not merely to the Jews, but to all people, or as the Saviour commanded, "*to every creature;*" hence, Simeon after clasping the Saviour in his arms, said: "Mine eyes have seen thy salvation, which thou hast prepared before the face of all people; a light to lighten the Gentiles, and the glory of thy people Israel." Luke 2: 30–32. But how can these be good tidings to all people if all are not saved? We answer, that those tidings deserve the denomination of good which propose any advantages to us, whether we avail ourselves of them or not. The quality of the tidings does not depend upon the treatment they receive. To deceive the unthinking, a play of words has been made upon the fact that ministers preach the doctrine of endless punishment, and it is very gravely inquired, "If such doctrine can be considered good tidings?" Now the design of the gospel is not to procure or threaten men with this punishment, but to offer them salvation from that to which they were already exposed. A man is exposed to a midnight assassin; a friend warns him of it, and points him out a way of escape. Is not such a warning good tidings to the man, although it apprizes him of great danger? Where there is no danger, there can be no deliverance. The gospel is indeed glad tidings to men, because they are greatly exposed, and in proportion as they discover their danger will they prize their deliverance. If a man is saved from the harmless bite of an insignificant insect, he will value it but little; but if he is saved from intense suffering, or an untimely death, it will forcibly impress his feelings. The gospel cannot be preached without pointing out the evils and danger from which it proposes to deliver those who receive it; and as the faithful minister finds a future judgment and endless punishment clearly revealed in the Bible, he urges the danger of these as a motive why men should embrace the gospel. Universalists scout the idea of being exposed by sin to any suffering beyond this life; hence, they can never value their gospel very highly, for they were never in any very great danger, and of course have never experienced any great deliverance. This accounts for the heartlessness found among its votaries when left to themselves. Such is the want of vitality in the system, that were New England wholly given up to this dogma it would soon die out, so far as organization and support of its ministry is concerned. The great vital principle of action in the order is, *opposition to others.* Remove this, and there is not enough in it to keep it alive a single year.

But the Christian sees in the gospel a great and glorious plan to rescue man from eternal death; and in Christ he sees a great Saviour dying for his sins and becoming "the author of eternal salvation unto all them that obey him," (Heb. 5 : 9); and all this the effect of great love. He has felt, too, his own personal exposure and wretchedness, and has been led to cry to God for salvation through Jesus Christ, and has found the gospel to be good tidings, for his is a great salvation. He now feels as no man with Universalist views can feel, for he is forgiven much and he loves much. Luke 7 : 47. Impressed with such views and feelings, he needs not the spur of opposition to keep him awake to duty, for the love of God is not merely talked of, but is shed abroad in his heart by the Holy Ghost; and this prompts him to deeds of noble daring and sacrifice for Christ and lost men, that they may receive the gospel too.

LXXIII. "*For this purpose the Son of God was manifested, that he might destroy the works of the devil.*" 1 John 3 : 8.

But what has the devil done? Has his work exposed men to a future hell? Universalists will not admit this for a moment. Well, what has Christ done by being manifested? Did he come to save from misery in the future world? It is denied by high authority among Universalists that Christ came into this world to save men in the next. (Sec. CV.)

1. According to this dogma, universal salvation is to take place in the next world by the resurrection. (Sec. I. and XCV.)

2. The works of either devils or men cannot endanger this salvation, as it was all made sure when God created man. (Sec. CV.)

3. Christ never came into this world to save men in the next.

With these positions, taken generally by the order, what force or consistency is there in bringing this text, as Mr. Whittemore, (*Guide*, p. 52,) and others of the order, are wont to do, to prove the salvation of all in eternity? Shall we so reflect upon the intelligence of these men as to count them ignorant of these contradictions in their arguments? Christ's coming that he *might* destroy the works of the devil, is expressive of the *design* of his advent, but is a very different thing from saying that he *will* save all men unconditionally. John in this same epistle, (1 John 1 : 9,) has clearly stated the conditionality of this destruction of sin. "*If we confess our sins*, he is faithful and just to forgive us our sins, and to cleanse us from all unrighteousness." In such penitent, believing hearts Christ destroys the works of the devil and qualifies them for heaven. That the finally impenitent will not be saved, because Christ was manifested that he might destroy the works of the devil, is also seen by the fact that to punish the sinner for his wickedness is not the work of the devil. After the sinner has slighted mercy and failed to comply with the conditions, and dying in that state, God's penalty must be inflicted, and there is no escape.

LXXIV. "*That in the dispensation of the fullness of times he might gather together in one all things in Christ, both which are in heaven and which are on earth.*" Eph. 1 : 10.

In an unrestricted sense, the text includes not merely human beings, but every created object, such as beasts, birds, fishes, reptiles, planets, &c. As none will contend that these things are included, we see that the text is to be understood in a restricted sense. John the Baptist came to "restore *all things*." Matt. 17 : 11. It was not his office to restore the universe to its original order, or to restore the whole human race to bliss; but to restore all things to be restored by his ministry. (Sec. XXX.) So God in the fulness of times will gather all things in Christ to be gathered. The idea is, that in the "fullness of times," when Christ shall have finished his work as mediator, when he shall deliver up the kingdom to the Father, (1 Cor. 15 : 24,) from whom he received it, (Matt. 28 : 18,) all the saints in heaven, and all the faithful then living upon earth, whether Jews or Gentiles by birth, shall be made to constitute one triumphant church, as they are in fact one family now. Eph. 3 : 15.

But bear in mind that it never was the design of God in the gift of his Son, that moral agents who fail to comply with the conditions of the gospel, should be gathered into the church triumphant. We learn by language equally strong, (Col. 1 : 20,) that God designed to "reconcile all things unto himself," by Christ. But we also learn from the context that the reconciliation takes place in this world, and that it is conditional, for the reconciled are exhorted to "*continue* in the faith," and not to be *moved away* from the hope of the gospel;" and the apostle, speaking upon the same subject, (2 Cor. 5 : 19, 20,) shows not only that the work takes place in this world, but conjoins this reconciliation with the moral agency of men; for while the ambassadors for Christ beseech, sinners are to become reconciled, which would be a work wholly uncalled for if all are to be reconciled unconditionally in a future state. (Sec. LXXV.) Furthermore, the Saviour has declared most explicitly that at the time specified by the apostle, instead of a gathering of the whole human race to constitute them happy forever, some shall be sent "away into everlasting punishment." Matt. 25 : 46. Paul teaches the same. 2 Thess. 1 : 9.

LXXV. "*And having made peace through the blood of the cross, by him to reconcile all things unto himself; by him I say, whether they be things in earth, or things in heaven.*" Col. 1 : 20.

This text simply informs us of God's design in giving his Son to die for the world, which was that he might reconcile all things unto himself by Christ. That the design contemplates in its provisions the reconciliation of all men to God, is admitted. But it does not follow from thence that all are, or ever will be, reconciled, for there are certain terms of reconciliation presented which men as moral agents are to comply with. That men can resist the means by which God designs to bring about this reconciliation is clear from what the apostle says in another place upon the same subject. Hear him : "To wit, that God was in Christ reconciling the world unto himself, and not imputing their trespasses unto them, and hath committed unto us the word of reconciliation. Now, then, we are ambassadors for Christ, as though God did beseech you by us; we pray you in Christ's stead, be ye reconciled to God." 2 Cor. 5 : 19, 20. Observe : Universalists bring the text at the head of this to prove, not that it is the purpose of God to make all holy and happy in this world, but in the future, for the resurrection is to usher all into bliss ; and they scout the idea that men in this world can do anything towards procuring or preventing their final salvation. (Sec. XCV.)

But it is the purpose of God that men shall be reconciled in this world, and for this intent ambassadors are sent. That this is correct we see by the scriptures following the passage, where we learn that some were then reconciled, (v. 21,) and that even after the reconciliation has taken place, final salvation is suspended upon the condition of perseverance, (v. 22, 23) ; for immediately after the apostle had expressed the pleasure of God concerning the reconciliation of all things, he adds : "And you *hath he reconciled* in the body of his flesh through death, to present you holy, and unblemished, and unreprovable in his sight; IF YE CONTINUE in the faith, grounded and settled, and be not MOVED AWAY from the hope of the gospel." With what propriety a passage can be brought which contemplates a reconciliation to take place in this world, in which man's agency is employed, both as ambassadors and recipients of the blessing, to prove that all will be saved in the future state, independent of human agency, by the resurrection, the reader must determine. The truth is, it no more teaches the salvation of all men in the eternal state, than it does the return of the Jews to Palestine.

LXXVI. "*Behold the righteous shall be recompensed in the earth, much more the wicked and the sinner.*" Prov. 11:31.

This text is adduced to prove that the righteous and the wicked experience a full retribution in this world. But does the passage assert this? It neither asserts or implies this; for to understand it in the absolute sense of the language, it affirms that the wicked and the sinner are *much more* than recompensed. Again: The Universalist construction makes the first member of the text deny that the righteous are recompensed in heaven, which contradicts the Saviour. Matt. 5:11, 12. Our opponents profess to believe in just rewards and punishments in this world according to works; that the wicked and the righteous suffer and enjoy all they deserve in this world as a result of their conduct. But the Bible says: "All things come alike to all: there is one event to the righteous and to the wicked; to the good, and to the clean, and to the unclean; to him that sacrificeth, and to him that sacrificeth not; as is the good so is the sinner." Eccl. 9:2.

This is asserted of men in this world, as the context shows. Taking this text alone, we see that a retribution in this world is positively denied; and if we allow the Universalist construction of Prov. 11:31, we have scripture arrayed point blank against scripture. We have not introduced this text because we believe that the Spirit designed to teach that there is absolutely no difference between the righteous and the wicked in this world, but just to show what might be done were we to use the same license Universalists do in applying scripture. They bring Prov. 11 : 31 to disprove future retribution, and with equal propriety we bring Eccl. 9 : 2, containing language more explicit, to disprove present retribution, and thus God's righteous administration is banished from both worlds ! Now what does this result teach us ? It shows us that to arrive at the truth, we should compare scripture with scripture. If we take these passages to the New Testament and compare them where the future condition of man is more clearly brought to light, we shall find that after death is the judgment, (Heb. 6 : 2 ; 9 : 27,) and that endless punishment awaits the finally impenitent. Matt. 12 : 32 ; 25 : 46. That God smiles upon the good here, and imparts an inward comfort that the wicked are strangers to, and that he frowns upon the ungodly, and thus gives each a foretaste of what awaits them in the future, is true ; but then the good often suffer here by the conduct of the wicked, while some of the wicked enjoy worldly comforts of which some of the pious are deprived. Even their own pious acts have often been the occasion of intense sufferings in this world. Ps. 34 : 19 ; John 16 : 33 ; Acts 16 : 22 ; 1 Cor. 15 : 19 compare with Job 21 : 7, 9 ; Ps. 73 : 3–12. Is this the way that each class is fully "recompensed ?" (See Sec. XLVI.)

LXXVII. "*Another parable put he forth,*" &c. Matt. 13 : 24–30.

With the exception of a few thoughts of our own respecting the commencement of the Christian dispensation, by permission of Rev. P. R. Russell, we present the reader with his able refutation of the Universalist interpretation of this parable, as found in his "Letters to a Universalist," p. 115–125.

He says : "This parable I regard as clearly teaching the probationary nature of time, and the reality of a judgment to come.

But this natural and obvious view of the passage, you object to, and refer me to standard authors among Universalists, for the true scriptural sense of this portion of our Lord's preaching. I will now examine the commonly received exposition of Universalists. Messrs. T. Whittemore and H. Ballou shall be our guides. They differ a little between themselves, but in the main agree. Let me then ask,

"1. What is meant by the field? Mr. Whittemore answers: 'Here the word *world* is a translation of the Greek word *kosmos*, which usually signifies the material universe. The world, therefore, is to be understood in its usual sense in the instance before us.' *Whittemore on Par.*, p. 96. Now, remember the field in which the wheat and tares were sown, is '*the material universe.*' A large field truly.

"2. What is denoted by the *tares?* Mr. Ballou shall answer: He tells us that the wheat represents sound doctrine, that is, Universalism, and the tares false doctrine, that is, the doctrine of future and endless punishment. Hear him: 'Nor are tares of a very different character from false doctrines, which make many appearances like the truth, as tares do like wheat, when in the blade.' Again: 'That it was the will of the Saviour that false doctrines should be imbibed [Monstrous!] until their fruits should come to maturity, is shown, in that he saith, "Let them both grow together till harvest."' *Ballou's Notes on Par.*, pp. 72, 68. A popular preacher of your denomination, a few months since, in preaching from this parable addressed his audience thus: 'My hearers, do you not sometimes feel a desire in your hearts, that all men may be holy and happy in the world to come? Yes. Well, *this is the wheat.* On the contrary, do you not at times feel a shudder at the thought that you may be seperated from your friends in eternity, and that any of them should sink in endless torments? Yes. Well, *this is the tares.*' That is, according to Mr. Ballou and Universalist authors in general, pure, *bona fide* Universalism is the wheat; and the doctrine of future punishment is the tares. Remember this.

"3. The harvest, or the end of the world, what does that denote? Mr. W. shall answer: 'It never should be forgotten that the end of the world, at which the harvest was to take place, was not the end of *kosmos*, the world said to be the field; but the end of *aion*, the age, and unquestionably referred to the conclusion of the Jewish state,' i. e., destruction of Jerusalem. *Notes on Par.*, p. 101.

"4. Our Saviour in his exposition of this parable, says: 'At the end of the world,' at the time of the harvest, 'the Son of man shall send forth his angels, and they shall gather out of his kingdom all them that offend, and them that do iniquity.' Who are these *angels* that the Son of man employs as reapers? Mr. W. will answer: 'It is certainly meant that the Roman armies were the messengers (angels) which God sent to destroy his rebellious people, the Jews.' p. 103. Remember then, the angels of Christ, were the *Roman armies*. They were the *reapers* of the field, 'the material universe.'

"5. Our Saviour says, in his explanation, that 'then' — (that is, at the end of the world), 'the righteous shall shine forth as the sun in the kingdom of their Father.' What does this denote, according to the new light shed upon the scriptures by modern Universalism? Mr. Whittemore will answer.

"'Their persecutors, the Jews, being destroyed (at the destruction of Jerusalem), and persecutions on every hand being abated and softened, they would experience comparative earthly felicity, and have an enlarged enjoyment of gospel peace and life. Separated from the hypocrites, the church would be pure!!' p. 104.

"We have now before us the Universalist exposition of the parable of the tares and wheat. It is furnished by two of your most popular divines, fathers and oracles of the order. It is unquestionably the best exposition of which the system is capable. Is it sound? Will it stand the *test* of examination? Look it over. The field is *the material universe* — the wheat is sound doctrine, that is pure unadulterated Universalism. The tares represent false doctrine; particularly the doctrine of future punishment; the harvest or end of the world, was the destruction of Jerusalem; the angels were the Roman armies; the exaltation of the righteous, was the *earthly felicity* which Christians enjoyed at the destruction of Jerusalem. To all this I object.

"1. It contradicts the exposition which the Saviour himself has given of this parable. After the multitude were sent away, the disciples came to Christ with this request: 'Declare unto us the parable of the tares of the field.' Now if Christ meant to teach that at the destruction of Jerusalem, he would by the agency of those ungodly, mercenary idolaters, the Roman soldiers, gather the doctrine of future punishment out of *the material universe*, and leave nothing but the doctrine of Universalism, he would have undoubtedly expressed it in clear and emphatic language. Did he do so? Look at his explanation of his own parable.

"'He answered and said unto them, He that soweth the good seed is the Son of man; the field is the world, the good seed are the children of the kingdom; but the tares are the children of the wicked one; the enemy that sowed them is the devil; the harvest is the end of the world; and the reapers are the angels. As, therefore, the tares are gathered and burned in the fire, so shall it be in the end of the world. The Son of man shall send forth his angels, and they shall gather out of his kingdom all things that offend, and them which do iniquity, and shall cast them into a furnace of fire: there shall be wailing and gnashing of teeth. Then shall the righteous shine forth as the sun in the kingdom of their Father. Who hath ears to hear, let him hear.' Matt. 13: 37–43.

"1. Here we are taught by one that cannot lie, (1.) That the good seed, or wheat, when ready for harvest, is not Universalism, but 'the children of the kingdom,' called 'the righteous,' in v. 43. Here a figure of rhetoric is used, called metonomy, in which the cause is spoken of as the effect, or the effect as the cause. The seed sown by Christ in person, or by the agency of his true ministers, is the truth; the crop, or result, is the 'children of the kingdom.' (2.) The tares in harvest are not false doctrines; but 'the children of the wicked one,' the natural product of false doctrines. False doctrine produces depraved hearts. Here the same figure is used as before. The wicked are frequently spoken of as the children of the master whom they serve, or the principles they adopt. They are called the '*children of disobedience;*' '*children of their father, the devil.*' Now, in saying that the tares and wheat, not when sown as seed, but when reaped in as a harvest, are false and true doctrines, you contradict Christ, who says: 'The tares are THE CHILDREN OF THE WICKED one;' the wheat, '*the children of the kingdom,*' '*the righteous.*'

"2. I object to your exposition again, *because it is absurd and nonsensical.* Look at it. Did Christ employ the Roman soldiers — a wicked and bloody set of men as ever lived — to purge his church and gather out of it all false doctrine? Did they, as a matter of fact, gather out the *tares* — the doctrine of future punishment — from the field, the *material universe,* and burn it up in fire? If so, then it follows that the Roman army which destroyed Jerusalem, a wicked crew of heathen monsters in human form, were the most successful preachers of Universalism which the world has ever beheld. They reaped down and burnt up the doctrine of future punishment, not only under the walls of the holy city, but through the *material universe.* Nothing but pure Universalism, of course, could have been left throughout *the material universe.*

"It is surprising that some ancient historian has not chronicled this wondrous harvest time of the Roman army, when they so effectually, as the 'mighty angels' of the Son of man, cleansed not only the sanctuary, but the *material universe* from false doctrine and wicked men. We should naturally suppose that Josephus, Philo, Tacitus, or Suetonius, or some other historian of those days, would have noticed so extraordinary an event. But no. They have left us in the dark, both as it respects the *modus operandi* and the fact of this marvellous circumstance. Besides, if the *tares* — false doctrine — were gathered out of the field, *the material universe*, and burnt up at the destruction of Jerusalem, is it not a little extraordinary, that the whole field, *the material universe*, was so quickly covered over again with tares? For it is a matter of fact, which you will not presume to deny, that the doctrine of future retribution, your *tares*, has been adopted, so far as we can learn from ecclesiastical and profane history, by the entire mass of Jews (the small sect of Sadducees excepted) and Christians, Pagans and Mahommedans, from the days of the apostles down to the beginning of the present century. Where did these tares all come from? I think your reapers must have acted the part of eye-servants, and left large patches of the old crop standing, with which the enemy seeded over the whole field again. Besides, it is a circumstance which I cannot account for, that the entire harvest of wheat, true doctrine — Universalism, gathered in by the angels, Roman army, should have been so lost, and that for nearly eighteen hundred years; for you are probably well aware of the fact, that the peculiar system of Universalism has not a single advocate in all antiquity. True, your authors tell us that *Origen*, *Clement of Alexandria*, and some other Christian fathers, were Universalists; but this is all deception. These men believed in the doctrine of a judgment to come. They were Platonic philosophers, and their error consisted in blending the speculations of that vain philosophy in relation to the preexistence and transmigration of souls with Christianity. (Sec. CXXXIII.)

"3. It is not true that the end of the world took place at the destruction of Jerusalem. The word *aion*, world, here, I admit, does not mean material world. It denotes age or dispensation, '*the gospel age, or dispensation.* The Jewish age, or dispensation, closed thirty-seven years before the destruction of Jerusalem. 'Now once in the end of the world (Jewish age) hath he appeared to put away sin by the sacrifice of himself.' Heb. 9 : 26. Now when did this take place? Not at the destruction of Jerusalem, for he had appeared, been sacrificed, and reascended to glory, between thirty and forty years before that event. The cross was the boundary line between the two dispensations; hence, the apostle shows the necessity of Christ's death in order to introduce the new dispensation. Heb. 9 : 16, 17. He then shows, as we have seen, that this had taken place, and thus the New Testament or gospel dispensation had taken the place of the Jewish. Christ, the great antetype of Jewish types, had been offered, Christian ordinances instituted, the gospel commission given, and the gospel had been preached all over the Roman empire, before the Jewish city was destroyed. Yet, to sustain other false positions, Universalism asserts that the Christian dispensation did not commence till Jerusalem was destroyed!!

"4. Mr. Whittemore's exposition as to what is meant by 'the righteous shining forth in the kingdom of their Father,' will not stand the *test*; for (1.) It is not true that the Jews, the enemies and persecutors of the Christians, were destroyed at the destruction of Jerusalem. Multitudes of the Jews survived the destruction of their city and temple, nor does it appear from the page of history, that their calamities purged their hearts of prejudice against Christ or his followers. (2.) It is not true that Christians, in consequence of the destruction of Jerusalem by the Roman army, experienced any remarkable degree of *earthly felicity*. On the contrary, the Christians in Judea were seperated forever from their unconverted friends, driven out from their houses and homes; their property given to the flames, and they were obliged to take shelter in *the dens and caves of the earth*. Is this 'shining forth as the sun in the kingdom of their Father?' Is this experiencing 'earthly felicity?' It is such 'earthly felicity,' such 'shining forth in the kingdom,' as Mr. Whittemore would be unwilling to receive as his reward for well doing. Let a company of furious savages be let loose upon the city of Boston — and with sword and torch in hand, let them butcher the helpless, burn the city,

Trumpet office and all, break up the editor's family, and chase him into the mountains of Vermont — and he would be the last man who would call such a retreat, such a disaster, 'shining forth as the sun in the kingdom of his Father,' or 'comparative earthly felicity!!' (3.) Nor is it true that 'the church was separated from hypocrites and became pure,' at the destruction of Jerusalem. No such fact can be proved from history. It is a fact *invented* to help out with this explanation. On the contrary, the church was more pure before than after the destruction of Jerusalem. While the apostles were alive, the church was more pure in doctrine and discipline, than at any period since. As these holy men, one after another, passed away, men continued to rise in the church, who 'brought in damnable heresies.'

"5. I cannot adopt your exposition of this parable, because it requires me to violate an important rule of biblical interpretation, viz.: *That every explanation of scripture should be regarded as false, which does not harmonize with well known facts, or with itself.* Well, now your exposition of this parable of the tares and wheat, does not harmonize with well known facts — well known historical facts are against it. It does not harmonize with itself; hence it must be false.

"6. I cannot adopt your exposition, because it is supported by sophistry and false application of scripture. 1 Cor. 3:12–15, is commonly brought forward to prove that the tares represent false doctrine, and not wicked men, and that while their false doctrines were burnt up at the destruction of Jerusalem they themselves will be saved. 'Now if any man build upon this foundation, gold, silver, precious stones, wood, hay, stubble; every man's work shall be made manifest; for the day shall declare it, because it shall be revealed by fire; and the fire shall try every man's work, of what sort it is. If any man's work abide which he hath built thereupon, he shall receive a reward. If any man's work shall be burned, he shall suffer loss; but he himself shall be saved; yet so as by fire.' 1 Cor.

3 : 12–15. Now, if you will consult the preceding context, you will readily perceive that the apostle is speaking here only of believers, those who have built their hopes upon Christ, the right foundation. 'For other foundation can no man lay than that which is laid, which is Jesus Christ; now *if any man build upon this foundation*," &c. Now as all men do not build upon this foundation, so the text affirms nothing as to their destination. Again: We are gravely asked, when we listen to Universalist expositions of this parable, if tares can become wheat, or wheat tares. I answer, Yes. Dr. Clarke tells us that tares are a bastard or degenerate wheat. Wheat, then, in oriental countries, sometimes degenerates and becomes tares, and by cultivation, like all degenerate plants, may be reclaimed. Tares, then, among wheat, very fitly represent degenerate men, who may appear like and with the righteous, but are unlike them at heart. But if tares and wheat were never convertible, still there would be no impropriety in employing tares to represent the wicked in the final judgment. Sheep cannot be converted into goats, nor goats into sheep, and yet Christ likens the righteous to sheep and the wicked to goats. This you will admit. So the argument built upon the false premises, that wheat can never become tares, falls to the ground.

"7. It is an outrage upon good sense, to call the Roman army, a class of human butchers, the *angels* of Christ. No where in the New Testament, are wicked men or devils spoken of as the angels of Christ.

"8. The Roman army did not at the destruction of Jerusalem, as a matter of fact, do either what Christ says is to be done at the harvest by his angels, or what Universalist expositors represent them as doing. They did not 'gather out of the kingdom of God all things that offend, nor them which do iniquity;' nor did they gather out of the church, or out of the whole or any part of *the material universe* false doctrines. If Universalism be true, they gathered out of the earth, I will admit, some thousands of wicked Jews, and gave them a passport by the sword to the world of the blessed.

"9. I reject your exposition of the parable of the tares and wheat, because this parable was evidently designed to represent the same event with the parable of the drag-net which Christ delivered on the same occasion.

"'Again: The kingdom of heaven is like unto a net, that was cast into the sea, and gathered of every kind; which, when it was full, they drew to shore, and sat down, and gathered the good into vessels, but cast the bad away. So shall it be at the end of the world: the angels shall come forth, and sever the wicked from among the just, and shall cast them into the furnace of fire: there shall be wailing and gnashing of teeth.' Matt. 13:47–50.

"Here the *bad fish* is evidently designed to represent the same thing as the *tares;* their being seperated from the good by the angels at the end of the gospel age, or world, cannot be said to represent the purging out of false doctrine, without giving the *lie* direct to the Son of God. 'Angels shall come forth and sever THE WICKED from among the just.' Can language be more plain?

"In fine, I have carefully examined your standard authors on this parable. I have frequently heard your preachers attempt to explain it away. I have also carefully examined the explanation which Christ has given of his own words as therein employed, and I find so much that is false in point of fact, absurd and contradictory in itself considered, in the Universalist exposition; while in the exposition given by the Saviour himself, I find so much that is natural, easy, and obvious to the common sense of mankind; that I hope you will not regard it as disrespectful to you, or fanatical in me, to wholly decline the adoption of your exposition, while I take that of the Son of God."

LXXVIII. "*For as much then as the children are partakers of flesh and blood, he also took part of the same; that through death he might destroy him that hath the power of death, that is, the devil; and deliver them, who, through fear of death, are all their life time subject to bondage.*" Heb. 2: 14, 15.

This passage is brought by Universalists to prove that sin and the punishment of wicked men will have an end, because the devil will be destroyed. But before this text can avail them anything, they must prove that destruction, in the sense here used, means annihilation, and this they cannot, do since, it is often said that the wicked shall be destroyed, who, they contend, will live in the enjoyment of bliss forever. See 2 Thess. 1: 9. But were we to admit, the annihilation of the devil, could that fact be brought in proof that all men will be saved? By no means, for the death that he has the power of is not spiritual or eternal death, but the death of the body, as will be seen by a moment's attention to the passage. It is presumed that no one supposes that the word *death*, which occurs three times in this passage, is to be understood in different senses. We ask, then, what death did Christ die? It was not a spiritual death, for he "did no sin." It was most certainly the death of the body; the death which was a consequence of his partaking of flesh and blood, verse 14. Then it must surely be the death of the body which the devil has power over, and Christ by his resurrection has so destroyed (not annihilated) him, as that he has lost that power, and hence all shall be raised from the dead. But this proves nothing in favor of the salvation of all men, for while we learn from the scriptures that by the resurrection the "vile body" shall be changed, (Phil. 3: 21,) it is nowhere asserted that the *vile soul* shall be changed by that event. That by the devil is meant sin personified, is assumption without proof. The apostle was not in the habit of adopting this blind method in speaking of sin, as all his epistles show. On the personality of the devil, see Section XCVIII. The promise of a seed to bruise the serpent's head (Gen. 3:15,) is sometimes presented in connection with this passage, which informs us that Christ took flesh, "that through death he might destroy him that hath the power of death, that is, the devil." "If the latter of these passages explains the former, then both were accomplished when Christ died and rose from the dead; and by destroying the devil the apostle does not mean a literal destruction, but a destruction of his power, by which he held the children of God in bondage through the fear of death, ver. 15. And the apostle applies this to the time which then was, and not to the future state. If then it proves universal salvation, it must be that all men are now, and have been for eighteen hundred years, saved, and the devil destroyed!" *Merritt.* It has been denied by Universalists that Christ ever came into this world to save us in the next (Sec. XXIX.) and Mr. Whittemore says, "The evils from which Jesus came to save men are in this world, and for this reason he came into this world to save them. *Guide*, p. 254. Yet he takes the passage we have been considering, which treats of Christ's coming into this world and his work, to prove the salvation of all men in eternity! *Guide*, p. 51. Truth never demands such zigzag work to sustain it.

LXXIX. "*And saw heaven opened, and a certain vessel descending,*" &c. Acts 10:10–16.

The following is Mr. Whittemore's whole argument to prove Universalism from Peter's vision. "Peter saw, in the vision of the vessel like a sheet knit at the four corners, that all men came down from heaven; that they are all encircled in the kind care of God, while here on earth; and, that *all will be drawn up again into heaven.*" *Guide*, p. 44. Well done, Mr. Whittemore! Reader, are you not captivated? All men came down from heaven, and are placed upon earth, and all will be drawn up again into heaven! So it seems that the whole race of man, all who have lived, now live, or may hereafter live, have once been holy and happy in heaven, and while in this place of bliss the Lord put them out and let them down to earth to suffer, as a race, six thousand years or more, and then he is to draw them all up to heaven again. How does this comport with the idea of a kind father, about which Universalists say so much? Would a kind earthly parent do thus? But the sufferings of earth are doubtless rendered less intense by the fact that but few remember that they once lived in heaven. We doubt if the author of the Guide, with all his acumen, has any recollection of it. People have, very generally, been in the habit of thinking that all have not lived upon this earth an equal length of time, hence the distinctions, in language at least, of old and young that have obtained. Many, too, have been in the way of thinking that some have already gone to heaven while others linger below. But progress is a characteristic of the age, and we now see by Peter's vision, while Mr. Whittemore holds the candle, that these views are all wrong, for the whole human race came down from heaven at the same time, remain on earth the same length of time, and will all be taken to heaven at the same time. This is Universalist divinity. Admirable! But to be serious. What instruction did this vision convey to Peter? Was it that all were to be saved in heaven? Nothing like it. It was this: "Of a truth I perceive that God is no respecter of persons; but in every nation he that *feareth him and worketh righteousness is accepted of him.*" Ver. 34, 35. Peter had conscientious scruples against associating and eating with the Gentiles, which of course would debar him from preaching the gospel to them. God took this method to divest Peter's mind of these scruples and prejudices, and he saw clearly that God would accept all of every nation who feared him and wrought righteousness. This is a very different thing from the salvation of all, whether they fear God and work righteousness here or not. To *fear* God does not sound well in Universalist ears. (Sec. LXIX.)

LXXX. "*And Enoch, also, the seventh from Adam, prophesied of these, saying, behold, the Lord cometh with ten thousand of his saints, to execute judgment upon all, and to convince all that are ungodly among them of all their ungodly deeds which they have ungodlily committed, and of all their hard speeches which ungodly sinners have spoken against him.*" Jude 14, 15.

The author of the Guide favors us with no light upon this striking passage. Mr. Balfour finds in it a prophesy of Jerusalem's destruction. But how false and absurd to say that the Lord came with ten thousand of his saints to execute judgment upon all at the destruction of Jerusalem. Did thousands of saints *come* with Christ to Jerusalem? Christ did not come himself at that event; (Sec. XLIII.) and as to his saints, he contradicts this absurd exposition by representing it as a time when they should flee from Judea into the mountains, (Matt. 24:16–20,) instead of coming with him, as those who wrest the scriptures assert. As this interpretation contradicts the Saviour, no more need be said to refute it. This passage refers to the great day of which we read so much in the scriptures, when Christ shall come as judge "*to execute judgment upon all,*" whether Jews or Gentiles. See Sec. XLIX.

LXXXI. "*Marvel not at this; for the hour is coming in which all that are in the graves shall hear his voice, and shall come forth; they that have done good, unto the resurrection of life; and they that have done evil, unto the resurrection of damnation.*" John 5:28, 29.

But few texts have given more trouble to Universalists than this, and many are the labored articles they have written to destroy its force. Sometimes it denotes a moral resurrection, and then again it is a figurative one, and had its fulfilment when Jerusalem was destroyed. We are favored with criticisms to show that the Greek word *anastasis*, rendered resurrection, does not always mean a literal resurrection from the dead, and that damnation does not necessarily imply endless punishment, together with the usual display of scripture references and orthodox authorities. Mr. S. Cobb, sees the Jerusalem catastrophe most clearly in the passage, and discourses thus: "When the terrible calamities began to break forth upon them, (the Jews,) then they waked from the dust; then were they called forth from their graves, or their secret places, in which they had been sleeping — they were roused from their dormancy. They came forth to a sense of their own shame, to the resurrection of their own condemnation — and suffered that dreadful punishment, of which Moses and the prophets, and the Son of God, had so repeatedly forewarned them. And this judgment did not affect the wicked alone; it affected the faithful disciples of Jesus, also. It called *them* forth into a more full enjoyment of life and happiness. They had been pressed down under grievous persecutions, and the calamities of war prevailed in all the land. And when every thing in the natural world appeared blackness and darkness, no doubt considerable darkness brooded over their minds." After assuming that a very wonderful change took place in the temporal and spiritual condition of Christians at the destruction of Jerusalem, Mr. Cobb adds, "Now this important change in the condition of the disciples, so wonderfully wrought, was as properly called their coming forth from the graves, through the authority of Christ, to the resurrection, as the redemption of the Jews from Babylonish captivity into their land, was called of the Lord by Ezekiel, the bringing them up from their graves, to inherit the land of Israel; and equally striking is the declaration, They that have done evil shall come forth to the resurrection of condemnation, to express the effectual arousing of the wicked and unbelieving from their graves of secrecy and their refuge of lies, to misery, shame and contempt. *Trumpet*, No. 669. In the same number of the Trumpet, Mr. Whittemore, speaking of Mr. Cobb's interpretation, says, "it is maintained by the Universalist denomination with hardly an exception." So Mr. W. endorses it in behalf of the order. From these expounders, then, we learn that "all that are in the graves" were Jews and Christians, and that these both experienced a resurrection at Jerusalem's destruction, the former to damnation and the latter to life. But were Jews and Christians raised then? Let us contemplate the Jews in the light of history. This informs us that Jerusalem was besieged six months by the Roman army, that eleven hundred thousand Jews perished in the city, and some hundreds of thousands out of it; that the city and temple were totally destroyed, that the Jews ceased to be a nation, were cast down from the high privileges they had hitherto enjoyed, and that large numbers of them were consigned to hopeless bondage. This must be called a resurrection! What is said about the Jews being "waked from the dust," "called forth from their secret places," &c., is mere home-made cloth, and proves nothing but the weakness of the cause it is designed to support. There is a beauty and propriety in the use of the figure in Ezekiel's vision, (Ez. 37:11–14,) it being there used to show that the Jews as a nation would be brought up out of their degradation and bondage in Babylon to the civil and religious privileges for which they were afterwards distinguished. But in the case before us, the reverse is the fact. They now became degraded instead of being raised. Their national character and privileges were now taken away instead of being restored. They now, keeping Ezekiel's figure in view, were sent down into their graves instead of coming forth from them. All must see the sophistry of producing Ezekiel's vision to patch up this interpretation. Again, these interpreters are quite sure that by John 8:21, "Ye shall die in your sins," is meant the death of the Jewish nation, which took place when Jerusalem was destroyed. *Guide*, page 164. So their exposition of John 8:21, and of John 5:28, 29, when taken together, amounts to this: the death and resurrection of the Jewish nation both took place at the same time and by the same event, viz.: the destruction of Jerusalem!! Error is ever inconsistent with itself.

But Christians also came forth from their graves to the resurrection of life when Jerusalem was destroyed. Now we ask in what sense Christians were dead and in their graves before that event? Were they spiritually dead? Then were they not Christians. Were they inactive in their Master's cause?—Never were Christians more active and devoted than before the destruction of Jerusalem. Such was their zeal, that the gospel, before that event, had not only "spread through the Roman empire, but even to India and Parthia." *Porteus' Evidences.* Was darkness brooding over their minds, as Mr. Cobb would have us believe? Of this there is no evidence whatever. What! is Christianity a mere creature of circumstances? Must gloom and darkness brood over Christian minds in times of temporal calamities? The martyrs were happy in the flames, and it is one of the chief glories of Christianity that it can render its recipients happy independent of outward things. They can "rejoice and be exceeding glad when persecuted." Matt. 5: 12. True Christians have done this in all ages of the church; but to serve a rotten system, it must be now made to appear that early Christians were a gloomy, disconsolate, wretched, inactive people who were represented by the Saviour as in their graves, needing the destruction of Jerusalem to raise them to life and make them happy! To say nothing of the perversion, we ask where is the man, knowing anything of the power of the gospel upon his own heart, who can for a moment believe this? But did not Christians experience some great temporal blessing at Jerusalem's overthrow? In Matt. 24: 9, which Universalists apply to this event, we learn what reward Christ's followers received at that time. "Then shall they deliver you up to be afflicted, and shall kill you; and ye shall be hated of all nations for my name's sake." See, also, ver. 16–18. Was this their reward for having done good? But it is said that they were raised to great privileges, and entered into great rest from persecution after the power of the Jews was broken. But what evidence is furnished of this? Just none at all; but on the contrary we learn that Christians were persecuted in a manner unparalleled for at least two hundred years after Jerusalem was sacked by the Romans. (Sec. XXVI.) Was this their resurrection to life? Universalists, upon this and a few other texts, would make it appear that deliverance from the Jewish power was a great blessing to Christians, and that the Roman power was not to be dreaded, for under it great rest and privileges were to be enjoyed; but in their work on Matt. 10: 28, they will have it that Christ is instructing his disciples not to fear the Jews, but to greatly fear the Roman power! (Sec. XCII.) And thus the serpent bites himself again. All must see at a glance the perversion of the text when applied to Jerusalem's destruction.

But some take the position that a moral or spiritual resurrection is intended in ver. 25, of this chapter, and that the same construction is to be given to verses 28 and 29. But this reduces the Saviour's language to nonsense. Hear it: "There is to be a spiritual resurrection; marvel not at this, there is to be a spiritual resurrection!" Such senseless tautology was never uttered by the Great Teacher, and the construction which requires it must be false. The text paraphrased upon this principle stands thus: "Marvel not at this, for the spiritually alive (they that have done good) shall come forth from their spiritual graves and be made spiritually alive; and they that are spiritually dead (have done evil) shall come forth from their spiritual graves and be made spiritually alive by a spiritual resurrection to damnation!!"

If the same resurrection is taught in ver. 25 that is in verses 28 and 29, then it must be obvious to all that the death and resurrection must be exactly the opposites the one to the other. If the resurrection is a spiritual or moral one, then the death is a moral death, i. e., a death "in trespasses and in sins." "To come forth from this death is to come forth to a life of purity and happiness." Well, then, "the hour is coming, in the which all that are in the graves of sin and moral death shall come forth; they that have done *good!*" What! done good? Dead and buried in sin, and yet be doing good? Is a man when dead and buried, *alive*, in the very sense in which he is dead? Dead in trespasses and sins, and yet the condition of their coming forth unto the resurrection of life, (that is, holiness and purity,) is their having done good, that is, having been *holy* and *pure*, while *dead* and *buried in sin*. But look at the other part of the verse. "They that have done *evil*, to the resurrection of *damnation*." Of course all that were dead, had done evil, if the death was a death in trespasses and sins. To come forth from this death, is to come forth to a life of holiness and purity, and yet this holiness and purity is the resurrection of damnation! May the good Lord deliver us from such holiness and purity. Such a construction resolves the whole passage into a mass of absurd nonsense." *Rev. C. Kingsley.*

The Universalist commentator assumes that a spiritual resurrection is intended, and of course denies that Christ speaks of the immortal resurrection. He says: "Whenever the sacred writers mention a retribution, they are silent in regard to a resurrection; and whenever they mention a resurrection to immortality, they are silent in regard to a retribution. If we interpret this passage, therefore, to mean a resurrection of mankind from natural death to immortality, some to happiness and some to misery, we must do it in defiance of the invariable usage of the New Testament writers." *Page in loco.*

Here it is asserted that a resurrection to immortality is never spoken of by the sacred writers in connection with a retribution. The falsity of this is seen not only from the passage under consideration, but also in Heb. 6 : 2, where Paul, in giving a summary of Christian doctrines, speaks of the resurrection in connection with eternal judgment. (Sec. LVI.) Mr. Page avails himself of Mr. Balfour's favorite rule of "*scripture usage*," a handy method by which to set aside a plain declaration of God, if he has not repeated it in the same language elsewhere. So the Saviour must not be understood to mean what he appears to mean in John 5 : 28, 29, because the scriptures nowhere else assert the same thing in the same form of language; as though God is not to be believed unless he announces the same thing in the same form a dozen times. Christ says: "God is a spirit," and Universalists profess to believe it. Now what is "*scripture usage*" upon this? God's nature and attributes are often spoken of in the Bible, but nowhere, save in John 4:24, is it asserted that "God is a spirit." Are we to conclude from this fact, that the spirituality of the Divine Being is not taught by the Saviour? By no means. Speaking of the words *graves* and *resurrection*, Mr. Page says: "It is certain that the two words are not thus connected in any other place in the New Testament."

This is said to bear against a literal resurrection. But we might with equal force say of the words *God* and *Spirit*, that "it is certain that the two words are not thus connected in any other place in the" *whole Bible*, and thus prove that God is not a spirit! But such work would be worse than trifling, as all must see, yet it is just the work of Universalist expositors. They assert, too, that all will be saved in the resurrection; but neither the word *saved* or *salvation* is found in connection with the word *resurrection*, when spoken of the immortal state, in either the Old or New Testament. Is it just to conclude from this, that none will be saved in the resurrection? If so, where is Universalism? We have met with another quibble, as follows: "If the passage refers to the immortal state, then all must be saved and all must damned, since all have done some good and all have done some evil." Now what of *force* there is in this lies equally against any other application. Is it referred to Jerusalem's destruction? Were each class, Jews and Christians, destroyed by the Romans, and each saved from that destruction? No more upon this need be said.

Another twist of the serpent is this: "If the immortal resurrection is intended, then only those will be raised who have done good or evil, and thus infants are excluded." In reply we say, If a Universalist Jerusalem resurrection is intended, then only those were to be raised who had done good or evil, and thus infants are excluded. But among the eleven hundred thousand that perished in that resurrection, (!) were there no infants? History informs us that mothers devoured their own infant offspring, in that dreadful siege, called by our opponents a resurrection. It does not follow that no infants will be raised, merely because they are not named by the Saviour; for observe, he does not say that those only are to be raised who have done good and evil, but *all* are to come forth from their graves. He then speaks of the retribution of moral agents, and omits naming infants for the good reason that he was addressing adults, and his words were designed to influence moral agents in all succeeding ages of the church; and this omission no more excludes infants from salvation, than women are excluded from the benefits of the Saviour's death by the assertion of Paul, that Christ "tasted death for every MAN;" thus omitting to name women.

One more subterfuge: "This cannot refer to the resurrection of the bodies of men, for multitudes of the dead are not in their graves at all." This is a most peurile objection. All must see that the general expression, "all that are in the graves," means all the dead, all within the empire of death, whether in the dust of the earth or in the sea. Observe, this was addressed to Jews, who believed in the resurrection of all men constituting two classes, denominated "the just and unjust." Acts 24:15. We learn from Josephus that the Jews believed that all men, the just and the unjust, would be raised and brought before God, the Word, or Christ, and be judged by him according to their works: that he should pass upon them a just sentence, "by giving justly to those who have done well an everlasting fruition; but allotting to the lovers of wicked works eternal punishment." *Dis. on Hades.* Paul declared he believed as the Pharisees did concerning the resurrection. (Sec. X.) Taking into connection the Saviour's words, and the belief of the Jews, can any be at a loss to know how they must have understood him? They must have understood him as teaching the resurrection in their sense, for he qualifies nothing. He gives no explanation, showing that he is using their doctrine of a future state as a figure to convey the idea of spiritual life and death in this world, or temporal calamities upon their nation. He gave the Jews (ver. 25–27) instruction relative to a spiritual resurrection, and his power and authority to execute judgment, because he was the Son of man or the Messiah. At this they were astonished, and the Saviour seeing it, said: "Marvel not at this, (for this is no more surprising than the doctrine of the resurrection, already admitted by you,) for the hour is coming in the which all that aré in the *graves* (making a distinction between those morally and those literally dead), shall hear his voice, and shall come forth; they that have done good, unto the resurrection of life, and they that have done evil, to the resurrection of damnation." "If the Saviour here is speaking of men dead in sin, and representing them as buried, he would, to have preserved sense, have represented the good as being alive. But both classes, the good and the evil, are dead; both are in their graves; both hear the voice of the Son of God; both come forth from their graves, the one to a resurrection of *life*, the other to a resurrection of *damnation*." This passage of itself is an ever-enduring refutation of Universalism, and the Bush theory of the resurrection. See Sec. LI. where a resurrection and judgment at the end of time are proved; also, Sec. XXVI. and LXI. on the coming of Christ, where the same is shown.

LXXXII. "*Thy kingdom come, thy will be done.*" Matt. 6:10.

"*Whatsoever is not of faith is sin.* Rom. 14:23.

In No. 634 of the Trumpet, is the following weighty affair thrown in by the editor:

"Partialists say that Universalism is the devil's doctrine; and yet they all pray that it may be true. Is this praying—'*thy* kingdom come, *thy* will be done.'"

The assertion that all pray that Universalism may be true, is very common, and as false as it is common. No understanding Christian ever prays that Universalism may be true, or false, or that any other doctrine may be so. Doctrines are principles of the Divine government, and no more to be changed than God himself is to be changed. God's truth is immutable, whatever that truth may be. Christians do not pray for the salvation of all men in the Universalist sense, for,

1. They believe there are millions of souls already saved, and, of course, for these they do not pray.

2. They believe there are millions of souls already lost: for these they do not pray.

When they use universal language in their prayers, they have respect to men who are on probation, and to certain scripture promises which are to be fulfilled through the instrumentality of the church and the agency of the Divine Spirit, whose aid is promised if asked, and not to the whole human race, i. e., all who ever have lived, now live, or may hereafter live on this earth.

In assuming that Christians pray for all men in the above named sense, Universalists connect with it Rom. 14 : 23, and consider it a great argument in favor of their views. The following is a specimen of this kind of sophistry, found in the Universalist Companion, for 1841 :

"If, then, we pray for the salvation of all mankind, and at the same time do not believe that our prayers will be answered, or, in other words, do not believe that all will be saved; do we pray in faith? And are such prayers acceptable to God? Ans. 'Whatsoever is not of faith is *sin*.' Rom. 14 : 23."

We have shown that Christians do not pray for the salvation of all men in the sense here named. We now ask, for what do Universalists pray? Their ministers stand up before the people, and pray for all men. What do they mean by it? Is it that all may be saved from an endless hell in the future state? No. They deny that men are exposed to such a punishment. Furthermore, they no more believe that our praying will in any way affect the salvation of men in the future state, than that whistling or swearing will effect its accomplishment. To admit that men are in any way exposed to endless punishment, would be fatal to their whole theory, as they well know. It is not, then, for the salvation of men in the future state that they pray. For what, then, do they pray, when they use universal language in their prayers? If they do not pray in reference to the future world, it must be that they have reference to the salvation experienced in this. Well, do they really believe, when they pray, that all men in the Universalist sense, i. e., all that ever have lived, and that now live, will come to the knowledge of the truth, and be saved in this world? Certainly they do not; for such a thing is impossible. Notice, then, they do not believe that all, or any men will be saved in the future state, in answer to prayer; for all will be saved independent of prayer, or anything else done here. Neither do they believe that all will be saved in this world. Reader, remember this when a zealous disciple of Universalism presents this *weighty* argument. Question him upon these points, and be careful to tell him that "*whatsoever is not of faith is sin.*"

Questions are sometimes put as follows: Can you pray that one soul may be damned to all eternity? and if you cannot, ought you to believe that for which you cannot pray? In answer to the first question we say, No; and to the last we say, Yes. Sufficient reason for these answers could be given; but to show the sophistry of such questions in a few words, we submit the following. The destruction of Jerusalem was a punishment divinely inflicted upon the Jews for their sins. No Universalist will deny this. They will have it, too, that Paul taught Jerusalem's destruction in the most of those vivid descriptions of judgment and punishment he has given in his epistles, but none will for a moment suppose that Paul desired, or would pray for, that dreadful calamity to come upon his brethren, the Jews; but the Jews experienced that calamity, notwithstanding. Now if the doctrine of endless punishment is false, because Christians cannot pray that men may suffer it, the doctrine of Jerusalem's destruction was false when Paul preached it, for the same reason, which is contrary to matter of fact; therefore all such *reasoning* is false. We are told that men suffer in this world for their sins, but are Universalists in the habit of praying that men may suffer? Think of these things, reader, when these questions are proposed.

For Universalist views of prayer, see Sec. CVII.

LXXXIII. "*The desire of the righteous shall be granted.*" Prov. 10: 24.

The following upon this is found in the Universalist Companion, for 1841:

"Do not the righteous desire the salvation of all mankind? Will not the desire of the righteous be granted? Ans. Prov. 10: 24. 'The *desire* of the righteous *shall* be granted.'"

The whole text reads thus: "The fear of the wicked, it shall come upon him; but the desire of the righteous shall be granted;" and it is dismembered to serve the purposes of Universalism. The text teaches a *personal* evil to the wicked, and a *personal* good to the righteous, and has no more reference to the salvation of all men, than it has to the damnation of all men. Let us take the same liberty with the first member of this text that these men do with the second, and see what it teaches.

Do not many wicked men fear future and endless punishment? Yes; for Universalists themselves assert that many wicked men believe the doctrine.

Will not the fear of the wicked come upon him? Ans. Prov. 10: 24. "The fear of the wicked, it shall come upon him." Then is endless punishment true.

Let us try the other member, and see what we can prove.

Do not the righteous desire that sin and misery may now cease throughout the world? Will not the desire of the righteous be granted? Ans. "The desire of the righteous shall be granted." This world, then, is a paradise!

Again, did not Jesus Christ, the *righteous*, desire the salvation of the Jewish nation, and evince that desire by his tears?

Will not the desire of the righteous be granted? Ans. "The desire of the righteous shall be granted," therefore, Jerusalem was never destroyed by the Romans, just as sure as Universalist logic is sound.

LXXXIV. "*And the Lord God formed man of the dust of the ground, and breathed into his nostrils the breath of life; and man became a living soul.*" Gen. 2 : 7.

"*Then shall the dust return to the earth as it was; and the spirit shall return unto God who gave it.*" Eccl. 12 : 7.

The following dialogue, manufactured by Mr. A. B. Grosh, a leading man in the denomination, was thought so valuable by Mr. Drew, that he copied it into his Banner.

"*Limitarian.* My dear sir, your doctrine is a dangerous, a very dangerous fallacy; and, if you take not heed, will result in the endless damnation of your immortal soul.

"*Universalist.* What is the soul? Is it that 'breath of life' which God breathed into the nostrils of man, when he 'became a living soul?"

"*L.* I think it is.

"*U.* You agree, then, with me, that whatever is immortal in man must have come from Deity — must, in fact, be *a part of himself.*

"*L.* I do. For he created all that *is* created.

"*U.* Very well. Now do you really believe that God will punish 'his breath'— a part of himself — to all eternity? [The Limitarian was silent, evidently unwilling to answer.] Now, my dear friend, the Bible teaches me that he will *not.* It says (Eccl. 12 : 7), 'the spirit shall return unto God who gave it,' when the body returns to dust.

"*L.* Yes, but that only refers to the souls of *good* men.

"*U.* And pray, from whom do the *wicked* receive their souls? Is it from *Satan,* that they must return to *him?* Or does Satan get that portion of Deity so completely under his control that he can hold it and punish it to all eternity, in despite of that Almighty Being, of whom and whose it is?

"*L.* Dangerous sophistry! Blasphemy! [Exit."

This is a choice specimen of Universalist divinity. The obvious design is to teach an old, heathen notion, that the soul of man is a part of God; and then, that endless punishment is false, because God will not punish himself to all eternity! That the soul is not a part of God, but was created, is evident from the scriptures, which declare that God made man in his own image. This, we conceive, was not spoken of the creation of the body, for that is no more the image of an intelligent, immortal, holy Spirit, than any other material substance. It was the soul that God made in his own image. Were it necessary, argument and scripture might be produced, to prove that God created the *whole* man, the soul as well as the body; but other considerations will show, in a few words, the absurdity of the idea that the human soul is a part of God himself. Admit for a moment this idea, and what follows? It follows that a part of the Almighty is scattered about in millions of parts in the form of human souls, and that these souls have been suffering more or less ever since the creation; for none doubt, that we know of, but what the souls of men suffer, as well as their bodies. "Will God punish a part of himself to all eternity?" is the *wise* question proposed in the dialogue. In answer, we say, that it requires no greater stretch of our credulity to believe that God will punish himself eternally, than it does to believe he can punish himself six thousand years, by inhabiting human bodies. Again, the notion is quite common with Universalists, that we are dependent upon the resurrection for a future existence; but if the soul is a part of God, that must be false, unless a part of God may be annihilated! Again, Universalists very generally deny the resurrection of the body; hence, all the future salvation so much talked of, pertains to the soul. But we ask, is it not both absurd and blasphemous to talk of *saving* a part of God? We read of the death of the soul, and the Scriptures count man a sinner. Is the body the sinner, or has the soul something to do with it; and if the soul has something to do in the matter, we ask, does a part of a holy God sin? Some have told us that all sin originates in the flesh, and that the soul is pure of itself, but is, by its connection with the body, forced into the service of the body, and thus sin is accounted for. But, we ask, is a part of the Almighty so pent up in the human body that it is obliged to do its bidding; or in other words, does the creature govern the Creator? No wonder that Mr. Grosh should represent the Limitarian as exclaiming "*Blasphemy!*"

But no soul will be punished to all eternity, because "the spirit shall return to God who gave it." Eccl. 12 : 7. Let it be observed that here nothing is said about the misery or happiness of the spirit. That all spirits will return to God, Christians believe, and they believe, too, that he will dispose of them according to their deserts, and that to the ungodly, "it is a fearful thing to fall into the hands of the living God." Heb. 10 : 31.

Thoughts might be given upon the attributes of God, to show the anti-christian character of the sentiment inculcated by the dialogue; but these brief hints are sufficient to show the reader that it wars with scripture, the nature of God, and common sense. This argument upon the soul, to prove their doctrine, was a very common one among Universalists a few years since, but we had supposed, like much of their former *truth*, it was now obsolete, and were surprised at meeting this new edition of it in the Banner. Anything and any way, only prejudice the people against evangelical sentiments, and induce them to believe, if possible, in Universalism.

One thought more. Stress is laid upon the phrase "*breathed into*," &c., as though the soul was a part of God on this account. The prophet, (Isa. 30 : 33,) speaking of Tophet, says, "the breath of the Lord, like a stream of brimstone, doth kindle it." Did a part of Deity kindle the fire in Tophet? All will see that this is simply an expression of God's agency in producing it. So with Gen. 2 : 7.

LXXXV. "*My counsel shall stand, and I will do all my pleasure.*" Isa. 46 : 10, 11.

Is it the design of the Spirit in this text to teach that the pleasure of the Lord is done in all things? By no means; for respect is had to a particular subject, and we are not to draw a general conclusion from a particular case, especially when the Bible declares (Ezek. 33 : 11), that some things take place contrary to the pleasure of God. What is God's pleasure in the case before us? The context explains as follows: "Calling a ravenous bird from the east, the man that executeth my counsel from a far country; yea, I have spoken it, I will also bring it to pass; I have purposed it, I will also do it," v. 11. This counsel or pleasure was to be executed by a *man*. If we turn to chap. 44 : 28, we shall see who this man is, and what the pleasure of the Lord is. It reads thus: "That saith of Cyrus, He is my shepherd, and shall perform all my pleasure; even saying to Jerusalem, Thou shalt be built; and to the temple, Thy foundation shall be laid." Here we see that God says of Cyrus, "he shall perform *all my pleasure*," i. e., all my pleasure concerning the rebuilding of Jerusalem and the temple.

The position taken by Universalists is, that God's will is always done; and their leading writers deny the freedom of the human will. Mr. Ballou says, "It is evident that will or choice has no possible liberty." *T. on Atonement*, p. 42. Mr. Rogers, following in his wake, says, "the notion of free-will is a chimera." *Pro & Con*, p. 290. Mr. Ballou, in showing that sin is intended for good, says, "It is not casting any disagreeable reflections on the Almighty to say he determined all things for good; and to believe that he superintends all the affairs of the universe, not excepting sin, is a million times more to the honor of God, than to believe he cannot, or he does not when he can." *T. on Atonement*, p. 40. Again he says, "Natural evil is the necessary result of the physical organization and constitution of animal nature," p. 31; and then he informs us that "moral evil or sin owes its origin to natural evil," p. 32; and also that "man is independent of his volitions, and moves by necessity," p. 64. Mr. Ballou is consistent with his theory when he says, "The Almighty had no occasion to dislike Adam after the transgression, any more than he had even before he made him," p. 104; and according to his deductions, "the Divine favor can neither be gained nor lost." *Exp.*, v. 1, p. 28. Says Mr. Whittemore, "Man cannot do what his Maker wills he shall not do, and he cannot leave undone what his Maker wills he shall do." *Trumpet*, No. 968. Other leading writers in the order might be added to this list, whose views are in harmony with these. (Sec. CIV.) Indeed, Universalism can be sustained in no other way than by resolving all the wickedness of the world into the sovereignty of God, and annihilating the moral agency of man; for if the above views are correct, a steam engine is as much a moral agent as a human being. Sin, by this view, is not merely reduced to a trifle, but there can be no such thing unless we come to the blasphemous conclusion that a holy God sins. These sentiments in fact make him the author of all sin and misery in the universe; and when viewed in connection with Bible declarations, charge him with the grossest acts of hypocrisy towards his creatures, to say nothing of cruelty in punishing them for what they cannot avoid. As a specimen of its application in proof of Universalism, the following syllogism is presented, taken from the Universalist Companion, for 1842:

"1. It is God's will for all men to be converted and saved.

"2. God's will will be done.

"3. Therefore all men will be converted and saved."

We find a set of syllogisms ready made at our hand, in the 5th No. of the "Sword of Truth," in answer to the above, by which its soundness may be readily tested. They are the following:

"1. It is the will of God that all men should keep sober.

"2. God's will will be done.

"3. Therefore, all men do keep sober, and the temperance

reformation is finished, just as sure as Universalist's arguments are sound.

"1. It is God's will that all men should embrace the truth.

"2. God's will will be done.

"3. All men do not embrace Universalism; therefore Universalism is not the truth.

"This cannot be retorted upon us, because we hold that many things transpire contrary to the will of God."

We will change the form of this fruitful syllogism, for it will answer almost every purpose.

"1. If the will of God is done in every act, and in every event, as the syllogism asserts, it follows that everything that is done, and everything that takes place, is in accordance with the divine will.

"2. Murder, robbery, drunkenness and whoredom, all take place.

"3. Therefore murder, robbery, drunkenness and whoredom, are all in accordance with the blessed will of God.

"Once more,

"1. Universalists ought not to be opposed to the fulfillment of the will of God.

"2. If the above Universalist syllogism be sound, murder, robbery, drunkenness and whoredom transpire in fulfillment of the divine will.

"3. Therefore Universalists ought not to be opposed to murder, robbery, drunkenness and whoredom."

Again,

"If God's will can but be done in everything, it follows that what does not take place, is not according to the will of God.

"All men do not pray, therefore it is not the will of God that all men should pray.

"All men do not believe the truth, therefore it is not the will of God that all men should believe the truth.

"All men do not keep his commandments, therefore it is not the will of God that all men should keep his commandments."

The Saviour said, (Matt. 7 : 21,) "Not every one that saith unto me Lord, Lord, shall enter into the kingdom of heaven; *but he that doeth the will of my Father which is in heaven.*" Here we have proof that the will of God is not done in all cases. A host of such texts might be adduced, were it needful. What is sin, but a transgression of the Divine law? and what is that law but a transcript of the Divine mind, or an expression of His will?

Thus these men array the God of truth against himself.

LXXXVI. "*He retaineth not his anger forever, because he delighteth in mercy.*" Micah 7 : 18.

Says the author of the Guide, p. 42, "A precious assurance! altogether at variance with the doctrine of endless misery." This forms one of those arguments by which the faith of a certain class of minds receives its *enlargement.* The prophet predicts the desolation of Israel, on account of the wickedness of the people. He is interceding in their behalf, after which God is introduced promising their future restoration to national privileges in this world. Then a chorus of Jews is introduced, singing a hymn of thanksgiving, beginning with the verse of which this text is a part. The reader will see by examination, that this was not spoken of all men, nor of the future state, but of the Jewish people in this world, "*the remnant of his heritage.*" But no matter for this, it can be woven in as occasion may require, with other texts, to deceive the people. We might, with at least equal propriety, bring Isa. 27 : 11, to disprove Universalism. It reads thus: "He that made them will not have mercy on them, and he that formed them will show them no favor." Here it is asserted of a certain class, that God *will not* have mercy on them, and that he will show them *no favor.* How will this comport with the idea of God's endless mercy and favor to all men? Reader, is not our argument as sound as Mr. Whittemore's?

LXXXVII. "*God shall wipe away all tears from their eyes; and there shall be no more death, neither sorrow, nor crying; neither shall there be any more pain; for the former things are passed away.*" Rev. 21 : 4. See also verses 7 and 8.

Paraphrased in accordance with Universalist views, the passage reads thus: "God shall wipe away all tears from the eyes of the whole human family; and to all there shall be no more death, neither shall they suffer any more sorrow, or crying, or pain; for the former things have passed away from the whole of Adam's posterity." But the reader will see at a glance that this happy state of things is not predicated of the whole human race, but of the inhabitants of the "NEW JERUSALEM," v. 2. "*There shall be no more death.*" This, with Universalist divines, is a kind of make-weight text to be thrown in at any time, like Lam. 3 : 31, and 1 Cor. 15 : 22. Mr. Whittemore has put it in capitals, and says, "Although we read in the scriptures of the *second death*, yet, if we read of *thirty deaths*, it would be no argument against Universalism, since the time is to come when "THERE SHALL BE NO MORE DEATH." *Guide*, p. 53. The substance of this, when connected with the facts in the case, is this: a certain class shall suffer no more death; therefore, none of the human family shall suffer any more death! Not very logical. But when is the happy state of things contained in the text to take place? Not in this world, as "none are saved from all moral evil here." *U. Ill. & Def.*, p. 261. "No man on earth is entirely free from sin." *Page, on Matt.* 7 : 23. It is in the future, then, that the blessings named in the text are to be enjoyed. We too admit the future-state reference of the passage, and we know, too, that if there is any meaning in language, it is descriptive of the bliss of the saints as distinguished from the state of the wicked (v. 8). Inspiration, after describing the exemptions and bliss of saints, says, "He that overcometh shall inherit all things (all the things just described); and I will be his God, and he shall be my son. But the fearful, and unbelieving, and the abominable, and murderers, and whoremongers, and sorcerers, and idolaters, and all liars, shall have their part in the lake which burneth with fire and brimstone; which is the second death," v. 7 and 8. It will be seen by examination, that there is not a single mark of future reference in v. 4, that is not found in v. 8. They both refer to the future condition of man, presenting two classes and conditions, according to character. One class are to experience "*no more death;*" but the other are to suffer "*the second death.*" One is freed from tears, sorrow, and pain; the other "shall have their part in the lake which burneth with fire and brimstone." Never was there a more gross perversion than using v. 4, or any part of it, to prove the salvation of all men. The fact that the system *demands* such work of its advocates to sustain it, should be considered proof demonstrative that it is not of God. Reader, beware of the "second death."

LXXXVIII. "*For it is impossible for those who were once enlightened, and have tasted of the heavenly gift,*" &c. Heb. 6:4–6.

The author of the Guide, p. 197, labors to show that this passage cannot mean what it seems to mean, because "the scriptures teach that all things are possible with God," and "that all will admit that God can do anything which does not involve in itself a necessary contradiction or impossibility." Very true, and the case named in the passage is just of that character. When the Bible declares that all things are possible with God, it is to be understood in a restricted sense; for it is evident from the nature of God, and also from the Bible itself, that it is "impossible for God to lie," and that "he cannot deny himself." Repentance is a work God has enjoined upon the sinner, without which he cannot be saved. But while none can repent without divine aid, it is also true that God as a moral governor, cannot coerce men into repentance. It must be voluntary on the part of man, or it involves a contradiction, arraying the Deity against himself by attributing to him a work which he has enjoined upon the sinner, and which none but a sinner can perform. The apostle speaks (2 Tim. 2 : 25) of God's giving repentance, by which we understand that he gives the means and opportunity, and not that he repents for the sinner. Man is not passive in this work, but an active agent, as the Bible and experience clearly show. But says the Guide, "If a man becomes incapable of repentance, he will be no longer a moral agent; nor will he be under obligation to do that which he cannot." To this quibble we reply, that the responsibility of a man before God who has lost his moral agency, or power of right action, depends upon how he lost it. If a man in the providence of God becomes insane, independent of his voluntary action, justice declares him not responsible. But if a man by his voluntary acts, hardens his heart, sears his conscience, grieves the Spirit, and hurls his own reason from its throne, justice requires that such a man be held responsible for acts committed while in such a state. Is the man who voluntarily deprives himself of the means to sustain his own family, in no way responsible for the poverty and wretchedness which may follow such an act? A man becomes beastly drunk, reason is dethroned, he burns his neighbor's buildings, and murders his own wife. Does not God hold him responsible for these acts? Civil law, even, holds him responsible, for the good reason that he had no right to abuse his powers by drinking to intoxication. God has given man powers as a moral being, but if he abuses them by acts of sin so as to destroy his reason, is it not just to conclude that God will hold him responsible in the day of judgment, not only for the evil he commits in such a state, but also for the good he fails to do, which he might otherwise have accomplished? Most certainly it is. Again; it is said by the Guide, that "Paul only meant that it was impossible for him, by his preaching to apostate Christians, to renew them again to repentance." Well, what is gained by this, supposing that it be admitted? Does it prove that their renewal *is* possible from some other source? Inspiration declares of such apostates that it is IMPOSSIBLE, that is, they are past recovery; it is impossible for any instrumentality or agency "to renew them again unto repentance; seeing they crucify to themselves the Son of God afresh, and put him to an open shame." But Universalism contradicts the Bible, and says it is possible. Which shall we credit, Universalism or the Bible. See Sec. IV.

LXXXIX. "*What must I do to be saved?*" Acts 16: 30.

Why does the jailer tremble and fall before Paul and Silas, proposing this important question? Did he fear the Roman law? This could not be, for that had not been violated; and this he knew, for Paul had just said to him, "Do thyself no harm, for *we are all here.*" Would he have consulted two poor missionaries of the cross, if the Roman law was all he feared? Then see the answer of Paul. "Believe on the Lord Jesus Christ, and thou shalt be saved." Was faith in Christ the way of salvation from the penalty of Roman laws? Faith in Christ was quite a sure way to incur that penalty. Paul had been whipped in the public streets of Philippi only the day before, and the jailer knew it; and now Paul directs him to believe on Christ in order to escape the Roman law! This is too absurd, even for Mr. Whittemore; hence, in his Guide, p. 175, he admits that the jailer in effect inquired, "What must I do to become a Christian?" But, lest it should be thought that he had any respect to the future world, a dust is raised about the word *saved*, and ten texts of scripture are produced to prove most conclusively what no one ever denied, viz: that Christians are said to be saved in this world, a fact with which all Christians are perfectly familiar; and what does it prove? Does it prove that the jailer had no thoughts of eternity, in the deep convictions he evinced? Much is said about universal salvation, which of course is to be experienced in the future state. Suppose we were to deny that there is any salvation in the future world, and then, to prove it, should make a great parade of text to show that men are said to be saved in this world, would it be honest? Yet this could be done with equal fairness. (Sec. LI.) The jailer was without doubt a believer in future retributions, for this doctrine was common not only among Jews, but also among Gentiles (Sec. CXXXII); and it is highly probable that he heard the praying and singing of the apostles, and knew something of their teachings; these, together with the earthquake and the Christian demeanor of the prisoners, were set home to his heart by the Holy Spirit. He now sees himself a sinner, and has such a discovery of his awful exposure, that he trembles, rushes in and falls down before Paul and Silas, and cries, "Sirs, what must I do to be saved?" Faithful Christian ministers, in all ages of the church, have witnessed the trembling power which sometimes seizes the guilty before God, in view of their lost condition. The jailer bears every mark of being strongly excited by fear, which completely refutes the idea so much dwelt upon by Universalists, viz: that fear has nothing to do with making men Christians; for observe, Mr. Whittemore admits that he desired at this crisis to become a Christian, and the history shows that he did become one.

XC. "*For as in Adam all die, even so in Christ shall all be made alive.*" 1 Cor. 15:22.

In this section we purpose to examine those texts in 1 Cor. 15, which are involved in the controversy with Universalists, passing over those which have no particular bearing upon the subject. As may be seen most clearly, the apostle is not proving how all men will be made holy and happy, but his subject is the *resurrection of the body*. To prove and illustrate this, the chapter was written. It will be seen, too, that this was addressed to Christians, to "beloved brethren," and after proving the resurrection, he very beautifully illustrates and explains what they, as Christians, might expect pertaining to their bodies in that state. This was called forth by the fact that some false teachers at Corinth denied the doctrine of the resurrection of the body. In the first part of the chapter he proves the resurrection of

Christ, and then shows the fatal consequences to the whole Christian system, if it be a fact that Christ has not risen, as follows: "Now, if Christ be preached that he rose from the dead, how say some among you that there is no resurrection of the dead? But if there be no resurrection of the dead, then is Christ not risen; and if Christ be not risen, then is our preaching vain, and your faith is also vain. Yea, and we are found false witnesses of God; because we have testified of God that he raised up Christ: whom he raised not up, if so be that the dead rise not. For if the dead rise not, then is Christ not raised. And if Christ be not raised, your faith is vain; ye are yet in your sins. Then they also which are fallen asleep in Christ are perished. If in this life only we have hope in Christ, we are of all men most miserable." Ver. 12–19.

Mr. Balfour (*Essays*, p. 193) denies the immortality of the soul, and contends that none who die have any conscious existence until the resurrection, which is yet future, and brings in proof of this, v. 18. That the apostle never designed to teach materialism in this passage, the reader will see by consulting the scriptures referred to a few pages forward in this section. He is showing, from ver. 12 to ver 19, the fatal consequences to the whole Christian system of denying the resurrection of the dead. Some, it seems, admitted the resurrection of Christ, while they denied that others would be raised. But the apostle shows them that consistency required that they discard the resurrection of Christ, and that they virtually did so by the doctrines they put forth. He then shows them, that occupying this ground they made Christ a deceiver, and the apostles false witnesses, and if the gospel could be thus stripped of the evidence it derives from the resurrection of its author, and the resurrection of the body be set aside, then every other doctrine pertaining to it must fall. Then the world must be left without Christianity, without any light respecting the future, and all must be as dark and dreary as Paganism. They had experienced present salvation from the guilt of sin, through the atonement; and some of their brethren had suffered all manner of indignities, and had died most cruel deaths in hope of a future life of bliss. But the apostle shows that if the resurrection of Christ is false, then all other Christian doctrines were of no avail; that their preaching was vain, and they "which had fallen asleep in Christ had perished," because they trusted in Christ to save them from their sins. But if he had not risen from the dead, he was himself a sinner, having been guilty of deception and falsehood, and had himself gone to perdition, and could never save them from the same fate. Furthermore, the doctrine of present justification was destroyed, for "your faith is vain, and ye are yet in your sins." Then, upon the principle that the Christian system is false, he shows the folly of those who, unlike some in our day who contend that conduct here takes no hold on the future state, were laboring and enduring with respect to a better world, he says: "If in this life only we have hope in Christ, we are of all men most miserable." We see by these brief thoughts that the idea taught, is not that there is no conscious existence unless the bodies of men are raised, but that a denial of the resurrection is equivalent to a rejection of the whole gospel plan, and thus the world would be left without any hope or just conceptions respecting the future. The apostle continues: "But now is Christ risen from the dead and become the first fruits of them that slept." Ver. 20.

"*Of them that slept.*" Are we to understand by this all mankind, or a particular class of persons? The latter, as is quite evident. This sense is fixed by ver. 18: "Then they which have *fallen asleep in Christ*," &c., that is, those who had died in his cause, perhaps as martyrs. The same class Paul names in 1 Thess. 4:16: "The dead in Christ shall rise first;" and the same that John refers to, Rev. 14:13: "Blessed are the dead which die in the Lord." The clause, "Christ the first fruits," will be considered in connection with ver. 23: "For since by man came death, by man came also the resurrection of the dead. For as in Adam all die, even so in Christ shall all be made alive. But every man in his own order: Christ the first fruits; afterwards, they that are Christ's at his coming." Ver. 21–23. What death did Adam die, or what death was introduced by him? "His death was simply moral; he died to innocence; there was nothing affected but his mind and heart; no change took place in his moral or physical constitution." *U. Ill. and Def.*, p. 76. But in what sense do all die in Adam? Some years since while delivering a course of lectures in one of the villages of Maine, we gave a public call upon Universalists for information respecting their views upon ver. 22. We knew that this text was often used to prove their doctrine, but could find nothing explicit, in the many books from their authors we had in possession, to show how *all die in Adam*. The next week an anonymous letter was received, supposed to be dictated by the Universalist minister of the place, in which we were informed that all men do not die in Adam, as we bathe in water or sail in a boat, but that Adam died to innocence, or died a moral death by sinning, and that all men by sin die as Adam did, and that by Christ all are to be made alive morally. According to this view, to die in Adam means simply to die as Adam did. Moral death, we suppose, is indicated Rom. 8:6: "For to be carnally minded is death." Also, Eph. 2:1: "Dead in trespasses and sins." Upon the hypothesis that a moral death and resurrection are intended, let us paraphrase the three texts and see what character is given the Saviour and his holy saints. "For since by Adam came moral death, by Christ came also the resurrection of the morally dead. For as in Adam all die a moral death, even so in Christ shall all be made morally alive. But every man in his own order in this resurrection from moral death to moral life: Christ the first fruits of the morally dead; afterwards, they of the morally dead that are Christ's at his coming!" And is it so? Was Christ the immaculate, who "did no sin," "dead in trespasses and sins?" Was he in his resurrection "the first fruits of them that slept" in moral pollution? And then are those who in the scriptures are denominated Christ's, morally dead? No; for "they that are Christ's have crucified the flesh, with the affections and lusts." Gal. 5 : 24. But to carry out the Universalist view of a moral death and resurrection, the passage is made to teach that which is both blasphemous and absurd, namely: That Christ was the first fruits of those who are raised from moral death and pollution, and afterwards those that are Christ's at his coming shall be raised from the same deplorable condition! Says Mr. Skinner: "Perhaps there is no better way of detecting the fallacy of a doctrine, than by looking at the difficulties into which it leads." *U. Ill. and Def.*, p. 171. We beg the reader to look at the difficulties into which Universalist interpretations lead in the subject under consideration. Adopt the truth, that the death and resurrection of the body constitute the apostle's theme, and all becomes plain and luminous in his reasoning. The reader need not be informed that ver. 22 is a text ever at hand to prove Universalism. This has, by the advocates of this dogma, been illustrated by scales. In the first scale is placed, "*As in Adam all die*," then "*even so*" under an even beam, and in the second scale, "*In Christ shall all be made alive.*" The object of this is, to show that just as much was gained by Christ as was lost by Adam; and this is doubtless true in the sense of the text. Now, if we can ascertain what is in the first scale, we can soon learn what is in the second. To get at this, let us inquire about what was Paul writing. Is he showing how all men became sinners in consequence of Adam's transgression, and how all men will be made holy and happy by Christ's obedience? Nothing of the kind. He is not illustrating the plan of salvation at all. Is Paul calling the attention of his brethren to the subject of spiritual death and spiritual life? By no means. This chapter, as all must see, was written to prove and illustrate the *resurrection of the body*, and this very naturally led him to show how men became subject to temporal death, which he does thus: "For since by man, i. e., Adam, came death, i. e. the death of the body, by man, i. e., Christ, came also the resurrection of the dead." Ver. 21. "For as in Adam (the man alluded to,) all die, even so in Christ shall all be made alive," i. e., shall be raised from the dead. Ver. 22. "But every man in his own order; Christ the first fruits, afterwards they that are Christ's at his coming." Ver. 23. No man, it would seem, need mistake the subject. It is not a resurrection of all men to holiness and happiness in heaven; it is not a resurrection to spiritual life, but the resurrection of the bodies of men, is the apostle's subject. He teaches us, most clearly too, by implication, that all will not be Christ's, at his coming to raise the dead.

It must be obvious to all, that the death of the body is taught by the first member of the text, and the resurrection of the body by the second, and nothing more. It is worthy of remark, that it is said (Phil. 3 : 21) of Christ, when he shall come to raise the dead, that he "shall change our vile body;" but it is nowhere said he shall change our vile soul; and we have yet to learn that anywhere in the Bible, anything is said equivalent to it. But suppose we go directly against the whole scope of the apostle's reasoning here, and admit that spiritual death is here intended; we then ask, do Universalists hold that all men were exposed to endless spiritual death or misery, by dying in Adam, and that all are to be, by Christ, raised to endless bliss? This they must admit, or the scale, containing the first member of the text, kicks the beam at once, and the "*even so*" is even nonsense. Will Universalists admit that Adam's sin affected his own future state, or that of his posterity? If they do, what becomes of that much cherished notion among them, that man's conduct here takes no hold on eternity? for if Adam's conduct took hold on the future state, then does the conduct of all men, inasmuch as the principles of God's moral government are the same respecting all men, as moral beings. There is no avoiding this. But, on the other hand, if the death, by Adam, takes no hold on the future state, then the life, by Christ, takes no hold on the future state, for it is "EVEN SO."

It is well known, that modern Universalists stoutly contend

against the idea that mankind are at all exposed to a future hell, either by Adam's or their own sins. Just to show how the use they make of this passage, when properly considered, wars with their own theory, let us inquire, what do they contend is taught by the last member of the text, or what is in the second scale? We are told, with great confidence, that it contains Universalism. Well, what is Universalism? It is this: *All men, by the resurrection, will be raised to endless bliss.* No Universalist will complain of this definition. This, then, is what the second scale contains. Now what must the first scale contain to balance it? Observe, it is "*even so.*" It must contain, then, that which is directly opposite. Well, what is that? It is *endless misery*, as all must see. There is no avoiding this, as the text is antithetical, strictly so. From this view of their interpretation of the last member of the text, we arrive at the following conclusion: by Adam, all were exposed to endless misery; by Christ, all are saved from endless misery. Now modern Universalists know that it would be fatal to their system to admit that men were ever exposed to endless misery; therefore they will not adopt the conclusion, although it grows legitimately from the premises they themselves furnish. Error is always inconsistent with itself. The doctrine of the text, as we have seen, is this: the temporal death of all men by Adam, the resurrection of the bodies of all by Christ, and thus the scales are even.

It will be seen from the above, that this text no more teaches the salvation of all men, than it does the restoration of the Jews to Palestine.

That some of our readers may have a better understanding of Universalist sentiments, and also see how they war with the scriptures, we shall present the views of two, who have been reckoned among their ablest divines, upon the resurrection. Mr. Balfour contends that man has no immortal soul, and can have no patience whatever with the idea of disembodied spirits. Hear him upon this point: "Man comes into the world and dies similar to the brute creation. God made man wiser than the beasts of the field, or the fowls of the air; and he has given him a promise of a resurrection from the dead: but to say he has given him an immortal soul, to be happy or miserable in a disembodied state, is traveling beyond the record." *Essay*, p. 97.

His doctrine is, that none that have died since the world began, have now any conscious existence, neither will they have until the resurrection, then all will be raised to a state of immortal bliss, irrespective of character here. This event he considers yet future. This materialism of his is abundantly refuted by the following scriptures, to which the reader is referred, to say nothing of many more texts. Eccl. 12 : 7 ; Matt. 10 : 28 ; Luke 16 : 19–31 ; 20 : 37, 38 ; 23 : 43–46 ; 24 : 36–40, where our Lord sanctions the doctrine of disembodied spirits ; John 11 : 26 ; 8 : 51 ; Acts 7 : 59 ; 2 Cor. 12 : 1–4 ; 5 : 1–9 ; Phil. 1 : 20–25 ; 2 Pet. 1 : 13–15.

The materialism of Mr. Balfour, we conclude, has never been very extensively received by the denomination, for such is the state of the human heart, while under the influence of modern Universalism, that the rule seems to be readily adopted that no doctrine can be true which does not afford its recipients the most pleasurable sensations respecting the future, whatever may be their character here.

In this fact is found a reason why the doctrine of a limited future punishment has been so generally rejected, which was at one time held by the denomination. (Sec. CXXXVI.) For the same reason Mr. Balfour's views have not obtained extensively among them. Errors of as great magnitude as Mr. B.'s are readily received by their people, if they are only in keeping with their *desires ;* but his errors have the misfortune not to be of this stamp. They desire to be happy immediately at death. But there is something very repulsive in the thought of going into a state of nonentity, perhaps for thousands of years, before heavenly bliss can be enjoyed. Hence their teachers, who are always accommodating men upon such subjects, and are always disposed to impart peace to troubled minds, have sought out an invention by which all men are to enter into bliss immediately when they die. So far as we can learn from their books and papers, the ideas which prevail most extensively among Universalists at the present respecting the resurrection, are, that it is not *general*, but *successive*, or as some say, *progressive*, and that the human body will never be raised. This resurrection, they conclude, has been going on, from the time of Adam down to the present. Some talk of it as though it took place at death, and others, as if to get rid of certain difficulties growing out of a death resurrection, would have a space of insensibility between death and the resurrection of some days' duration. The following extract is taken from a sermon by Mr. J. B. Dods, who has been one of the most *noted* divines in the order, and from all we can gather, we think it contains very nearly the sentiments of many of the Universalists upon this subject:

"We have already shown that the resurrection of the dead was to be at the sound of the last trump. And as that trump commenced sounding at the end of the Jewish age, when Christ came in his kingdom, I deem it sufficient to establish the fact, that the dead are continually rising in this *last*, this *gospel day.* But the question presents itself — were any of the human family raised immortal before that period? To this question I give an affirmative answer. I firmly believe, that the dead have been rising immortal from Adam to the present day, for God has never changed the established order of the universe. I believe that the dead are raised without any *miracle*, in the common acceptation of that term, as much as I believe that we are born, and die, not by a *miracle*, but according to that constitution of things which God has immutably established from the beginning. I believe this doctrine of Christ to be founded upon the unchanging principles of philosophy, but so mysterious, that man in his present existence cannot comprehend the subtle causes and effects by which he shall put on immortality." *Trumpet*, No. 718.

These views are certainly more anti-scriptural than Mr. Balfour's, for with all his absurdities, we must give him the credit of one correct thought, viz.: a future general resurrection; but in these we cannot discover even one truth. These views war with the scriptures, (ver. 20 and 23,) which declare Christ to be the first fruits. According to this hypothesis, the first fruits appeared many ages before Christ, for men had been rising from the dead ever since Cain killed Abel, or four thousand years before the Saviour's resurrection. The apostle, as if he here foresaw that some would attempt to teach that the phrase "first fruits" has reference to *rank* and not to the *order* of the resurrection, has established the fact that Christ is the first in the immortal resurrection, by language which cannot be frittered away. In Col. 1:18, he calls him "the first born from the dead," and in Acts 26:22, 23 he says:

"Having therefore obtained help of God, I continue unto this day, witnessing both to small and great, saying none other things than those which the prophets and Moses did say should come:

"That Christ should suffer, and that he should be the first that should rise from the dead, and should shew light unto the people, and to the Gentiles."

"Here Christ is declared by the inspired apostle to be "*the first that should rise from the dead.*" A progressive resurrection stands opposed to those scriptures, which speak of the event as yet future. See Mark 12:23, 24; Luke 14:14; John 5:28, 29; Acts 24:15; 1 Thess. 4:14–17. Others might be named, but these texts are enough to establish our point. Again: This resurrection is to take place at the coming of Christ 1 Thess. 4:14–17; 1 Cor. 15:23. Did Christ come at the resurrection, thousands of years before he assumed human nature? Does he now come at the death of every individual? Are the scriptures referred to, and other similar ones fulfilled, in this way? Preposterous! Mr. Balfour, in contending with those who hold that the resurrection takes place at death, has the following:

"When shall the resurrection of the dead take place? Some say it takes place at every man's death. But certainly Martha did not think so, for she said concerning Lazarus—'I know that he shall rise again in the resurrection at the last day.' She probably borrowed the phrase *last day*, from what she heard our Lord say, (John 6 : 39, 40–45,) where he four times spoke of the resurrection, as being in the last day. If the resurrection is at a man's death, she ought to have said: 'I know that he rose four days ago,' for Lazarus had been four days dead. But she spoke of the resurrection and the last day as simultaneous events. It appears to me, that the resurrection, the last day, the period called the end, and the coming of Christ, all refer to the same period. But how many years, or ages until it arrives, the Bible, so far as I understand it, does not inform us, and I have no desire to be wise above what is written." *Essay*, p. 179.

Again, in speaking of Christ's conversation with the Sadducees, he says:

"In concluding my remarks on these passages, I would merely notice, that if the resurrection takes place at a man's death, both our Lord and the Sadducees speak as if they had been of a different opinion. The Sadducees speak of it as a future event, thus: 'In the resurrection therefore when they shall rise.' So did our Lord, for he says: 'For when they shall rise from the dead, they neither marry, nor are given in marriage.' But would either of them have spoken in this manner, had they believed that every man is raised at his death? It is easily perceived that this would have entirely altered the shape of the Sadducees' question." *Essay*, p. 187.

Mr. Balfour's arguments upon this point are sound, as all must see.

Upon the hypothesis of Mr. Dods, and others, the body is never to be raised. But we ask, was not the resurrection of Christ the pattern of ours as well as the pledge? Was not Christ's literal body raised? or was his only the resurrection of the spirit? Said he to his astonished disciples after his resurrection, "Handle me and see, for a spirit hath not flesh and bones as ye see me have." Surely, if the scriptures (Luke 24:37–43) do not teach that the Saviour's material body, the same body that died upon the cross, and was put into the sepulchre, was raised, what can they be relied upon teaching?

Another thought. Did the resurrection of Christ take place when he died? Certainly not.

Should it be thought that a progressive resurrection militates no more against the idea of Christ's being the first fruits, than the resurrections which took place when the Saviour was upon earth, such as that of the widow's son and Lazarus, we answer, these have no connection with the resurrection taught by Christianity. In these cases there was divine power exerted, or a miracle performed, to restore natural life in this world. This is a very different thing from the Christian resurrection, by which all men are to be raised, and the righteous to be glorified with their Saviour in heaven. We know not that any ever contended that these form a part of the Christian resurrection.

Again: Universalists have written much to prove that Christ came at the destruction of Jerusalem. Will they give ver. 23 such a reference? If so, then the resurrection took place and death was destroyed at the destruction of Jerusalem!

"Then cometh the end, when he shall have delivered up the kingdom to God, even the Father; when he shall have put down all rule, and all authority, and power." Ver. 24.

"Then cometh the end," that is, when Christ shall come to raise the dead. By "the kingdom" is to be understood Christ's mediatorial kingdom, which shall be restored to God the Father when he (Christ) shall have put down all rule, and authority, and power which opposed itself to his government. See on verses 27 and 28.

"For he must reign till he hath put all enemies under his feet." Ver. 25. This is a willing subjection say Universalists, and they will have it that it surely indicates the salvation of all men. But we see nothing whatever to warrant such an assumption. Remark, he must reign, not till he makes all men holy and happy, but till he hath put all his enemies *under his feet.* This is an allusion to the practice of conquerors who trod upon the necks of their conquered enemies. This, however, was preparatory to their destruction, and not to their restoration, as may be seen Josh. 10 : 24–26.

"The last enemy that shall be destroyed is death." Ver. 26. Or as some would render it, "The last enemy, death, shall be destroyed." Keep in mind the apostle's subject, which is not a moral resurrection, and consequently it is not moral death which shall be destroyed. His theme is the resurrection of the body; hence, the death spoken of is animal death, or the death of the body. What Paul asserts, is simply this: "Death, the last enemy of our physical nature shall be destroyed by the resurrection. But what has this to do with making all the race holy and happy in heaven? Just nothing.

"For he hath put all things under his feet. But when he saith all things are put under him, it is manifest that he is excepted which did put all things under him. And when all things shall be subdued unto him, then shall the Son also be subject unto him that put all things under him, that God may be all in all. Ver. 27 and 28.

To say that the subjection named is a spiritual and willing one of all moral beings, is taking for granted what should be proved. It is mere assumption. When a sovereign has subdued his rebellious subjects, are we to understand by it that all are to be restored to favor, that none will suffer? A strange conclusion that. Great stress has been laid upon that part of the text which says: "That God may be all in all." But it should be remembered that it is said of Christ, (Eph. 1 : 23,) that "he filleth all in all;" also, in Col. 3 :11, "Christ is all and in all." Christ is now sovereign, as he has not yet delivered the kingdom to God the Father; and in the government of it he is now "all in all," yet millions are unsaved. This being the case, the sovereignty may be transferred to the Father, and he become all in all, in the sense of government, which is the sense intended, and still a portion of the human race may remain unsaved. Observe: it is said, "*Then shall the Son be subject unto him, that God may be all in all,*" which implies that if the Son should not deliver up the kingdom and become subject, God could not be all in all in the sense intended in the text. This plainly shows us that reference is had to authority in this passage, and not to the salvation of all men, and that by God's being all in all, nothing more is meant than that he will then govern the universe in his own person, as he did before all power in heaven and earth was transferred to Christ. Matt. 28:18. Thus we see the passage yields no support to Universalism.

"But some man will say, how are the dead raised up? and with what body do they come?" Ver. 35. This is not the language of a sincere inquirer after truth, but of an objector. It is the language of one who intended to make the most direct and positive denial of the doctrine. From the argument of the apostle it appears that the objection was based upon the fact, that the body after death becomes decomposed, and mingles with other elements, as if the objector had said: The dead can never be raised up, for the thing is unreasonable and impossible, as the body becomes decomposed, its matter is scattered and its identity is destroyed. Now, this is in substance the reasoning of a large portion of Universalists at the present time, against the resurrection of the body.

Prof. Bush, a few years since, came to their aid, and has written a book against the resurrection of the body, in which he says, (p. 40): "The resurrection of the body, if my reasoning and expositions are well founded, is not a doctrine of revelation." Again he says, (p. 70): "The resurrection body is that part of our present being to which the essential life of the man pertains." "It constitutes the inner essential vitalities of our present bodies: and it lives again in another state because it never dies." Again, (p. 170): "Let it (the resurrection) be understood as an event which transpires with every individual believer, as soon as he leaves the body."

We have rarely if ever found, even among Universalist writers, more bare-faced skepticism connected with a professed regard for the Bible, than is found in the book from which these extracts are taken. Everything in the Bible must bow to his rational deductions, as he calls them. Speaking of the body raised, he says: "It lives again in another state, because it *never dies.*" If we look at this chapter, and elsewhere in the Bible where the resurrection is taught, we shall find that it is the *dead* that are raised. We think it would puzzle Mr. Bush, with all his philosophy, to show how they are raised *from the dead* who *never die!* We have shown on ver. 23, the anti-scriptural character of the notion, that the resurrection takes place when a man dies, which need not be repeated here. The resurrection is not to be accounted for upon philosophical principles, but is an effect produced by the immediate agency of God. It is to be considered in the light of a miracle and in no other, and certainly the man who lays any claim to a belief in Christianity must admit that God can perform a miracle. Then, "why should it be thought a thing incredible with you, that God should raise the dead?" Acts 26:8.

What though the body be decomposed, and form new compositions, or be scattered to the four winds, is not Almighty power and skill adequate to the task of raising the same identical body? "Cannot the chemist take a piece of gold coin into his laboratory, file it to powder, dissolve it with acids, alloy it with other metals, grind it again to powder, throw it into the fire, and mingle it with soot, ashes, and charcoal, and yet bring out the same fine gold? And cannot he mold it again in the same die, and be perfectly sure that it is the very same gold? And is the God of all power and wisdom, whose vast laboratory is the *universe*, less skillful than the creatures he has made? And cannot *he*, who is intimately present to every particle of matter, who knows every particle by *name*, and whose power has brought every particle into *being*, collect together again the scattered fragments of the human frame, although mingled with the elements, and driven to the four winds of heaven. May we not reply to those making this objection to the resurrection of the body, "Ye do err, not knowing the scriptures, nor the *power of God.*" *Rev. C. Kingsley.*

"Thou fool, that which thou sowest is not quickened except it die: and that which thou sowest," &c. Ver. 39–49. Paul answers the objection named ver. 35, and says: "Thou fool! objectest against the resurrection of the body, because it is dead, and *decomposed,* and mingled with the dust. But your own experience shall condemn you; for the very seed you sow, whether *wheat* or other grain, never rises out of the ground except it die and become decomposed, the very objection you allege against the resurrection of the body. You talk of the body as being a mass of loathsome corruption. But even the grain you sow becomes the same in this respect. But you do not sow the body that shall be, as to this circumstance, but naked grain which putrifies in the earth; but God giveth it a body such as pleases him, differing as to the circumstances just mentioned, but composed of the same matter. It comes forth from corruption new and beautiful. So is the resurrection of the dead. The body that is sown or buried in the earth is not the same body that rises again, as to its frailty and tendency to corruption and dissolution, though composed of the same matter; for (ver. 42–44) "it is sown in *corruption,* in a state of decay: "it is raised in *incorruption.* It is sown in *dishonor;* it is raised in *glory.* It is sown in *weakness;* it is raised in *power.* It is sown a natural body," the subject of all these weaknesses; "it is raised a spiritual body," subject to none of them. For "there is a *natural* body," namely, that which was sown, "and there is a *spiritual* body," namely, that which rises again, very different as to its circumstances, but composed of the same substance. This we conceive to be the true state of the apostle's argument, without ever being intended to give the least sanction to the "germ" doctrine. Any comparison may be tortured and spoiled by tracing analogies which were never intended. The point of comparison is a state of decay and corruption, in both the grain and the body, and the coming forth out of a state of corruption to new life and vigor. It was God who gave the grain such a body as pleased him; and the God that could do the one could do the other. "It is sown in *corruption*, it is raised in incorruption." What is sown in corruption? Why the *dead body*, carrying out the metaphor of the grain. "It is raised in *incorruption*." What is raised in *incorruption?* Why that which was sown in *corruption*, namely, the *body*. What else was sown in corruption? Was the resurrection body of the new theory ever sown or buried in corruption? It was never sown or buried at all, for "it escapes from the body before it is consigned to the dust." It never was corruptible at all; for "it is *immortal* in its own *nature*." It was never *dead* at all; for "it lives in another state, because it never dies." It never had any *body* at all; "it is only called a body because of the poverty of human language." "It is sown in dishonor, it is raised in glory." What is sown in dishonor? Why, the body, in a state of dissolution, when it becomes food for worms. "It is raised in glory." What is raised in glory? Why, that which was sown, or buried, in dishonor, viz., the body. "It is sown in weakness, it is raised in power." What is raised in power? Why, that which was sown in weakness, viz., the body. "It is sown a *natural body*, it is raised a *spiritual* body." What is raised a spiritual body? Why, that which was sown a *natural* body. What else is sown or buried, but the *natural body?* It is the same *natural* body which becomes changed to a *spiritual* body by the resurrection from the dead." *Rev. C. Kingsley.*

Mr. Kingsley, in the work from which this extract is taken, is combating the denial of the resurrection of the body by Prof. Bush; hence, some of these points which have a bearing upon the Universalist controversy are unnoticed. We add a few thoughts.

The apostle in this passage is treating upon the spiritual corporeity of the resurrection body, which differs radically from flesh and blood, and is contrasting it with the gross animal putrefactive corporeity of the present state. It has been asserted that by "*the dead*," (ver. 35,) all the dead are meant. But admitting that the apostle puts into the mouth of the objector the question, "How are *all* the dead raised up?" it would by no means follow, that what is said in the rest of the chapter is true of all men. But it is not admitted that the phrase, "*the dead*," necessarily means all the dead. If Universalists contend that it does, let them never refer to Rev. 20 : 12, 13, where the expression occurs four times, to Jerusalem's destruction again. *Guide*, p. 240. The sense is to be determined by the connection in which the expression is found. It is obvious that Paul means by "*the dead*," those who had fallen asleep in Christ, (ver. 18,) who are Christ's at his coming, (ver. 23). What follows was addressed to "*brethren*," and the use of the pronoun *we*, as we find it, shows us that he was speaking of Christians only.

"*It is raised in glory*." Are we instructed by this that all men, the wicked as well as the righteous, are to be raised in glory? This is the assumption, but it is without proof. The proof is all to the contrary. Observe: The resurrection named in this chapter is to take place at the coming of Christ. Ver. 23. That all men are not to be raised to glory at Christ's coming, is evident from 1 Thess. 1 : 7–10, where a marked distinction is made between Christ's saints and the wicked. (Sec. XLI.)

We are not to make the inspired apostle contradict himself. In Acts 24 : 15, speaking of the Pharisees, who were accusing him of heresy, in repelling the charge, he says: "And have hope toward God, which they themselves allow, that there shall be a resurrection of the dead, both of the just and unjust." Now, what did the Pharisees allow? Did they allow that all men would be raised in glory? By no means. They held that the righteous only would be raised in glory; and as Paul declares he believed with them upon this point, he of course is teaching nothing contrary to this in the chapter under examination. (Sec. X.)

We must not contradict the Son of God. Where has he ever informed us that all shall be raised in glory? Nowhere. But he has informed us that the wicked shall be raised to damnation, (John 5 : 29,) which is quite another thing. Where in all the Bible is it to be found, that all men are to be glorified with Christ at the resurrection? It is not to be found; but wherever the subject is named, it is confined to saints. Take the following, (Col. 3 : 4): "When Christ, who is our life, shall appear, then shall ye also appear with him in glory." *Ye.* Who? All men? No; but Christians, as may be seen by the context. Rom. 8 : 17. "If so be that we suffer with him, that *we may be glorified together.*" This, too, is spoken of Christians, and none else. Phil. 3 : 20, 21. "For our conversation is in heaven; from whence we look for the Saviour, the Lord Jesus Christ: who shall change our vile body, that it may be fashioned like unto his glorious body." Here again the same idea is presented, namely: That Christians are those who are to be glorified with Christ when he shall come to raise the dead. Observe, too, it is not the vile soul which is to be changed, but the vile body, and this agrees with the subject of this chapter. As then, the righteous dead only are the subjects of this glorification, nothing is gained by it for the doctrine of Universalism.

"Now this I say, brethren, that flesh and blood cannot inherit the kingdom of God," &c. Ver. 50–52. Here we learn that "flesh and blood cannot inherit the kingdom of God;" that is, in its frail perishing state, hence the need of a change. But what shall become of those who are still living when Christ shall come to raise the dead? Paul reveals the mystery. "We shall not all sleep, that is, all will not die, but we shall all be changed in a moment, in the twinkling of an eye." The idea is, that the change that will pass upon the bodies of the living, will make them precisely like those of the dead after the resurrection. It will be seen, too, that the change and resurrection are simultaneous events, which forever destroys the doctrine of a progressive resurrection. Paul speaks of the same resurrection, 1 Thess. 4 : 14–17. The reader will find this transcribed in Sec. XXVI., also a quotation from Mr. Whittemore, admitting that it refers to Christ's coming to raise the dead.

In comparing 1 Thess. 4 : 14–17 with this chapter we find the following points of resemblance.

1. *Cor.* The coming of Christ is taught. Ver. 23.
   Thess. "We which are alive and remain unto the coming of the Lord." Ver. 15.
2. *Cor.* The resurrection of the pious dead is the theme. Ver. 52.
   Thess. "The dead in Christ shall rise." Ver. 16.
3. *Cor.* In stating the order, they that are Christ's are to be raised first." Ver. 23.
   Thess. The dead in Christ shall rise first. Ver.16.
4. *Cor.* The death of the body is called a sleep. Ver. 51.
   Thess. "Them also which sleep in Jesus shall God bring with him." Ver. 14.
5. *Cor.* The bodies of the living saints are to be changed when Christ shall come. Ver. 52.
   Thess. "Then we which are alive and remain shall be caught up together with them." Ver. 17.
6. *Cor.* The change of the living and the resurrection of the dead, are to take place instantly at the coming of Christ and the sound of the trump. Ver. 52.
   Thess. "The Lord himself shall descend from heaven with a shout, with the voice of the archangel, and with the trump of God." Ver. 16.

No man can well mistake the apostle. He is describing the same event in one epistle that he is in the other. How utterly at variance is this description with the doctrine that every man is raised when he dies. Some have asserted that all men are to be changed in the twinkling of an eye (ver. 52) from sin to holiness. This change is not predicated of all men, and if it were, it would prove nothing in favor of such a view, for it is not the soul which is to be changed, but the body. But Christians are the class the apostle is speaking of.

"For this corruptible must put on incorruption," &c. Ver. 53, 54. In these verses we learn that when the saints are raised that this corruptible mortal body will put on incorruption and immortality, and in this will be fulfilled "the saying that is written, Death is swallowed up in victory." What death? Why the death of the body, which is corruptible and mortal, as the whole connection shows. How false the notion, that the body is never to be raised; for what is this corruptible and mortal to be raised, if it is not the body?

"O death, where is thy sting? O grave, where is thy victory? The sting of death is sin," &c. Ver. 55–57. Here death is personified, and is said to have a sting, which is sin. What is meant by this? Its most obvious meaning is this: *Sinners fear to die because of their sins.* The tormenting fear of death, then, produced by sin, is its sting. But we ask why, upon Universalist principles, should the vilest wretch in creation fear death? This theory asserts that, "so far as admission to endless glory is concerned, the saint and sinner stand on a perfect level." *U. Ill. and Def.*, p. 266.

So we see that the most polluted sinner is just as well prepared for death, so far as the future is concerned, as the most holy saint, and has in reality no more to fear. This one idea, "the sting of death is sin," when properly considered, overthrows of itself the no future punishment theory. This theory stands directly opposed to the idea that the sting of death is sin, and therefore must be false. The apostle exclaims: "Thanks be to God, which giveth us the victory," &c. *Us.* Who? All men? No, it is Christians he is speaking of.

"Therefore, my beloved brethren," &c. Ver. 58. This verse closes up the apostle's argument, and in it he connects man's conduct in this world with his eternal state; for in referring to what he had been saying concerning the resurrection of the righteous dead, he says: "Therefore, my beloved brethren, be ye steadfast, unmovable, always abounding in the work of the Lord, forasmuch as ye know that your labor is not in vain in the Lord."

This exhortation harmonizes with the apostle's own practice, who was willing to sacrifice every worldly consideration, "if," says he, "I might by any means attain to the resurrection of the dead." Phil. 3 : 11. What did he mean by this? Did he fear that he would not be raised at all? That cannot be it, for he has declared (Acts 24 : 15) most positively that he believed in the resurrection of all men. It was the blissful resurrection of the just to which he aspired. What should we think of a Universalist minister in our time, who, in speaking of his labors and sacrifices, should assign as a reason for his so doing, his anxiety "to attain to the resurrection of the dead?" What should we think, were he to exhort others to labor and steadfastness in reference to a future state? Think? why we should think he was either playing the hypocrite, or that he had renounced his Universalism. Yet Paul is called a Universalist!

We have thus passed through that portion of this chapter which treats of the resurrection of the body. This is called the *Magna Charta* of Universalism. But where is that doctrine taught in it? Where is it once said that all shall be saved in the resurrection, or that which is equivalent to it? The place cannot be shown; but on the contrary it lies with great weight against certain doctrines advocated by Universalists with great zeal, as the following will show:

1. It is asserted in this chapter that, "By man came death." But Universalism teaches that man was created mortal, and would have died if he had never sinned, and so death is attributed to God and not to man, and thus the apostle is contradicted.

2. Universalists very generally discard the resurrection of the body. But Paul teaches it most explicitly in this chapter, as we have shown.

3. Universalists very generally teach a progressive resurrection; that men have been rising from Adam to the present time. But in this chapter it is represented as instantaneous.

4. Universalists teach that all will be Christ's in the resurrection. But the apostle speaks of those who "are Christ's at his coming," thus making a distinction between those who are his and those who are not.

5. Universalists very generally deny the second personal adven of Christ to raise the dead. But Paul teaches it, as we have seen. (Sec XLI.)

6. Universalism teaches that, "As there is no intimation of any difference of situation, or any distinction in the plentitude of their blessedness, we are authorized to believe that the resurrection state is one of equality." *Scrip. Doc.*, p. 42. But Paul makes a distinction even among the righteous in the resurrection. Ver. 41, 42.

7. Universalism says: "The phrase 'kingdom of God,' we have already frequently explained in these pages. It signifies the moral reign of Jesus upon earth." *Guide*, p. 182. But Paul uses the expression to designate the future state. Ver. 50. This must be admitted, unless the resurrection named and its predicates take place in this world; a position which would at once destroy all the capital Universalists wish to make out of the chapter.

8. Paul teaches that the sting of death is sin. Universalism teaches that sin is no more its sting than holiness, as we have seen.

9. Universalists scout the idea that our actions here, affect our future condition. Mr. Whittemore thinks it "is alike reasonable with saying that a man who sows a field of grain in Massachusetts, shall reap the harvest from it in the State of Ohio." *Trumpet*, No. 635. But Paul, as we have seen, exhorts his brethren to labor in reference to the future world.

In at least these nine particulars, are Universalist teachings at war with the evangelical teachings of Paul in this chapter.

And here we add, that with the same liberty Universalists take with certain phrases and texts, an ingenious man could, with some good degree of plausibility, deprive this whole chapter of its future-state reference. (Sec. CXXIII.) As Mr. Whittemore has furnished us a rule, (Sec. CXV,) let us now apply it to this chapter. Is it said that all men shall be holy and happy *in eternity?* Is it once said that all men shall enjoy endless bliss *beyond the grave?* As this is not said, we conclude nothing like it is meant in this chapter. Observe, we do not adopt this rule, but only apply it to show how the demand for a particular phraseology, that Mr. Whittemore makes, will destroy his own proof texts.

XCI. "*But they which shall be accounted worthy to obtain that world, and the resurrection from the dead, neither marry, nor are given in marriage; neither can they die any more: for they are equal unto the angels; and are the children of God, being the children of the resurrection.*" Luke 20 : 35, 36; Matt. 22 : 30; Mark 12 : 25.

The assumption is, that all men by the resurrection are to be made equal unto the angels, and are to die no more. But the reader will see at a glance, that what is here asserted by the Saviour is not spoken of all men, but of a particular class, "*they which shall be accounted worthy.*" This passage and Matt. 22 : 30; Mark 11 : 25 are parallel texts. They occur in our Lord's conversation with the Sadducees. The rule laid down for the interpretation of parallels, is this: "Where parallel passages present themselves, the clearer and more copious place must be selected to illustrate one that is more briefly and obscurely expressed." *Horne.*

All who acknowledge the divine authority of the scriptures, will see that this rule is a just one, as the Holy Ghost would express nothing unimportant or untrue. The text in Luke is the more full and copious, and among other things not found in Matthew and Mark, is this: "*But they which shall be accounted worthy to obtain that world and the resurrection from the dead.*" This part of the text stands directly in the way of these expounders, so they must get rid of it, by hook or by crook. To do this, the rule named is trampled under foot, as all will see, by the following comment upon these texts, from the "Guide to Universalism," p. 155 :

"John makes no record of our Lord's conversation with the Sadducees on this subject at all. Now what shall we do? We find, that two or three Evangelists who report this discourse, make no mention of the qualification found in Luke. But what then? Are we, therefore, to say that what Luke reported is not true? No, certainly not. What we are after is the weight of evidence as to the importance of that qualification. And that weight is as two to one against the importance of the words in question. We say against the *importance*, because had Matthew and Mark considered them important, (as the objection we are noticing certainly is,) it is hardly rational to conclude they would have omitted them altogether. The most probable conclusion is, that, whatever we may understand by the words now, Luke did not intend by his report to give a sense to the conversation, which the other Evangelists did not receive or record. They ought to be understood as harmonizing."

Here you have it, reader, with all its beauties. Mr. W. would not say, that what Luke says is not true. No, that would be showing the cloven foot of Infidelity too plainly. But he makes a dust about the *importance* of the qualification, if possible, to destroy the force of the Saviour's words. But there they stand faithfully recorded, and with mighty weight, too, against the Universalist perversion of this passage. Mr. W. knows this, hence his labor to render them unimportant. To labor to make them unimportant, is virtually to labor to fix upon the Saviour the character of a trifler. To say that all men *shall be accounted worthy*, is to make the Saviour utter nonsense. Why is the qualifying phrase thrown in, if there is no distinction in the future world?

It will not be admitted that the Saviour taught by implication in this passage, that a part of mankind would never be raised from the dead, as that would be fatal to Universalism; for, according to that theory, if they are not raised, then are they annihilated; and, if annihilated, then are they not saved.

With this text before us, one of three things must be admited: either Christ used words without meaning, or he taught that some would never rise from the dead, or else he had respect to some particular condition or resurrection in the future world. To adopt the first of these is impous, and to adopt the second is fatal to Universalism. The third is equally fatal to this dogma, but contains the truth, for every candid mind must see that the Saviour, in his reply to the Sadducees, referred to the preparation necessary in order to enter that blissful spirit world where the souls of the righteous go after death, and to the resurrection of the just, or the righteous dead — the same resurrection to which Paul aspired, (Phil. 3 : 11,) who was willing to sacrifice everything the world calls good and great, "if," says he, "*I might by any means attain to the resurrection of the dead.*" (See Sec. CVI.)

Now Paul was under no fearful apprehension that all would not be raised, for he has declared his belief in the resurrection of all men, (Acts 24 : 15); but he knew there was danger of his failing of the resurrection of the just, and it was *this*, he labored to secure. Again, there is a portion of the passage in Luke, which Universalists often press into their service. It is this: *neither can they die any more,*" "*are the children of God, being the children of the resurrection.*" Neither Matthew or Mark record these saying; therefore, according to Mr. Whittemore's logic, they can be of but little *importance;* yet this same man, and others of like faith, find it very convenient to pervert them, and make them very *important* in teaching their errors! Take the following oft-perverted, yet much-relied-upon text, by Universalists, to prove their doctrine: "And I, if I be lifted up from the earth, will draw all men unto me." John

12 : 32. This is recorded only by John. Matthew, Mark and Luke have said nothing about it. Is it therefore of but little importance? All will see the wickedness of adopting such a method with the scriptures, and how large a portion of the gospels must wilt away into *little importance* under such an interpretation.

The Saviour is not speaking to the Sadducees upon the subject of happiness after death, but upon the subject of marriage. The objection in their minds is not a supposed difficulty as to moral character in the resurrection, but as to conjugal relations. He tells them that they err, not knowing the scriptures nor the power of God; for in the resurrection they neither marry nor are given in marriage, but *concerning marriage,* are as the angels in heaven. This is true of all in the future state, whether good or bad; but the Saviour, as before stated, is speaking only of the good or worthy. But do men merit the bliss of heaven? The word *worthy,* as here used, is not to be understood in the sense of merit, but of suitableness, the same sense it bears in Rev. 3 : 4 : "They shall walk with me in white, for they are worthy;" that is, they are suitable or qualified. From the context we learn that the audience of the Saviour was a mixed multitude of disciples, Pharisees and Sadducees. None of them were Universalists. The Sadducees denied a future existence, and the Pharisees believed in a resurrection and endless punishment. The Saviour not only meets the objection of the Sadducees concerning the resurrection, but he also exposes their error respecting the immortality of the soul, by proving that doctrine true from the Pentateuch, the five books of Moses, which they professed to receive. In doing this, Universalists will have it that he preached their doctrine most clearly to his hearers. If he did, he was understood by them, for it would be a severe reflection upon the Great Teacher to say that he failed to make himself understood. But is there any evidence that they so understood him? Observe: Universalists have told us that the great cause of our Saviour's ill treatment by the Pharisees, was his Universalism. Well, now, here are his shrewd opposers, the Pharisees, believers in endless punishment, who are present for the express purpose that "*they might take hold of his words.*" Ver. 20. Do they raise any objections to his words on this occasion? None at all; but express their unqualified approbation thus: "*Master thou hast well said.*" Ver. 39. Would these *Partialists* have spoken thus, if he had taught them Universalism in this connection? Never. Christ exercised his whole ministry among believers in endless punishment, but he never came in collision with them upon this point, or rebuked the doctrine in a *single* instance. (Sec. CXXXII.) How unlike the course pursued by Universalist ministers in our time. What would be thought of a minister of that order who should remain silent upon the doctrine of endless punishment, and should use such a qualifying expression as "they which shall be accounted worthy to obtain," when speaking of the future state? With these facts before us, all must see that using this passage to prove the salvation of all men, is a most palpable perversion. (See Sec. CXXIII.)

XCII. "*And fear not them which kill the body, but are not able to kill the soul; but rather fear him which is able to destroy both soul and body in hell.*" Matt. 10:28; Luke 12:4, 5.

We have in the Guide, p. 92, on this declaration of the Saviour, a specimen of the treatment those texts receive which are directly opposed to Universalism. Says the author, "This passage is, confessedly, difficult of construction." Very difficult for Universalism, we admit. He then favors us with quibbles, questions, negatives, and Greek criticisms. He tells us again and again what it does not mean, but leaves us staring about to learn what it does mean. He informs us that "various explanations of this passage have been given by Universalists," and refers us to a string of authors, whose productions probably not one in a hundred of his readers will ever see. Failing to find in the Guide how the author would construe the text, we betake ourselves to files of the Trumpet, and are more successful. We find it as follows: "*Fear less them which can torture you, but have not the power lawfully to take life, than that power which is able to destroy you utterly in Gehenna.*" Mr. W. then adds: "Jesus did not tell his apostles to fear that *God* would destroy them utterly in Gehenna. On the contrary, in the same connection, he exhorts them to have confidence in God, and to have no fear that he would forsake them. They might reasonably be afraid of men, who had power according to the laws, to destroy them in Gehenna, the place of legal punishment near Jerusalem: but they were expressly told not to be afraid of God, in whose sight they were precious. At the time Jesus uttered these words, the Jews were in subjection to the Romans, and had not the power themselves lawfully to take life. The power of burning in Gehenna, or the valley of Hinnom, had passed out of the hands of the Jews; hence Jesus directed them to fear that power less which could only torture them, without destroying life, than the power which could destroy both body and life in Gehenna, or the valley of Hinnom." *Trumpet*, No. 678. Here Mr. W. denies that the fear of God is enjoined, but says that the expression "*fear him*" refers to the Roman power. Mr. Balfour expresses himself as follows: "Who then is referred to by the word *him*, whom the disciples were commanded to fear? God, we think, is the being; and is designated by what he is able to do, in the next words." *Inq.*, p. 142. So Mr. W. and Mr. B. are at variance. Who shall decide? Again, says Mr. B., "If it is said the civil magistrate is the one referred to, I then ask, can he kill soul and life, which others could not do? Could he "destroy both soul and body?" If so, then God himself could do no more than this. But, unless it can be shown that destroying both soul and body in Gehenna, was a punishment inflicted by the civil magistrate in our Lord's day, it is not at all probable that our Lord referred to him." *Inq.*, p. 141. Correct, Mr. Balfour. It is a mere assumption, destitute of any foundation in history, either sacred or profane, that the valley of Hinnom was a place for inflicting punishments, either by Jews or Romans, in our Saviour's time.

A writer in the Trumpet paraphrases the text on Mr. W.'s principle, thus: "And fear not them (i. e. the Jews) which can only torture the body, but are not able to take the life; but rather fear him (i. e. the Roman power) which is able to torture your body, and destroy your life in hell (*gehenna*)." *Trumpet*, No. 948. The doctrine inculcated by Mr. Whittemore, is this: Fear not God, neither fear the Jews, but greatly fear the Roman power? But to destroy the force of John 5: 28, 29, against their doctrine, Universalists are under the necessity of representing the Jews as those to be feared; and that when their power should be broken, great favors might be expected of the Roman power? (Sec. LXXXI.) Again, did our Lord adopt this blind method to inculcate the *duty* of *fearing men* upon his disciples? In justice, however, to Mr. Whittemore, we state that he seems to have abandoned his explanation in the Trumpet; for in his Guide, he asks, "Does it say that God will destroy both soul and body in hell? No: it says he is able to do so." So now God, and not the Romans, is the one referred to. This discrepancy between Mr. W. in the Trumpet, and Mr. W. in the Guide, grows out of the fact, doubtless, that the text is so "*difficult of construction.*" But does not God's ability, here admitted, teach most conclusively that there is a hell? Has an officer authority to put a man into prison, while there is no prison in existence? Certainly not. Mr. W. in the Guide, regards the Saviour as merely asserting the power of God, and not his determination to punish after the death of the body. The sentiment of the passage then, is this: "Be not afraid of them that kill the body, but after that have no more that they can do; but I will forewarn you whom ye shall fear; fear him which after he hath killed, hath power to cast into hell; yea, I say unto you, fear him, for he will never do it. That is, *fear him of whom ye have nothing to fear!!* There is nothing to fear; God only has the power, but he will never use it. Did the Saviour utter such solemn nonsense as this? Yet to this is Mr. W. driven in his war with God's truth.

But it is said by some, that *soul* in the text, means *animal life.* Now all know that animal life dies with the body, which reduces the passage to this absurdity: "Fear not those who kill the life, but cannot kill the life!" Did the Great Teacher mean this? Never. Mr. Page, in his commentary, furnishes no less than five different explanations of this text, some of them as diverse from each other as light is from darkness, given by W. E. Manly, J. B. Dods, H. Ballou, S. Cobb, and H. Ballou, 2d. This class of writers seem to be well agreed upon one point, viz: that the text must be murdered; but they are far from being satisfied with each other's manner of doing it. Their expositions look so absurd to themselves, that they are constantly endeavoring to mend each other's work, and if possible render them more plausible. But what is all this work, but an evidence of their warfare with the plain and evident teachings of the word of God, to get rid of the doctrine of a future hell? The passage is a very plain one, and teaches

1. That the soul is immaterial—that the body may be killed while the soul shall survive uninjured.

2. That there is such a place as hell, into which soul and body may be cast and destroyed.

3. That in the discharge of their duty the disciples were not to fear men, who could only kill the body; but they were to fear God, who is able to cast both soul and body into hell.

The word *Gehenna*, which in this text is translated *hell*, has been a subject of no small amount of labored criticism. Mr. Balfour has occupied no less than two hundred and forty pages of his Inquiry in his peculiar way, to show that the word in our Lord's time was not used to signify a place of future punishment. The Rev. Andrew Royce, in a valuable little work entitled "Universalism a Modern Invention," has taken hold of the subject with the hand of a master. His manly and conclusive reasonings contrast very strikingly when compared with the low criticisms, sophistries, perversions, and appeals to the prejudices of the irreligious, with which Mr. Balfour's book abounds. Mr. Royce lays down the following just rule of interpretation :

" *Words and phrases are to be understood in their usual and known signification, of the age and country in which they were spoken or written, unless the writer or speaker expressly attaches some other meaning to them,*" p. 15.

The propriety of this rule is shown, and some of the passages out of the twelve in which the word Gehenna occurs in the New Testament, are given, and then the history of the word is presented as follows :

" Now *what was the known and usual signification of Gehenna among the Jews in the days of Christ?*

" Universalists have told us that Gehenna was, in the days of our Saviour, the name of a valley near Jerusalem, where the filth of the city was deposited, where perpetual fires were kept burning, and where malefactors were executed ; and that when Christ used the word Gehenna, he had reference to punishment inflicted in this valley, or to other temporal calamities symbolized by punishment in this valley. Almost the whole of this statement is false. But the truth is this : The eastern section of the pleasant valley which bounds Jerusalem on the south, was anciently called the *Valley of Hinnom,* in the Hebrew tongue, *Ge Hinnom* (Josh. 15 : 8). In this valley, more than seven hundred years before Christ, the idolatrous Jews set up the image of the god Moloch, a horrid idol-god of the Ammonites, and to it they sacrificed their children by fire, (2 Chron. 28 : 3,) contrary to the express command of God (Lev. 18 : 21). About six hundred and eighty years before Christ, the good king Josiah abolished this horrid practice, and defiled the valley of Hinnom. 2 Kings 23 : 10. Henceforward the filth of the city was deposited there, and fires were kept burning to consume it. This valley now became a loathsome place, with its dead carcases perpetually breeding worms ; and its fires continually burning, became, in the mind of the Jew, a fit emblem of that place of future woe into which the wicked are cast after death. After this valley began to be considered an *image* of the regions of woe in another world, in process of time, by an easy transition very common in language, the Jews began to call those regions themselves *Gehenna* — a name derived from *Ge Hinnom*, the ancient Hebrew name of the valley. Probably for centuries before Christ came, the Jews had been using Gehenna as the name of the place of future punishment.

"We assert, then, that Gehenna was familiarly used by the Jews in the days of our Saviour, as the name of the place of future punishment — that this was its customary and known signification at that time," pp. 18–20. In proof of this position, extracts are furnished from the Talmuds and Targums, the works of Jews, who lived near the time of Christ. Mr. Royce says, "Indeed, I *find no evidence* that Gehenna was used in any other sense in the days of our Saviour. I find no evidence that there was any place on earth called Gehenna, in the days of Christ. That six or seven hundred years before Christ, there was a place near Jerusalem, called in the Hebrew of that age *Ge Hinnom*, is evident enough; that the *word* Gehenna was derived from the *words* Ge Hinnom, is also very clear. It is quite certain that the *word* Gehenna was used in the days of Christ, as the name of the world of woe. But I find no evidence that there was *ever* any place *on earth* called Gehenna." "But we have other reasons for believing that Christ employed Gehenna to designate the place of future woe. It evidently, in all the instances in which he uses it, denotes *some kind* of punishment. But where is the evidence that men were punished in the valley of Hinnom in the time of Christ or afterwards? Men were in no danger of punishment in any Gehenna *on earth*, yet our Saviour threatened wicked men with the condemnation of Gehenna. Further; the Gehenna of which Christ spake was where the 'fire is not quenched.' But were there perpetual fires in the valley of Hinnom in the days of Christ? There is certainly no evidence of it. That fires were frequently kindled in this valley, to devour the filth deposited there after it was defiled by the order of King Josiah, several hundred years *before* Christ, is probable enough; but there is no evidence that fires were unceasingly burning in the valley of Hinnom, in the days of Christ," pp. 23, 25. Mr. Royce is doubtless correct; for Universalists have never been able to produce evidence that there was such a place of punishment known by such a name in the days of Christ, near Jerusalem. All they have ever produced is the unsupported opinions of some modern commentators. The reviewers of Mr. R., it seems admit that the Targums and Talmuds are good evidence as to the meaning of Gehenna at the time in which they were written, but assert that most of the eminent critics now agree that the Targum of Jonathan Ben Uzziel, from which most of the extracts furnished by Mr. R. were made, could not have been completed till some time between two and four hundred years after Christ. To this Mr. R. replies, "This is not true. 'Most of the eminent critics' do not agree in any such thing. Only three or four are named, and three or four are not most of the eminent critics on this subject, as we proceed to show.

"1. Prideaux says that it is the general opinion, both among Jews and Christians, that this Targum 'is as ancient as our Saviour's time, if not more ancient.' 2. The Jewish historians positively assert it. Prideaux mentions particularly Zacutas, Gedalias, David Ganz, Abraham Levita, and others. 3. Prideaux, with the older critics generally, place it near our Saviour's time. 4. Calmet, author of a 'Historical and Critical Dictionary of the Bible,' places it at the same time. 5. The celebrated Orientalist and Biblical critic, Gesenius, than whom none can be a better judge, considers this Targum as ancient as the time of Christ. 6. Horne, in his 'Introduction to the critical study of the Scriptures,' says that this Targum was written about fifty years before Christ. 7. Wolfius, in his 'Bibliotheca Hebraica,' as quoted by Horne, says that Jonathan flourished a short time before Christ. 8. Parkhurst, the author of Hebrew and Greek Lexicon, quotes this Targum as evidence of the meaning of Gehenna, which I presume he would not have done, had he not supposed it nearly as ancient as our Saviour's time. 9. The editor of the 'Encyclopedia of Religious Knowledge,' after consulting, it should seem, the various authorities, places it about thirty years before Christ. 10. Professor Stuart says, 'The later Hebrew, the Talmudic and the Rabbinic, was not so late, but that it preceded the time when the New Testament was written.' It is true that doubts have been expressed by some in relation to the antiquity of this Targum. Horne says, 'From the silence of Origen and Jerome concerning this Targum, both Bauer and Jahn date it much later than is *generally* admitted.' " pp. 124, 126. In reply to this, our author introduces an argument from Prideaux, showing most conclusively that the reasons for such doubts were without weight: and then exposes a falsehood put forth by the editor of the Trumpet, viz: that " 'According to the testimony of the most learned men, the earliest of the Targums brought forward was not written till very many years after the death of Christ. In regard to the most important of all — the Targum of Jonathan — the most learned of the German critics agree that it was not written till three or four hundred years after the death of Christ.' Now this statement contains more than one falsehood. 1. 'The most learned men' do not testify that this Targum was not written till very many years after the death of Christ, as we have just seen. 2. The most learned of the German critics do not '*agree*' that it was not written till three or four hundred years after the death of Christ. Gesenius is as learned as any of them, and he places it before Christ. 3. *None* of the German critics '*agree*' that it was not *written* until three or four hundred years after the death of Christ. Some of them, it is true, suppose it mainly a *compilation* of earlier Targums, and not *completed* till between one and three hundred years after the death of Christ." pp. 130, 131.

Concerning the use of the word Gehenna, Justin Martyr, who wrote about fifty years after the death of John, says, "Gehenna is the place in which those are punished who lead unrighteous lives, and disbelieve what God has declared by Christ." Justin had the advantage of instruction from those who had conversed with the apostles, and doubtless learned the sense of Gehenna from that source. "It may be further remarked that it is obvious that Gehenna, in the language of the Jews of our Saviour's time, was the name of the place of future punishment, *from the fact that there is not the least evidence that they had any other name for this place.* The reader should be careful not to confound Gehenna with Hades. Hades was understood to be the world of spirits *generally*, in which were both the righteous and the wicked; but Gehenna was the place of future punishment, as Paradise was the place of future bliss. That the Jews believed in a place of future punishment, none deny. By what name, then, did they call it? Wherever the word is found in ancient writings, unless we except the New Testament, it uniformly stands for the place of future woe. The presumption, therefore, is certainly very strong that this was its *exclusive* meaning. If, then, Universalists deny that this word signified the place of future punishment among the Jews of our Saviour's day, it rightfully devolves upon them to show by what name they did call this place; or, if they had no *name*, by what *circumlocution* they expressed it. Besides, it is incredible if the Jews of Judea had another name for the world of woe, that it should not have appeared in the New Testament. If our Saviour had believed in such a place, he would of course have spoken of it under the name which it bore with his countrymen. If he did not believe in such a place, he would have used the name for the purpose of refuting the doctrine." pp. 130, 133.

The word Gehenna does not occur in Josephus, Philo, or the Apocrypha. To this Mr. R. replies, "The reason why this word does not occur in Josephus, shall be given in the words of Hosea Ballou, 2d. 'He sought to avoid the Hebraisms and peculiar phrases of the Jews, and to attain the classic purity of the Greek and Roman style.' Gehenna was a word *originating* and used only, in the language of Judea of our Saviour's time, which is the reason why it does not occur in Philo or the Apocrypha, all of which were written in Alexandria, and in the Greek. Mr. Whittemore, with his characteristic candor, says, 'If this word signifies the place of endless misery, how does it happen that all the apostles preserved so entire a silence in regard to it? Let Mr. Royce answer this, if he thinks it safe to attempt it!' I think it entirely 'safe' to say that if Gehenna is mentioned ten or twelve times in the New Testament, in the sense of future punishment, the doctrine is established, and not the less established because it is not mentioned one hundred times more. I think it 'safe' also to say that, since Gehenna is a word of the dialect of Judea of our Saviour's time, in writing to people out of Judea, whether Jews or Gentiles, the apostles would not have been likely to have often used the word Gehenna, for to such a people it would have conveyed no definite idea. They could, as they have already done, teach the doctrine of future punishment without naming the place of such punishment." pp. 138, 139. Following up his opponents, Mr. R. says, "Our Vermont reviewer, following Mr. Balfour, contends that the passages in the New Testament in which Gehenna is found, have exclusive reference to temporal calamities. This he infers from several propositions which he *assumes* to be true. These will be first examined. 1. He says, 'This (Gehenna) is a Hebrew or Old Testament word.' This is not true. This word does not occur in the Hebrew Old Testament, or in any translation of it. The words of which it is compounded are there, but Gehenna is not there. 2. 'Its meaning in the New Testament must be learned from the Old.' This is not true. If this word were found in the Old Testament, it does not certainly follow that it has the same meaning in the New. Paradise is found in the Hebrew text of the Old Testament, (Neh. 2 : 8; Cant. 4 : 13; Ecc. 2 : 5,) and *always* as the name of a place in another world. As many, and just about the same arguments may be adduced to prove that Paradise does not mean a place of bliss, as that Gehenna does not mean hell. 3. He adds: 'The writers of the Old Testament use this term to signify, 1st, a valley near Jerusulem; and, 2d, in a figurative or emblematic sense, to describe the temporal miseries which God was to bring on the Jews for their sins.' Neither of these assertions is true. The writers of the Old Testamant, as we have seen, do not use the word at all; and they never used *Valley of Hinnom*, from which this word is derived, in a 'figurative or emblematical sense.' I know that Mr. Balfour asserts this, but it is only his assertion, as we shall see. The passages referred to, as instances of the use of the term Valley of Hinnom in this figurative sense, are in the 7th and 19th chapters of Jeremiah. They are the following: 'And they have built the high places of Tophet, which is in the Valley of the son of Hinnom, to burn their sons and their daughters in the fire; which I commanded them not, neither came it into my heart. Therefore, behold the days come, saith the Lord, that it shall no more be called Tophet, nor the Valley of the son of Hinnom, but the Valley of Slaughter; for they shall bury in Tophet till there be no place.' Jer. 7: 31, 32. 'They have built also the high places of Baal, to burn their sons with fire, for burnt offerings unto Baal, which I commanded them not. Therefore, behold the days come, saith the Lord, that this place shall no more be called Tophet, nor the Valley of the son of Hinnom, but the Valley of Slaughter, and I will make void the counsel of Judah and Jerusalem in this place, and I will cause them to fall by the sword before their enemies.' Jer. 19: 5, 6, 7. Are the words *Valley of the son of Hinnom* used figuratively here? Are they in the least turned from their literal meaning? Every intelligent child should know better. I should have been pleased if our reviewer had informed us precisely *what* figure is used here. It must be readily discerned by every reader of these passages, that Tophet, or Valley of Hinnom, is mentioned by the prophet *simply* as the place in which the Jews had been guilty of idolatry, and in which their dead bodies should be buried in multitudes, when God, for their iniquities, should send them upon their enemies; and that, on account of this, it was to be called the Valley of Slaughter. It was a literal prediction, and was exactly and literally accomplished in the days of Jeremiah. In proof, read Lamentations.

"Thus we perceive that *every one* of this reviewer's three or four propositions are totally untrue. They are mere *naked assertions*. He does not attempt to prove one of them true. And yet, precisely such, and *no better*, is the foundation of all the various interpretations which the Universalists have given of those passages in which Gehenna is found.

"The absurdity of his argument will be fully seen by laying it out in full view. '*Hence*,' he says, (that is, from the preceding falsehoods,) '*Hence*, when Christ used Gehenna, speaking in the idiom of the Jewish prophets of the Old Testament, he signified by it, first, punishments in the literal valley of Hinnom; or second, temporal judgments coming on the Jews, symbolized by the valley and everything connected with it.' Accordingly, the passage which *reads* thus: 'And if thy hand offend thee, cut it off; it is better for thee to enter into life maimed, than having two hands to go into Gehenna, into the fire that never shall be quenched,' (Mark 9:43,) is interpreted to *mean* thus: 'It is better for thee to enter into the life or enjoyment of the gospel, or Christ's spiritual kingdom in this world, feeling as if thou hadst made a sacrifice of interests as dear as a hand, an eye, or a foot, than remain out of the gospel kingdom in possession of these interests, and fall under the dreadful judgments coming on the Jews who reject Christ, which are symbolized by Gehenna; for the fire of those divine judgments shall not be quenched or stayed in its progress, but shall effectually destroy the Jewish people.' Now strip this argument of all its sophistry, and it stands thus: Christ's words which plainly *say* one thing, must be interpreted to *mean* another and a totally different thing;

because more than five hundred years before Christ, dreadful calamities were visited upon the Jews for their idolatry, in exact fulfilment of the predictions of Jeremiah. What can be more absurd than this! For, as we have seen, the calamities in which the Jews were involved when their country was depopulated, and themselves dragged into captivity, five hundred years before Christ, or the language of Jeremiah by which these events were foretold, have no more connection with the language of Christ in which Gehenna is found, than has the calamity of Noah's flood. Nor does it appear from the subject or connection, that he had any more reference to the destruction of Jerusalem, than to the destruction of Lisbon.

"If the valley of Hinnom, mentioned by Jeremiah, had been in *his* day a place in which dreadful punishments were inflicted; if he had actually used it figuratively, to signify temporal miseries coming on the Jews as a people; if Jesus Christ had used the same words, in a similar connection, and in reference to a similar subject; there might have been some foundation for the above argument. But such are not the facts. Jeremiah spoke of *Ge Ben Hinnom*, our Saviour of *Gehenna*. Jeremiah spoke of *national* sins, and explicitly and literally predicts *national* punishments. Jesus Christ spoke of *individual* sins, and makes no allusion to the time, place, or circumstances of temporal punishment. In short, there is no more connection between the events indicated in these respective passages, than between any two events whatever." pp. 139–144.

By these extracts from Mr. Royce, the reader will see the sophistry and perversion of Universalists upon the word Gehenna. If anything more were necessary to show the absurdity of the figurative interpretations of those passages where the word occurs which Universalists contend for, it is found in the fact that they are not at all agreed among themselves with regard to their meaning, as we have before stated in this section.

The places where the word occurs in the Bible are as follows: Matt. 5:22, 29, 30; 10:28; 18:9; 23:15, 33; Mark 9: 43, 45, 47; Luke 12:5; James 3:6.

Mr. Witherell, who it seems stands high in the order as an expositor of Universalist doctrines, speaking of Gehenna, says: "I am aware that it is contended that this word came by degrees to be used to signify a place of punishment. Well, because a majority of professing Christians have come, by degrees, to believe that the word *Gehenna* signifies a place of endless punishment, is that any proof that the sacred writers used it to express such an idea? No. We are not to judge of the meaning of words, by what they have come by degrees to signify; but we should endeavor to ascertain what idea the writer meant to convey by them." pp. 20, 21.

Here we have a sample of the false issues so common with this class of writers; and in this case it discovers either an uninformed head or a bad heart, either of which is not very creditable to those editors and ministers who have so "cordially approbated" his work. (Sec. IV.) We fearlessly assert that no author who is a believer in future punishment, ever put forth the sentiment, that "*Christians have come, by degrees,* to believe that Gehenna signifies a place of endless punishment." This is a "false fact," created to serve the cause of error. The truth is this, as has been shown: Gehenna was in use among the Jews of our Saviour's time, to designate the place of future punishment, and the Saviour used it in the same sense. This is what Mr. Royce and others have asserted and proved, and not that "*Christians* have come, by degrees," &c.

XCIII. "*Not of works, lest any man should boast,*" &c. Eph. 2: 9, 10.

When Christian ministers have urged the importance of repentance, faith, and holiness here, in order to heaven hereafter, Universalists have denied that these are at all necessary in order to secure future bliss, and a crafty use is sometimes made of this text to serve their purpose. The following is an illustration: "Immortal happiness is the free, unpurchased gift of God, and every person must receive it as such; for it is 'not of works, lest any man should boast.'" *Witherell*, p. 28. According to this writer, the apostle is speaking of salvation in the immortal state. Will he abide his own construction? Then is the immortal salvation conditioned upon faith, as may be seen by the context, which reads thus: "For by grace are ye saved through faith; and that not of yourselves, it is the gift of God. Not of works, lest any man should boast." v. 9, 10. If the salvation of the text is in the immortal state, then is future salvation secured "*through faith*," which contradicts modern Universalism. But if only present salvation is intended, then we have but another instance of gross perversion; for the apostle is made to say, by this writer, that immortal happiness is not of works, lest any man should boast, when the passage asserts no such thing. Christians never assume that either present or future salvation is merited by their works, They are often grossly misrepresented by Universalists upon this point. There is a vast difference between meriting salvation by works, and using the means which God has ordained to secure the salvation which he freely gives. The latter, true Christians do while they acknowledge that it is all of grace.

XCIV. "*There was a certain rich man, which was clothed in purple and fine linen*," &c. Luke 16:19–31.

This portion of Holy Writ has proved a great source of trouble to modern Universalists, and volumes have been written by them to put out the light here shed upon the future destiny of man. With them, this is a parable. To prove this, and that the cutting off the Jews from gospel privileges, and the exaltation of the Gentiles to these privileges is intended, Mr. Rayner has put forth a book of *nine* lectures! It is not the design to enter into a lengthy refutation of this view, but only to give the reader a clue to the perversion of this scripture in their hands.

Says Mr. Whittemore, "By the death of the two individuals is intended the change which was then about to take place in the circumstances of the Jews and Gentiles. The Jews were soon to be deprived of their national privileges, because they had not made a good use of them, and were to be cast into outer darkness, and suffer the most tremendous evils that had ever befallen any nation. On the other hand, the Gentiles were to experience a change equally great. They were to be brought to a knowledge of God, and of that gospel which was preached, originally, to Abraham." *Notes on P.*, p. 235.

"In the history, as recorded by the inspiration of God, both the rich man and Lazarus died. But, if the interpretation of Universalists be true, only one died — the beggar was already dead. And when the rich man died, by losing his spiritual advantages, the beggar by obtaining them, of course came to life. In the room of placing the rich man in hell, and sending Lazarus into Abraham's bosom, the Saviour, on the ground of Universalism, would have placed the beggar in the rich man's house, adding to his splendor and his sumptuous fare, and then placed the rich man at the gate, to beg a few crumbs from Lazarus' table. Such was actually the change which took place, if the death of the rich man was the loss of his spiritual privileges, and the death of the beggar was the conversion of the Gentiles to the faith of Abraham." *Smith*, p. 103. There would be a shadow of plausibility in the Universalist interpretation, if the rich man only was represented as dying. But how the exaltation of the Gentiles to gospel privileges can be considered a death, requires a Universalist to understand; for, on their ground, the Gentiles died as well as the Jews.

Again: "There was a certain beggar named Lazarus, (Gentiles,) which was laid at his gate full of sores; and he desired to be fed with the crumbs which fell from the rich man's (Jews) table." v. 20, 21. So the Gentiles were begging of the Jews. Now when we consider the dependent relation the Jews held to the Romans, we can scarce conceive of anything more absurd than the idea that the Saviour is representing the Gentiles as begging of the Jews, and desiring to be fed with crumbs which fell from their table. What favors have the Gentiles asked of the Jews, either political or religious? The rich man (Jews) says, "Father Abraham, have mercy on me, and send Lazarus, (Gentiles,) that he may dip the tip of his finger in water and cool my tongue." "This, as Universalists teach, signifies the great desire on the part of the Jews, to be blessed with the gospel by the means of the Gentiles. But in what age have they expressed such a desire? They have never acknowledged, up to this hour, that the Gentiles have the faith of Abraham. They have never solicited instruction from them, nor desired the consolations which the Gentiles enjoy." *Smith*, p. 103.

"Between us and you there is a great gulf fixed; so that they which would pass from hence to you cannot; neither can they pass to us that would come from thence." v. 26.

If the rich man in torments represents the Jews cast off from gospel privileges, and if Lazarus in Abraham's bosom represents the Gentiles in possession of them, as Universalists assert, then it follows that if a Jew "*would pass*" over and become a Christian, he cannot, neither can a Christian embrace Judaism if he "*would.*" But is there any such impassable gulf or decree that Jews cannot become Christians if they will, or Christians become Jews? This interpretation makes the Saviour mock the Jews in sending the gospel to them; and how foolish was Paul, laboring and weeping over them to convert them to Christianity. This nonsensical and absurd explanation is contradicted by the fact that some have apostatized to Judaism from Christianity, and also by the fact that thousands of Jews have become Christians.

The rich man (Jewish nation) had five brethren he was desirous should be warned, that they might shun the torment he was then enduring. Query. Were there five other Jewish nations in danger of being cast off from gospel privileges? Who were the "five brethren?" Echo returns, who?

In noticing these points, we are complained of by Universalists for making too much of circumstances connected with this account; for these, it is said, are not to be brought against the "main design." But Mr. Ballou, the father of modern Universalism, has noticed the circumstances very minutely, and has stated their meaning in his peculiar way, (*Notes*, p. 252–256,) and Mr. Rayner and others have turned the circumstances against the sense given to the passage by evangelical Christians, with all the art they are capable of. Some have gone so far as to deny its future reference, because of the circumstance of the rich man and Lazarus represented as having eyes, finger, and tongue, and thus placing themselves by the side of atheists, who reject the God of the Bible, who is pure spirit, because he is said to have eyes, ears, mouth, arm, &c. Such seem not to understand that things spiritual and eternal are represented to us in this world by visible and material objects. This faulting us for meddling with the circumstances, arises from the fact that they are all against them. But the circumstances involve no more difficulty than their "main design." With them, the Saviour's main design was to illustrate the admission of the Gentiles to gospel privileges, and the rejection of the Jews. But where do they learn this? Has Heaven given them a special revelation upon this point? Surely there is nothing in the passage or its connection, that in the least indicates it. No common reader of the Bible would receive even a hint of it there. It is unnatural and false, manufactured to get rid of the solemn import of the passage.

The main design of the Saviour appears to have been to present the difference in the future world between a wicked rich man and a righteous poor man. In proof we submit the following:

In the context the Saviour was discoursing, not about giving the gospel to the Gentiles, or rejecting the Jews, but on the subject of avarice. He told the Jews that they could not serve God and Mammon, rebuked them for their worldliness and self-righteousness; and "the Pharisees also, who were covetous, heard all these things, and derided him." Ver. 14. He then introduced the subject of the rich man and Lazarus, instructing them that their state in hades, if they were covetous and served Mammon rather than God, would be one of torment, notwithstanding their wealth, while the righteous poor would enjoy bliss. This is natural and easy, and applies with force to the subject. Another consideration which goes to give it a future state reference, is the belief of those to whom it was addressed. Says Mr. Balfour upon this passage, "Our Lord was reasoning with the Pharisees, who believed the popular opinion, that in hades there was a place of torment." *Inq.*, p. 83.

This being the fact, how, we ask, must they have understood him? This is a parable, say Universalists. Admitting this, what is gained to their cause? Just nothing; for parables are founded on facts and not on fiction. Examine every one of the Saviour's parables in the New Testament, and it will prove true in every instance, unless this must be considered an exception. Take the following:

"The kingdom of heaven is like unto leaven, which a woman took, and hid in three measures of meal, till the whole was leavened." Matt. 13:33. Now this is founded not upon fiction, but fact. Women, leaven, meal, are all real things, and not fictitious. And then there was such a practice common as is here stated, viz., for women to put leaven into meal. If there were no women, no leaven, no meal, and if women never put leaven into meal, then this parable would be lame and forceless. If we should admit that Christ intended to illustrate the giving of the gospel to the Gentiles, and the rejection of the Jews by this, what would follow? It would follow that this, like other parables of the Saviour, is founded upon acknowledged facts. Among other facts, the following are recognized, whatever the scope or design intended, viz., that there are such men as rich men and beggars, and that some of the former fare sumptuously and are clothed in purple and fine linen, while some poor beggars lie at their gates covered with sores; that there are such animals as dogs, such a thing as death, such beings as angels, and such a place as hell, (hades,) where departed souls are tormented. Now if these are not facts, then has the Saviour founded one parable upon fiction; and that, too, without disabusing the minds of his hearers, who were laboring under the belief of this fiction. Would a Universalist minister in our day base a parable upon torments in the future state, without first informing the people that it was all fiction? So far from this are they, that they spend much of their time in efforts against the doctrine, in holding it up as the greatest of errors. But in no *single* instance do we find the Saviour, or any of his apostles, so employed, notwithstanding they passed their days on earth in the midst of those who believed and taught the doctrine. Compared with moderns they were very inefficient Universalist ministers! (Sec. CXXXII.)

The truth is, Christ has shown us here, in terms that few ungodly men can contemplate and be at ease, that there is a world of woe. He has raised the curtain that intervenes between that dark world and this, and exhibited to us how fearful a thing it is to be lost. He teaches us that our destiny is fixed at death, and that if sinners will not yield to the persuasions and heed the warnings they have in this world to escape the "place of torment" by the means which God has provided, none others will be employed, neither would it avail anything in their case should one be sent from the dead.

It has been asserted that there is no evidence that the rich man was bad, or that Lazarus was good. That the rich man was wicked, and the poor man good, is implied through the whole passage. Indeed, what of force there is in this, lies with all its weight against applying it to Jews and Gentiles. The rich man, with Universalists, is the Jewish people, who are to be cast down and punished for their wickedness. The rich man is a type of this wicked nation. Was he good or bad? No more need be said.

XCV. "*For therefore we both labor and suffer reproach, because we trust in the living God, who is the Saviour of all men, especially of those that believe.*" 1 Tim. 4 : 10.

That the reader may have a fair sample of the perversion of this text, we present the following extract:

"And it is no less true than strange, that the apostles were persecuted for preaching this same doctrine of universal salvation. Will the reader take Paul's word for the truth of this? Hear him: 'This is a faithful saying and worthy of all acceptation, for therefore we both labor and suffer reproach, because we trust in the living God, who is the Saviour of all men, especially of those that believe.' Now God is the Saviour of no more than he saves, and hence, if Paul can be credited as to the cause of his labor and reproach, it was for believing and preaching the salvation of all men." *Trumpet*, No. 805.

Universalists would render this passage subservient to their cause in two ways:

1. By assuming that the apostles suffered reproach for preaching Universalism; than which, nothing can be more false. Whatever was the nature of, or however extensive, the salvation, it was not for preaching it, that they suffered reproach; but it was for *trusting in the living God,* as all must see, who will give a moment's attention to the language. The phrase, "*living God,* is applied in the scriptures to the true God, to distinguish him from the dead gods of the heathen. 1 Thess. 1 : 9. Paul, Timothy, and others, preached him, and exposed the folly of those who worshipped idols. Acts 17 : 16–30. Their work was a crusade against idolatry, and for this they suffered reproach.

2. Universalists assume from this text, that all men will be holy and happy in the future state. But has Paul said any such thing in the passage? Let us see. That God *is* the Saviour of all men, we firmly believe.

1. He is the providential Saviour of all men living. Acts 17 : 28.

2. He is the gracious Saviour of all men. John 1 : 9; Tit. 2 : 11, 12.

See, also, Sec. XXIX., where Rom. 5 : 18, 19 is examined. Universalists hold that all men will be saved in the future state by the resurrection. Speaking of the common salvation named in this passage, Mr. Williamson says: "Well, then, if man's resurrection from the dead depends upon God alone, and no human power can effect it, so must the state and condition of man depend equally upon God, and be equally beyond the reach of human agency." "The truth is, that man can by his faith and works do something towards ameliorating his condition here; but he cannot procure his resurrection from the dead, and if he cannot procure the thing itself, much less can he procure any modifications of it. *All* that man is, and *all* that he *can be* in the resurrection, he must owe to God alone; his feeble work cannot reach one line beyond the grave." After speaking of what is to be accomplished by the resurrection, he adds: "This is the salvation which God has prepared for a world, and in this sense God is the Saviour of all men." *Expo. and Def. of U.*, pp. 167–169.

Mr. Whittemore says: "This heavenly image which we lost, we obtain back again at the resurrection of the dead." "They will be children of God, bearing a moral likeness to him. This will be the state of all who shall be raised from the dead." *Guide*, pp. 37 and 44.

Reader, can you believe that the apostle, in the text under consideration, meant to say, that God *will become* the Saviour of all men in the resurrection state, especially in the present life, of those that believe? This you must believe, if you receive the construction Universalists put upon the apostle's words. They refer one branch of it to the future state, and the other to the present life, which is wholly unauthorized. They tell us that the special salvation pertains to this life, and the common to the future. Now if we receive it as true that God will become the Saviour of all men in the future state, while he is the special

Saviour of those that believe in this life, then is the salvation of this life greater and more glorious than the salvation of heaven; for God is the Saviour *especially* of those that believe, i. e., he is their Saviour in a higher sense than he is the Saviour of all men. None will deny but the Bible represents the salvation of the heavenly state as infinitely greater than the salvation of believers in this life, however holy they may be. But Universalists, by referring one part of this text to the future, and the other to the present life, have made the heavenly salvation the lesser, or common, while the greater, or special salvation, is in this world! We ask, by what authority do Universalists take their dissecting knife, and cut this text into two portions; referring a part to the future state, and a part to this world? The most superficial thinker upon the subject will see, that it either wholly refers to this world, or else it wholly refers to the future. We deny the future state reference of any part of it. The apostle was speaking of what *then* existed. He first states that he and his brethren suffer reproach, for trusting "in the living God." He then states that God IS (not *will be*, in the resurrection), the Saviour of all men, especially of those that believe.

It is true, that those who experience this special salvation through faith, if they continue in the faith, will be saved in the future world; for Paul, in view of death, could say, (2 Tim. 4:7, 8): "I have kept the faith; henceforth there is laid up for me a crown of righteousness," &c.

Mr. Williamson, speaking of the word "*especially*," says: "The idea is, that this word limits the salvation of God to believers alone. Now Paul wrote to Timothy saying: 'The cloak that I left with thee at Troas, bring with thee when thou comest, and the books, but *especially* the parchment.' There is precisely as much reason in saying, that Paul did not want the cloak and books, because he said '*especially*' the parchment, as there is in saying, that God is not the Saviour of any but believers, because the text says especially of them that believe;

and if I tell you that Paul wanted both the cloak and books, you ought to object at once, and remind me that he said he especially wanted the parchment." *Expo. and Def. of U.*, p. 166.

This is what is called in logic, a "false issue." It is based upon the assumption that it is denied that God is the Saviour of all men; whereas, no Christian writer, to our knowledge, ever did so; but on the contrary it is contended, in opposition to Universalists, that he *is* the Saviour of all men, and not that he *will become* such in eternity.

It will be time enough to use this illustration when we deny that God is the Saviour of all men, and when Universalists shall have proved that it indicates the salvation of all in the immortal state. The book and parchment illustration is just no illustration of the case.

By the quotations it will be seen that Universalists consider the resurrection of all men as equivalent to the salvation of all men. To express their views, then, the text should read: "Therefore we both labor and suffer reproach, because we trust in the living God, who will raise all men from the dead, especially those that believe!"

A writer in the Banner (Sept. 4, 1842) made quite a flourish over our admission, that God *is* the Saviour of all men, and called us "an unconscious Universalist." He bases his argument upon the immutability of God, thus: "Now if God *is* the Saviour of all men, of course he always will be the Saviour of *all*, from the fact that he changes not. We should think that any man without his logical glasses, could discover from the nature of God, that whatever he *was*, he *is*, he always *will be*." By applying his own logic it will be seen that Mr. J. H. S. is an unconscious believer in the endless anger of God. "God IS angry with the wicked every day." Ps. 7:11. Now, if God *was* angry with the wicked when the Psalmist wrote, he is *now* angry with the wicked, and "always *will be*." God's anger then is endless. Paul, speaking of the vengeance of God, says: "It is a fearful thing to fall into the hands of the living God." Heb. 10 : 31.

Now if it *was* a fearful thing to fall into the hands of God, because of his vengeance, it *is now*, and "always *will be*" for "he changes not." But how does endless vengeance comport with the endless salvation of all men? (Sec. XVIII.) The same application might be made to 2 Kings 22 : 13; Ps. 5 : 5; 11 : 5, and a host of other texts. If the man has proved anything by his argument, he has proved Universalism to be false. One step more. If the unchangableness of God secures the salvation of all in the immortal state, because he is the Saviour of all now, then for the same reason the salvation of heaven and of this world must be exactly the same, not only in nature, but also in degree; for according to the argument, what he is to his creatures as Saviour now, he always will be; and as there is now much of sin and misery in existence, while God *is* the Saviour of all men, so there always will be, for "he changes not." If this argument is sound, nothing is gained by any of our race in exchanging worlds, and so Paul was mistaken when he said, "to die is gain." No more need be said to show the weight of such an argument.

We see, then, that using this text to prove the salvation of all men in the future state, or to prove that the apostles were persecuted for preaching Universalism, is a gross perversion of its clear and evident teaching.

XCVI. "*Then said Jesus unto them, take heed and beware of the leaven* (*doctrine, ver.* 12) *of the Pharisees and of the Sadducees.*" Matt. 16 : 6.

Mr. Whittemore, referring to this text, says: "Jesus warned the people against the doctrine of the Pharisees, who are well known to have believed in endless punishment." *Guide*, p. 42.

We know that the Pharisees believed in endless punishment; and we also know that it is a gross perversion of our Lord's words to say, that in this text, his disciples are warned against this doctrine. An Atheist might, with just as much propriety, force these words into his service, by saying: "Jesus warned the people against *the doctrine* of the Pharisees, who are well known to have believed in the *being of God*," and thus prove that the Saviour was an Atheist, and that he taught his disciples Atheism! Give us the liberty taken with this text, and we will take the position that a Christian ought not to believe in the being and unity of God, a general providence, the immortality of the soul, a resurrection, or eternal bliss; and should any call in question such unbelief, they shall be silenced with, "beware of the doctrine of the Pharisees," for they held all these doctrines. Had the Jews been asserting their doctrine of eternal punishment, or calling in question our Saviour's Universalism, there might be some propriety in considering the warning as against future punishment; but nothing of the kind appears in the context.*

This warning appears to have been directed against the superstitious and hypocritical teachings of the Jews about signs. The Jewish people, it is well known, were desirous of the appearing of the Messiah; but by the erroneous doctrines which had obtained among them, relative to the manner of his coming and the nature of his reign, they were led to reject him, and still to look for the signs of his appearing. Hence the Pharisees and Sadducees insultingly and hypocritically ask him for a sign, ver. 1. Our Saviour, after upbraiding them with dullness of apprehension, and calling them hypocrites, and a wicked and adulterous generation, seeking after a sign, declares, "There shall no sign be given unto it, but the sign of the prophet Jonas." See ver. 3 and 4. Christ had already wrought miracles in their presence sufficient to demonstrate his Messiahship, and but one

* Mr. Thayer, a Universalist minister, in his late work, asserts that endless punishment was the popular doctrine, both of Jews and Pagans, in the Saviour's time, and, also, that the Saviour maintained a position of "*entire silence*" toward it. *His. of E. Punishment*, p. 137.

more was necessary to fulfill the scriptures, to take away the scandal of the cross, and to establish his religion; that was his resurrection from the dead, which was typified in the case of Jonah.

Of such doctrine as this, that led the people to shut their eyes against all the evidence of his Messiahship, and still to look for the coming of their deliverer, Christ would have his disciples beware; but not of the doctrine of future and eternal punishment.

We may observe, too, that this warning was against the doctrine of the Sadducees, as well as Pharisees; but it is well known that the Sadducees no more believed in endless punishment, than they did in Universalism. They, too, were the enemies of our Lord, as well as the Pharisees. In Luke 12 : 1, the Saviour warns his disciples against "the leaven of the Pharisees," which he says is "hypocrisy." But we think his meaning in Matt. 16 : 6, is given above; for, says Paul, (1 Cor. 1 : 22): "The Jews require a sign."

We assert, *That while the Saviour exercised his ministry among believers in endless punishment; that he never pointed it out as an error, or warned the people against it in a single instance, and that this omission can never be reconciled with the idea that he was a teacher of Universalism.* The text here examined is the only one we have ever seen produced to disprove this position, and with what force the reader can judge. See Sec. CXXXII.

XCVII. "*And this I say, that the covenant, that was confirmed before of God in Christ, the law, which was four hundred and thirty years after, cannot disannul, that it should make the promise of none effect. Is the law then against the promises of God? God forbid.*" Gal. 3 : 17–21.

In answer to an objection raised by himself, that Universalists keep the threatenings of God concealed, Mr. Williamson quotes these texts, and says: "I know, as well as you can know, that there are many threatenings in the law, but I tell you that these are not against the promises; and when you explain them in such a manner as to make them conflict with the promises, you pervert them." Mr. W. then goes on to state, that endless punishment cannot be true, for it is against the promises, taking for granted what he would do well to prove, viz., that God has promised to save the whole human race in the future state. And then refering to Rev. 21 : 4, he adds: "Here is the covenant, it promises with the most solemn certainty, that there shall come a time when there shall be no more death, neither sorrow, nor crying, neither shall there be any more pain." *Ex. and Def. of U.*, p. 144.

This writer perverts Gal. 3 : 17–21, by making it teach that God covenanted with Abraham to make all the human race holy and happy in eternity, when no such promise was ever made. (Sec. I.) The apostle in the chapter shows that justification by faith is promised in the covenant, and that the Gentiles, as well as the Jews, might become heirs if they would believe in Christ. Mr. W. perverts Rev. 21 : 4 by forcing it to teach that there shall be no more death, sorrow, crying, or pain, for any of the human family; whereas this is affirmed of *the inhabitants of the New Jerusalem* only. Turn to it and read what precedes and follows. See, also, Sec. LXXXVII, where it is examined.

That which requires such gross perversions to sustain it, cannot be the truth of God.

XCVIII. "*Then was Jesus led of the Spirit into the wilderness to be tempted of the devil,*" &c. Matt. 4 : 1–11; Luke 4 : 1–13 : Mark 1 : 12, 13.

The doctrine of the existence of the devil enters so far into the essence of Christianity, that those who deny it generally deny all the peculiar and fundamental doctrines of the Bible. No man is properly acquainted with the condition of his race until he sees that "the whole world lieth in the wicked one."

1 John 5 : 9. See *Clarke in loco.* Ministers do not execute their high commission until they turn men " from the power of Satan to God." Acts 26 : 18. " For this purpose the Son of God was manifested, that he might destroy the works of the devil. 1 John 3 : 8. Only the existence and works of the devil can account for the advent and death of the Son of God. A man's religious sentiment may usually be detected by what he holds respecting the devil. If he will have it that the devil means evil propensities, carnal mind, or persecuting Jews, you may generally class him with the so called *liberals*, which in general is but another name for modern infidels. One grand device of the devil is to beget a disbelief in his own existence, for he knows that " in vain the net is spread in the sight of any bird." Prov. 1 : 17. This done he springs his snare, and his victims " are taken captive by him at his will," boasting all the while of their superior liberty and light, and crying out, " no personal devil." To this class of men, and especially those of them who are obliged to profess a regard for the Bible in order to teach their errors, the Saviour's temptation has ever proved a source of trouble. As a theological curiosity, and a specimen of the treatment of this subject by the visible father of American Universalism, we present the following from Mr. Ballou. He inquires :

" But what means the scripture, which speaks of a devil ? one who was a liar from the beginning, &c. I answer : I have no objection to believing that there is such a devil as the scriptures speak of. He is called the old serpent, and is the same I have described which beguiled the woman in the beginning ; and it is the carnal mind, which is enmity against God. Any person who is wholly dictated by a fleshly mind, may justly be called a devil, as in the case of Judas and Peter. As our Lord said to the Jews, also, " Ye are of your father, the devil ; and the lusts of your father, ye will do." But says the objector, do you think our Saviour was tempted by the powers of the flesh, when it was said, he was tempted by the devil ? I ask in my turn, for what is this particular circumstance introduced? If we cannot prove, from our own experience, that we are tempted by some other being than our own fleshly appetites, would it be anything more than a speculative belief, to admit another tempter? But says the objector, that does not answer the question. Then let us look at his temptations; when he hungered, he was tempted; by what? and to what? Answer, by hunger, to turn stones into bread. Here was a fleshly appetite. When he had a view of all the kingdoms of the earth, and their worldly glory, he was tempted to avail himself of them. Here was natural ambition, such as gave rise to the victories of an Alexander. When on the pinnacle of the temple he was tempted to cast himself down, as it was written concerning him, that God would give his angels charge over him, &c. Here was that passion which gives rise to presumption, and wishes to avoid duty. But it is said, the *devil taketh him about*, thus and so; not literally, however, for there is no *mountain* in the *world* that commands a *prospect* of but a *small part* of the *kingdoms* of the *world*. The *exceeding high mountain* on which our Redeemer stood, when he saw all the kingdoms of the world, and the glory of them, was the mountain of *human pride*. Remember, when a person is *on* a mountain, the mountain is *beneath his feet*. So was this mountain of *human pride beneath the feet* of our sinless Redeemer." *Ballou on Atonement*, pp. 51, 52.

Here is Universalist theology with all its beauties. The exceeding high mountain is the mountain of human pride, and by the assistance of the devil (Matt. 4 : 8) the Saviour has got human pride beneath his feet!! But what is this devil? Mr. B. has just told us that "*it is the carnal mind, which is enmity against God.*" He has told us, too, that this mountain of human pride was "beneath the feet of our *sinless Redeemer.*"

It comes to this, then; the sinless Redeemer's carnal mind, which is enmity against God, placed him in such a position that human pride was beneath his feet. Abominable! Did the

Saviour have a carnal mind or enmity to God urging him on in this direction? Is it by the carnal mind that victory is gained over human pride? Was the holy Saviour inflated with human pride before his conflict with Satan? Mr. Ballou flatly contradicts himself by first saying that the devil is the carnal mind, which the Saviour must have had in order to be tempted by it, and then calling the Saviour the "sinless Redeemer." The fact is clear that there is no possible way to get rid of the idea of a personal devil in the temptation of Christ, without making the Saviour a sinner, which is to contradict the Bible. 1 Peter 2:22; Heb. 7:26; 1 John 3:5; Rev. 3:7.

Let us apply Mr. Ballou's theory to that important passage found Eph. 6:12: "For we wrestle not against flesh and blood, but against principalities, against powers, against the rulers of the darkness of this world, against spiritual wickedness in high places."

This is given by the apostle to prepare his brethren to stand against "the wiles of the devil." Ver. 5. Says Mr. Ballou, "Any person, who is wholly dictated by a fleshly mind, may be justly called a devil." But the apostle says, in striving against the devil, "we wrestle *not with flesh* and blood." So we see that Mr. B. and the scriptures are at odds again.

Apply the Universalist theory of personification to Matt. 8:28–34, where it is stated that the devils besought the Saviour that, in case he cast them out, he would suffer them to go into a herd of swine. "And he said go; and when they were come out, they went into the herd of swine," &c. In this account, who besought Christ to suffer them to enter into the swine? Were they evil principles, fleshly minds, carnal natures, or insanity? Did these, or any of them, leave these men and enter the swine? Preposterous! Says Dr. Clarke upon this passage: "Certain *doctors* in both sciences, *divinity* and *physic*, gravely tell us that these demoniacs were only common *madmen*, and that the disease was supposed, by the superstitious Jews, to be occasioned by demons. But, with due deference to great characters, may not a plain man be permitted to ask, by what figure of speech can it be said that "two diseases *besought* — *went out* — *filled a herd of swine* — *rushed down a precipice,*" &c. What silly trifling is this! Some people's creeds will neither permit God nor the devil to work; and, in several respects, hardly to exist. For he who denies divine inspiration will scarcely acknowledge diabolical influence." Well might Dr. Clarke call this "silly trifling!" Whatever might be thought of their opinions, such men would certainly command more respect for themselves were they to come out boldly, as did their former brother, Abner Kneeland, and cast aside the whole book of God. That the Universalist denomination is rife with skeptical views, concerning some of the plainest teachings of the Bible, is well known to many. Its advocates have been for a long time warming and nourishing the serpent Infidelity into vigorous life. Thus strengthened in the order, he has grown rampant, and it has been with some degree of difficulty that the leaders have prevented a full exhibition of his ugly proportions to the gaze of those without. A resolution passed by the Boston Association of Universalists, at Cambridgeport, Nov. 1, 1847, furnished the occasion for their tearing the masks from each other's faces. The resolution was against certain rank Infidel sentiments, which some, more bold than the rest, had begun to proclaim openly. (Sec. CXVIII.) The aggrieved brethren subsequently published "A Statement of Facts," showing most clearly that they had adopted no new method to dispose of offensive scriptures; that Mr. Ballou long before this had been as infidel as they were. As an illustration of this, Mr. J. W. Hanson, whose name, with others, is appended to the document, and is still a minister of the order, gives the following anecdote.

"The following incident is related by the respectable physician mentioned therein, who is ready to vouch for its substantial accuracy: In the year 1814, Father Ballou preached in the old township of Dunstable, and was entertained by Mr. Hunt, father of Eben Hunt, M. D., now of Danvers. On reaching the house at the close of the services, an older brother of Eben's, who was said to be somewhat skeptical, said to Mr. Ballou: 'What do you make of the account of the devils which were driven into a herd of swine?' 'Ah!' said the old gentleman, 'I was always sorry they put *that* story in!'"

The infidelity here developed needs no comment. Hear Mr. Hanson again in this same document:

"That the principle which, when logically carried out, results in Rationalism, is very general in the Universalist body, is veritably true. Rev. A. A. Miner was asked, during the recent session at Cambridgeport, if he believed that Christ cast out devils from a human body; he answered: 'Most assuredly I do.' The reply was, 'You are the first Universalist I ever heard say so.' Rev. L. R. Page replied, 'And you are the first I ever heard deny it.' This conversation needs to be explained to convey a correct idea. There is not a single Universalist preacher who believes that Christ ever cast out devils or demons from a human being. They believe that those who were operated upon by the Saviour were *insane* or *epileptic*. And yet the Bible says nothing of the sort. Whenever, therefore, a Universalist discovers the word *demon* or *devil*, as *he does not believe in such*, he exercises RATIONALISTIC PRINCIPLES, and calls it *insane*. Why does he then fault those who apply the same principle to other subjects? The Jews believed that literal devils possessed men, and Christ used their precise phraseology. The Universalist *Commentary* may say that Christ cured men of *epileptic fits;* the BIBLE says he cast out *devils.*" *St. of Facts*, *Feb.* 5, 1848.

Here it is contended, not by an enemy to Universalism, but by one of its advocates in good standing in the order, and now editor of the Gospel Banner, in Maine, that the Bible teaches just what Christians have ever believed concerning the Saviour's casting out devils, and that Universalist preachers do not believe it. What is all this but an admission that the Bible and Universalism stand opposed to each other? Yet these men, who thus assert their own supremacy over the Bible, stand up behind it and preach to the people! With such license and recklessness, what matters it to them whether they take their text from Sinbad the Sailor or the Bible, other than that they can more successfully deceive the people by the latter?

The text in James 1 : 14 is brought against the personality of the devil. It reads thus: "But every man is tempted, when he is drawn away of his own lust, and enticed." The argument amounts to this: James says, men, when tempted, are drawn away by their own lusts; therefore, there is no personal devil to tempt men. This is as logical as the following: Floods sometimes destroy buildings; therefore, buildings are never destroyed by fire! The objection based upon this text vanishes when it is understood that no Christian contends that the devil is the only source of temptation. It by no means follows that because men are drawn away by their own lusts, that there is no personal devil who exercises an agency in tempting the fallen race of Adam.

It has been urged that the Saviour called Peter, Satan, (Matt. 16 : 23,) and Judas a devil (John 6 : 70.) Well, suppose that Judas, by a figure of speech, for his wickedness was called a devil; and Peter, for his opposition to the Saviour's prediction concerning his death, was called Satan: does it follow that there is no real or personal devil? The idols of the heathen are called gods, and the Psalmist says of wicked judges, "Ye are gods" (Ps. 82 : 6); but does it follow that there is no real or true God? Says Mr. Hare, "When it is so plain a fact that there is an infernal devil and spiritual Satan, it can answer no purpose to quote a hundred texts of scripture to prove that men or women are sometimes called devils, (i. e., calumniators,) or satans (i. e., adversaries). The existence of ten thousand human devils, and earthly satans, brings no evidence that there is no chief of demons, nor spiritual devil or hellish Satan." *Errors of Soc.*, p. 54. What would be thought of us, were we to set up an argument against the existence of God, based upon the fact that images and men are called gods in the Bible? A graceless work, truly; but no more so than the work of Universalists upon the subject under consideration. A cunning Atheist could say as many smart and witty things against the Bible account of the being of God, as any Universalist can against the existence of the devil.

We are sometimes charged with believing in an "omnipresent and almighty devil." When Universalists attack this "castle in the air," we admit that they are sure to demolish it. Christians believe in no such being. In Matt. 4: 10, 11, the terms devil and satan are used to designate the same being; and in Luke 11: 15, this Satan, the Devil, Beelzebub, is called the chief of demons; hence our Lord attributes to him a kingdom. Luke 11: 18. This chief has subordinates, (Matt. 25: 41,) and these are very numerous, as we are given to understand. Luke 8: 30. From these and many other Scriptures which might be adduced, we are authorized to conceive of Satan as the head of a vast spiritual dominion; and thus account for the extent of the agency he exerts in tempting and seducing the world, and that, too, without conceiving of him as omnipresent. When Napoleon made Europe tremble with the terror of his arms, his power extended far beyond his personal presence, and what was accomplished by his armies, was attributed to him. So with Satan's legions; what they accomplish is attributed to him. How rapidly spirits move, is not for us to determine. It is possible they move as quick as thought: at any rate, Satan is represented as very active, "going to and fro in the earth." Job 1: 7; 1 Pet. 5: 8.

"Should the impossibility of a finite being tempting many persons, in different places, at one time, leave an apparent difficulty on this subject; it must be noticed, 1. That the devil has many demons under his direction. 2. That we do not precisely know what relation a spirit has to place. 3. That though the power of Satan is not infinite, it may be very great. 4. That we are not sure that evil spirits may not produce effects which often remain when those spirits are no longer immediately present. We know that a moral principle once imbibed often produces effects for a long period after the departure of the person from whom it has been imbibed." *Errors of Soc.*, p. 57.

It is asked, "why does God permit a subordinate being to accomplish so much mischief as is attributed to the devil?" We in turn ask, why does God permit so much mischief as is attributed by Universalists to the "principle of evil," or "carnal mind?" Moral evil exists, and is produced by subordinate beings; and if its existence reflects ingloriously upon the Divine government, it matters but little how it has obtained in the world, that is, so far as the honor of the Divine administration is concerned. We learn from the Bible that both men and devils have an agency in producing it. A hundred unanswerable questions might be proposed concerning the origin of the devil, and his work; and as many, equally unanswerable, might be propounded concerning the origin and existence of the "principle of evil." What important truth is there in the Bible but may be destroyed by this process, if admitted to be correct? Take the existence of God, which Universalists profess to believe in common with others, and who does not know that questions may be proposed upon this subject to almost any extent, such as no sane man would think of answering. "Fools may ask questions that wise men cannot answer" upon this, as well as other subjects. Negatives and artful questions concerning things clearly revealed in the Bible, have formed the stronghold of infidelity the world over; and Universalism has reaped a rich harvest from this soil, in its opposition to truth. The question with the Christian is not what does skepticism say concerning heaven or hell, God or the devil, but, WHAT DOES THE BIBLE SAY?

But it is inquired, "Does piety depend upon the belief of a devil?" Not Universalist piety; but true piety depends much upon it. Mark it, reader; when you find a man who will deny the existence of the devil, with all the evidence the Scriptures afford of the fact, that man's mind is prepared to deny any other doctrine, no matter how clearly revealed, if it is not in accordance with his feelings. Christian piety includes the duty of believing the truths and warnings of God's word. It includes the duty of resisting the devil, that he may flee from us (Jas. 4 : 7) ; it consists in the exercise of watchfulness, which acquaints us with his devices (2 Cor. 2 : 11) ; and in holding fast the shield of faith, wherewith we shall be able to quench all the fiery darts of the wicked one (Eph. 6 : 16). These are the influences that are upon the hearts of pious Christians, prompting to watchfulness, prayer, and zeal in the cause of Christ ; and the best heads and hearts that ever adorned the world, have been under such influences ; being conscious, by the struggles they had with the powers of darkness, of the personal existence of the devil. But those who are blinded by the god of this world, and are under the influence of the spirit that now worketh in the children of disobedience, (Eph. 2 : 2,) who are led captive by the devil at his will, (2 Tim. 2 : 26,) have no such conflicts, and it is not very strange that in their pride and self-procured blindness they should deny his existence, and see in those scriptures which reveal his being, the "carnal mind," "principle of evil," or "evil personified," or anything or nothing, as a depraved imagination may dictate.

One thought more. It is abundantly admitted by Universalists themselves, that the Jews in our Saviour's time, believed in the existence of personal devils or demons. Mr. Hanson, as we have seen, has asserted this. Speaking of Christ, Mr. Balfour says, "he spoke of demons as real beings ; of Beelzebub, as the prince of devils or demons ; and of Satan, or the devil, as an evil being" (*Essays*, p. 67) ; and Mr. Hanson asserts that "Christ used their (the Jews) precise phraseology" respecting them. Now the question is, was it any part of the Saviour's mission to point out and correct the errors of the age in which he lived ? Mr. Whittemore shall answer. "Our Saviour, when on earth, labored hard to root up the plants which his Father had not planted. He knew that error was injurious to man, and that he performed an act of kindness and duty in exposing it. It would be a task far too arduous to mention all the instances recorded in the New Testament, of Christ and his apostles pointing out and contending against the errors of the age in which he lived." *Trumpet*, No. 750. The Jews believed that devils were real beings, and not diseases or evil personified, as Universalists assert. Now if this were false, and if, as Mr. W. asserts, the Saviour was so careful to point out and contend against the errors of the age, we might reasonably expect to find some clear and decided opposition to this error, on the part of Christ and his apostles. But what is the fact? We assert, without fear of contradiction, that not a single instance is to be found in the Bible where this doctrine is held up as an error; but on the other hand, as Mr. Hanson says, Christ used the same phraseology that the Jews did respecting it. Why did not the Great Teacher rebuke and expose this error, if it were one? Why *seem* to favor it, by the use of such language as has deceived the church for eighteen centuries? Christ, say Universalists, came to save men from ignorance; and yet he left the Jews, among whom he labored during the years of his incarnation, in the most profound ignorance respecting the personality of the devil, and by adopting their "precise phraseology," has entailed this ignorance upon the church for eighteen hundred years! How unlike is this to the course of Universalist teachers in this age, who are prompt in apprising people that there is no personal devil, and wonder at and pity the credulity that can receive such a doctrine; and then, as if to cap the climax of absurdity, they claim to be the only true successors of the Saviour in the ministry! The same views are applicable to this, that we have taken of the Saviour's treatment of the doctrine of endless punishment. (Sec. CXXXII.) To the sincere inquirer after truth, no more need be said to show the falsity of Universalist views upon this subject.

XCIX. "*The wages of sin is death; but the gift of God is eternal life, through Jesus Christ our Lord.*" Rom. 6 : 23.

The author of the Guide, in constructing an argument upon Rom. 5 : 18, says, "We find 'the free gift came upon all men unto justification of life.' This free gift is eternal life. See Rom. 6 : 23." Thus he uses the last member of this text to prove Universalism, or that all shall enjoy endless bliss in the future world. The passage, it will be seen, presents an antithesis; and if the eternal life named in the second member of the verse means endless bliss, as Mr. Whittemore admits by the use he has made of it, then the death in the first member is endless death. Observe, the death here named is contrasted with endless life, and "as no medium can be found between life and death, the death incurred by sin could not make eternal life necessary, unless that death were otherwise eternal. If mankind are not exposed to eternal death, they have already eternal life, and God needed not to give it by Jesus Christ; for this would be to give only what they already possess. In other words, if eternal life is the gift of God by Jesus Christ, then eternal life was forfeited; which is the same as to say that the penalty of eternal death was incurred." *Errors of Soc.*, p. 284.

An effort has been made to turn the last member of this text against the conditionality of salvation, because eternal life is the *gift* of God. A false issue is often raised upon this subject. Christians are represented as expecting to merit heaven by their good works, while Universalists are so evangelical as to receive it as a gift. This is false. Christians constantly affirm that all merit is in Christ. They do not, however, believe that eternal life is bestowed unconditionally; hence they urge the duty of a compliance with the conditions, and a use of the means to secure it. Does this destroy the idea of a gift? A man is starving; a friend offers him bread on the conditions that he will take and eat. He complies with these conditions, and is saved from starvation. Was not that a gift? And would a man in his senses think he had merited the bread merely because he had taken and eaten? Surely not; but he would count that man his benefactor who bestowed upon him the gift. Man, as a moral being, has power to receive or reject the gifts of God. Are not all our temporal blessings equally the gifts of God? Yet these gifts are sometimes rejected, perverted, and turned into curses. Forgiveness of sins, eternal life and blessedness, are the gifts of God, to be received, however, on the conditions of repentance, faith, and obedience (John 3 : 14–16); for while it is declared that Christ "became the author of eternal salvation unto all them that obey him," (Heb. 5 : 9,) it is also declared of him who rejects Christ, that he "shall not see life; but the wrath of God abideth on him." John 3 : 36.

C. "*For our light affliction, which is but for a moment, worketh for us a far more exceeding and eternal weight of glory; while we look not at the things which are seen, but at the things which are not seen: for the things which are seen are temporal; but the things which are not seen are eternal.*" 2 Cor. 4 : 17, 18.

This is the language of contrast. The afflictions of the Christian are light when contrasted with the evils of sin, here and hereafter. They are but momentary, when contrasted with endless duration. It is also the language of holy confidence under sufferings. They "work for us a far more exceeding and eternal weight of glory." Observe; these afflictions do not work for the Christian mere transient, temporal rewards, but an ETERNAL WEIGHT OF GLORY. But Universalism contradicts this, by asserting that all rewards and punishments are temporal — that they are received in this world, and end with this life. But Christians look for their reward in the future, and not to things seen which are temporal, but to things which are not seen, but which will be realized in the eternal state. This too is the language of degree. "A *far more exceeding* and eternal weight of glory." The obvious sense is, that our doing and suffering here for Christ will enhance our future glory. But American Universalism teaches that the most devout and holy man that ever lived, shall have no higher bliss in the future than Julian the apostate, or any other polluted scoundrel. "All shall be equal," is the motto. How utterly at variance is this with the words of Paul; yet he is called a Universalist!

CI. "*The Son of Man goeth, as it is written of him; but wo unto that man by whom the Son of Man is betrayed! it had been good for that man if he had not been born.*" Matt. 26:24.

Dr. Clarke comments as follows upon this passage: "Can this be said of any sinner, in the common sense in which it is understood, if there be any redemption from hell's torments? If a sinner should suffer millions of millions of years in them, and get out at last to the enjoyment of heaven, then it was well for him that he had been born; for still he has an *eternity of blessedness* before him. Can the doctrine of the *non-eternity* of hell's torments stand in the presence of this saying? Or can the doctrine of the *annihilation* of the wicked consist with this declaration? It would have been well for that man if he had never been born! Then he must be in a state of conscious existence, as non-existence is said to be better than that state in which he is now found." *Clarke in loco.* We are told in argument, to get rid of the force of this text, that this was a common proverb among the Jews. Admitting it to be so, it does not abate its force when coming from the Saviour. These words are not merely a common proverb, but a *divine truth*, when uttered by him in whose mouth was no guile.

CII. "*And if children, then heirs; heirs of God, and joint heirs with Christ; if so be that we suffer with him, that we may be also glorified together. For I reckon that the sufferings of this present time are not worthy to be compared with the glory which shall be revealed in us.*" Rom. 8:17, 18.

This is spoken, not of all men but of Christians who are led by the Spirit of God, (v. 14,) and who suffer in the cause of

Christ. It is declared that the sufferings of this present time are not worthy to be compared with the glory which shall be revealed in us, i. e., as a result of our suffering with him here. None need mistake the sense of this passage. It has been the solace of suffering Christians for eighteen centuries. It connects our present conduct with our future destiny, which Universalism impiously denies. Of like import is 2 Tim. 2 : 11, 12. "It is a faithful saying; for if we be dead with him, we shall also live with him; if we suffer, we shall also reign with him; if we deny him, he will also deny us." Here is a conditional promise of reigning with Christ, and being owned by him at last. Such must be "dead with him," i. e., die to sin. Such must own him before the world, and be willing to suffer for his sake, if they would be owned of Christ; for "if we deny him, he will also deny us."

CIII. "*The soul that sinneth, it shall die.*" Ex. 18 : 4.

This text and some others of like import are produced by Universalists to prove the doctrine of no-escape from merited punishment. Such scriptures were evidently designed to set before the sinner the penalty of the law, and to show him what he is to expect in case he continues impenitent; but were never designed to teach that there is no remission of punishment in case of penitence. This may be illustrated by civil government. Go to the statute book, and we shall find that the law expressly declares, "He that committeth murder or treason, shall die for it;" and yet in that same book there is a discretionary and gracious power lodged with the executive to pardon, which always means the remission of the penalty of the law. So in Heaven's statute book it is declared, "The soul that sinneth it shall die," "God will by no means clear the guilty," &c., and yet in the same book there is a merciful provision, called the gospel, presented to our view, in which Jesus Christ is "set forth to be a propitiation through faith in his blood, to declare his righteousness for the *remission of sins that are* PAST, through the forbearance of God; to declare, I say, his righteousness: that he might be just, and the justifier of him which believeth in Jesus." Rom. 4 : 25, 26. God says, "When I say to the wicked thou shalt surely die; if he turn from his sins, and do that which is lawful and right; if the wicked restore the pledge, give again that he had robbed, &c., none of his sins that he hath committed shall be mentioned unto him." Ez. 33 : 14–16. Observe, *none of his sins that he* HATH *committed* shall be mentioned unto him. Now what is meant by this declaration, if it is not that on condition of penitence and reformation, the sinner shall be exempted from deserved punishment for past sins? (Sec. LXX.)

"That salvation is of grace, that the whole gospel system is of grace, is everywhere taught in the Bible. But if the sinner actually endures the whole penalty of the law, he owes nothing to justice, and therefore cannot be indebted to grace. For it should be recollected that the gospel is emphatically called grace, because it is mercy shown to sinners — it is favor conferred upon the undeserving and the ungodly. But those who by dint of suffering have borne the whole penalty of God's law, and thus discharged all its claims, cannot say, 'by grace I am saved,' but 'by suffering I am delivered;' and now strict justice demands that I should be admitted into heaven. Their song, therefore, will not be the song of redeeming grace, for they are under no obligations to grace. Does the criminal praise the lenity and clemency of that government which has inflicted upon him the whole demerit of his crime? Does he ever think he owes his enlargement to the mercy of that government? Neither can a sinner who has suffered the curse of the law to its full extent, ascribe his deliverance to mercy. There is not a particle of mercy in it. If men had seriously set themselves to work to devise a system directly opposite to the Bible, it is clear they could not have hit upon one more suited to their purpose than this." *Dr. Fisk.* That all punishment is not disciplinary, may be seen Sec. CIV.

CIV. "*Though he cause grief, yet he will have compassion according to the multitude of his mercies; for he doth not afflict willingly, nor grieve the children of men.*" Lam. 3: 32, 33.

The Jews are chastised by being cast off as a nation, for their departures from God. The Prophet predicts that God would yet have compassion, and deliver them from Babylon and restore them to their own land; for, "Though he cause grief," &c. From this it is assumed that all punishment is amendatory, and that endless punishment is false. *Guide*, p. 42.

That God uses disciplinary punishments, is enforced from every Christian pulpit. These chastisements are inflicted both upon the righteous and the wicked, with a design to bring the latter to repentance, and preserve the former in the way of duty, and improve them in holiness. "While administering this discipline, God appears as a father correcting his children for their good, mingling the assurance of his love with every stroke, and showing himself ready to forgive their iniquities when they submit; but threatening heavier punishments if these prove ineffectual. That these chastisements are also called punishments in the Scriptures, we do not deny; but that they are different, both in the degree and design of them from capital punishments, or punishments, properly so called, we affirm. Even in this world, when his creatures have proved incorrigible, God has made this difference in the character of his punishments. When he destroyed the antediluvians, Pharaoh and his host, the inhabitants of Sodom, &c., he did not inflict a disciplinary punishment, that is, a punishment designed for their good; for he took them away in his wrath from the place of repentance, and from the means of reformation." *Merritt.* The Bible represents man as sinning against God; but Universalism represents him as sinning against himself only.

Says Mr. Williamson, "God brought us into existence of his own good pleasure, and without our knowledge or consent; and he is bound, by the principles of his own nature, to do us justice; and he has no right, in the nature of things, to do an injury. The right to punish for sin, has its foundation in the fact that sin is an evil and bitter thing, and its practice productive of evil to man." *Exp. & Def.*, p. 66. Mr. W. informs us that he speaks this with reverence; but really, we should not have discovered it in the sentiment. "The right" (!) of God to punish sin, is based upon the fact that it is productive of evil to man; and such punishment looks continually at the good of the sufferer. But if this be so, then the law was made exclusively in reference to the happiness of man, irrespective of the Lawgiver and the dignity of his government, which presents an anomaly not to be charged upon a divine and perfect administration. In accordance with this, there are no wastes to be repaired, no insulted dignity to be vindicated, no injurious influence to be counteracted, except so far as it relates to the sinner himself. Man is diseased, and the penalty of the law or punishment is the remedy; and yet this remedy is called a curse, and furthermore, Christ came to redeem man from this curse, or remedy! "Christ hath redeemed us from the curse of the law." Gal. 3:13. Now what is the curse of the law but its penalty? Says Mr. Skinner, "A just punishment is as essential for our welfare as anything that love can do — a remission of such a punishment would be a curse instead of a mercy." *U. Ill. & Def.*, p. 250. If this is correct, then Christ has redeemed us from that which is as essential for our welfare as anything that love can do! Or, in other words, he came not to bless us, but to curse us by redeeming us from the curse. Such is the theology of Universalism. "The law curses men, but the curse blesses them!" The Bible speaks of certain characters "who shall be punished with everlasting destruction." 2 Thess. 1:9. With what is the sinner here threatened? Why, shocking to relate, it is that which is as essential to his welfare as anything that love can do! "Much more, then, being now justified by his blood, we shall be saved from wrath through him." Rom. 5 : 9. Wrath of course means punishment. We are instructed, then, that Christ saves us from a merciful remedy for our spiritual disease ! "Jesus which delivered us from the wrath to come." 1 Thess. 1 : 10. That is, he has delivered us from a manifestation of the love and mercy of God ! God sends strong delusions upon those "who believe not the truth, but obey unrighteousness," and for what purpose ? Is it to bless and save them ? Inspiration declares that the design of such infliction is not the good of the sufferer, but "THAT THEY ALL MIGHT BE DAMNED." (2 Thess. 2 : 10–12,) and this damnation is incurred for not loving "the truth, that they might be saved," (v. 10,) and thus damnation stands opposed to salvation, instead of being a means to secure it, as Universalism asserts. Now if all punishment looks to the good of the sufferer, and is not a curse but a blessing, then God *promises* the *blessing* of damnation upon those "who believe not the truth, but have pleasure in unrighteousness !" So it seems that the damnation which stands opposed to salvation, must be hereafter numbered among the "exceeding great and precious promises" of which the Scriptures speak !!

The assumption that all punishment is designed for the good of the sufferer, is completely overthrown by this passage alone. Look at the case of Pharaoh and his host, and the ungodly Sodomites already named, also Ananias and Sapphira. Acts 5 : 1–10. These wicked people were hurried into eternity in consequence of their sins. Was this designed to reform them ? As well might we say that a man was hung to reform him. These, and similar inflictions, have taken place from time to time in the history of the world, to vindicate the government of God, to let the world know that he is not insensible to passing events, and as a warning to the living. It is asserted that the Jews were punished for their sins when their city was destroyed by the Romans. But was this only designed to reform the sufferers ? Was this as essential for their welfare as anything that love could do ? Was the Saviour so unwilling that they should be blessed with such love and mercy, as to weep in view of it? Luke 19:41. Was the death of eleven hundred thousand Jews in the siege of Jerusalem, designed only to reform those who suffered it? There is but one way for Universalists to meet this, and that is to bring forward their doctrine that death ends sin, and that all shall be as the angels of God in the future; and thus death *reformed* the Jews into this state. But how will this harmonize with the idea that no man escapes any deserved punishment? Is it replied that dying was their punishment? But how could that be, if it ended their sins, and introduced them to heaven? And then, do not good men die as well as bad? And then again, why this *partialism* in the case of the Jews, as seen in the fact that thousands were sent off to heaven during the siege, while to thousands of others, no more guilty, the gate of heaven was shut, and they were left to suffer their hell in this world for scores of years? What justice, love, or mercy, is there in this? And yet this is Universalist theology. Is it replied that this was a national punishment, and designed to reform the Jews as a nation? But why, according to Universalist notions, should there have been a national punishment at all upon that people for rejecting the Messiah nearly forty years after he left the earth? According to this dogma, every man is punished for his individual sins as soon as he commits them. (Sec. XLIX.) Nations are composed of individuals, and if every individual is punished to the full extent, then the whole nation is punished to the full extent. Every Jew, then, suffered immediately all the punishment that was due him for rejecting Christ, and thus the whole nation had been punished. And yet God inflicts a punishment upon this very people, involving individual suffering for the very crime for which they had all been punished to the full extent, nearly forty years before! This is a logical result of Universalist teachings, and stands directly opposed both to the mercy and justice of God. We deny that the punishment upon the Jewish nation was designed to reform it; and all know that if it was, it has proved a total failure for eighteen hundred years.

The passage in Luke 13 : 24–28, Universalists generally refer to the Jerusalem catastrophe. Now whether this is referable to the future state or to Jerusalem, it matters but little in this argument, for in either case it stamps with falsehood the notion that all punishment is designed to reform the sufferer. Here we beg leave to introduce Mr. Whittemore as a witness. He remarks upon this scripture thus : " 'Strive to enter in,' that is, do not wait, but seek *now* to become my disciples ; for the time when you will have the opportunity of seeking is short ; many will seek to enter into my kingdom when it is too late, and therefore will not be able : they will seek when they see the calamities that are coming upon them ; but then I shall have risen up and shut the door, and their time for gaining admittance will be passed. Now all this is literally true ; for when Jerusalem was destroyed, the Jews ceased to enjoy Gospel privileges, and thus the door of the kingdom was closed against them." *Guide*, p. 148.

Mr. W. is right, unwittingly right, that is, so far as the principle of the divine administration is concerned. Now look at the plight into which Universalism is thrown by this. The Jews are punished in this instance for rejecting the gospel kingdom, and this punishment is designed to reform them ; and yet by this very punishment they are put beyond the possibility of reform ; for says Mr. W., " When Jerusalem was destroyed, the Jews ceased to enjoy gospel privileges, and thus the door of the kingdom was *closed* against them," and so closed, that even should they seek to enter in they would not be able ! How serpentine is error. We are instructed in this passage, that when sinners are punished in consequence of having spurned the offers of mercy, and neglected the day of visitation, God does not intend their reformation and happiness. He will then say, it is too late, " I know you not," " depart from me all ye workers of iniquity." Of like import is Prov. 1 : 24–28. It is false, then, that all punishment is designed for the good of the sufferer. Again : " The sinner is represented as being punished according to his *works*, not according to his *wants*. Every man is represented as receiving '*according to that he hath done in the body*,' and not according to *that which is necessary to save him*. Christ says, 'Behold I come quickly, and my reward is with me to give unto every man *according as his works shall be*,' not *according to what is necessary to bring him to repentance*. Again, the sinner is said to be *cursed*, to be *punished*, to endure *wrath*, *wrath without mixture*, *indignation*, *fiery indignation*, to *perish*, to be *destroyed*, &c. Now if all these mean no more than what is for the sinner's good — no more than what is essential for his best interest — no more than what unmingled mercy deals out, as the most tender physician administers a bitter medicine to a patient, there were never greater misnomers. Then are wrath and love the same; then between vengeance and mercy there is no difference; then is punishment the means of salvation from sin, the cause of punishment, and an effect proves a remedy for its own cause; then is a curse a blessing, and death leads to life!" *Lee.*

If all punishment is designed to reform the sufferer, then it is the will of God that all should reform when he inflicts it; and to adopt the Universalist views, concerning the attributes of God and the absolute character of his will, it would follow that all do reform when punished; for who has not heard their argument upon, "Who will have all men to be saved." Upon this it is said that the wisdom and power of God are equal to his will, and therefore all will be saved in the future.

Now this argument is equally valid to prove that all men are saved from sin now, for none can doubt but God wills it, especially if he punishes them only to reform them. But scripture and matter of fact contradict this. We are informed, that "evil men and seducers wax worse and worse, deceiving and being deceived." 2 Tim. 3:13. Now this class of wicked persons, as Universalism asserts, were punished all their sins deserved on the commission of every sin, and yet so far were they from being reformed that they waxed worse and worse. Look at drunkenness and other vices of our age, and how often do we witness an illustration of this. See Isa. 1 : 5 ; Jere. 5 : 3 ; Rev. 16 : 9. We introduce the insufficiency of punishment to reform, in order to consider it in connection with mercy. When we assert that if there is no remission of punishment in the gospel plan, then there is no mercy, we are told that the mercy of God is seen, not in withholding, but in inflicting the punishment, and that to withhold punishment would be a curse instead of a mercy. In contrasting human government with the government of God, Mr. Skinner says of the latter: "God has all wisdom and power, and can do all his pleasure. He is never like earthly governments, reduced to the necessity of choosing between two evils. Hence, if one is doomed to endless pain, it is because God desired it. It is no removal of the difficulty to say, he has threatened endless misery; and if the sinner will incur the penalty, we are not to charge the blame upon God, or accuse him of vindictive feelings in executing his threatening, for he foresaw and was able to avoid this result; he might with perfect ease and honor to himself, have so arranged his government as to secure the obedience and happiness of all. Consequently if there is infinite evil in the penalty, it is because God desired it, and had infinite malignity towards the sinner." *U. Ill. and Def.*, p. 195.

This argument is made by Mr. S. to prove that endless punishment is unjust and cruel, and that all punishment is amendatory. The reasoning is sophistical, and, furthermore, if it does anything it completely overturns the discipliniary punishment, for which Mr. S. is contending. Let us apply it. "God has all wisdom and power, and can do all his pleasure. He is never like earthly governments, reduced to the necessity of choosing between two evils. Hence, if any one is doomed to suffer in this world, it is because God desired it. It is no removal of the difficulty to say, he has threatened punishment in this world, and if the sinner will incur the penalty, we are not to charge the blame upon God, or accuse him of vindictive feelings in executing his threatenings, for he foresaw and was able to avoid the result; he might with perfect ease and infinite honor to himself, have so arranged his government as to secure the obedience and happiness of all in this world without punishment. Consequently, if there is sin and punishment in the world, it is because God desired it, and exercised malignity towards the sinner." It will amount to nothing to say, that this suffering is but a means to secure the good of the sinner, for Mr. S. has told us that God "is never reduced to the necessity of choosing between two evils," and of course is not under the necessity of punishing men for their good, for he could have so arranged his government as to secure that good without it. This mode of argument is adopted by the whole tribe of Universalists, and yet it lies with all its force against their cherished notion of disciplinary punishment. It stands opposed to matter of fact, viz.: the present sufferings of our race; therefore, must be false. On this method in argument, see Sec. CXIV.

The conclusion from this argument is, that God punishes sinners unnecessarily in this world, which is, to say the least of it, unmerciful, and yet Mr. S. talks largely in his book about the mercy of God in punishing the sinner! The truth is, Universalism drives mercy completely out of the divine administration. Mr. Skinner, as do Universalists generally, resolves all the actions of men into the sovereignty of God. He says: "The will of God is absolute. The will of kings is absolute; and God is the king of kings and lord of lords. He does all things after the counsel of his own will. Of course when he made man and gave him the power which he possesses, he did everything according to his own will. It will avail nothing to say, man is a moral agent; for why should God give him an agency which would defeat his own will? This would be planning against himself. Nothing is more evident than that an expected result of a voluntary act, proves that it was desired." *U. Ill. and Def.*, p. 174.

Here we learn the fatalism of Universalism, "whatever *is*, is right;" everything is according to the will of God. (Sec. LXXXV.) Speaking of the mercy of God to man, Mr. S. adopts the following definition: "Mercy has been defined to be that benevolence, mildness, or tenderness of heart, which disposes a person to overlook injuries, or treat an offender better than he deserves." p. 202.

In the same book he asserts as follows: "Justice will have all its demands; every man shall suffer to the full extent of his deserts. There is no remission of punishment, either on account of the Saviour's death, or the sinner's penitence." p. 249.

Mr. S., by these views concerning the will of God and punishment, represents all the leading writers in the order. We could give the same in substance from the works of a dozen or more in our possession. Now with these doctrines, where can there possibly be any mercy in the system? Mercy, says Mr. S., "is to treat an offender *better than he deserves.*" Then he says: "Every man shall suffer *to the full extent of his deserts.*" No mercy, then, according to Mr. S.'s own showing. We have seen that punishment often fails to reform, and that some under its infliction wax worse and worse. Is there mercy in continuing to punish such, when God not only knows it is so, but willed it should be so? Observe: "An expected result of a voluntary act, *proves that it was desired.*" There can be no mercy in such a procedure. But why should the sinner be punished at all for wrong doing? He has not been guilty of wrong doing unless it is wrong to do the will of God. Mercy, we are told, is seen in punishing the sinner to reclaim him. Reclaim him from what? Why from being and doing just as God wills he should be and do! So distant is this from being merciful, that it is downright cruelty. By this strange system the Deity is arrayed against himself. He wills the sin, and wills the reformation of the sinner, and inflicts stripes to effect it. The sinner waxes worse and worse under the stripes, till rotten ripe in pollution he falls into the grave, and all this in accordance with the will of God! With these views of Universalists before him, the reader can judge with what propriety those scriptures are presented to prove Universalism, which speaks of the mercy of God. From what has been presented, we think it sufficiently clear that all punishment is not designed to reform the sufferer. We should be careful to distinguish between God's judicial punishments and his paternal chastisements. The sinner has not sinned against himself, but against God. To be sure, he has brought upon himself misery, and is without hope. God's law is vindicated in his final punishment, if he spurns the offers of mercy and dies in his sins. It is equally vindicated through Christ, if he repent of his sins, believe and obey the gospel, and is thus saved from the punishment of past sins. Rom. 4:25, 26. The penalty by which that law is vindicated, however, is not designed for the final benefit of the offender. God has indeed appointed its proclamation *a priori*, for the benefit of the governed, by the prevention of crime. In this sense we have no objection to calling it reformatory, as its proclamation operates as a warning to sinners. But it is not inflicted, *a posteriori* for the final benefit of those who disregard the divine authority. It avails nothing for Universalists to present an array of scriptures to prove that God sometimes inflicts reformatory punishment, and that some have been benefitted by such punishment. This is admitted.

The point at issue is this: Universalists assert that *all* punishment is for the good of the punished. This we deny, and have given some of our reasons for so doing. With what force the reader must judge. Many more might be added, had we space to spare. See Jere. 16:13; 13:14; 1 Sam. 6:19. Were these inflictions designed to reform the sufferers?

CV. "*That he by the grace of God should taste death for every man.*" "*He died for all.*" "*Who gave himself a ransom for all.*" Heb. 2:9; 2 Cor. 5:15; 1 Tim. 2:6.

These, and other texts of like import, are in frequent use in Universalist writings to prove their doctrine. By their use the construction put upon them is this: "Christ tasted death that he might save every man in the future state." "He died for all, and gave himself a ransom for all, to secure the salvation of all men in the future world." We say this is the construction, because they would not think of quoting them to prove that all are saved in this world. It is in the future state that all are to be saved.

Christ's vicarious atonement is discarded by the order generally. Says Mr. Skinner: "The whole system of vicarious atonement is false." *U. Ill. and Def.*, p. 120. So say they all, from Father Ballou down to the dimmest satellite. Indeed, there is not a leading writer among them who admits that Christ's death was at all necessary to save men in the immortal state; and yet they continue to use these scriptures (*Guide*, p. 34) in this way, because there is universal language employed, and the people can be deceived by it. On the contrary, Mr. Ballou says: "That Christ came into *this* world to save us in *another*, is contrary to all the representations found in the scriptures." *Lec.*, p. 14.

Mr. Whittemore says: "The truth is, we do not read one word in the Bible about saving men from punishment in the future state. The evils from which Jesus came to save men are in this world, and for this reason he came into this world to save them." *Guide*, p. 254.

And yet in this same Guide, Mr. W. uses the above named scriptures to substantiate the doctrine of the salvation of all in the future world, because Christ gave himself a ransom, and died for all in this world! Much is said by this class of writers about Christ's saving all men. But is there any such thing as Universal salvation by Christ, according to their own positions? What, according to these men, was the great object of Christ's mission. Mr. Williamson says: "The witness does not go into court to make truth. He goes there, to testify to what is already true. So Jesus, in our view, came not to make anything true, that was not so before; but he was the faithful and true witness, who came to make known the truth, as it was in the beginning, is now, and ever shall be, world without end. He came to reveal the character and purpose of God." *Exp. of U.*, p. 16.

Says Mr. Skinner: "Jesus bore witness to God's rich provisions of grace; to that eternal life which he had prepared for the world. This was the great purpose of his mission." But when did he prepare this for the world? "When he created he prepared and secured salvation for his children." *U. Ill. and Def.*, pp. 264, 265.

Here is Universalist theology. Christ never came to save men in the future world, for they were never lost, or in danger of being lost there, for their salvation was prepared and secured when God created them. Christ's death and mission has nothing to do with procuring, modifying, or in any way affecting the happiness of our race in heaven. All would have been thus saved if Christ had never visited our world, for this was all made sure when God created man, and "Christ came not to make anything true that was not so before." The bliss then of the future state is, to say the least of it, a *Christless* thing. According to this view, Christ is *not* the *author* of eternal salvation (Heb. 5 : 9) to any; and the holy ones in heaven (Rev. 7 : 10) are in no way indebted to Christ for their glorified state. It will be seen that *Universalism denies that Christ is the Saviour of a single soul in heaven.* Yet these same writers, who put forth these sentiments, produce John 4 : 42, "Christ the Saviour of the world," to prove that all will be saved in the future state! (Sec XXIV, also Sec. XXI.)

We are informed that the great object of Christ's mission was to testify to what was already true; to teach the resurrection and remove ignorance and sin from men in this world. Men are ignorant of the character and purposes of God. The Saviour came to enlighten them, to bear witness to the truth. Well, what is the truth? Why, Universalism. Nothing else, surely. Christ came to remove the ignorance of Partialism from the world, and to convice them by his resurrection that all would be raised from the dead to a blissful state. But universal salvation in this sense has not been secured by Christ, for millions have died, and millions are now living, who have never heard of him, and there are millions more who have had the Bible, containing the history of his mission, who could never learn Universalism from it. And as for sin, all know that men are not universally saved from it here, and, furthermore, according to leading Universalists, Christ never did, nor never will, save a single individual entirely from sin; for, says Mr. Skinner, "None can be fully saved from all moral evil here." *U. Ill. and Def.*, p. 261.

Now if none are saved from all moral evil here, and if Christ came to save none in the future, as Mr. Ballou and others assert, then he saves none from all sin any where. What wretched work these crafty yet blind guides make with salvation. UNIVERSAL SALVATION!! Salvation from what? Not from sin in this world, as we have seen. Is it from ignorance? No; for darkness covers the earth, and gross darkness the people. Is it from future suffering? No; for none have ever been exposed to this. Is it from punishment in this world? No; for every one must suffer the full penalty. Is it from sin in the world to come? No; for there is no condition for man there, but "that in which he is as the angels of God in heaven." Is it from a future hell? There is no such place, say these men. Is it from the grave? No; for the popular doctrine with Universalists now is, that the body will never be raised. Is it from nonexistence? Men were never in danger of this, for this was guarded against at the creation, as Mr. Skinner asserts. Says one writer: "I know of no salvation for them if their system is true, unless it be a salvation of all persevering Universalists from believing the gospel. Such a system may, with much more propriety, be denominated universal damnation, than universal salvation. It universally punishes all, and universally saves none." *Russell.*

CVI. "*If by any means I might attain to the resurrection of the dead.*" Phil. 3 : 11.

This text stands directly opposed to Universalist views. Paul lived and labored that he might secure a blissful resurrection, and thus connects his present conduct with his future destiny. The only writer we have noticed who has attempted to destroy the force of this passage, is Mr. Harris. After quoting John 5 : 24, he says: "This refers wholly to the spiritual change or resurrection wrought in believers, by the power of the gospel in this life;" and he will have it that the text under consideration refers to the same resurrection. *Future Life*, p. 178.

We are to believe, then, that the holy apostle Paul, who had been favored with such a wonderful conversion, and had been *raised* up with others to sit together in heavenly places in Christ Jesus, (Eph. 2 : 6,) had not as yet experienced a spiritual resurrection by the power of the gospel in this life, but was laboring to attain to it! What an exhorbitant demand Universalism makes upon the credulity of its votaries!

Dr. Clarke remarks thus: "*The resurrection of the dead.*" That is, the resurrection of those who, having died in the Lord, rise to glory and honor: and hence St. Paul uses a peculiar word, which occurs nowhere else in the New Testament. This glorious resurrection, and perhaps peculiarly glorious in the case of *martyrs*, is that to which St. Paul aspired. The word αναςασις signifies the *resurrection* in general, both of the just and of the unjust; εξαναςασις may signify that of the *blessed* only." See Sec. XCI.

CVII. "*But if ye being evil, know how to give good gifts unto your children, how much more shall your heavenly Father give good things to them that ask him?*" Matt. 7 : 11.

This passage is sometimes used to show that God, who is much better than earthly parents, will not inflict endless punishment. The sophistry lies in representing God as a father only, and as being influenced by the same motives and feelings that frail, erring, earthly fathers are. All divine truth is alike immutable. God is not only declared to be our father by creation, (Mal. 2 : 10,) but it is revealed with equal clearness that "the Lord is our judge, the Lord is our lawgiver, the Lord is our king." Isa 32 : 22. God stands in both the parental and regal relation to his creatures. But the great effort of Universalism is to destroy the latter relation, and to *exalt* the former to human imbecility! (Sec. XV.)

Observe: This bestowment of good things is not upon all men, but upon "*them that ask him.*" The Saviour in this and the four preceding verses, is showing the willingness of God to bestow certain blessings in answer to prayer, a doctrine which, if we may credit some of their leading authors, Universalists have but little faith in. *It is not believed by them that he is a prayer answering God.*

Speaking of prayer, Mr. Skinner says: "The change which our devotions are intended to make is upon *ourselves*, not upon the Almighty. Their chief efficacy is derived from the good dispositions which they raise and cherish in the human soul." *U. Ill. and Def.*, p. 332.

Again: "*The whole effect of prayer and every other religious duty*, must be upon *ourselves*, and not upon the supreme and independent Creator." "It should be considered a great privilege, as well as a great duty. *Not*, let it be repeated, with the view that it will effect any sort of change in the Supreme Being, in his disposition, in his will, or in his purposes." *U. Manual*, pp. 27, 39.

In keeping with these views, Mr. Ballou says: "The necessity and utility of religion, according to common opinion, is, on the one hand, to obtain or secure the divine favor; and on the other, to be screened from the displeasure of the Almighty. But if our deductions are allowed to stand, it is very clear, that *the divine favor can neither be gained nor lost.*" *Exp. of U.*, p. 28.

All must see that such a view makes prayer utterly useless, so far as the divine being is concerned. He answers no prayer, for prayer effects no change at all in his conduct towards us, but is, in its effect, *wholly confined to ourselves.* How completely is the Saviour contradicted by these sentiments. Christ says that our heavenly Father *gives* good things to them that *ask* him. Not so, say these men; the man who asks gives the good things to himself!

Universalist views being correct, Elijah must have found himself in a sad condition in his contest with the prophets of Baal. He builds his altar, puts on the wood, and the bullock cut in pieces, and pours on his barrels of water. Now, for the demonstration to confound Baal's prophets, and to show that there is a God in Israel. Elijah prays thus: "Lord God of Abraham, Isaac, and of Israel, let it be known this day that thou art God in Israel, and that I am thy servant. Hear me, O Lord, hear me; that this people may know that thou art the Lord God." 1 Kings 18 : 36, 37. God answered the prayer; the fire came down, consumed the materials, and licked up the water in the trench, and the people cried, "The Lord he is the God! the Lord he is the God!"

This is false, says Universalism, for "*the whole effect of prayer must be upon ourselves,*" and God was no more moved by Elijah's prayer, than Baal was moved by the prayers of his blind worshipers.

Christ uses the parable of the unjust judge (Luke 18 : 1–8) to illustrate and enforce the duty of prayer. The judge is not disposed at first to grant the widow her request, but she continues to importune, and he changes his purpose and bestows the favor she asks. A bad illustration, says Universalism, for the "whole effect of prayer must be upon ourselves." A correct illustration would be this: the woman is improved somewhat by her own effort, while the judge is as unmoved by her entreaties as a stone, neither changing his purpose or granting her request. This illustrates the Universalist view of prayer, as all will see.

And thus this dogma, as ever, is arrayed against Christ. So we might go on through the Bible and show the antagonism of Universalism to its teachings concerning prayer.

"*The divine favor can neither be gained nor lost,*" says Mr. Ballou. Universalist ministers stand up before the people and profess to ask favors of God. What is meant by it? Are they sincere? Do they believe he will grant favors, or is it only to be seen of men? With such views, what a farce is a Universalist prayer! The Bible teaches that God bestows blessings in answer to prayer. Universalism teaches that prayer is a self-stimulating and re-active process of man; or in other words, that men bless themselves by praying. Quite a difference.

That the natural tendency of pure sentiment, offered with sincere and reverential feelings, is salutary to some extent upon both those who pray and those who listen, we readily admit. But the position, that this is all of prayer, is highly infidel in its character, contradicting the Bible and the experience of ood men in all ages of the church. With such views before us, from their leading men, we are not surprised to hear Mr. Smith, who was a popular preacher of the order for twelve years, assert as follows:

"No minister of the sect, whom I ever knew, maintained family prayer. I have known many to ridicule the custom, but no one to observe it. I have often been in families of the principal advocates of Universalism, and passed the night. They have been at my house. I found no family devotions at their dwellings. They expressed no surprise at not finding an altar at my fireside."

Persons have lived in the families of some of their leading ministers for months, and never heard the voice of prayer in their houses. When their brethren in the ministry called to pass the night, they abounded with witty anecdotes about the Partialists, but never prayed.

Now how has it been with Universalists? Have they considered these sinful neglects? No. They have boasted of them as virtues. Their prayers were secret, such as Christ enjoined; they were not like the old Pharisees, praying, joining church, fasting, and all that, to be seen of men. One would have supposed that persons, who had said so much about praying to be seen of men, would have had no public prayers at all, and thus evinced consistency. But these men, notwithstanding all they have said about praying to be seen of men, are seen standing praying in their pulpits from time to time; but this has doubtless been much against their inclination, and would have been abandoned before now, if public opinion would have borne them out in it. A few years since, Robert Smith, a Universalist preacher, an editor in Hartford, Conn., gave out in public that he should pray no more when he conducted public service. He contended that such prayer was wrong; that offering prayer in connection with a sermon, was a tribute to Orthodoxy that he was unwilling to pay. He offered a reward of one thousand dollars to any man who would prove that the Saviour ever made a public prayer. Mr. Grosh, of Utica, an editor and minister in the order, says he preached several months without public prayers.

Since quite a number of their ministers have renounced the doctrine, and Mr. Smith's book has been so extensively circulated, showing the blighting influence of Universalism, the leaders have found it necessary to change their course somewhat. Policy dictates that the denomination should appear more pious. Prayer books have been published, and a part of their ministers, and a few of their people, have been induced to set up something like family worship. It seems, however, that Mr. Cobb had been in the habit of "lifting up his voice in thanksgiving and praise" in his family, and after Mr. Smith's exposure, he published this to the world in his paper, which called forth a rebuke from Mr. Drew, editor of the Banner, as follows:

"We do not suppose this is a *very* unusual thing amongst Universalist ministers; but all do not choose to publish it. Some, it may be, have so *literally* practised upon the precept of Jesus requiring secret prayer, as to have kept their practice so much of a secret that the world has not known it." *Banner, Jan.* 16, 1841.

Mr. Drew, it seems, was one of those modest persons, who have ever been very secret about their prayers! Being greatly devoted to the interest of the order, however, and the leaders judging it expedient to appear more pious, "before men," he cheerfully sacrifices his modesty, commences repeating the Lord's prayer on the Sabbath in his house, and tacitly sanctions his Bro. Cobb's Phariseeism, by publishing to the world his own prayers, as follows:

"Every Sabbath day, when we are at home, and at an hour when we are not officiating in the church, we gather our family of little ones around the domestic hearth-stone, read the sacred scriptures in course, each reading a portion, say the Lord's prayer together, and then gather around the organ, and with heart and voice, raise our united voices together, in praise to him who is the God and Father of all the families of the earth." *Banner, Feb.* 4, 1843.

How long Mr. D. continued this we are not informed. Here is Phariseeism, with a witness! After all the ridicule they have heaped upon others, there is no class of men who make a more ostentatious display of their religious doings than do these same Universalists.

A few years since great efforts were made to get up prayer meetings in the denomination; but with their views of prayer, these doubtless appeared so farcical to themselves, as well as to others, that in most cases they have been abandoned, and in some instances praise meetings (!) have taken their place, the exercises consisting chiefly in praising Universalism and denouncing evangelical truth. Indeed, if God, as Universalism asserts, is, from his own nature, necessarily impelled to acts of love towards all his creatures, whatever their character, where can be the necessity of prayer? We might as well pray for him to be omnipotent, or omniscient, as for him to be gracious. Universalism is a prayerless religion, and its influence in this respect is seen in every community where it exists. On praying for all men, see Sec. LXXXII.

CVIII. "*For our conversation is in heaven; from whence also we look for the Saviour, the Lord Jesus Christ; who shall change our vile body, that it may be fashioned like unto his glorious body.*" Phil. 3:20, 21.

This passage stands directly opposed to the notion that the body is never to be raised, and must, if possible, be destroyed in some way. The last effort we have met with to do this, is found in Harris's "Future Life." He says, "The apostle does not say that Christ would change "*vile bodies*," but "*vile body*," which was the *church;* for the apostle has told us that the *church* is the *body* of Christ." p. 192.

Christ's body then, the church, is the "vile body" meant by the apostle, and when Christ comes from heaven he is to change his own body and make it like his own body!! Well, who belong to this church? All men, of course, if Universalism is the truth, and Mr. Ballou, in a sermon on Eph. 5:25–27, has asserted, "that all men belong to the church of Christ." *Select Ser.*, p. 133.

But when is Christ to come and change his vile body? Mr. Harris, on the same page, states that it was to be changed at the coming of Christ in his kingdom; and on page 190 he quotes Bush, to show that his "second coming commenced with that new order of things, which is, in the main, to be dated from the destruction of Jerusalem — which is to be considered as continuing through the whole period of the dispensation."

Admitting Mr. Ballou's position, that the whole human race compose the church, this interpretation of the text amounts to the idea, that the whole human race are to be changed and made like Christ's glorious body, under the dispensation which commenced with the destruction of Jerusalem. So the millions of our race who had died and were exalted to bliss, prior to the destruction of Jerusalem, are to be changed with the rest of the *vile body* subsequent to that event!! Paul must mean the church, because he says our vile *body*, and not vile *bodies*. What paltry quibbling this. The honest minded reader will see at a glance the character this work gives Universalism and its advocates.

CIX. "*Abraham called upon the name of the Lord, the everlasting God.*" Gen. 21 : 33.

The Hebrew *olam*, and Greek *aion*, *aionios*, have been discussed so much that they have become, to some extent, *naturalized* to the mind of the common English reader, especially so, to those acquainted with the controversy these words have elicited. Most have witnessed, too, with what an air of triumph the fact is stated, by Universalists, that the word everlasting is applied to things of limited duration, as, the priesthood of Aaron, the hills, and the possession of the land of Canaan by the Israelites. The priesthood has passed away, the hills are not endless, and the seed of Abraham have long since ceased to possess the land of Canaan; therefore, the word everlasting does not mean endless. Our limits forbid an extensive article upon this subject. A few hints only will be given, just to furnish the reader a clue to the sophistries employed to destroy the true meaning of language.

If everlasting in its true or original sense does not mean endless, because it is sometimes applied to that which ceases to exist, then by the same process in argument it cannot mean less than endless, because it is applied to the existence of God, which is absolutely endless, as all admit. We see, then, that the sense of the word is not fixed by the subject. The subject only determines whether it is used in a proper or an accommodated sense, in that particular instance. No point has been more clearly shown, by those able men who have controverted Universalist views upon this subject, than this, viz., that the proper meaning of the Greek noun *aion*, and its corresponding adjective *aionios*, is endless. Dr. Clarke, on the text at the head of this section, remarks as follows:

"The Septuagint renders the words *Theos aionios*, the ever existing God. From this application of both words, we learn *olam* and *aion* originally signified ETERNAL, or *duration without end*. *Aion*, according to Aristotle, and a higher authority need not be sought, is compounded of *aei*, *always* an *on*, *being*. Hence we see that no words can more forcibly express the grand characteristics of eternity than these. It is that duration which is *always existing*, still *running* ON, but never *runs* OUT. In all languages, words have, in process of time, deviated from their original acceptations, and have become accommodated to particular purposes, and limited to particular meanings. This has happened both to the Hebrew *olam*, and the Greek *aion*; they have been both used to express a limited time, but in general a time the limits of which are unknown; and thus a pointed reference to the *original ideal meaning* is still kept up. Those who bring any of these terms, in an accommodated sense, to favor a particular doctrine, must depend upon the good graces of their opponents for permission to use them in this way. For as the real grammatical meaning of both words is *eternal*, and all other meanings only accommodated ones, sound criticism in all matters of dispute, concerning the import of a word or term, must have recourse to the grammatical meaning, and to the earliest and best writers of the language, and will determine all accommodated meanings by this alone. Now the first and best writers in both these languages, apply *olam* and *aion* to express *eternal*, in the proper meaning of that word; and this is their proper meaning in the Old and New Testament, when applied to God, his attributes, his operations, taken in connection with the *ends* for which he performs them, for *whatsoever he doeth it shall be forever*. The word is with the same strict propriety applied to the duration of the rewards and punishments in a future state, and the argument that pretends to prove, and it is only pretence, that in the future punishment of the wicked the worm *shall die*, and the fire *shall be quenched*, will apply as forcibly to the state of happy spirits, and as fully prove that a point in eternity shall arrive, when the repose of the righteous shall be interrupted, and the glorification of the children of God have an eternal end."

In keeping with Dr. Clarke's views are the words of the Saviour, Matt. 25 : 46 : "These shall go away into everlasting punishment, but the righteous into life eternal." The word *aionion* is here rendered everlasting in the first member of the text, and eternal in the second. Now, if in the first member it is used in a limited sense, then it must be in the second, which limits the bliss of the righteous. Mr. Whittemore seeing this, has resorted to a most wretched perversion, which is, that the "eternal life" means the spiritual life of the believer in this world, and does not refer to the future state. To be righteous in a religious sense, which is the sense here, is to possess spiritual life, as all must admit. The Saviour, then, is made to utter the following : "*The spiritually alive in this world, shall go into spiritual life in this world!*" Such senseless tautology is not to be charged upon the divine Saviour. None but a man who had a bad cause to sustain, would thus pervert the words of Christ. The Saviour in this passage instructs us that the bliss of the righteous, and the punishment of the wicked will be equal in duration.

For Dr. Clarke's remarks upon this text, and Dr. Huntingdon's rebuke to Universalists for trifling with language expressive of endless duration, see Sec. XLI.

Mark 3 : 29 : "But he that blasphemeth against the Holy Ghost, hath never forgiveness, but is in danger of eternal damnation." Here forgiveness and damnation are set over against each other. Hence, if a man is never forgiven, he must be damned endlessly, and thus the unforgiven are in danger of eternal damnation. Another evangelist (Luke 12 : 10) says of this blasphemy, "*it shall not be forgiven.*" Now an *aionon* punishment for a sin that *hath never forgiveness*, and that ***shall not*** *be forgiven*, must of necessity be endless in duration. There is no avoiding this.

It is often said by Universalists, that the term endless is nowhere applied to punishment in the Bible. But why this stress upon the word endless ; why prefer this word to everlasting, eternal, forever and ever, which are the strongest terms used in reference to a future state ? The obvious reason is, because the Bible employs them to express the duration of the sufferings of the wicked.* The term *endless* is nowhere in the scriptures applied to the punishment of the wicked, and the same may be said of the happiness of heaven. The word is used by the apostle in reference to Christ's priesthood, (Heb. 7 : 16) : "Who is made, not after the law of carnal commandment, but after the power of an endless life." But it is not said that any shall have this life. But suppose *endless*, the word of their choice, was to be found in the Bible connected with the punishment of the wicked, would it stand before their criticisms with the license they take? By no means; for they could pervert it with the same ease that they now do the term everlasting, for the term endless, too, is used in a limited sense. Timothy is cautioned against "endless genealogies." 1 Tim. 1 : 4.

It discovers either great ignorance or depravity to make such a demand for the term endless in connection with punishment, when, if it were found, its true sense would no more be admitted by Universalists, than the true sense of everlasting is now admitted by them. And if the term endless is necessary to prove endless punishment, is it not equally so to prove endless salvation? We have only to apply their own rules in argument to the bliss of heaven, to deprive it of its endless duration. Is it said that such scriptures as, "There shall be no more death,"

* Our opponents admit that the doctrine of endless punishment was popular with the Jews in the time of Christ. But what word or words were in use among them, to express the duration of punishment, if those under consideration were not used for that purpose? Universalists would confer a favor by giving information upon this point.

(Rev. 21 : 4,) " Neither can they die any more," (Luke 20, 36,) prove endless bliss ? We reply, that these no more prove endless bliss, than, " Shall not see life," (John 3 : 36,) " I will love them no more," (Hosea 9 : 15,) " Will show them no favor," (Isa 27 : 11,) " Shall not be forgiven," (Luke 12 : 10,) disprove it. Mr. Morse, a Universalist minister, as quoted by Mr. Lee, p. 192, says, " The word *aionios* is equivalent to long, lasting, or everlasting." The design of this was to make the impression, that the word is as correctly rendered by *long* as by everlasting, which is false. The absurdity of this rendering will be seen by applying it to John 3 : 15, " Whosoever believeth in him shall not perish, but have eternal life." No Universalist will contend that this eternal life, which is conditioned on believing, is future bliss, for our belief or unbelief can neither gain nor forfeit that, according to their system.

Now if " eternal life," in this text, may with propriety be rendered " long life," then it speaks this : " Whosoever believeth in Christ shall not perish, but have *long* life in this world ! " But is it true that a belief in Christ secures long life in this world ? So far is this from the truth that thousands have shortened their days by believing in Christ. Stephen believed in Christ. Did he have long life in this world ? We might introduce a host of texts to show up this assumption. No more need be said upon this point.

Sometimes, when it serves their turn, Universalists will have it that *aionios* may be properly rendered by *age-lasting* ; hence, we read in their books of age-lasting correction, &c. Let us apply this to 2 Cor. 4 : 18 : " We look not at things which are seen, but at things which are not seen : for the things which are seen are temporal : but the things which are not seen are eternal," i. e., *age-lasting*. Things which are only age-lasting are of limited duration, and therefore must be temporary. The passage, then, is reduced to the following nonsense : " We look not at the things which are seen, for they are temporal ; but we look at the things which are not seen, for they are temporary ! "

Did the apostle mean this? Nothing is more obvious than that he meant endless duration by the term under consideration. The scriptures denote the brevity of human life by such expressions as "grass," "weaver's shuttle," "shadow," "vapor," "few days," &c. But when they speak of punishment, they never assert that its duration is as the grass, weaver's shuttle, shadow, vapor, or a few days; but, on the contrary, we find the strong terms, everlasting, eternal, and forever, are applied to it. As we have seen, some who deny future punishment have asserted that *aionios* is equivalent to *long*, *age-lasting*. They assert, too, that none escape the punishment due for their sins. To show this in its true light, let us suppose a case. A man dies in the act of wilful murder. Now, if there is no future punishment, when and where does he suffer long, or age-lasting punishment for that last sin? Is "eternal damnation," "everlasting punishment," inflicted in the brief space of human life, which is as the shadow or vapor? Is it inflicted in a few years, months, days, or it may be a few seconds after the sinful act, or even, as Mr. Whittemore will have it, (Sec. XLIX,) while sin is being committed? No more need be said to show the violent wresting of the scriptures upon this point.

Speaking of the terms in question, Prof. Stuart inquires: "If, then, the words *aion* and *aionios* are applied sixty times (which is the fact) in the New Testament, to designate the *continuance* of the future happiness of the righteous; and some twelve times to designate the *continuance* of the future misery of the wicked; by what principles of interpreting language does it become possible for us to avoid the conclusion that *aion* and *aionios* have the same sense in both cases?" Again he says, "The result seems to me to be plain, and philologically and exegetically certain. It is this: either the declarations of the scriptures do not establish the facts, that God, and his glory, and praise, and happiness are *endless*; nor that the happiness of the righteous in a future world is *endless*; or else they establish the fact, that the punishment of the wicked is *endless*. The whole stand or fall together. There can, from the very nature of antithesis, be no room for rational doubt here, in what manner we should interpret the declarations of the sacred writers. WE MUST EITHER ADMIT THE ENDLESS MISERY OF HELL, OR GIVE UP THE ENDLESS HAPPINESS OF HEAVEN." *Exeg. Essays*, pp. 56, 62.

Blank Atheism, or no future life whatever for any of our race, is a clear and logical result of Universalist arguments upon future punishment.

CX. "*The earnest expectation of the creature waiteth for the manifestations of*," &c. Rom. 8 : 19–23.

The following, with the exception of the application of Mr. Whittemore's rule at the close, has been kindly furnished for this work by Rev. Charles Munger.

"Does this passage teach the final salvation of all men? This is the question now at issue. The answer depends wholly upon '*the creature*,' and its deliverance. What the creature is, and what its deliverance, must be determined by the essential conditions of the entire passage and the context. Taken in the order of the apostle, they seem to be these :

"1. The creature waiteth in earnest expectation for the manifestions of the sons of God. Ver. 19.

"2. It was made subject to vanity, not willingly, but in hope. Ver. 20.

"3. It shall be delivered from the bondage of corruption into the glorious liberty of the children of God. Ver. 21.

"4. The creature is not the same as the sons of God, but a thing or class distinct. The last statement is important. If the creature is the same as the sons of God, then the passage refers only to these, and of course has nothing to do with Universalism. If it is not the same, then this fact is a very important condition or feature, which must be regarded in the interpretation. The distinction, as we have just seen, is absolutely essential to the claims of Universalism. It is perfectly apparent, also, from the structure of the passage, and the distinction of terms; thus: the *creature itself also* shall be delivered into the liberty of the children of God. Ver. 21.

"The whole creation groaneth, and not only they, (it, for the antecedent is neuter,) but ourselves also which have the fruits of the Spirit, even we ourselves groan waiting for the adoption. Ver. 22, 23.

"The supposition that the passage teaches Universalism rests upon the three following assumptions.

"1. That the passage is not figurative.

"2. That the creation includes every human being.

"3. That its deliverance is from sin into conscious enjoyment of holiness and happiness eternal.

"The first statement, though exceedingly important, they never argue, but assume. The second they usually argue thus: The same creature which was made subject to vanity, shall be delivered. True, the creature is the same in both verses 20 and 21, but to assume that it means the human race in ver. 20, and therefore it does in ver. 21, is a mode of reasoning not very conclusive, though quite characteristic. But, secondly: 'Dr. McKnight decides that the creature in the passage signifies every human creature.' *Guide*, p. 47. Very well, Grotius, Michaelis, Luther, Tholuck, Rosenmuller, Bloomfield, Doddridge, Benson, Knapp, Robinson, Hodge, with many other 'learned friends,' decide that it means no such thing, but on the contrary 'the visible creation.' Thirdly, it is argued 'that the creature,' ver. 21, is equivalent to 'the whole creation,' ver. 22, and that this last expression signifies every human being in Mark 16 : 15, and therefore it does here.' Let us examine first the fact, and then the logic. The passage referred to is this: 'Go ye into all the world and preach the gospel to every creature.' Does this expression here include, Universalists themselves being judges, the millions of human beings who were dead, and, according to their views, in heaven, if not elsewhere, when it was spoken? Does the term, every creature, in this commission, include absolutely every individual of the entire race? Evidently not. Universalists interpret the commission to refer to the age then present. Thus the 'important fact' upon which they rest their cause, is *not* a fact, and the argument is invalid. But suppose it were a fact that the expression in this single instance signified every human being, does it follow logically that it certainly does in Rom. 8 : 19–23? Paul says, that in his day 'the gospel was preached to every creature which is under heaven.' Col. 1 : 23. Here the same expression is used, both in Greek and English; but it includes only a small part of the human race. And shall we say, therefore it does in Rom. 8 : 19–23? This argument from a single use is certainly as good in one case as another. Again: In Col. 1 : 15, the same expression comprehends 'all things created,' and therefore by the same rule it does in Rom. 8 : 19–23. The logic which thus proves and disproves the same thing must be false, and the conclusion based upon it is no better. The supposition that the term 'creature' signifies every human being, then, is without any valid proof, the arguments on which it depends being invalid. That it is untrue, is proved by the essential conditions of the passage, as above mentioned. Take that one, for instance, which is not only essential to the identity of the passage, but, as before shown, absolutely necessary to the claims of Universalism, viz.: That 'the creature' is distinct from 'the sons of God.' If it is distinct, then the creature is not the entire race absolutely, for the sons of God are a part of the race, and distinct from 'the creature.' If it is not a distinct class, then the passage refers only to the sons of God, and has nothing to do with Universalism. What is affirmed of '*the creature*' is not true, in fact, of every human being, and therefore the creature cannot have this interpretation. The Universalist depends upon the literal construction of this language. We cannot admit the figurative without destroying his scheme. But it is not literally true that every human being awaiteth in earnest expectation for the manifestations of the sons of God — was made subject to vanity, not willingly, but in hope. It is not true literally that every human being has an idea even of the adoption — the redemption of our body — and therefore they cannot in patience wait for it. Thus the position that 'the creature' is every human being, must be abandoned because it is without proof, and also contrary to essential conditions of the passage.

"There is but one hope left for Universalism in this passage, and that is a 'forlorn hope' indeed. Does the advocate of the doctrine attempt to reconstruct his scheme upon the basis that 'the creature' includes all that portion of the human race not comprehended in the class called the sons of God, i. e., the wicked? Then it will be a difficult task to show, that what is affirmed of the creature is true of the wicked, and still more difficult to sustain the main position with the evidence which the importance of the case demands. Hard as the task is, it must be done and done well, or the passage must be given up. For unless the apostle intended to teach that the wicked, all the wicked, shall be delivered from sin into the glorious liberty of the sons of God, he did not teach Universalism in this text. This is precisely the thing that must be proved. This is Universalism, and Paul did so teach, say its advocates, in this passage. But that he did not is further evident,

"1. From the design he had in view in introducing the present sufferings and future glory of the sons of God. It was simply this: To comfort them in their afflictions and to prevent their apostasy from the faith and practice of the gospel. He employs these powerful motives. 1st. If we are children, then heirs; if we suffer with him we shall also be glorified together. Ver. 17. 2d. The sufferings of this present time are not worthy to be compared with the glory to be revealed, not in all, but '*in us.*' Here he presents the future glory of the saints with its limitations and conditions, 'if children,' and 'if we suffer with him.' Then he writes thus, (if the term creature includes the wicked): The wicked also earnestly expect this glory, and they were made subject to vanity, sin, and death; not willingly — not by their faults; and in fact they also shall inherit the glorious liberty of the children of God. Ver. 19–21. Thus his entire argument is rendered null, and the motives void by the subsequent announcement, that it will be the same in the end with those who deny Christ as with those who confess him, even unto death. Had he designed to induce apostasy from the restraints of the gospel, and give full license to sin, this was the doctrine to do it. But as such was not his design, such was not his doctrine.

"2. That Paul did not teach here, that the wicked shall be co-heirs with the saints, is evident from the following explicit statements in the context. Compare the context with the doctrine of the text, as explained by Universalists:

"*Context.* 'If any man have not the spirit of Christ, he is none of his.' Ver. 4.

"*Text.* 'All are his, whether they have his spirit or not.'

"*Con.* 'If children, then heirs.' Ver. 17.

"*Text.* 'All are heirs.'

"*Con.* If we suffer with him, we shall also be glorified together. Ver. 17. Compare 2 Tim. 2:12: 'If we suffer we shall also reign with him; if we deny him, he will also deny us.'

"*Text.* We shall all be glorified with Christ, whether we suffer with him or deny him. Thus Paul is made to contradict himself.

"Look once more at the context and compare Paul's testimony there with this interpretation of the text, and see how his language and this doctrine neutralize each other:

"*Paul.* The carnal mind is not subject to the law of God. Ver. 7.

"*Univer.* True it *is* not, but it *shall* be, in every case, without exception.

"*Paul.* If any man have not the spirit of Christ, he is none of his. Ver. 9.

"*Univer.* If any man have not the spirit of Christ he need not fear, for he shall have it.

"*Paul.* If ye live after the flesh, ye shall die. Ver. 13.

"*Univer.* True, ye shall die, but ye shall live afterwards, for whether flesh or spirit be your choice here, eternal life is your certain portion hereafter.

"*Paul.* As many as are led by the spirit of God, they are the sons of God. Ver. 14.

"*Univer.* All are the sons of God; and if not, they *shall* be.

"*Paul.* The spirit beareth witness with our spirits, that we are the children of God, and if children, then heirs — heirs of God and joint heirs with Jesus Christ. Ver. 16, 17.

"*Univer.* Rom. 8 : 19–23, and, in fact, the whole Bible beareth witness that we, even we, 'who are filled with all unrighteousness, fornication, wickedness, covetousness, maliciousness, envy, murder, deceit, malignity, backbiters, haters of God, covenant breakers, implacable, unmerciful,' (Rom. 1 : 29,) are co-heirs with the saints, and shall be delivered into the glorious liberty of the children of God.

"Thus we have compared the doctrines of the context with the text as explained by Universalists, and we can now see how false the apostle was to his own statements, and how he utterly destroyed the logical decency, as well as moral effect, of his discourse, upon the supposition, that in the text he teaches that the wicked shall be delivered from sin into the glorious liberty of the children of God. Neither can we avoid these contradictions and absurdities in any possible way, but by denying that he taught Universalism in this passage, or, indeed, any other; for the result is the same if he has taught it anywhere. The argument with the Universalist is now closed. We have shown that every position which he has taken, or can take, from which to deduce his doctrine, is false. We have shown that the term creature does not mean the entire race of man, nor yet the wicked portion of it. But it must mean one or the other of these, or the passage cannot possibly teach Universalism. The true import is very apparent from a comparison of the positions already established. We have seen that the creature must be something made subject to vanity. It must be then the material earth, or its inhabitants. We have shown that it is not man, in whole, or in part. It must, therefore, be the earth and irrational creatures, or *one* of them. There may be a distinction between 'the creature' and 'the whole creation,' or every creature; the former designating a part, the earth; the latter, the whole, the earth and irrational creatures. If so, the promise of redemption is restricted to the 'creature,' the earth. It is not said that the whole creation shall be delivered, but only 'the creature.' That the earth is to be delivered from the curse, and will share the glory of the children of God, according to its nature and as it did before the fall, is certainly not denied, but frequently intimated in the scriptures. 'It is certainly in harmony with the design of the apostle, in a bold figurative expression, to give an idea of the future glory of the saints by representing it as so transcendently excellent as to excite the earnest desire of the entire creation, animate and inanimate.'

"Neither is the method singular, for 'the scriptures frequently speak of the creation as a sentient being, rejoicing in God's favor, or trembling at his anger, speaking abroad his praises, &c., as Paul here represents it as longing for the great consummation of all things. Again: 'It is agreeable to scripture to speak of the earth as cursed for man's sake; as made subject to vanity, not on its own account, but by the act of God in punishment of the sins of men. Finally, it is according to the word of God to represent the creation as participating in the blessings and glories of the Messiah's reign. Isa. 31:1; 29:17; 32:15, 16; 2 Pet. 3:7-13; Heb. 12:26, 27.' *Hodge.*"

One thought more. Mr. Whittemore has adopted a rule in argument, (Sec. CXV,) which, if correct, we have a right to avail ourselves of. Let us apply it here. Does the passage say that *all our race* shall be delivered from the bondage of corruption in the *immortal state?* Does it say that *all men* shall have the "liberty of the children of God" *in eternity?* Does it say that there is *no punishment after the resurrection of the dead?* "As nothing of the kind is *said,* we presume nothing like it is meant." *Guide,* p. 72.

This mighty battering ram, of Mr. Whittemore's constructing, when turned upon Universalism, beats down the whole citadel, walls, tower and all, for it can be brought to bear with destructive force upon *every* text produced to sustain that doctrine.

CXI. "*And I saw the dead, small and great, stand before God; and the books were opened,*" &c. Rev. 20 : 12–15.

Mr. Whittemore sees Jerusalem's destruction in this passage. *Guide,* p. 240. But by what stretch of language it can be made to appear that the dead, small and great, stood before God, and that the sea gave up the dead which were in it, and that death and hell delivered up their dead, and that every man of them were judged according to their works at Jersalem's destruction, we have yet to learn. The phrase "*the dead*" in 1 Cor. 15 : 35, includes all the dead, say Universalists. If this phrase must mean all the dead, then it is to be so understood in this passage. The connection determines this to be the sense here. But were all the dead at Jerusalem to be judged when the Romans besieged that city? Furthermore, there is no valid evidence that this book was written before that event. Says Horne, "We conclude, therefore, with Dr. Mills, Le Clerc, Basnage, Dr. Lardner, Bishop Tomline, Dr. Woodhouse, and other eminent critics, in placing the Apocalypse in the year 96 or 97." *Introd.,* Part 2, p. 382.

We might take up every point in the passage, and show the violent wresting by such a construction as is given by the Guide, but will leave it with the good sense of the reader, after giving Dr. Chauncey's view of the text. He paraphrases the 12th verse thus: "I then beheld in my vision the dead raised, both high and low, young and old; and they stood before the throne of God, and were judged in a most fair and equal manner, according to their works, whether they had been good or evil. And that this retribution might be *absolutely universal*, taking in the whole race of men, the dead, without distinction or limitation were raised again to life, whether they died and were buried in the sea, or whether they died on the land, and were buried in the grave; all in the invisible state of the dead were brought to life, and judged according to their works." *Salvation of all Men*, p. 376. Dr. Chauncey was a Universalist, according to Mr. Whittemore's definition, (*Guide*, p. 16,) but it never once entered his mind that Jerusalem's destruction was the theme of Inspiration here.

CXII. "*Lord, are there few that be saved?*" &c. Luke 13: 23–30. Upon this passage, we take the liberty to copy the following from *Ressell's Letters*.

"Now if Christ had been a Universalist preacher, here was a happy opportunity to assail the popular error upon the subject of the future destiny of the wicked, and to set at least one person right. But did Christ preach to him Universalism? Far from it. Look at the case. It is evident he did not teach Universalism,

"1. From the question which was proposed to him by one of his hearers. Did you ever know an instance in which one of the hearers of a Universalist preacher, ever applied to his minister to get his opinion as to how many would finally be saved? Why the very fact that he is a Universalist answers the question. If Christ taught the doctrine that all men were equally and immortally happy upon entering the eternal world, his hearers would have all known this to have been one of the peculiarities of his faith, and they would as soon have asked him how many gods there were, as whether few would be saved.

"2. If up to this time Christ had taught Universalism ambiguously and with reservation, *now* that the question is fairly submitted to him, and seeing he must have come from heaven — not to save men from perdition, for they were never exposed to future sufferings — but to teach Universalism, it would seem all ambiguity and reservation must be laid aside, and we shall have and unqualified declaration that all men will be saved. Go to any Universalist preacher with the question whether few or many are to be saved, and he will answer it at once, and in such language, too, as cannot honestly be misunderstood.

"3. But the manner in which Christ answered this question, clearly shows that the Son of God regarded the man who asked the question, as in danger of losing his own soul. Hear the answer of Christ. Let it ring in your ears with all its awful solemnity, and sink down into your heart. 'Strive to enter in at the strait gate; for many, I say unto you, will seek to enter in, and shall not be able. When once the master of the house is risen up, and hath shut to the door, and ye begin to stand without and to knock at the door, saying, Lord, Lord, open unto us; and he shall answer and say unto you, I know not whence ye are: Then shall ye begin to say, We have eaten and drunken in thy presence, and thou hast taught in our streets. But he shall say, I tell you I know not whence ye are; depart from me, ye workers of iniquity. There shall be weeping and gnashing of teeth, when ye shall see Abraham, Isaac, and Jacob, and all the prophets, in the kingdom of God, and yourselves thrust out. And they shall come from the east, and from the west, and from the north, and from the south, and shall sit down in the kingdom of God.'

"Mr. Whittemore in his Guide, in which he says, 'every threatening is explained,' has given this text the ingenious 'go by.' He quotes 7 : 13, 14, attempts an explanation, refers to Luke 13 : 24 as a parallel text, and passes along. But your preachers and authors who *have* attempted an explanation of this text, tell us that the inquirer did not seek information as to the number who would enjoy salvation in the world to come, but how many there are saved now in this world; that is, he wished to know whether there were few or many righteous persons in this world. A grave question, truly! The answer of Christ is referred to the famous destruction of Jerusalem. It was then and there the door was shut to the Jews, and opened to the Gentiles; it was then and there that Abraham, Isaac, and Jacob, and all the prophets, were seen in the kingdom of God, while they themselves were thrust out, &c. To all this I object,

"1. If the inquirer wished to know the state of morals and religion, it is not a little singular that he should have gone to Christ to have ascertained the state of society around him. He had been brought up in society, and had daily opportunities of observing the characters of his fellow men. He knew men were to be judged by their fruits, and he could have formed a very satisfactory conclusion as to what portion of society were then pious, without going to Christ with the question. It is an unnatural question to be asked under the circumstances.

"2. In the answer of our Lord, nothing is said adapted to teach the inquirer that Jerusalem was to be destroyed at all, much less that the master of the house was to rise up at that time and shut the door of the kingdom of heaven. If this was the illusion, the inquirer cannot be supposed to have understood it.

"3. As a matter of fact, it is not true that Christ, the master of the house, shut the door of grace or glory against the Jews, either at, or any time since the destruction of Jerusalem. The Jews and Gentiles, since the crucifixion, stand on a dead level as to religious rights and privileges. Christ has broken down the middle-wall of partition, and his gospel was before the destruction of Jerusalem, and has been ever since, 'the power of God unto salvation to every one that believeth, to the JEW first, and also to the Gentiles.' Rom. 1 : 16.

"4. The persons said to be excluded here from the kingdom of God, are not the Jews as a nation, but '*all the workers of iniquity*.' Does *all* in the vocabulary of Universalism mean *all?*

"5. If the kingdom of God (v. 28) denotes the gospel kingdom, which Universalist expositors tell us was fully set up at the destruction of Jerusalem, then it is not true that Abraham,

Isaac, and Jacob, and all the prophets, were ever in the kingdom of God at the destruction of Jerusalem; nor can it be true that they will ever be in that kingdom. How, then, can it be true that any of those who heard Christ on this occasion, did see those Old Testament saints in that kingdom? Besides, the most if not all present on this occasion to hear Christ, were in eternity before Jerusalem was destroyed. How, then, could they see Abraham and all the prophets entering into the gospel kingdom in this world? These are mysteries. The more I examine your explanations, the more supremely ridiculous and contradictory they seem to me. The truth is never thus inconsistent and contradictory."

CXIII. "*No murderer hath eternal life abiding in him.*" 1 John 3:15.

In reply to the idea that suicide cannot be punished unless there be punishment in the future state, Mr. Whittemore says, "It supposes the sin of suicide to consist in the overt act, after which the sinner cannot be punished. On the contrary, the sin consists in the *intention* to do the deed; and every person not morally blind, can see punishment enough for this in that horrid state of mind which could induce the intention. This state of mind may have existed for a long time prior; it may have been continually growing worse." *Trumpet*, No. 676. The sin lies in the intention, and the punishment for that intention consists in that state of mind which induced it, and "*and may have existed a long time prior.*" Or, in other words, God punishes for sin before it is committed, and as a man must be counted innocent till he commits sin, God by this method is charged with punishing the innocent, and thus neither mercy or justice have a place in his administration! Such is the theology of Universalism. (Sec. LX.)

Various devices have been sought out to show how suicide is punished without future retribution; but Mr. A. B. Grosh, a great man in the order, solves the whole difficulty by showing, in his way, that suicide is no crime. To the question, "How do you reconcile cases of suicide with your doctrine of all-sufficient punishment in this life?" he answers thus:

"I suppose that the scriptures regard it as under one of the following heads:

"1. Either they class it under the head of *murder* — 'thou shalt not kill,'— in which case the penalty, the *whole* penalty, the *only* penalty, *after* the act, I can there find on record against murder, is inflicted on the criminal *in the very act of transgression;* viz.: by man his blood is shed. I am not very sanguine in this opinion, (i. e., that it is murder,) inasmuch as there is no appearance of malice in the offender against himself; for the apostle says, 'no man ever yet hated his own flesh;' consequently the act is scarcely murder.

"2. Or the scriptures consider it as the act of none who are of *sound mind,* and therefore accountable beings. In the cases where suicides are recorded, the act itself is never condemned, or even named as a *criminal* one. It seems *entirely omitted* in the various and frequent lists of actions forbidden to be practised.

"3. In conclusion, believing the object of punishment to be salvation from sin, I can conceive of *no use for it for this act* more than for any other. There is no danger that suicide will ever be committed in the immortal state. As to the mental guilt, let it be shown that the suicide had an evil *intention,* and that he was of perfectly sane mind in forming it, and that it is necessary for his salvation to be punished after death, and there is no one that will object to his receiving all that is necessary. *As this cannot be done,* no more than I can prove the negative of the proposition; and, above all, as the Bible is silent on the subject; I think it best becomes us not to *dogmatize* upon it." *Mag. & Adv.*, vol. 8, p. 358.

Some infidels have advocated the right of man to commit suicide when he pleases, inasmuch as he has no agency in bringing himself into the world. Is the doctrine set forth by Mr. Grosh any better? He labors to prove that suicide is no sin, and of course needs no punishment; and Mr. Whittemore will have it that sin is punished beforehand! We leave these views with the reader, as specimens of the work of two leaders in the order, a work every way worthy of the cause it is designed to sustain. More disciples would avail themselves of the liberty of cutting their way to their fancied heaven through their own throats, were it not for weakness of faith. (Sec. CXXXVIII.)

PART II.

MISCELLANEOUS ARGUMENTS.

CXIV. The arguments built upon the perfections of God against the truth, are perhaps as deceptive as any. God, say Universalists, possesses unbounded goodness, and of course will seek the greatest good of his creatures; and his infinite wisdom and almighty power can accomplish all his goodness dictates: as endless punishment cannot be for the good of his creatures, the doctrine is false. Now this specious argument, so often employed, lies with all its weight against matter of fact, viz: the present sufferings of the human race. It avails nothing to say that their present sufferings shall result in their good; for, reasoning from the attributes of God, as Universalists are wont to do, we might ask, is a being possessed of infinite wisdom, power and goodness, under the *necessity* of first making the human race suffer six thousand years before he can make them perfectly happy? All will see that, if our knowledge of God's attributes is to be the basis of doctrine, then no human suffering could ever have existed; for none can doubt but Omnipotence could have created men, at first, as happy as any ever will be, and have kept them so. But matter of fact teaches us that he has not done it; therefore all such reasoning must be false. Suppose a being, adopting the Universalist mode of argument, to have existed prior to the creation of man. It is announced to him that God is about to create a race of beings called men, and that they are to exist in a sinful, suffering state for six thousand years, or more, and then he is to make them all holy and happy; that some of the race shall live and endure this thirty, fifty, one hundred, and some even nine hundred and sixty-nine years (Gen.

5 : 27) ; that they shall suffer from wars, slavery, famine, poverty, disease, intemperance, *partialism*, and innumerable other evils; that even tender infants, before they know right from wrong, shall often suffer the most extreme agonies for weeks and months together; but that this suffering is all disciplinary, and necessary for the ultimate happiness of the race. How would such a being meet this? He would reply, I cannot believe a doctrine which reflects so ingloriously upon my Heavenly Father, and is so at war with his attributes; for,

1. His power and wisdom are infinite, therefore he can do His pleasure, and none can hinder.

2. His goodness is unbounded, which of course will admit of no unnecessary suffering on the part of his creatures, but will make him delight in their perfect and undisturbed happiness.

3. Having such power and wisdom, such suffering is unnecessary, for he can create and keep them just as happy as he can possibly make them after they have suffered six thousand years; therefore such a suffering race will never exist.

Such reasoning, as plausible as it may appear, would have been false, for such a suffering race is now in existence; and as it is compatible with the attributes of God for the human race to suffer six thousand years without our seeing a reason why, it may be so for some of them to suffer endlessly. We might extend our remarks and illustrations had we space, but enough has been said to give the reader a clue to the sophistries of these men upon this subject. (Sec. CIV.)

Their appeals to human sympathy are equally deceptive and fallacious. Say they, "You are possessed of more goodness than your God, for you would not punish one of your children endlessly." To such it is replied, You are possessed of more goodness than your God, for when your child is suffering by disease, or otherwise, had you the ability, you would relieve it in a moment. God has such ability, but he does not relieve it; the innocent child suffers on. So you see how much better you are than your God. Again; you cast about you, and witness the untold agonies of the human race, suffering from various causes; and while you contemplate these, your heart is moved with compassion, and had you the ability, you would put a stop to these evils at once and forever, and spread peace, joy, and permanent happiness throughout the universe. God possesses such ability, yet the suffering continues. So you see how much better you are than your God. By this mode of argument many are deceived; making human sympathy a rule by which to judge of God's moral government, is most preposterous; and for finite man to make his views of the divine perfections, which he can never fully understand, the basis of doctrines, is always to plunge himself into the vortex of error. Infinity can never be fully comprehended by a finite mind; and, as in reasoning upon other subjects, we cannot arrive at just conclusions, unless we understand the premises, so with this. God has revealed to us that he is almighty, holy, wise, just and good, but we can never so understand these infinite perfections, as to be able to learn from them, aside from what the Scriptures reveal, what is, and what is not consistent with them. If Universalism is taught in the Bible, it is true, whether we can see a reason in the divine attributes for it or not; and so with endless punishment. But for finite and depraved man to rise up, and tell us from the divine attributes what must and what must not take place, is as unseemly as it would be for a child of three years to be found dictating and expounding the laws of an empire.

The same deceptive course is pursued concerning the will of God. (See Sec. LXXXV.)

CXV. "We call upon the writers who adduce these passages in support of the doctrine of endless misery, to bring forward some text like this: The wicked shall perish *in the immortal state;* into smoke shall they consume away *in the immortal state;* the transgressors shall be destroyed *beyond the grave;* the end of the wicked shall be cut off *in eternity.*" *Guide,* p. 67.

This, by its author, is adopted as a rule by which to set aside scriptures brought against his doctrine, and we find him applying it as follows: "Prov. 14 : 32. 'The wicked is driven away in his wickedness; but the righteous hath hope in his death.' In order to express the common doctrine which is inferred from this passage, it should read, 'the wicked is driven into endless punishment in the future world;' but as nothing of that kind is *said*, so we presume nothing like it is meant." On Eccl. 12: 14, he asks, "Is it said, 'God shall bring every work into judgment' in the future, immortal existence? No such statement is made." Again; Ps. 49 : 14, 15, "Is there one word intimated in regard to punishment *after the resurrection of the dead?* Not a syllable." With such a rule, who can wonder that Mr. Whittemore is always victorious in controversy!

Suppose we make the same demand, and call upon Universalists to produce texts like these: all men shall be as the angels of God *in the immortal state;* all men shall be holy and happy *beyond the grave;* all men shall be saved *in eternity;* and then assert that, because none of these expressions are appended to any texts they bring to support their doctrine, that nothing like them is meant? In this way not only is future punishment destroyed, but future bliss; and thus the world is left without any hope of a future life.

In No. 1005 of the Trumpet is the following scrap, thrown in by the editor:

"Last week's 'Recorder' has an article entitled 'Unpardonable Sin.' We will give the editor of the 'Recorder' *fifty dollars*, if he will find such an expression in the scriptures."

Doubtless this passed for a very weighty argument, with many of the readers of that print. We are told, too, in their writings, that the phrase "*eternal death*" is not found in the Bible; and from the frequency of this statement by some of their divines, we conclude they deem it of great importance in sustaining their system. We admit that the exact phrase "eternal death," is not in the Bible, but the phrases "*eternal damnation*," "*everlasting destruction*," and "*everlasting punishment*," are in the Bible; and we conclude that eternal death is antithetically expressed in Rom. 6 : 23; also, that the doctrine expressed by this phrase, is clearly taught in other parts of the scriptures. The argument of the Universalists is this: the expressions "*unpardonable sin*," and "*eternal death*," are not in the Bible; therefore the doctrines they are used to express are not in the Bible. Is this sound? Let us see, by applying this rule in argument to some of the expressions in use by Universalists, and see how it works. In their writings we find the following: "*future state*," "*immortal state*," "*immortal existence*," "*all will be holy and happy*," "*Deity*," &c. All will see that we could very safely offer "*fifty dollars*," to any one who will find either of these expressions in the Bible. The argument stands thus, then: these expressions are not in the Bible; therefore the doctrines they are used to express are not in the Bible. Thus, by the magic wand of its own advocates, is Universalism swept by the board, and the existence of God, too. All discerning men will see that there is no argument in this: but the advocates of this dogma use it because they know that unthinking men may be duped by it.

But supposing the phrase "eternal death" was found forty times in the Bible, would Universalists allow it a future-state reference? Not they. The same sophistry which deprives the phrase "eternal life" of its future-state reference, could, just as easily, be employed on the phrase "eternal death." It discovers great wickedness to harp so much upon the absence of the phrase "eternal death," to prove their doctrine, denying, as they do, the future-state reference of the phrase which is its counterpart. (Sec. LXVIII.)

We have been told, for the hundredth time, that St. Paul never used the word hell in his preaching. The following is a specimen:

"It is a singular fact that St. Paul, from all that appears in the whole history of his *thirty years'* preaching, did not once use the term HELL, to a solitary individual, saint or sinner. To be sure, he made use of certain other expressions, which are usually considered, in our day, as relating to endless punishment; but if hell, as commonly understood, is the place of punishment, it is a singular and wonderful fact that Paul the Apostle, and the chiefest of all the apostles, never once uttered it to an individual! Query. What would be thought of a minister in our day, who should preach *thirty years*, and never once threaten his impenitent hearers with the punishment of *hell?* Answer me that. What would be thought of him?" *U. against P.*, p. 265.

Here the reader has one of Mr. Fernald's *facts*, with all its comely proportions. This is a very fair specimen of the honesty and logic of Universalist divines. Notice the crafty attempt to make the impression on the minds of the unthinking, that we have a history of *all* Paul's preaching for *thirty years*, whereas we have not so much as he probably preached on one occasion, when he continued his discourse till midnight. We are aware of the difference that exists between "the whole history," and the history of the whole of a thing. But did this man mean that this distinction should be noticed? Why does he ask, "what would be thought of a minister in our day, who should preach *thirty years*," &c. Then mark his italics. All will see the deceptive design.* But Paul "did not once use the term hell, to a solitary individual." This man, however, admits that he used "certain other expressions which are usually considered, in our day, as relating to endless punishment." Yes, and not only in our day have they been so considered, but by the brightest ornaments of the Christian church, from the time of the apostles to the present. But admitting that we have a history of the whole of Paul's thirty years' preaching, are there not some other singular and wonderful facts connected with it? The most of

* We see the same kind of deception relative to the Saviour's three years ministry, in Thayer's recent work on Endless Punishment, p. 117.

those vivid descriptions given by Paul in his writings, of judgment and punishment, are by Universalists referred to Jerusalem's destruction; yet in *no single* instance do we find the expression, Jerusalem, or destruction of Jerusalem, in connection with such descriptions. This is true, too, of all the rest of the epistles where such descriptions are found. Aside from a few short passages in the Gospels, no one would ever learn from the New Testament, that the destruction of Jerusalem by the Romans, was even so much as thought of by primitive Christians. Now we ask, is it not a singular and wonderful fact, that Paul the Apostle, and the chiefest among the apostles, and all the rest of the apostles, too, while they were preaching and writing about the destruction of Jerusalem so much, they never uttered the phrase "*destruction of Jerusalem,*" to a single individual! Now if Paul could teach the punishment of the Jews at Jerusalem without naming the place, then he could teach the punishment of sinners in hell without naming the place. Query. What would be thought of a Universalist minister in our day, who should preach *thirty years*, and never once use the phrase, "*destruction of Jerusalem?*" Answer me that. What would be thought of him?

The following is from Mr. S. R. Smith:

"The doctrine of the future punishment of the wicked, that is, after death, is in no instance unequivocally asserted in the Bible. It is merely inferred from a few passages, which certainly admit of a different construction. Surely, if true, it is too important to rest merely upon conjectnre. *Scrip. Doc.*, p. 29.

This is from a Sunday School book, and by such a method do they deceive the young. The argument stands thus: The exact phraseology that S. R. Smith here employs respecting future punishment, is not in the Bible; therefore, there is no future punishment taught in the Bible! Let the Universalist, if he can, place his finger upon the passage in the Bible where it says, "all men shall be saved after death." This he cannot do. We assert, then, that "the doctrine of the final salvation of all men, that is, after death, is in no instance unequivocally asserted in the Bible. It is merely inferred from a few passages, which certainly admit of a different construction. Surely, if true, it is too important to rest merely upon conjecture." Universalism, then, is a fable.

All who write and speak of doctrines, are in the habit of using language, the exact form of which is not found in the Bible; and none are more in the habit of this than Universalists themselves. But of us they demand the precise phraseology of the Bible, or else, forsooth, the doctrine is false! One instance more. Mr. Skinner, speaking of the judgment says, "Not an instance can be found, in all the Scriptures, where it is declared to be in eternity." *U. Ill. & Def.*, p. 229. Paul says that the judgment is after death (Sec. XX.): but then, as the exact expression "*in eternity*" it not appended, there can be no judgment in eternity! We beg leave to inquire where, in all the Bible, is it declared that "salvation is in eternity?"

Do not these men see the forceless character of such arguments? It would be a severe reflection upon their intellects to say they do not. Why, then, do they use them? Because the depraved and ignorant can be deceived by them.

CXVI. "Ministers uniformly speak of the wicked as having gone to hell, and the virtuous to heaven. Why then call them back from their respective places to judgment?" *U. Ill. & Def.*, p. 235.

Reasons could be given for a judgment, were it necessary. But suppose we cannot tell why God will have a general judgment, does that disprove it? It is not for us, as receivers of a revelation, to call in question the Divine procedure, as there may be a reason in the mind of him whose thoughts are far above our thoughts for such an event, even though we cannot see it. It becomes us to inquire, what say the Scriptures? and not to be cavilling. (Sec. CXXXIX.) The Bible evidently teaches that good men enter bliss at death, (Phil. 1:21–23,) and that wicked men enter into misery. Luke 16 : 23. It also teaches a general judgment after death. Rom. 14 : 10; Heb. 9 : 28, 29. It is the very genius of Infidelity to call in question God's revealed truth. Is there nothing difficult of solution in Universalist views? Why does evil exist? Could not the Almighty with equal ease have created man with a constitution incapable of sin and suffering? Or could he not, by his Almighty fiat, put an end to these at the present moment? Questions of this character to any extent, might be asked by skeptics.

The judgment is in this world, say Universalists, and takes place immediately. "Now is the judgment of this world," is a text ever at hand to prove that there is no future judgment, because all are judged *now*. (Sec. LI.) Christ uttered these words nearly forty years before Jerusalem was destroyed. Says Mr. Whittemore, "At the destruction of the Jewish nation, there was a general judgment among the nations of the earth." *Guide*, p. 187. Now if the Jews and all others then living were judged forty years before Jerusalem was destroyed, what call was there for a general judgment when that event took place? (Sec. CIV.) When Universalists shall have harmonized these portions of their theology to the satisfaction of the candid, they may, with a better grace, call in question what God has revealed concerning a general judgment in the future world.

CXVII. In an effort to show that Universalism is not a new doctrine, a writer in the Universalist Companion for 1844, says, "But after all that has been said about new things, what has self-styled orthodoxy itself to boast of in this respect? To hear its believers talk, one would think that the doctrines they profess have been in existence thousands of years. But what saith history on this subject? If we except the Greek and Roman churches, all existing denominations are of comparative recent origin, having mostly arisen since the era of the Reformation." p. 35. He then goes on with some parade to show when the

Lutherans, Episcopalians, Baptists, Methodists and Presbyterians, originated as denominations. He commences with the origin of doctrines, and then shuffles off on to the origin of denominations! A false issue in argument may deceive the people, but the cause of truth never requires it. Christians have never condemned Universalism because the denomination embracing it is a new one, but because the doctrines are new, being such as were not taught by Christ, his apostles, or the primitive fathers. (Sec. CXXXII.) He has reiterated, too, the old historical falsehood so common in the order, viz.: that Tertullian was the first who openly asserted the doctrine of endless punishment in the Christian church. (See Sec. CXXXIII.)

CXVIII. Universalists have boasted much of the spread of their doctrine in Germany. This Universalism, of which they have said so many good things, has at length visited them in New England, producing not a little trouble in their camp. This Universalism, or Rationalism as it is called, is so open, and its atheistical character so visible, that it was not so well suited to the order in New England, especially just at a time when its leaders were laboring hard to impress the world with the falsehood that Universalism is *bona fide* Christianity. That this has obtained extensively in the body, is asserted by Mr. G. Severance, a minister in the order. He says, "within a few years, Rationalism has become very much diffused in American literature. It has found its way into many of our (Universalist) societies." *C. Freeman*, July 18, 1851.

Creeds, Universalists could have no patience with, and true liberality had its abode with them only. Believe or disbelieve what you will, only believe in the "main point," viz.: that all will ultimately be saved, and you are a Universalist. This has been the profession. But a few years since, expediency demanded that a creed be manufactured for those among them who had become too bold in propagating the good German Universalism; so at the "Boston Association," held at Lynn, Nov. 1847, the following was introduced:

"Resolved, *That this Association express its solemn conviction, that in order for one to be regarded as a Christian minister, with respect to faith, he must believe in the Bible account of the life, teachings, miracles, death and resurrection of the Lord Jesus Christ.*"

After some manœuvering, fearing lest the resolution would not be adopted, its friends succeeded in carrying an adjournment to meet in four weeks, in Cambridgeport, when the resolution was adopted by the Association. Those among the aggrieved by its adoption, were J. M. Spear, C. Spear, D. H. Plumb, W. M. Fernald, J. W. Hanson, J. Prince, B. H. Clarke, and W. G. Cambridge. These have published a "Statement of Facts," in which they complain of great illiberality. Mr. Plumb says: "I stand now just where I stood six years ago, when I obtained letters of fellowship, and was ordained. No questions were asked me then in regard to belief. I believed in universal salvation then, and I do now. This was regarded as the only real essential of a Universalist. The manner in which he was induced to believe it — how it would be brought about — what would intervene between the present and its final accomplishment, were all regarded as questions of secondary importance, and were never to my knowledge put."

In this document they complain that they were wronged, inasmuch as they had introduced no new principle of interpretation, but had only employed one which had always been in the order; and examples are given from leading Universalists. (See one furnished by J. W. Hanson, in Sec. XCVIII.)

In all this these men are correct, and as Universalist ministers, they surely had cause of complaint. The theory has ever been propagated by Rationalistic principles, from Ballou on the Atonement, to the last author. Its very life depends upon murdering the Bible. Says Mr. Cambridge, in the sheet named, "Universalists have harped continually in relation to using the sacred gift of reason in the investigation of truth —

the teachings of the Bible, &c. But how is it now? They do not say in so many words that reason is carnal, but their actions show that they are driven to the disagreeable necessity of eating their own words."

But what was the design of this resolution? Mr. Prince inquires, "Does it cut off any from the ministry? Some who voted for it, say that they regard it only as an *expression of opinion*, not as a measure virtually to exclude any one in particular from the fellowship of the order, or as an attempt to drive any one away from the Universalist ministry. Had they viewed it otherwise, they say they should not have voted for it."

The action amounted to this, then: men who were declared by the resolution not to be Christian ministers, were permitted to remain in good and regular standing in the Universalist ministry! But what was the real design of the resolution? Mr. Prince shall tell, who is now a minister in the sect, as are the most of them whose names are attached to the document. He says, "I express it as my solemn conviction, that the whole movement, which has resulted, (after the mountain labor, and 'flourish of trumpets' in the announcement,) in the generation of a 'Resolve,' was an endeavor to erect a screen between the Universalist denomination and the other sects, to hide from their eyes the fact, which has been daily growing more and more apparent to the gaze of the world, that the Universalist body is to a considerable degree tinctured with Rationalistic ideas of the Bible, of miracles, and of the subject of inspiration in general. And I have no doubt it was thought that a movement of the kind would have a tendency to overawe the minds of some of the younger brethren, who have recently ventured to give free utterance to their convictions, in the pulpit. But, as far as the movement is intended to disguise the fact of the existence and operating influence of the *spirit* of Rationalism in the sect, it will signally fail. The screen is too thin — it has too many loop-holes — and the other sects will either peep through or look over it, with a half-suppressed titter, if indeed they are able to preserve anything like an approach to gravity!"

Doubtless Mr. Prince is correct in his view of the subject. This "statement of facts" has so raised the screen, that without difficulty the outsiders have a fair view of the serpents that nestle over in the dark swamp of Universalism. They present a view of Universalist ministers as they are, and not as they are seen in the pulpit. As they have raised the screen, let us look again. Mr. Fernald, in the same sheet, reports Mr. Ballou, senior, as saying to him, "That we could not, with our reason, believe in miracles as above the workings of nature; that it was *best not to say much about it;* that if any were so imprudent as to broach it now, they would have to bear all the brunt of the battle, and those who come after would reap all the good. On relating the impression I received from this conversation to a talented clergyman, he remarked that he agreed with the venerable gentleman; that he did not call him weak or fearful, for not promulgating these views; but on the contrary this was a a proof of his wisdom; that he probably had not seen the time when the world could bear these views, and so had not proclaimed them."

Again Mr. F. says, "One of the most popular clergyman in the denomination, not sixty miles from Boston, assured me, in his study last spring, that he did not believe that Christ was ever raised bodily from the dead." Mr. Fernald contemplated preaching to a society, and was about to send word to them by a minister of the order as follows: "Please tell the people that I am a Rationalist; that I do not believe in the miracles as above nature — many of them I do not believe in at all — not even the bodily resurrection of Christ. 'Fernald,' said he, 'don't send any such word. Go tell them that you are a Christian, and there are not ten men in the society that will care what you believe.' Such was the advice and remarks of this highly esteemed clergyman." Mr. F. asserts that those entertaining these views are not the obscure and uninfluential alone, but that they "are among the first in the order — the most talented, the most influential and popular." Here we see the gross infidelity and black hypocrisy of Universalism. Much more of the same sort might be presented from this revelation of depravity, did our limits admit.

In the Trumpet of Aug. 25, 1855, a disciple writes to the editor, and appears to be in a famishing condition for Universalism as preached by "Father Ballou," and says: "I have heard a young man who is in formal fellowship with the Universalist denomination, declare in the pulpit, that he did not believe that God rested on the seventh day after the creation, as related in Genesis. That he did not believe that Christ existed at all before he was born in Palestine, or that there was anything miraculous in his birth, more than in the birth of any other individual."

Now in what respect does this young man differ from Ballou? He is a little more imprudent or honest in proclaiming his thoughts from the pulpit, that is all. Sentiments equally infidel are found in Ballou's writings in abundance. (Sec. XCVIII.) Will he be disfellowshipped for these rank infidel sentiments? More prudent they would like to see the young man, but are not such *bigots* as to disfellowship a minister of theirs for so small an affair!

CXIX. "No instance of persecution can be pointed out, in all the history of the church, which can be justly attributed to those who believe that God will at last have mercy upon all." *Guide*, p. 261.

If Mr. Whittemore meant to say that no individual of his faith has ever persecuted, his statement is false. Instances not a few could be given, where Universalists have treated members of their own families most brutally for embracing religion among other sects. If he meant to say that Universalists as a body have never persecuted, it is no more than can be said of several other sects, who believe in endless punishment. The Methodists, and some of the Baptist sects have never persecuted. But does this prove that they never would, if hitched on to the corrupting car of state? By no means. And is a mere belief in Universalism so potent to remove depravity, that no persecution might be expected from its votaries did circumstances favor it? Their verbal persecution, the low slang and bitterness with which they have followed Christians, clearly indicate to what they would resort, had they the power, to destroy "Partialism." It will be time enough for Universalism to boast of its pacific character when it shall have once had the rod of power in its own hands without using it.

We are often cited to the bloody deeds of Papal Rome and the persecutions under the Episcopalians and Puritans. These, it is said, were perpetrated by believers in endless punishment, and not by Universalists; and the conclusion is, that Universalism must be the child of heaven. But cannot Atheism prove itself in a very good condition in the same way? The sects named as persecuting were Christians and not Atheists; therefore, Atheism must be the true theory! Not a few of those who have instigated persecutions no more believed in endless punishment than Mr. W. does; but in consequence of the unholy connection of church and state, as found in some parts of Christendom, they have persecuted those who differed from the religion of the state, for worldly purposes, regardless of their own religious views concerning the future condition of man. How does it happen that we, as a nation, have a constitution protecting us in our religious rights? Are we indebted to Universalism for this? Indeed, Mr. W.'s idolized form of Universalism is less than forty years old, (Sec. CXXXIII,) and it is well known that when the people of the United States adopted the constitution, there were but few to be found calling themselves Restorationists, and that all, or nearly so, of the different sects were receivers of the doctrine of eternal punishment. Yet from such a people is transmitted to us a constitution securing religious liberty to all, Universalists not excepted. Away then with such a miserable sophism as stands at the head of this section.

CXX. When we speak of the anger, hatred and vengeance of God, (Ps. 7 : 11; 11 : 5; Rom. 12 : 19,) we are informed that we are not at liberty to attribute human passions to him. We admit that we are not to attribute anger and hate to God in the same sense that man is excited by these passions. But in revealing himself to us God has sometimes used a figure called anthropopathy, by which he attributes human passions to himself, as being the most appropriate ideas of his ways to us, of which we can have any conception, especially when disconnected with everything weak and sinful found with these passions in man. If we do not impute to him something like human passions, and thus follow his own example, we give up revealed truth for philosophical ignorance. Universalists seem not to be aware that compassion, mercy, pity, desire, and love are all human passions, which they readily attribute to God, and that we may err as greatly in our views of these, as in our views of the other class. They hesitate not to infer from the promptings of these passions in man how they must be exercised in God towards his creatures, and thus they make them the same in God that they are in man. When we imitate God by speaking of his indignation, fury, wrath, anger, and vengeance, we are charged with making God a vindictive tyrant. Might we not with equal propriety charge our opponents with representing God as a weak old man in his dotage, or as some cracked-brain swain, ready to melt away with love? What we ask of Universalists is, that they desist from this mode of reasoning upon the sterner passions which God has attributed to himself, or else that they show their consistency by extending the same mode of reasoning to the milder one. If they do this their false appeals to human sympathy and parental affection will become powerless. God's anger, love, and immutable justice all harmonize. See Sections XV. and XXXVII.

CXXI. In the propagation of their doctrine, Universalists make the largest professions of liberality and love for the truth.

They are willing to " hear both sides ; " and Christians are often asked, why they are unwilling to hear Universalists preach, to read their books, and listen to their sermons ? In answer we say,

1. Christians are to " have no fellowship with the unfruitful works of darkness, but rather reprove them." Eph. 5 : 11.

2. The reason why they are unwilling that men should hear Universalists, and read their books, is, not because they fear the truth, but because they fear their sophistries and perversions. They are so, for the same reasons that they are unwilling their friends should hear avowed Infidels lecture, and read their works. They know that such is the opposition of unrenewed minds to God's truth, and their inclination to error, that it is no uncommon thing for men to be exceedingly skeptical respecting the plainest scripture truths, yet, at the same time, manifest an astonishing credulity in receiving almost any absurdity which is offered in opposition to them. This is true of Infidels generally, and it is strikingly true of modern Universalists.

One cunningly devised falsehood in favor of inclination, and to palliate sin, will, upon a certain class of minds, have more weight than ten honest and solid arguments rebuking sin and craning men up to their duty to their God. Universalism is a powerful appeal in favor of depravity, and against God's penalties. It says to irreligious men, " Just what you *desire* the future state to be, it shall be, irrespective of your conduct here." The young, some of whom have but a limited knowledge of the Bible, are often captivated by arguments, as forceless in reality as a feather ; just because the doctrine is in harmony with their feelings, and gives them the largest indulgence they could ask in sinful pleasure.

CXXII. " Preach your own doctrine and let others alone," is a saying quite too common among Christians. If by it, however, is meant that a minister should not evince a pugnacious spirit, that he should not be a lover of controversy, that he should not magnify minor differences between evangelical Christians,—if this is what is meant, we have no objection to it. But if by it is meant, that a man who is set for the defence of the gospel should only teach his own doctrine, and never expose destructive error, we demur. So did not the Lord Jesus Christ, so did not Paul. Suppose a very alarming disease prevalent in your town, and the skillful physician is applying a remedy with great success. While he is doing this, a quack comes along with large professions of skill, administers a medicine which is exactly the reverse of the successful one, and is proving fatal to all who take it, and some of your own dear friends are by it sent down to the grave. The faithful and successful physician analyzes the spurious medicine, comes out fearlessly, and shows the public its destructive properties, and what it is doing. Would you oppose his course, under these circumstances, and cry out, "Administer your own medicine and let other medicines alone?" No, certainly you would not. The world is diseased by sin; the gospel is the remedy. Universalism is a spurious gospel. By the showing of its own advocates, it is opposed, in every essential point, to evangelical Christianity. (Sec. CXXXV.) If an error, as we believe it is, it is a most fatal error. Its advocates are administering their opiates, and many sinners are put to sleep in their sins, and may never be aroused till they wake up in hell. And has the minister done all his duty, when he has merely preached his own sentiments? Before Heaven, we think not.

Perhaps there are but few ways in which they have deceived Christians more, than by their professed love of opposition, for the benefit they derive from it. That they would be pleased with opponents unacquainted with their theory in its modern shape, (Sec. CXXV,) and who have not the ability to expose their serpentine windings, we doubt not. But however much they may bluster at the time, they know full well that an able exposure of their system, and the dishonest means by which it is supported, done in a right spirit, is always an injury to their cause.* Hear what A. C. Thomas says upon this subject:

"I do not coincide in opinion with those who declare, that opposition tends to the advancement of Universalism. On the contrary, I am satisfied that, had it not been for opposition, Universalism would be, at this day, the predominent religious profession in the United States." *Trumpet,* No. 1056.

This is from one of the most pugnacious among them, and one who is well acquainted with the effects of opposition upon the order.

In exposing Universalism, wisdom is necessary, as well as in the discharge of every other ministerial duty. When there are but few of this order in a place, and they have no regular preaching, it might be unwise to give them so much importance as a formal course of lectures would seem to. But where there is an organization, and a minister leading souls to destruction, we do not believe it is wisdom, or duty, for a Christian minister to look calmly on and do nothing. After suitable preparation, let him call the attention of the people to a course of lectures, and fearlessly, in the spirit of Christ, expose the infidel character of the system, and all the dishonorable methods by which it is supported; and also its destructive influence upon the cause of true piety.

Or if there is wanting that kind of ability and taste, of which many able ministers are destitute, for an exposure of this character from the pulpit, let them keep their people informed by the circulation of suitable books and tracts upon the subject. The Universalist papers are filled with doctrinal matter, and they are, with an industry worthy of a better cause, pushing their doc-

* The same argument which forbids an effort against the system, because of the spasmodic zeal it awakens, lies with all its strength against revivals; for nothing renders Universalists more desperate than the outpouring of God's spirit among the people. But shall we not labor for, and welcome revivals, lest they should start up and do something out of the ordinary course? Let the people have light, either from the pulpit or the press, or both.

trinal books and tracts into almost every place. (Sec. CXL.) The people must have light, and especially the church. In the absence of this, we shall occasionally find a morbid sympathy springing up in some minds in favor of this dogma, or they may be captivated by it through our neglect. Let Christian ministers do their duty in this respect, and there need not be any fear of the result. Every minister will of course choose his own method of doing this work, but let it by all means be done. Wavering minds will be established in the truth, and Christians will clearly see the antichristian character of Universalism.

Corroborative of Mr. Thomas's view is the decline of Universalism in Maine. There is no State in the Union where there has been so much decided and open opposition to this error by lectures, discussions, and publications, as in this State. What has been the result ? We cannot give their number of church members, as they are not in their statistics. Church organization, in which they engaged with so much zeal a few years since, was an uphill business, and we hear but little about it now. There are a few localities where there is some show of prosperity, growing mainly out of the wealth connected with it ; but Universalism, as a whole, is greatly on the decline in Maine. This is evident from the decrease in the ministry.

The statistics of the order are before us in the Universalist Companion. In 1844, there were seventy-seven preachers in the State. In 1855, there are fifty-seven. So there is not only no gain for eleven years, but actually a decrease during that time of *twenty* ministers.

The following description is given of the cause in Maine by the Corresponding Secretary of the Maine Convention of Universalists. He says :

" Many societies are without preaching, where were apparently promising congregations. Indeed there is no part of the State, where we may not meet with meeting houses, dedicated to the preaching of doctrines of the Reconciliation, which now stand unoccupied, seeming to say to us in saddened tones, ' Is it nothing to you all ye that pass by?' " *Banner, July* 16, 1854.

CXXIII. Universalists bring our Lord's conversation with the Sadducees, (Matt. 22 : 30; Mark 12 : 25; Luke 20 : 34–36,) in proof of the salvation of all in the future state. We admit that the immortal resurrection is here revealed, but deny that the salvation of all is here taught. See Sec. XCI., where Universalist assumptions are exposed. To illustrate their work upon numerous other passages, we will just show the reader how a *twistical* Universalist could deprive this of its future state reference, if he found it for his interest to do so. In doing this we have only to apply the same mode of argument and definition of terms to this passage, that Universalist divines do to others where the same expressions are found.

1. "*This world,*" and "*that world,*" Luke 20 : 34, 35. By "this world" is meant *this age*, that is, the Jewish age; and by "that world" is meant *that age*, that is, the Christian age, after the destruction of Jerusalem. *Guide to U.* See also Sec. IV.

2. "*Resurrection*" (anastasis). This is the same word which occurs in John 5 : 29 and Luke 14 : 14. "It does not necessarily signify restoration to life after natural death." *Notes on Par.*, p. 165. As the resurrection of the just took place when Jerusalem was destroyed by the Romans, (Sec. LIV,) and as all that were "in the graves" were raised at the same time, some to damnation and others to life, (John 5 : 29; Sec. LXXXI,) and as the same word occurs in the conversation with the Sadducees, it must refer to the same event.

3. "*From the dead.*" This refers to Jews and Christians at the Jerusalem calamity, for they must have been in some sense dead, or they could not have come forth from their graves at that event. (Sec. LXXXI.) It is clear then that no reference is made to the future state of man.

4. "*Neither can they die any more.*" Our ablest divines,

such as Mr. Whittemore and Mr. J. B. Dods, have shown most conclusively, (*Guide*, pp. 164, 223,) that John 8 : 21, and Rev. 21 : 8, have particular reference to the national death of the Jews when Jerusalem was destroyed. The true sense is this: The Jews having died a national death, can die no more as a nation. All must see that the future state is not intended.

5. "*They are equal unto the angels.*" Our greatest men have made it as clear as a sunbeam, that the "mighty angels," 2 Thess. 1 : 7, "and *all* the *holy* angels," Matt. 25 : 31, (Sec. XLI,) mean the polluted heathen, or the Roman armies. *Notes on Par.*, p. 103. Surely it cannot be necessary to go into the future world to become equal to such angels!

6. "*They are as the angels of God in heaven.*" Matt. 22 : 30. Does the word *heaven* carry it into the future state? By no means, for another of our great men says: "It is believed that there is no one place in which the word is used in the Bible, where it obviously means life, or happiness, or the place of these after death." (Sec. LIII.) This, then, makes nothing against our position.

7. "*Neither marry or are given in marriage.*" As we have shown beyond dispute, that this resurrection took place when Jerusalem was destroyed at the end of the Jewish age, all must see that it must have been impossible to have entered into the conjugal relation in such a season of consternation. This saying was literally fulfilled at that time.

8. "*And are children of God, being children of the resurrection.*" We have shown again and again that all men are now the children of God; hence, the Saviour never meant to say that the immortal resurrection would make them children. Dr. Campbell has shown, that agreeable to the original import of the word *anastasis*, (resurrection,) "rising from a seat is properly termed *anastasis*; so is awakening out of sleep, or promotion from an inferior condition." *Notes on Par.*, p. 161. Since, then, there are so many resurrections in this world, we are not

obliged to confine this expression to Jerusalem's destruction, and as all are the children of God here, it is not referable to the immortal resurrection. The true sense, as here employed, is obviously this: To denote the process by which men are raised from non-existence to manhood, and thus they are children of God, being children of the resurrection. Do we not often inquire, where such and such a man was raised? Another and sufficient reason why this passage has no reference whatever to the future state, is, it will not stand the test of Mr. Whittemore's infallible rule. (Sec. CXV.) Let us apply it. Does it say that all men shall be as the angels of God in the *immortal state*? Does it say that all men shall be holy and happy *in eternity?* Does it say that this resurrection is *after death?* "As nothing of the kind is said, we presume nothing like it is meant."

Here we have that which is as truthful and conclusive as most Universalist expositions. With their license we can deprive all their proof texts of their future-state reference, and tumble the most of them into Jerusalem. Apply their interpretations to the expressions, "*resurrection,*" "*die,*" "*death,*" "*Christ's at his coming,*" "*the end,*" and "*kingdom of God,*" which occur in 1 Cor. 15, and that can with equal ease be deprived of its future reference, and thrown into the destruction of Jerusalem. Can that be the truth of heaven which relies for its support upon such a method with the Bible?

CXXIV. It has been asserted that evangelical Christians hold that a belief in endless punishment constitutes a Christian. This is false. They constantly assert the possibility of holding the truth in unrighteousness. What we contend for is this, that the doctrine is taught in the Bible; that it is a fundamental one in the Christian scheme; that it is one of those weighty motives, which God designs should be brought to bear upon sinners to arouse them to seek for that work of grace, without which they cannot be Christians, believe what they will. When the doctrine of endless punishment is given up, other important doctrines are usually abandoned, and all the motives for a prayerful, godly life soon go by the board. The usual result of discarding this doctrine is, other gross errors and irreligion.

> " The breach, though small at first, soon opening wide,
> In rushes folly with a full-moon tide;
> Then welcome errors of whatever size,
> To justify it by a thousand lies."

These words of Cowper find an illustration in the Universalism of America. The same disposition which prompts a man to disbelieve eternal punishment, will prompt him to a disbelief of every other Christian doctrine which his reason cannot fully compass, or which is not in accordance with his feelings. These are the reasons why we contend for the doctrine, and not that simply believing it constitutes a Christian. Depravity is the same, whether found in connection with orthodox or heterodox views. The question is, which is calculated to bring a sinner to Christ for a removal of that depravity, that doctrine which says that God's favor cannot be gained or lost (Sec. CVII.); that, so far as the future is concerned, the saint and sinner are on a perfect level (Sec. XC.); or that which threatens sorrow here and a positive evil in the world to come, in case of continuing to disobey the gospel? We assert that the latter is the reformatory doctrine, because it is taught in the Bible, and the salvation of sinners by the labors of its advocates illustrate it. Ingenious men may give an air of plausibility to some points connected with the Universalist theory, but they can point to none reformed and made pious as a result of teaching it. Their reformed men are generally at a distance, in some other town. Should the Maine Liquor Law be extensively adopted, it will doubtless render hundreds more respectable who vociferate for Universalism, by cutting off their *spiritual* supplies. But such reforms must be credited to the *law*, and not to *their* gospel.

CXXV. There are many very able ministers who well understand the truths of the Bible, and know that Universalism is false, who are, nevertheless, somewhat ignorant of the crafty methods resorted to for its defence. The difference between these and Universalist teachers, is this: The latter exert all their ingenuity to destroy the obvious meaning of certain portions of the scriptures; while the business of the former is, to enforce the truth as they find it in the Bible, and, under God, to make men pious. The objects to be secured by the two are very different; and it is not to be considered a disparagement to a good minister of Christ, if he is to some extent unacquainted with the wiles of such men. Such uninformed persons, however, should be cautious how they engage in controversy with men whose sole business is to shuffle the word of God, as truth might suffer by their inability to defend it, or to expose the sophistries arrayed against it. One part of their craft is, to represent an opponent as a giant in the ranks of the opposition; and if he is a D. D., all the better, if he is only ignorant of their tactics, or has not the power timely to command his own resources. If such discussions are ever necessary, none should join issue, but such as have *studied* the last edition of Universalism, so that they can say with Paul, "We are not ignorant of his (their) devices." See Sec. CXXII.

CXXVI. A while since, a mighty effort was put forth to make the world believe that John Wesley was a Universalist. A story has been told in which it is stated that he said he "fully believed Universalism but had not made known the fact to the world, thinking the time was not yet ripe for the promulgation of the sentiment." A writer in the "Newark Eagle," who signed himself "Verity," said, "He (Mr. Wesley) did not answer a work written by Sir George Stonehouse. He and others had promised to do it. But he excused himself by saying it would occupy so much of his time that he could not acquit his conscience before God. That this is a mere subterfuge, is self-evident."

So says Mr. "Verity." The first story fixes the charge of hypocrisy upon Wesley, and the second of lying. Whittemore, in his history, names Wesley in connection with Stonehouse, but not as a Universalist then or at any subsequent period. But, on the contrary, he represents him as saying to Stonehouse, "Better you had died, George, before you had written that book." p. 237.

Taking into the account Wesley's profession and labors till the day of his death, the whole effort amounts to this: John Wesley was a *good* Universalist, a base hypocrite, and a confounded liar! A brilliant trinity of attributes, well harmonized, created by the advocates of Universalism for the benefit of the craft; but vain is the attempt to tack them on to John Wesley. The world knows too much of him for that. John Wesley a Universalist!

It is a very common thing for the leaders in the order to assert that their doctrine prevails extensively in other sects. Mr. Boyden, in a sermon before the U. S. Convention, says: "I am fully persuaded if the secrets of all hearts were laid open, we should find thousands who are supposed to be men in orthodoxy, so called, but really are babes in Universalism." *Banner, Nov.* 2, 1844.

That is, many who profess to be strong orthodox, are in reality Universalists.

A writer in the Universalist Companion, for 1852, says: "Even among orthodox sects, many members, and not a few clergymen, secretly hold our views."

Brown, in his History of Universalism, p. 337, gives the following: "A Calvinistic clergyman declared, 'I am a believer in Universalism; I do believe all will be saved; but it will not do to preach it.' Why, sir? 'I cannot get supported handsomely and comfortably if I was publicly to avow this doctrine.'"

Mr. Brown will have it that there are many more Universalists of this class in the ministry of Christian churches. Mr. Whittemore, in his Modern History of Universalism, furnishes us quite a list of these concealed Universalists. Among them he names (p. 383) J. Huntington, D. D., of Coventry, Conn., who, as he states, wrote a book in the prime of his life, called "Calvinism Improved," teaching Universalism. The manuscript he kept by him during his life, and made provision in his will for its publication after his death. *Brown's Hist. of Univ.*, p. 339. Here then is a Universalist, with a manuscript by him for years, containing his real sentiments, and yet all the while sustaining the relation of pastor to a Congregationalist church, and receiving his salary from those who think him a believer and teacher of orthodox views. In this transaction we have a clear evidence of his belief in Universalism, and also an illustration of its blighting, withering influence upon the moral feelings of its recipients. Then look at the case just presented from Brown's History, of a man who was a Universalist, but preached among the Calvinists to get a comfortable support! And we are informed that there are many such Universalists in other sects. What gross hypocrisy!

Could an enemy have given Universalism a worse character than is here given it by its friends? And shall we be charged with slander, if we say the doctrine is demoralizing. O, Universalism! "Out of thine own mouth will I judge thee." In view of the hypocrisy of Universalists upon this subject, a thought occurs, viz.: No *believer* in a future judgment and endless punishment will ever be found professing to be a Universalist all his days, or publishing anonymous books advocating the doctrine. With such a belief he would feel that such wicked reservation and deception would meet him in the judgment, and send his soul to an endless hell. Such deception upon such a subject, in connection with such a belief, cannot *possibly* exist. Reader, which think you is the truth of God, that which *admits* of such deception upon this subject, or that which *absolutely* forbids it?

One thought more. All are aware that their editors have seized with great avidity upon the defections in the membership and ministry of Christian churches, given them the highest coloring possible, and published them to the world as the fruits of Partialism. But what authority have they for this, since there are so many of their own faith, both in the membership and ministry of these same churches? It would be a very natural conclusion that such unprincipled men are just the men to commit other deeds of wickedness.

But why are the eyes of these gentlemen constantly turned to the Christian church for the influence of their sentiments? We beg of them to look for a moment in a less honorable direction. Look at the ungodly throng of profane, drunken, gambling, Sabbath breaking men, to be found more or less in every place where Universalism obtains. Some of these rally for its support, and others do nothing but *illustrate* it. They pay no support to its ministers, and seldom listen to its preaching. It is enough for them to know that Universalist societies are formed, houses built, and that men are abroad calling themselves gospel ministers, teaching that "God is *not* angry with the wicked every day," and the impossibility of sinning enough to incur any more punishment than shall be for the sinner's good. With such influences upon them they are wise enough not to pay money to ministers for a bill of indulgence, when they can have it gratis.

We beg of these men to look in this direction and witness the influence of *their* glad tidings to depravity upon this class of persons. We think the influence upon these will be found to be no better than it is on those in the Christian churches, of which they boast. It may be said that such are not Universalists. But they are not shaken off in this way. Speak to one of them about his duty to God and the danger of his soul, and he will draw forth his bill of indulgence with as much confidence as any poor Papist of Luther's time ever did. He is not to be frightened, for God is too good to send his creatures to hell. And although in morals he is waxing worse and worse, and his physical nature is fast sinking by his vices, yet his cherished faith tells him he is only ripening for glory!

CXXVII. *Twistical.* As this word is used a few times in this work, the reader shall have its history. A few years since Messrs. Drew and Whittemore got into a quarrel through their respective papers, about the character of the notorious J. B. Dods, in which the former said of the latter, (*Banner, March* 11, 1843): "We have for a long time, as have also most of our brother editors and preachers, been aware that Bro. Whittemore, when his mind has become warped by prejudice against *friends*, as well as foes, is one of the most unfair and twistical writers connected with our cause. But we were never called to experience so complete and final proof of his disregard of common fairness and fraternal courtesy as we find in his last paper. We will just say that in only fifty lines of his editorial remarks, embracing the close of his first column on his third page, we counted and marked no less than thirteen errors, which, if intended, are, to speak plainly, *falsehoods;* or, if not intended, are mistakes of too serious a nature to be committed by a man who professes to understand his subject."

Observe: This is not from an enemy to Universalism, but from one of the fraternity. Now this same Mr. Whittemore has written a book called "The Guide to Universalism," a book of great popularity in the order, in which he professes to explain all the principal texts which are thought to oppose Universalism. From our knowledge of his writings, we think Mr. Drew exceedingly happy in his effort at coining a word. It is highly expressive, especially in its application to Universalist divines, and should find a place in the next edition of Webster's Dictionary, for that purpose if no other.

CXXVIII. State prisons have been visited, and it is said the most of the prisoners, when questioned, were found to be believers in endless punishment; and the conclusion is, that this doctrine is productive of vice, while Universalism is highly conducive to virtue. Now suppose an Atheist were to visit these same prisons, and ask each convict if he believed in the being of God; doubtless the answer in almost every case would be in the affirmative. Then, according to the reasoning of Universalists, we should come to the grave conclusion, that a belief in God is detrimental to morals, while Atheism is favorable to virtue!

A statement has been extensively circulated, in Universalist prints, that the "Legislature of Ohio selected at one time a Methodist chaplain for the prison, on account of there being more Methodists than any other class among the prisoners." It is also stated that the prisoners were consulted in the choice. The evident design is to make the impression, that the convicts named were Methodists when they entered prison. This needs no refutation. Admitting what is said concerning the choice of a chaplain to be true, it is only a mark of the wisdom of both the Legislature and the convicts to choose an evangelical man instead of a Universalist. What good could Universalism do them? What good results from it to wicked men out of prison? Does it reform them? Never. If modern Universalism is true, evangelical teaching could do them no essential injury; but, on the other hand, if evangelical sentiments are true, Universalist teaching might do them an irreparable harm. Since, then, Universalism cannot boast of infallibility, that system may be false and ours true; this being the case, no wise man would reject evangelical Christianity, and throw himself upon Universalism, for that would be running an unnecessary risk. Let evangelical religion be embraced with all the heart, and such are safe, whether Universalism be true or false. Shrewd prisoners, away from the exciting influence outside the prison walls, and having time for reflection, with their Bibles before them, may see the worthless character of Universalism, and find the best of reasons for choosing a Christian minister to instruct them. As it respects those who once professed religion, they were brought to the prison, not by evangelical principles, but by *acting in opposition to them,* as they will all testify. The just retributions of eternity were, at that time, removed from their minds. Their crimes are in no way chargable to evangelical sentiments. But the truth is, many Universalists do find their way into the state prisons, though if inquired of might not admit a belief of it, for it is no uncommon thing for the most zealous supporters of the dogma to reply in the negative, when questioned upon this subject, assigning as a reason that they "*are not good enough to be Universalists.*" Now these exalted views of Universalism, and this extreme modesty, may sometimes obtain in the state prison as well as elsewhere.

But Universalists are often found in the state prison. Rev. J. B. Finley, who was sometime chaplain of the Ohio prison, and perhaps the very man who was chosen at the time named, in his "Prison Life," speaking of the convicts, says:

"Among the number was an old man, whom I knew many years ago; and he was then a villain, which he is up to this day. He professes to believe in God, in a future state, and in heaven; but affirms that all men as soon as they die go directly to the world of everlasting happiness. In other words this old veteran among scoundrels is a notorious Universalist." p. 133.

"Universalism has been the means of bringing many of my miserable charge to their present ruin; and I feel called upon to give it my most severe rebuke, from this Golgotha, where the skulls of its slain victims are so profusely strown." p. 27.

Speaking of hardened Infidels in the prison, he says, that he found the "most of them had gone to infidelity through the convenient door-way of Universalism." p. 31.

For aught we know, not a few of those in the prisons, who profess to believe future punishment, are Universalists at heart, for if believers in the doctrine can play the hypocrite in Christian churches, (Sec. CXXVI,) they can do the same in the state prison, especially if they wish to aid a minister of the order in making a report against "Partialism." We have no confidence in these prison reports from Universalist ministers. They make them to serve their errors, and their bill of indulgence gives them all the latitude they wish in the work.

CXXIX. The great numbers that have been converted from the Partialist ministry, as it is called, to Universalism, is an important item with editors of the order, to be kept before the people. But do they ever inform their readers of the vast disproportion that exists between their ministry and all others put together? No; for this would destroy all their capital. According Dr. Baird's Report of Religion in America, before the Evangelical Alliance in Paris, Aug. 5, 1855, which was prepared with great care and accuracy, the Protestant evangelical ministry in the United States, number as follows:

Episcopal, 1,714; Congregationalist, 1,848 settled, and 479 without charge. Different orders of Baptists, 8,525; Presbyterian, all orders, 5,889. Different denominations of Methdists, travelling and local ministry, 22,198; Lutherans, 980; Mennonists, 250; Moravians, 28. Cast these figures and we have an aggregate of 42,111. Add to this 822 licentiates among the Presbyterians, as reported by Dr. Baird, and the professors in colleges and seminaries, many of whom are ordained ministers, and also the ministry of the orthodox Quakers, numbers unknown, and there cannot be less than 43,000 ministers in the evangelical churches in the United States. But for our purpose, and not to overrate numbers, we will call the number 40,000.

According to the Universalist statistics for 1855, they have in the United States 646 preachers, 39 of which are marked as "formerly belonging to the Partialists." Now the question is, if 39 have been converted to Universalism out of 40,000 believers in evangelical doctrines, how many must be converted from 646 Universalists to evangelical views to make it equal? Figures will show that if *one* only can be found who has left the

Universalist ministry, and is now a minister in an evangelical church, that one is *more* in proportion than the thirty-nine, of which Universalists boast. Can *one* be found? Why then do they not, like honest men, state the vast disproportion here set forth? The reader can easily judge why. See Sec. CXXXIV. and CXXXVII.

CXXX. "Would it be merciful in God to suffer endless punishment? that is, would it be merciful to the sufferer? Can that be just which is not merciful? Do not cruelty and injustice go hand in hand?"

"We freely admit that the infliction of endless punishment upon sinners, is not a merciful act, but is directly opposed to the exercise of mercy. The claims of justice and mercy never conflict with each other; and hence, though we admit that endless punishment is not merciful, we deny, at the same time, that it is any violation of mercy. Justice and mercy are distinct principles, and may be exercised conjointly, or one may be exercised without any manifestation of the other, and yet without violating either. When God chastises his children, as in the case of all corrective and sanctified afflictions, justice and mercy are both displayed; justice, because the punishment is what we deserve, and mercy because it is sanctified to our good. When God forgives sinners without punishment, as in the case of the Ninevites, mercy is displayed without any manifestation of justice in the case, yet justice is not violated. When God cuts off the sinner, as in the case of the old world, the Sodomites, and many others which might be mentioned, he displays his justice without any manifestation of mercy,,yet there is nothing unmerciful in it, since mercy claims nothing in these cases, they being no longer subjects of mercy.

"The idea that Universalists make so prominent, that every act of the divine administration must be an act of mercy, to save his government from impeachment, has no foundation in the Bible. The scriptures make a clear distinction between mercy and justice, between grace and wrath, and between blessings and curses. An act of mercy never flows from simple justice, but is an offspring of goodness, while wrath never proceeds from mercy, but is insulted justice taking vengeance upon the guilty. The Bible does not pretend that mercy and justice are equally displayed in the case of every subject of the divine government; 'Therefore hath he mercy on whom he will have mercy, and whom he will he hardeneth.' Rom. 9 : 18. 'For he shall have judgment without mercy that hath showed no mercy.' James 2 : 13.

"These scriptures, together with many more which might be produced, show that every act of the divine administration, is not an act of mercy.

"But it is asked: 'Can that be just which is not merciful?' This has been already answered above, but we will answer it again by saying, Yes, an act may be just without being merciful. We have just quoted a text which says certain characters shall have judgment WITHOUT MERCY. Now, judgment without mercy cannot be merciful, yet it must be just. There are many cases in which an action may be just and not be merciful. It may be that justice requires that the murderer shall be hanged; but it is not an act of mercy even to a murderer to hang him. A rich man may lend money to a poor man, and justice may require the poor man to pay it again, but mercy does not require it, since the rich man is better off without it than he is with it. 'He that despised Moses' law died WITHOUT MERCY.' Heb. 10 : 28. Was there not justice without mercy? But it is asked, 'Do not cruelty and injustice go hand in hand?' Not necessarily; an act may be cruel without being unjust; or an act may be unjust without being cruel. It would be unjust for a poor man to cheat a rich man out of a bushel corn, but it would not be cruel. On the other hand it might be very cruel for a rich man to take a poor man's last bushel of corn to satisfy a just debt, but it would not be unjust.

"In all this, it should be borne in mind, that the injustice of endless punishment is taken for granted, without any effort to prove it. If it could be proved that endless punishment would be unjust, then it might be proved that it would be unmerciful; or if it could be proved that it would be unmerciful, that is, contrary to the claims of mercy, then it might be proved that under the circumstances of the gospel, that it would be unjust: but until one of these points is proved, independently of the other, no advance is made in the argument. It amounts to this: Endless punishment is unjust because it is unmerciful; and it is unmerciful because it is unjust. Such arguments cannot convince those who have minds to think for themselves. If indeed it may be called argument, it is *argumentum ad ignorantiam, ad captandum vulgus*. An argument founded on the ignorance of fact to ensnare the vulgar." *Sword of Truth.*

CXXXI. "Universalism will do to live by, but it will not do to die by." There could be no greater mistake. The only thing to be determined is this: is it true or false? If false, it will do neither for life or death. Religious error is never conducive to a sound morality, while religious truth is. Universalism is false; it is an evil tree, and therefore cannot bring forth good fruit. It is hoped that the senseless saying, "It will do to live by, but not to die by," will never again be uttered by any lover of truth. We need the same religion in life that we do in the dying hour. As it respects the boasted support of Universalism in death, it is all a delusion. A mere willingness to die is no sure evidence of Christian truth or character. Heathen devotees are willing to die; and Infidels, regardless of the future, have sometimes been willing to die. Men with consciences "seared with a hot iron," and hearts steeped in crime, have also evinced a willingness to die. Some Universalists have so long resisted God's spirit and rejected his truth, that they are left to "believe a lie," (2 Thess 2:10–12,) and some die while under this delusion.

Others among them who have made less progress in their warfare with God, have been aroused to a sense of their danger on the very verge of eternity, finding it to be a fearful truth, that Universalism "will not do to die by." When a poor sinner is thus awakened, it calls into requisition all the skill his Universalist attendants are capable of to keep it from the public ear, and also to prevent intercourse with Christians. Many such have been smuggled out of the world without a Christian to counsel them, or to offer a prayer in their behalf. It is known that a powerful influence often goes out from the death-bed scene, in opposition to their sentiments; hence unnecessary restrictions are often imposed to prevent Christians from visiting the sick and dying, and warnings have been hushed which would have carried conviction through whole neighborhoods. There is no end to the deceptions used to produce the impression that Universalism yields true support in death.

CXXXII. *Was the belief of endless punishment common both among Jews and Gentiles in our Saviour's time?*

Universalists shall speak for themselves, as their testimony will not be doubted upon this point.

"The Pharisees, it is well known, believed in the endless punishment of human souls." *Lectures by W. N. Fernald*, p. 79. "It is generally admitted that the Jews, in our Saviour's day, maintained the Pagan notion of immortal happiness for the righteous, and undying pain for the sinner." *Letter in the Trumpet of Feb.* 3, 1838, *by W. C. Hanscom, a Universalist minister.* "That the Pharisees believed in a punishment after death, we do not deny." *Whittemore's Notes on the Parables*, p. 62. "Jews and heathen believed in endless punishment." *Balfour's Essays*, p. 326.

The following will show how extensively it prevailed among the Jews when our Saviour, the greatest of teachers, sojourned among them. Mr. Balfour, in his *Inquiry*, p. 260, where he attempts to show that the Jews obtained their views of endless punishment from the heathen, says: "The introduction of this and other heathen opinions among the Jews was gradual, but in the days of our Lord had become general, with perhaps the exception of the sect of Sadducees." This sect composed but a small part of the Jewish nation.

Were Christ and his apostles Universalists? Were they believers in no future and eternal punishment?

Most assuredly they were, if Universalism is true. If they were not, then it is false. No time need be spent to prove this. Christ and his apostles, then, being Universalists, spent their time and preached among those entirely opposed to this doctrine, and believers in endless punishment.

Was it any part of the work of Christ and his apostles to point out and rebuke the errors of the age in which he lived?

Mr. Whittemore shall answer:

"Our Saviour when on earth labored hard to root up the plants which his Father had not planted. He knew that error was injurious to man, and that he performed an act of kindness and duty in exposing it. How careful was he to point out the errors which men had imbibed. '*Ye have heard*,' said he, 'that it hath been said, an eye for an eye, and a tooth for a tooth. *But I say unto you*, resist not evil, &c. *Ye have heard that it hath been said*, thou shalt love thy neighbor, and hate thine enemy. *But I say unto you*, love your enemies, bless them that curse you, do good to them that hate you, and pray for them which despitefully use you and persecute you.' He detailed some of the errors of the Scribes and Pharisees, relative to swearing by the gold of the temple, and the gilt upon the altar; and called them blind guides. He was careful also to point out the errors of their conduct, as well as of their opinions. The apostles followed our Saviour in their practice. 'Paul and Barnabas had no small dissension and disputation with' 'certain men which came down from Judea,' and taught the brethren that they could not be saved, except they were circumcised after the manner of Moses. They endeavored to root up a plant which God had not planted. It would be a task far too arduous to mention all the instances recorded in the New Testament, of Christ and his apostles pointing out and contending against the errors of the age in which he lived." *Trumpet*, No. 750.

Here it is admitted, yea, contended for, by Mr. W., that the Saviour was *careful to point out the errors which men had imbibed*, and that so *numerous* are the instances where Christ and his apostles have pointed out and contended against the errors of the age in which they lived, that *it would be a task far too arduous to mention all that are recorded in the New Testament.*

Do Universalists of our time deem endless punishment the chief of errors, and do they vigorously and incessantly oppose it?

Mr. Drew, one of the great men of the order, shall answer:

Speaking of the doctrine in question, he says (*Banner*, Feb. 2, 1841): "*We believe it to be the greatest error of our times — one fraught with the worst results to society.*" "*Put all the other errors of the world into one, and this would not equal in magnitude that to which we refer.*" "*Is it any longer a wonder to your mind, reader, that we as Universalists should employ so much of our time in preaching and writing against that grand error? Nay, but we must do it.*" In keeping with these extracts, are their pulpits and presses generally. This is but a sample of what might fill volumes, indicative of the views, feelings, and labors of these men.

Have we any account whatever that Christ and his apostles treated the doctrine of endless punishment as an error, by rebuking it, showing its fatal effects, and cautioning the people against it?

Now here is the Great Teacher, who has come from heaven to teach Universalism, and called and commissioned his apostles to engage in the same work. Mr. Whittemore says of him that he was *careful to point out the errors which men had imbibed;* and so numerous are the instances where Christ and his apostles have contended against the errors of their age, that *it would be a task far too arduous to mention all that are recorded in the*

New Testament. They commenced and exercised their ministry among believers in endless punishment, an error so great that Mr. Drew says of it, " Put all the other errors of the world into one, and this would not equal it in magnitude." Now we ask, may we not expect to find something very explicit, decided, and pointed from the Son of God, in opposition to this error ; something that shall make the matter clear to the church in all after ages, something at least analogous to the efforts against it by modern Universalist preachers ? We should certainly expect this. But what is the fact ? It is nowhere to be found in all the Scriptures that Christ, or any of his followers, ever spent a moment's time in disproving the doctrine, or in portraying to their hearers its dreadful effects, or in warning them against it. *We boldly assert that not a single instance of this character can be found.* Let Universalists produce one, if they can.

To what shall we attribute this silence ? Could not the Saviour perceive the dreadful effects of this error, as well as men in our day ? Or perceiving, had he no heart to feel as well as they ? Had pity left the Son of Man ? And what is still more surprising, he did explicitly point out and correct other errors which were as the pebble to the mountain when compared with this, if we may believe the smallest part of what its opponents say of it. He faithfully exposed the errors of the Pharisees ; such as their superstitious observance of the Sabbath, their washing of hands and pots, their making long prayers, the inconsistency of their " tithing the mint, anise and cummin," while they neglected the weightier matters of the law, and many other things : but he wholly passed over this great error. The apostles too, were often found opposing errors of little consequence compared with this, if Universalism is true. " How boldly and explicity Paul opposes the sentiment, that ' by the deeds of the law men could be justified in the sight of God.' With what a masterly argument he overthrew the Sadducean heresy, that ' there is no resurrection.' How fearlessly and directly he denounced the heresy of Hymeneus and Philetus, that ' the resurrection was already past.' Indeed, a very considerable portion of the Epistles of Paul is taken up in opposing the prevalent errors of the times." In the book of Acts, too, we find prevailing errors exposed, and faithful reproof administered and caution given, by different apostles. Also, in the Epistles of James, Peter, John and Jude, we find the errors of the times pointedly rebuked and glaringly exposed. But nowhere in the book of Acts, or any of the Epistles, do we learn that they ever rebuked the doctrines of a future judgment, and an endless punishment. How unlike modern Universalists, whose chief labor consists in exposing what they call their dreadful effects, and appealing to the sympathies of men respecting them!

Let us further inquire,

Did the Saviour and his apostles teach a future judgment and eternal punishment? Did they use language calculated to confirm those they addressed in these errors, if they were such?

To this we reply, they most certainly did. To say nothing of the impression Matt. 25 : 31–46 always makes upon the mind of the unsophisticated reader, we think there is not one, at all acquainted with Jewish belief relative to a future state, but must be convinced that our Lord's Jewish hearers, when he uttered this passage, must have understood him as teaching a general judgment, and endless bliss and misery. See an extract from Josephus, Sec. XLI.

"In hell (*hades*) he lifted up his eyes, being in torments." Luke 16 : 23. Mr. Balfour admits, (*Inq.*, pp. 74–79,) that when our Saviour spoke these words, "the opinion prevailed among the Jews that there were torments in Hades;" and he will have it that our Lord speaks in accordance with popular opinions. The Saviour then, instead of opposing a dangerous and prevailing error, speaks in accordance with popular opinion upon the subject. How then must his hearers have understood him? He qualifies nothing. He must have been understood as teaching torments in the invisible or spirit world.

For understanding the language of the Bible, the following common-sense rule is given by an eminent writer:

"The meaning of a word used by any writer, is the meaning affixed to it by those for whom he immediately wrote. For there is a kind of natural compact between those who write and those who speak a language; by which they are mutually bound to use words in a certain sense: he, therefore, who uses such words in a different signification, in a manner violates the compact, and is in danger of leading men into error." *Horne's Introd.*, vol. 1, p. 325.

It is obvious that this rule applies with force to the subject under consideration. As a few out of the many, the reader is referred to the following texts. Mark 3:29; Luke 12:4, 5; John 5:28, 29; Matt. 10:15–28; Rom. 2:4–16; 14:10–12; Heb. 6:1, 2; 9:27, 28; 2 Thess. 1:7–10; 2 Pet. 2:4–9. If the belief of those to whom these texts were addressed is considered, and also the labored, unnatural, and absurd interpretations Universalists are under the necessity of giving to destroy their force, what candid mind, we ask, but must see that Christ and his apostles not only *did not* oppose the doctrines of future judgment and endless punishment, but that they actually *did sustain* them by their own teachings?

Let us again inquire,

Did either Jews or Gentiles oppose Christ and his followers for teaching the future salvation of all men, or for rejecting the opposite doctrine?

There is not a single instance in the Scriptures where they met with such opposition. Universalists have often asserted that Christ was opposed for the same cause they are now, viz.: his Universalism. But this is mere assumption, without any foundation either in the history of our Lord or the Pharisees. That the Pharisees were the enemies of Christ, is well known; and as such, accused him of many things, such as his being an enemy to Cæsar; as in league with Beelzebub; a blasphemer, &c. On his trial, Pilate said to him, "Behold how many things they witness against thee;" but we look in vain to find that they ever charged him with holding and teaching no future and eternal punishment for the wicked. The Pharisees being his enemies, and the doctrine of eternal punishment being generally believed, both among Jews and Gentiles, might we not reasonably suppose that Christ's being a "perfect Universalist," would have occupied a prominent place in the charges brought against him from time to time. But upon this point there is a dead silence. He never complained of the Jews for holding the doctrine of eternal punishment, neither did the Jews of him for holding the salvation of all men. The same is true of all his apostles, who labored both among the Jews and Gentiles. For instance, look at the charges brought against Paul at different times; but never is he charged with teaching the salvation of all men. In the vindication of his character from heresy (Acts 24:15), he says: "And (I) have hope toward God, which they (the Jews) themselves allow, that there shall be a resurrection of the dead, both of the just and unjust." What did the Jews allow? None will assert that they allowed, or believed, that all men would be ushered into bliss by the resurrection. But they did believe that the just and unjust would be raised, and judged; and that one class would be welcomed to bliss, and the other sentenced to endless punishment. This was Paul's belief. All are aware of the great labor of Universalists to portray before the people the dreadful consequences of the doctrine of eternal punishment. *But be it known that there is not a single precedent for this course in all the Bible.* They have not produced one, for the good reason that they cannot.

Let it be observed, that while they fail to give *one* text to show that either our Saviour or any of his apostles ever came in collision with either Jew or Gentile upon the doctrine in question, they do bring a solitary text in which they profess to think Christ warned his disciples against it. It is this: Matt. 16:6, "Then said Jesus unto them, beware of the leaven (doctrine, v. 12,) of the Pharisees and of the Sadducees." Universalists will have it that this means, "beware of the doctrine of endless punishment." But did the Sadducees believe that? See Sec. XCVI., where the true sense is given, and the perversion exposed.

There is one text more they sometimes bring, to prove that Paul and others were persecuted for preaching their faith. It is 1 Tim. 4 : 10 ; "Therefore we both labor and suffer reproach, because we trust in the living God, who is the Saviour of all men, especially of those that believe." That this is a perversion may be seen, Sec. XCV.

A favorite argument to prove Christ and his apostles Universalists, may be briefly stated thus :

The Pharisees hated Christ and his apostles; the Pharisees were Partialists; therefore Christ and his apostles must have been Universalists. Their disciples often use this argument in substance, if not in form, and they obtain it from their teachers; for none can sit long under their ministry, without learning from them that the hatred the Pharisees bore to Christ and his apostles, was on account of their Universalism. This, you will see, is a very easy method to prove people Universalists. Let us try it again. The Pharisees hated all heathens; the Pharisees were Partialists; therefore the millions of heathen must have been Universalists. So you see that by this simple process, not only Christ and his apostles are made Universalists, but all the heathen.

Other grounds of difference, besides a point or two of doctrine, may call forth hatred. Papists have persecuted Protestants, and put them to death, yet they have ever agreed upon some points of doctrine. We do not contend that Christ taught or sanctioned all the doctrines of the Pharisees. Christ called them hypocrites, a generation of vipers, and threatened them with the damnation of hell, and claimed in opposition to their views to be the Messiah. Yet Universalists, it would seem, can see no possible reason why the Jews should have hated Christ, unless he was a Universalist! They will have it, too, that our Lord's

Universalism was shockingly offensive to the Jews, and yet in all their controversy with him, and their proceedings against him, it is not so much as once charged against him, or even named!

Let the reader weigh well the following thoughts:

1. Our Lord and his apostles, whose business it was to establish truth and overthrow error, spent their time upon earth among believers in endless punishment.

2. Deriving our knowledge from the Bible, they never exposed or rebuked the doctrine in a *single* instance.

3. If they were Universalists, they taught the doctrine, and it must have been known to the Jews. Charges of heresy were from time to time brought against them by their Jewish enemies; but in no *single* instance, either formally, incidentally, or accidentally, are they charged with holding the salvation of all men.

4. They used the same language in the presence of the Jews, that the Jews did to teach some of their prominent doctrines of a future state; or, as Mr. Balfour says, they spoke in accordance with popular opinions.

Now to what shall we attribute their conformity in language to Jewish belief, and the complete absence of any collision either with Jews or Gentiles upon the doctrines in question, and their failure to rebuke a future judgment and endless punishment, by a single direct attack or exposure.* Had they not as much love for human kind, and sympathy for suffering humanity, as modern Universalist ministers? Were they so blind that they could not see the fatal effects of this great and alarming error? Or were they wanting in courage to speak out and warn the people? Who so blind as not to see that if Universalists have the truth upon this subject, Christ and his apostles were sadly deficient as Universalist ministers? Or rather, who so blind as not to see that Universalism is glaringly false, that Christ and the apostles taught no such doctrine, but were believers and teachers of end-

* Mr. Thayer, speaking of endless punishment, says, "It was the popular doctrine of the day in the time of the Saviour, a part of the common faith of Jews and Pagans." Mr. T. also asserts that Christ maintained towards it a position of "*entire silence.*" *Hist. of E. Pun.*, p. 137.

less punishment? Do Universalist ministers sometimes say eloquent things concerning the example of Christ? Suppose they were to imitate it, would they ever clamor against endless punishment? Would they ever appeal to human sympathy, and raise arguments from the attributes of God against the doctrine? And suppose they were to use the same language Jesus did, without qualification, would they ever be taken for teachers of Universalism? Truly this is an age of improvement, for these moderns are far in advance of the Master!

Think upon the facts stated in this section, reader, and be a Universalist if you can.

CXXXIII. "The doctrine of endless misery, that inhuman dogma, which is common to both Arminians and Calvinists, was first openly asserted in the Christian Church by Tertullian, in the third century. Until this time, no declaration of any such doctrine as endless misery by any professed disciple of Jesus, is known to have been made." *Univ. Almanac*, 1844, p. 36.

This appears to be a common stock idea with Universalist writers, but it is a historical falsehood. Mr. H. Ballou, 2d, some years since published what he called the "Ancient History of Universalism," in which he states concerning Tertullian, as follows: "He is thought to have been the first Christian writer who expressly asserted that the torments of the damned will be of equal duration with the happiness of the blest." p. 80. Looking to Mr. Ballou as an oracle, he has by this statement misled all who have put their trust in him. If Mr. B. had no knowledge of such an important work as Justin Martyr's Apology, he was not qualified to write church history: if he had a knowledge of this work, then there was a wicked concealment of facts. Justin was one of the most learned of all the early Fathers, and among his valuable works are his Apologies, or what would be called in our times defences of Christian doctrines and practice, the first of which he addressed to the Roman Emperor Antoninus Pius, about A.D. 150. This, translated by

Rev. W. Reeves, London, 1709, is before us, from which we give the following extracts:

He says, "*Moreover we say, that the souls of the wicked being reunited to the same bodies, shall be consigned over to eternal torments, and not as Plato will have it, to the period of a thousand years only; but if you will affirm this to be incredible or impossible, there is no help for you, but you must fall from error to error, till the day of judgment convinces you we are right.*" p. 26.

The word *eternal* is evidently used here to distinguish between the endless punishment believed by Christians, and the limited one taught by Plato, the heathen philosopher.

Again he says, "*I must tell you likewise, that of all men living we are the greatest promoters of peace, and bring you in the most powerful auxiliaries to establish it in your dominions, by teaching that it is impossible for any worker of iniquity, any covetous or insidious person, any one, either vicious or virtuous, to hide himself from God; and that every one is stepping forward into everlasting misery or happiness, according to his works.*" p. 31.

Observe, "*every one is stepping forward into everlasting misery or happiness.*" Is the word *everlasting* used in a borrowed sense here? Then is the happiness of the righteous limited. All must see that it is used in its proper sense, to signify endless duration.

Once more he says, "*When we assert departed souls to be in a state of sensibility, and the wicked to be in torments, but the good free from pain and in a blissful condition, we assert no more than your poets and philosophers.*"

"*But the ringleader and the prince of evil spirits, is by us called the serpent, and Satan, and false accuser, as you may easily find from our scriptures, who together with all his hosts of angels and men like himself, shall be thrust into fire, there to be tormented world without end, as our Christ hath foretold.*"

"*For, tell you I must, that if you persist in this course of iniquity, you shall not escape the vengeance of God in another world.*" pp. 49, 59, 127.

Remark, "tormented world *without end, as our Christ hath foretold.*" All must see that endless punishment is declared by Justin to be a doctrine taught by Christ and believed by Christians; for he is not giving his own belief merely, but the doctrines of the Christians generally. This apology was written at least fifty years before Tertullian flourished.* A few years since, (1846,) we published a work containing an examination of the Ancient History, by Ballou, and the Modern History, by Whittemore, in which their errors upon this subject were exposed. The following is a synopsis of our investigation down to A.D. 210.

Barnabas, who lived in the time of the apostles, says of Christ, "*after the resurrection he will judge the world.*" "The way of darkness is crooked, and full of cursing, for it is the way of *eternal death with punishment.*"

Clemens Romanus, a fellow laborer with St. Paul, says, "If we disobey his (Christ's) commands, nothing shall deliver us *from eternal punishment.*"

* Mr. H. Ballou, 2d, in his History, attempts to show that Justin believed in the eventual annihilation of the wicked. This he does by quotations from his Dialogue with Trypho, the Jew. It is well understood that his Dialogue was written some years after his First Apology. This Mr. Ballou himself asserts as follows: "The Dialogue with Trypho was written certainly after the First Apology, but perhaps before the Second, which is generally placed at the year 162." *Anc. Hist., p.* 56. *Note.* Whatever may have been Justin's views when he wrote his Dialogue, he has most certainly testified in favor of endless punishment in his First Apology, which was written years before. Observe, it is from the First Apology we quote; and futhermore, he was not giving his own opinions merely, to the Roman Emperor, but the doctrines of Christians generally, at that time. Why did not Mr. Ballou furnish some extracts from Justin's First Apology, to show his readers what Christians believed respecting endless punishment, a day of judgment, the coming of Christ, &c., only fifty years from the death of St. John, and while Polycarp, the disciple of John, was still alive? He probably was not anxious for his readers to know these things.

Ignatius, who was acquainted with St. Peter and Paul, says of some, "*They shall not inherit the kingdom of God*," "*shall depart into unquenchable fire*."

Polycarp, a disciple of St. John, talks of Christ's coming to "*judge the quick and the dead*," of the "*eternal fire of God's judgment reserved for the wicked in the other world*."

Justin Martyr, who lived at the time of Polycarp, and had doubtless seen St. John, testifies abundantly, as we have seen, in favor of future judgment and endless punishment.

Hermas, about A.D. 150, or before, taught the possibility of such an apostasy as that there could be no return, that they might *depart from God forever*."

Tatian, (A.D. 170,) taught that there will be a "*resurrection and judgment at the end of the world*," that some will "*undergo death in immortality*."

The Epistle of the Churches of Lyons and Vienna, (A.D. 177,) says this of one: that she, "recollecting the *eternal punishment* in hell, reproved her tormentors."

Authenagoras, (A.D. 180,) teaches that "*at the day of judgment rewards and punishments will be distributed to mankind as they have done well or ill*."

Theophilus, (A.D. 181,) advises one to study the scriptures, that he might *shun eternal torments*."

Irenæus, (A.D. 180–190,) in giving the sentiments of all Christians, and stating that they were received from the apostles and their immediate disciples, asserts a *general resurrection and judgment*, when the wicked shall be sent into *everlasting fire*, and the righteous into *life and glory forever*."

Clemens Alexandrinus, (A.D. 190–196,) taught a future hell, and that the same means would be used there for the salvation of men that are used here. He was probably a Restorationist.

Tertullian, (A.D. 200–204,) taught a *future judgment and eternal punishment*."

Minucius Felix, (A.D. 210,) asserted the *eternity of hell torments*.

The reader may rest assured, that down to this period (A.D. 210) no Christian writer is known to have asserted that there will be no future judgment, or no future punishment; that our conduct here cannot affect our future state; or that by the resurrection all are to become holy and happy. Such sentiments were not known in the early days of Christianity. Mr. Ballou, in his history, has not attempted to show that one of the above named notions are to be found in any Christian writings down to this period; but says of them, (*Anc. Hist.*, p. 83,) "*That there was a future state of suffering they all agreed.*"

We should like, would space afford, to give large extracts from our former work; but a few statements upon which the reader can rely as the result of investigation must suffice.

Clemens Alexandrinus, already named, and Origen, (A.D. 230,) taught Restoration, obtaining it not from the Bible, but from the Platonic philosophy; and Origen propagated it by adopting the allegorical method with the scriptures.

After Origen, there is no declaration on the part of any Christian writer whose works have come down to us, that Universal Restoration was his belief, or the belief of others, until 134 years from the time Origen flourished; which was A.D. 230, or 111 years after his death, which took place A.D. 250. The writings of Titus, bishop of Bostra, A.D. 364, are the first named by Mr. Ballou as containing the doctrine, after Origen.

8. That although we find the doctrine in the writings of a very few men in the fourth century, yet it never was so extensively received as modern Universalists would have us believe; but that in addition to the 134 years from Origen to Titus of Bostra, there are at least two periods, one of 50 and another of 170 years, in which Mr. Ballou can produce no trace of the doctrine. Since the Reformation by Luther, some of the Anabaptists, Unitarians, and others, both in Europe and in this country, have held the doctrine of Universal Restoration, down to the present time; but they have always been few in number, compared with Evangelical Christians.

As it respects the sentiments, that man's conduct here cannot affect his future state, and that all will be rendered holy and happy by the resurrection, neither Mr. Ballou nor Mr. Whittemore has produced a single instance, showing that they were held by any professed Christian, from the time of St. John down to the commencement of the present century. It remained for men in the nineteenth century to produce these errors, and call them Christian doctrines.

Mr. Whittemore had access to the library of the Harvard University, which contains as large, if not the largest number of theological works, of any library in the United States. Doubtless Mr. Ballou had the same privilege with Mr. Whittemore, in the preparation of his work. How long Mr. Ballou's work was in preparation, we are not informed; but Mr. Whittemore has told us that he was upwards of five years in collecting materials for the Modern History, and that he steadily pursued his purpose, without regard either to labor or expense. None will doubt but what these men did the very best they could for Universalism, and for modern views in particular. Now with all their years of persevering labor and research, and with all the advantages of the extensive library in Cambridge, how many have they found professing to be, and received by the people as Christian ministers, who have had the boldness to openly avow and advocate the doctrine that all men will be saved, without any suffering beyond this mortal life? How many such men have they found among the thousands of ministers named on the pages of the Harvard College library, from the time of St. John down to the commencement of the present century? We answer, NOT ONE, according to their own showing! Samuel Richardson (*Mod. Hist.*, p. 71), was so far from boldly advocating the doctrine, that he kept himself behind the curtain, sending forth his work without his name, if indeed, he was the author of the work attributed to him. Some have thought he was not.

Mr. Whittemore occupies four pages and a half of his Modern History with an account of Richard Coppin, who lived about the middle of the sixteenth century. Well may he make much of him, for it is the *first* instance of which we have any account in history, of the public vindication of the doctrine of the salvation of all men, without any future suffering. He is named in none of the church histories before us, save Mr. Whittemore's. He appears to have been a reckless fanatic, very like the Come-outers of our day, and we have no account that he was ever recognized as a gospel minister by any body of professed Christians whatever.

The doctrine, that all men, irrespective of their character, or agency, shall be saved without any future sufferings, was openly avowed and advocated for the first time, by a man calling himself a Christian minister, about thirty-seven years ago. Hosea Ballou, the elder, was that man. Strange that the world should have been destitute of a true gospel minister so long!

Mr. Ballou advanced his scheme of no future punishment about 1818. There is one thing in this man's history worthy of remark. He states that during a reformation, he became interested in religion, and joined the Calvin Baptist Church, of which his father was the minister, in Jan. 1789, being then in his nineteenth year. He says of himself: "From that period to the present, I have been a constant student of the science of divinity."

The fall before he was twenty-one he commenced preaching Universalism. So it appears that he *studied about twenty-nine years, twenty-seven of which he was a preacher, before he found out that the Bible taught no future suffering!!* Surely this is slow work for a constant student of divinity, especially if Universalist sentiments are taught as clearly in the Bible as Mr. Whittemore would have us believe, when he says, (*Trumpet*, No. 646): "*We are not ashamed to boast, that of all the opinions in Christendom, ours grow the most naturally out of the sacred writings!!*" That Universalists had been very anxious to get rid of the doctrine of future judgment and punishment, is evident from the account given by Mr. Ballou himself, which is as follows, (*Fut. Retrib.*, p. 182) : "When I lived in Portsmouth, N. H., some fourteen or fifteen years ago, (about 1817 or 1818,) I was made exceeding glad, by discovering in my study on Heb. 9 : 27, 28, what I now believe to be the true application and use of the passage. I immediately communicated my thoughts on this text, and all accepted the exposition with approbation and delight."

About this time, Messrs. Turner and Ballou held a controversy in the Gospel Visitant, in order to satisfy themselves, in which, says Mr. B., "We agreed to do the best we could; he in favor of future punishment, and I the contrary."

"While attending to this correspondence, I became entirely satisfied that the scriptures begin and end the history of sin in flesh and blood; and that beyond this mortal existence, the Bible teaches no other sentient state but that which is called by the blessed name of life and immortality."

This account of Mr. Ballou's early life we find in the Modern History of Universalism, pp. 433–438.

CXXXIV. The less informed in the order are led to believe, by the glowing accounts in their papers, that Universalism is about to take the world by its rapid increase. Let us look at this idea in the light of facts. All things taken into the account, the progress of this error has not been very rapid in this country. By the statistics of the order for 1855, it appears that they number in the United States six hundred and forty-six ministers. How many members, we are not informed. To say nothing of the many evangelical denominations, besides the Methodists, that are increasing with great rapidity, and whose missionaries are belting the earth, let us take a comparative view of the Methodist and Universalist denominations. Although John Murray held scarcely any thing in common with modern Universalists, yet they proclaim him the father of Universalism in America. He landed upon our shores in 1770. Methodism commenced in America by the labors of Philip Embury, a local preacher in New York, in 1766, four years only before the arrival of Murray.

From the statistics of the Methodist Episcopal Church, for the same year with the Universalist statistics named, we find the following: Members, 755,916; traveling preachers, 4,474; local preachers, 6,061. The statistics for the M. E. Church South for the same year, stand thus: Members, 542,851; traveling preachers, 1,741; local preachers, 4,455. Taking these together, which, till a few years ago, were one denomination, we have a membership of 1,298,767, and a ministry, traveling and local, of 16,731.

We have not only the M. E. Church and the M. E. Church South, but there are the Protestant Methodists, the Wesleyans, and other smaller branches of the Methodist family in the United States, whose statistics are not at hand, all holding the same doctrines with the larger branches named. The ministry in all these, according to Dr. Baird, (Sec. CXXIX,) number 22,198. In the absence of a report of numbers we can only judge of the progress of Universalism by its ministry. By their own showing, there are now (1855) 646 in their ministry in the United States, of course not including the British Provinces. Take 646 from 22,198 and it will be seen that Methodism numbers *twenty-one thousand five hundred and fifty-two* more in its ministry than all the Universalist ministry in our land! By statistics, as reported in the Universalist almanacs, we see that in 1844 there were on the continent, including the United States, Canadas, New Brunswick, and Nova Scotia, 646 ministers, the same number they now report for the United States alone. In 1855, on the same territory, there are 651, being an increase of *five* in the Universalist ministry during eleven years!

We have not statistics at hand to show the increase of the Methodist ministry; but it is some thousands in the eleven years, for we find its increase in the two leading bodies the last year to be 783. That is, the increase of the ministry in the M. E. Church and the M. E. Church South the past year, is *one hundred and thirty-two more than all the Universalist ministry in North America!* Now, if the small increase of five ministers in eleven years indicates, as it doubtless does, the general state of the cause, we cannot conclude that Universalism is in a very prosperous condition.

Figures will show that on a comparative view the numbers are as one to thirty-four and a half. That is, for every Universalist minister there are thirty-four Methodist ministers, with fractions in our favor, in the United States. We are also without data to furnish the increase of the ministry in all the evangelical orders during the eleven years named; but have their present numbers (Sec. CXXIX) amounting to forty thousand, which gives for every Universalist minister, at least sixty-one evangelical ministers in the United States. Universalism has done great mischief in the world, and its progress has been considerable when contemplated by itself; yet when compared with the great increase of our population, and the progress of truth, it has been but little.

If Universalism did spread as rapidly as many of its votaries are induced to believe, it would not of itself be evidence of its truthfulness. Methodism has far outstripped it in numbers; but we should never think of contending that Methodism must be true solely on account of its rapid increase. If a doctrine spreads rapidly, and the reception of it has a transforming influence, changing the character and habits of wicked men into those of virtue and piety, we may safely conclude that it is of God, that it is true. But, where shall we look for such results from the spread of Universalism? We ask, where?

For the state of the cause in Maine, see Sec. CXXII.

CXXXV. Christians, because they cannot fellowship Universalists, are often charged with bigotry. We deny the charge and submit the following:

If evangelical Christians hold the fundamental truths of the Bible, then the doctrines which stand directly opposed to these must be infidel in their character. None, we think, will dispute this. That they do hold the truths of the Bible they firmly believe. The question we now propose, is this: Is the Universalist system antagonistical to the whole system of evangelical Christianity? Leading men in the order shall answer this. Mr. Williamson says:

"I have no disposition to conceal the fact, that there is a wide and irreconcilable difference between us and our opposers; nor can it be denied, that if we are right they are wrong; not merely in some points, but radically, and I had almost said totally wrong. This is a truth with which we are well acquainted; and that man pursues a mistaken policy, nay, even a wicked course of hypocrisy, who attempts to conceal this fact. There is no manner of use in endeavoring to make it appear, that there is but a shade of difference, between us and other denominations; for there is a difference, high as heaven, wide as the earth; a difference as hopelessly and utterly irreconciliable, as light and darkness; and there is no disguising the obvious truth, that if one system is true the other is false, desperately and hopelessly false, I had almost said, in its whole length and breadth." *Exp. and Def. of U.*, p. 215.

Such is the strong language of a distinguished Universalist minister, relative to the perfect opposition of the two systems. Mr. Grosh, another great man in the order, says: "Our faith, as of old, is opposed in every material part, that can effect the honor of God and the happiness of man, to the faith of the religious world." *Mag. and Advocate*, p. 349.

Abundance of similar testimonies are before us in their periodicals. We select the following from other leading men. In the Trumpet for Dec. 12, 1835, is an article on the "Tendency of Universalism," taken from the Gospel Banner, in which the following is found:

"The tendency of Universalism is, obviously, opposite to that of Partialism. They are clearly and plainly opposite sentiments; and, of course, must be opposite in their tendency and influence. If one of them is true, and productive of beneficial ɔ quences, the other is not; and vice versa. Both of them cannot be sustained by the word of God, if that word is itself worthy of credence; for 'a house divided against itself cannot stand.' If, therefore, the word of God is divided, and presents opposite and conflicting sentiments, it cannot sustain the test of critical examination, and should at once be abandoned."

This is doubtless from Mr. Drew, then editor of the Banner, as no correspondent is named.

Again: In the Banner of Nov. 2, 1844, is a sermon by J. Boyden, delivered before the United States General Convention of Universalists, in Baltimore, and in speaking of the opposing sentiments with which Universalism had contended, he says: "How difficult then to establish a doctrine so diametrically opposed to all the leading and long cherished opinions of the age!"

The Trumpet is before us for August 18, 1838, in which Mr. Whittemore quotes the following from Mr. Royce, who, in contrasting Universalist with Orthodox views, says:

"Universalism has 'a different God, a different Christ, a different spirit, a different sinner, a different sin, a different atonement, a different grace, a different pardon, a different salvation, a different resurrection, a different judgment, a different punishment, a different hell, and a different heaven — in fine, a difference with respect to all the essential doctrines of Christianity.'"

After quoting the above, Mr. Whittemore uses the following very emphatic language:

"*To this we give our assent.* Mr. Royce is *right.* We *confirm his words*, that Partialism is, in *every sense, a very different* doctrine from Universalism. *He cannot represent the difference to be too great.*"

Here it is contended, by these prominent men in the order, that their religious belief is in all respects entirely opposite to that of Christians in general; that the difference is "*as high as heaven, wide as the earth, and as hopelessly irreconcilable as light and darkness; that there is no disguising the obvious truth, that if one system is true the other is false, desperately and hopelessly false*; that Universalism "*is opposed in every material part to the faith of the religious world;*" that it is "*diametrically opposed to all the leading and long cherished opinions of the age;*" and of the two systems it is said: "*If one of them is true and productive of beneficial consequences, the other is not; and vice versa,*" and we "*cannot represent the difference to be too great.*"

The unqualified testimony here given, that Universalism is diametrically opposed to evangelical Christianity in every essential point, is correct; and we call the special attention of those professors of religion, who have been somewhat deceived by their goodly words and affected piety, as occasion may require, and are beginning to have a morbid sympathy for the system, to the statements of these leading advocates. With these facts before them, what view can enlightened Christians take of the system? They must either acknowledge their own system infidel in all its essential features, or else they must look upon Universalism as a system of infidelity, having assumed the Christian name to give it more force. This we conceive to be its true character.

By its own showing, the two systems are complete antipodes, and Mr. Drew, just quoted, says: "If one is true, and productive of beneficial consequences, the other is not; and vice versa."

Professing, as they do, to be a complete "*opposition concern,*" what shall we think of their oft repeated efforts to brand us with the character of bigots, because we cannot fellowship them as Christians? Do they really think that it would be an act of Christian liberality for others to fraternize with them, and thus endorse their religious character and sentiments? Might we not inquire, "What concord hath Christ with Belial? or what part hath he that believeth with an Infidel?" 2 Cor. 6:15.

Must we aid the incendiary in kindly the flames to burn the house over our own heads in order to be liberal? And are we to be accounted bigots because we cannot unite with this class of people in a religious capacity? In a *religious* capacity, we say, for we would live on terms of good neighborhood with them, as men and citizens. We would unite with them, the same as we would with other irreligious men, to rescue our fellow beings from temporal evils.

We would as readily seize hold with a Universalist minister to pull a man from the water or fire as any one else. But we can do nothing knowingly to endorse his sentiments, or to recognize him as a gospel minister. We cannot look upon him as one of Christ's ministers, or his gospel as Christ's gospel. We would love Universalists as those for whom the Saviour died, and do them good. We would deprive them of none of their rights. Yea, more, if their rights were in danger, we would aid them in securing them.

We, too, have rights. We claim the right of exemption from the charge of bigotry, because we cannot unite with those whose sole business is to destroy that which we consider more valuable than life itself. It is most conscientiously believed, that no enlightened Christian can unite with Universalists in a religious capacity, any more than he can with the disciples of Tom Paine. Is this bigotry? Then was the loving and beloved John a bigot. He says: "If there come any unto you, and bring not this doctrine, receive him not unto your house, neither bid him God speed. For he that biddeth him God speed is partaker of his evil deeds." 2 John 10, 11.

Surely the errors to which John refers could not have been more inimical to the gospel of Christ than are Universalist doctrines. It is only infidel liberality that makes God's truth of so little value, and glaring and poisonous error so harmless, that all who choose to call themselves Christians must be so considered, whatever the doctrines they may hold and teach. We believe no man can understandingly embrace Universalism, and be a Christian, any more than a man can understandingly embrace Mormonism, and still remain a Christian.

There may be some deluded persons who have been drawn among them unwittingly, who retain, for a while at least, something of their Christian character; but, as a general thing, they soon become imbued with the spirit of the order, which we conceive to be nothing less than a war with Jehovah's attributes and penalties. But is it right to class all in the denomination with Infidels? This we have not done. Many are with them who are not yet, neither do they mean to be Infidels, for they are not enlightened to see the true character of the system. But it would be a severe reflection upon the intellectual character of its leading advocates, were we to say the same of them; and we think no Christian man capable of tracing all their windings, and detecting their perversions of scripture, can sit down to their books without becoming established in the opinion, that their leading writers have no manner of faith in the Bible as a divine revelation, in the proper sense of that term, but are Infidels at heart, and have brought forth this system and baptized it with a Christian name, the more successfully to oppose vital godliness, and to make money by preaching and writing it.

That they use the Bible and profess a regard for the Christian faith, is well known. How they use the Bible has been shown in these pages; and as to the profession, that changes nothing. Theodore Parker, and his compeers in Infidelity, profess a high regard for pure Christianity.

Chubb, a noted Infidel, entitled one of his Infidel tracts, "*The True Gospel Asserted.*" Universalists preach and write some smart things against Infidelity, while its chief elements are found in their own system. (Sec. CXVIII.) In forming this estimate we look more particularly at what is denied concerning God the Father, Christ the Son, his nature and offices, the Holy Ghost and his work, and the condition and wants of man. We look at the treatment the Bible receives, and the baneful influence of the doctrines inculcated, (Sec. CXXXVII,) in producing irreligion, general skepticism, and nothingarianism.

Now what is the obvious duty of Christians in respect to this system of error? Let its votaries be treated with the same kindness that all other unconverted men are entitled to, but do nothing which shall seem to bid them God speed in their work. Build no meeting houses with them, neither open any for them to disseminate their doctrine. Yield to no expediency in this matter; it will always prove bad in the end. Some Christians, to please their friends, have occasionally accompanied them to Universalist meetings. The influence of this goes to confirm them in their errors.

If our friends have been deluded by the system, it is a weighty reason why we should give no countenance to it whatever. Let direction be sought of God, in the closet, and a Christian will seldom be found under the poisonous droppings of a Universalist sanctuary. A conscientious and strict disfellowship is demanded by the love we should bear for Universalists themselves, for a world lying in wickedness, and for "the church of God which he hath purchased with his own blood."

Napoleon's policy was to make those upon whom he made his aggressions pay the expenses of his wars. Universalists pursue a similar course of policy in getting up fairs, levees, and Sabbath School exhibitions, for which a fee of admittance is required, the object of which is to sustain Universalism. Some Christians are induced to attend, not fully realizing what they are doing, and thus they aid the enemy in his warfare against the armies of the living God. Christians, beware how you cast you influence and pay your money!

CXXXVI. Twenty-four years ago, Mr. Whittemore, after laboring to show that it availed nothing against modern Universalism for the opponents to refute the opinions of Origen, Relly, and Winchester, said, (*Trumpet, April* 1, 1831): "Universalists now know of no condition for man beyond the grave, but that in which he is as the angels of God in heaven."

Here no future punishment is declared to be a denominational sentiment. He has shown, too, in his Modern History of Universalism, pp. 439–441, that there were but few, comparatively, as early as 1829, among their preachers or people who believed in any future punishment whatever. But some have entertained the opinion that they are about to abandon the no future punishment scheme, and go back to Restorationism. What evidence is there of this? We are aware that there has been a little controversy through their papers concerning future punishment, pro and con. This, we conclude, is a kind of sham fight, the design of which is well understood by their leaders. We have known a few of their preachers, who were said to be believers in future punishment, but never heard of their preaching it. To make such a presentation occasionally may answer their proselyting ends, especially when it is desirable to bring about a marriage between the Universalist and Unitarian denominations in certain localities.

The sum and substance of the instruction imparted concerning the future is this: "Just what you desire the future state to be it shall be." Will their people desire punishment after death? Not they. If there is punishment after death, then in preaching it there must be appeals to their fears concerning it. Would their ministers be allowed to do this? We doubt if there is a Universalist congregation in our land that will tolerate the enforcement of future punishment by their minister. He may be permitted to hold it as a private opinion, but he must not preach it. After all, we conclude that this doctrine hangs rather loosely about those ministers in the order, who assert a belief in it. They fraternize with those who deny it, and appear perfectly at home with them.

To a mind unenlightened upon the subject, the doctrine of limited future punishment does not at first present so glaring an absurdity as no future punishment; and it is a fact that the most of those who apostatize from the truth, do not embrace the no future punishment scheme, at first, but believe in future punishment and restoration. To help forward this class, these preachers doubtless find it convenient to have a set of reserve doctrines, the public advocacy of which would not be tolerated by full grown Universalists.

Their first great labor is to prevail upon men to abandon endless punishment; this gained, they then, like the leaders of the French Atheism, initiate them into other degrees, and soon they reach the sublime climax of modern Universalism, namely: *Religion is designed only for this world; so far as the future is concerned, the saint and the sinner stand on a perfect level; all shall be made holy and happy by the resurrection.*

Some of the order, when hard pressed with the absurdity of no future punishment, have stated that the number of believers in future retribution is numerous in the denomination. If this is so, why are we not informed in what part of the Bible the doctrine is taught? Why is it not preached from their pulpits? Why is it not taught in their books? We have in possession a large number of books, sermons and tracts, from their ablest ministers, and in them all there is not a single effort to teach future rewards and punishments; but on the other hand the doctrine is uniformly combatted by these authors, and the future-state reference of those texts, which Restorationists formerly employed to teach future punishment, is denied. We called a short time since at the Universalist book store in Boston, and inquired if there was a book on sale in which future punishment is taught, or if any one in the denomination had issued such a book. The man in attendance said he knew of no such book issued among them. Their approved catechisms, used in their Sabbath Schools, do not teach it. They are before us by Balch, Bacon, Skinner, Adams, and S. R. Smith, not one of which even intimate that there is anything whatever to be dreaded by the sinner in the future world; but on the contrary, the last named author combats the doctrine. Now if the belief of future punishment is common in the order, why is it not found in their catechisms, designed to indoctrinate their children? And why from their pulpits do they not point out the scriptures and enforce the doctrine by them? Probably those who profess to believe it, hold it as a mere philosophical speculation, and are not over-anxious that it should have any practical effect, save to cover up one of the absurd features of Universalism, or to gain the favor of Unitarians.

A few years since, Mr. Drew, (*Banner, Nov.* 18, 1844,) speaking of some of his brethren in the ministry, who believed future punishment, says of them: "Their desire for the peace of the order has caused them to be more careful than some of different views have been, as to committing the order to their opinions."

That is, they have, very generally, said nothing about a future hell, to which they believed their fellow men exposed; but have been in closest union with, and have suffered their fellow travelers to eternity to be deceived by those who were teaching no future punishment, and that for the sake of "the peace of the order!" What shall we think of the honesty and benevolence of such teachers as fail to apprise men of such danger.

CXXXVII. All that modern Universalism professes to do for man is confined to this world. Its doctrines are productive of the purest morality. This is the profession. Does it accomplish what it professes? Pages might be filled with the testimony of such men as Charles Hudson, Adin Ballou, Dean, Todd, Whittaker, Smith, Bailey, Dow, Turner, and others, who have left the order and have given us the result of their observations concerning the baneful influence of the system, as put forth by Ballou and Whittemore.

Those ministers, who left them in 1831, calling themselves Restorationists, have presented the deleterious influence of modern Universalism from what they themselves had witnessed, in as deep colors as any anti-Universalist ever did. But for our present purpose we prefer to give statements from the pens of those who are now in fellowship with the order. Twenty years ago the editor of the Trumpet, in furnishing an account of his visit to the Maine Convention of Universalists, and of the resolves reported and passed by that body, says:

"*They declare the cause of Universalism worthy the support of men of piety and religious feelings; and recommend to the societies in Maine, that no man known to be addicted to the habits of drunkenness, or gambling, or profane swearing, or who is an unbeliever of Christianity, should be appointed to office in the societies.*" *Trumpet, July* 11, 1835.

From this we readily learn what class of men rallied for the support of Universalism at that time. Observe: There is nothing said in the resolution about private members, only the officers! This was passed *thirty-six* years after the organization of the Maine Convention. What shall we think of the sin-killing power of Universalism, when, at so late a period in its existence, it was found necessary to pass such a resolution?

A few years later, and we find Mr. W. C. George, a minister of the faith, writing as follows:

"There is, I fear, too much of disrelish among Universalists to practical preaching. Too many who call themselves Universalists, are glad to have our ministers hew our opponents in pieces, very much as Samuel did Agag, and to illustrate and defend the great doctrine of human salvation; but when he exhorts them to abandon bad habits, and to live good lives — when he preaches repentance and reformation, why *that* is very good, but then the orthodox are always harping about religion and morality; and *we* want the people to hear our doctrines." *Banner, March* 27, 1841.

If it is a self-evident fact, that those who love the practice of Christian morality do take pleasure in hearing it taught from the pulpit, what is the conclusion we are to draw from the statement of Mr. George?

A few years after this, Mr. J. George, of the State of New York, said by Mr. Drew to be one of their best ministers, writes as follows:

"I will notice a few particulars in the character of our denomination, which, for myself, in the light of the gospel, I can neither approve or countenance." The first thing Mr. G. names is, "A want of attention to the vital claims of religion upon the heart. It is a shameful truth, that this important demand of the gospel is almost entirely neglected in the denomination. Vital piety, a new heart, and a prayerful and holy life, as the first obligation of the New Testament, has but few advocates in the order."

Again, Mr. G. says: "There is among us a contentious, wrangling, controversial spirit, which is certainly uncalled for. There are multitudes professing a faith in Universalism, who seem to think that they have performed their duty religiously by a boisterous defence of their faith in controversy, and by giving their orthodox neighbors a severe and unmerciful castigation. There is a notorious lack of public spirit in the denomination. The missionary cause, and that of education is wofully disregarded and neglected, and the true catholic spirit is almost extinct among us. There is an unwillingness to make any sacrifice for the intellectual and spiritual improvement of others, and this is to be attributed to a want of *vitality*, of deep religious feeling and devotional spirit among us."

These extracts are taken from a June number of the Gospel Banner of 1819. This is not from an opponent, but a voluntary confession of a friend and minister of the order, who would be interested to represent the matter in the most favorable light. Yet such is the corruption and irreligion in the denomination, that he is obliged to speak out most truthfully. Mr. G. should become sensible of one more fact, namely: That these evil fruits are legitimate; that Universalism is a bad tree, and can never bear good fruit.

We see in the light of these facts why it is that Universalist papers have contained so much scurrility against Christian denominations, and why the editors of the order have seized with so much avidity upon the real or supposed defections in the ministry and membership of Christian churches, spreading them before the world to meet the cravings of their patrons. It is to pull others down on a level with themselves, in the public mind, that they do this. It answers as an apology for their own sins.

The vastly superior numbers in all the Christian denominations over their own, both in the ministry and membership, afford them great advantage in collecting this offal. Facts could be given, were it necessary, concerning not a few of their ministers, which, on a relative view, would place the order in no very enviable light.

A few figures will show that, on a comparative view of numbers, (Sec. CXXXIV,) for every individual case of immorality among them, there should be at least thirty-four among the Methodists to render it equal, and sixty-one in the ministry of the evangelical churches of the country. (Sec. CXXIX.) The same view may be taken of the respective memberships, only there is a far greater disparity in numbers here than in the ministry. A few years ago, some of the leaders in the order became quite zealous in church-forming, but the effort was looked upon with but little favor by the most of their people, and some of their ministers; for since all men are the dear children of God, why should such a division line be drawn between children of the same family? There was evidently too much Partialism in the idea for well instructed Universalists, and the thing has succeeded so poorly that they do not attempt to furnish the number of church members in their statistics.

A vast majority of the most zealous among them assume no church resposibilities; and when persons of this class commit deeds of wickedness, why then, forsooth, they were never Universalists! Christians, acting in accordance with the New Testament, form churches, extend their labors to the low and vicious, as well as the moral, seek their conversion to God, and when conversion is professed, gather them into churches, and strive to throw around them those influences which have a tendency to keep them in the narrow way which leads to heaven.

Thousands are thus saved to themselves, to their friends, and to the world, for usefulness. Among those thus gathered may be some hypocrites, perhaps Universalists at heart, (Sec. CXXVI,) or some may fall away and commit wicked deeds, and the churches be obliged to expel them, and what then? Why, such cases are taken up and published in Universalist papers as the fruit of Partialism!

Taking into the account their paucity of numbers, and the very few who assume church responsibilities, it will be seen that theirs is a mere Indian warfare with the armies of the living God. What a fine opportunity it would afford them to build up their people, not in holiness, but in hatred to others, if for every immoral minister among them, sixty-one such were found in other denominations. Others, when a defection occurs, bring the offender to trial and suspend or expel, if found guilty, and by this it becomes more extensively known, and soon finds its way into Universalist and Infidel papers. But Universalists are so *charitable* that some of their ministers, known to be guilty of immoral acts, continue to preach as though nothing had happened. To such an extent has this been carried, that even Mr. Drew, a few years ago, was compelled to utter his complaint as follows:

"We have seen too much of this false mercy — this real injustice — among Universalists. They have not dared to deal with their dishonest men, lest the public should find out that they had bad men amongst them!" *Banner, Jan.* 31, 1841. If Christians desired such food for a *spiritual* growth, and their ministers and editors were base enough to joyfully deal it out to them, a black list could easily be furnished, three to one in proportion, from the ranks of the Universalist ministry. Think of these facts, reader, when you chance to take up a Universalist paper, and see some doleful account of the "fruits of Partialism."

Modern Universalism has had its birth and being amid the largest religious freedom, and has used its license to the full extent, as the world knows. Its advocates have traveled, preached and printed at their will. With great zeal they have explained their doctrines, and caricatured evangelical sentiments. They have converted some to their views, and induced many to hate evangelical sentiments and operations, and yet with all these advantages we find the wretched state of things described by the writers we have quoted. The cause of this is told in a few words, namely: *Universalism is not of God.* Its motives are not those which God has furnished to move the heart to penitence and piety. Preaching the love of God to sinners, at the expense of other revealed truths, never did or can produce love to God in the heart. On the other hand it will produce irreligion as surely as a constant presentation of the harsher truths in the abstract will produce fanaticism. The world has witnessed an illustration of the former in Universalism, and of the latter in Millerism. It would have been well if the votaries of each of these delusions had heeded the words of Christ to the devil, where he says: "Man shall not live by bread alone, but by EVERY WORD that proceedeth out of the mouth of God." Matt. 4 : 4.

All the doctrines of revelation should have an influence upon the heart to give it a proper religious balance. It is not a presentation of the abstract idea that God is love, that produces love to God in the human heart. The sinner must first see his disease and danger, and with penitence and faith receive Christ as his Saviour; and then, and not till then, is the love of God produced in the heart; not by hearing that God is love, but by the Holy Ghost. Rom. 5 : 5.

But it may be asked, if Universalism is thus baneful in its influence, how is it that some respectable men are found in the denomination? We answer: That they are so upon the same principle that some, who openly profess Infidelity, are persons of many good qualities, in many respects good citizens, and kind neighbors. We are all aware that there are some such Infidels, yet no Christian thinks of attributing these good qualities of theirs to Infidelity, but they possess them in *spite* of Infidelity. Notwithstanding their hatred to Christianity, they are greatly indebted to it for its moulding and elevating influence upon their own character. If their birth and education had been in a heathen land, they would doubtless have been as debased as millions now are who possess minds naturally as good as their own. Now these respectable Universalists occupy the same position in respect to true Christianity. Many of them are children of praying parents, and all have had the advantages of a general Christian influence and instruction, and were the same respectable men, *before* they had any connection with Universalism, and some of them still retain this character, in spite of Universalism and their opposition to truth. This system had no agency in giving them this character. It is a fact, too, that not a few of this class are not aware of all the absurdities which must be believed, and all the truth which must be rejected, in order to be a consistent modern Universalist.

CXXXVIII. The bugbear of insanity and suicide caused, as they say, by the doctrine of endless punishment, is an important matter to be kept before their people by Universalist editors.

"The occasions of insanity are various as the numerous subjects which claim the attention of the mind. In most cases, the cause, near or remote, is in the constitution, *latent* until revealed by some casual circumstance, which imparts a sudden or unusual excitement to the mind. In very many instances, the direct occasion is known to be a hereditary pre-disposition to insanity, which is almost sure to show itself at a particular stage of mental development, under all circumstances. In general, any subject which attracts attention, and excites the mind beyond what is consistent with health of body or mind, tends to destroy the harmony of the mind and produce insanity. In some countries, cases of insanity are much more numerous than in others. Climate, diet, and customs, become inducing causes, by the influence they exert over physical and mental developments. The exciting cause of insanity, in a great majority of cases, are either of a business character, or arise from sudden and calamitous change, of one kind or another, in worldly circumstances or prospects. Recent investigations of this subject in Paris confirm these remarks, and so does the last report from our own State (New York) Asylum. Out of sixteen hundred and nine cases, only one hundred and fifty-two are put down as occasioned by 'religious anxiety,' leaving fifteen hundred and fifty-seven to be referred to other causes. Out of fifty professional men affected with insanity, only eight were clergymen. That religious anxiety does in some cases lead to insanity, I have no disposition to deny; but this fact is no argument against the causes of this anxiety. To suppose it is, would compel us to condemn all mental discipline, and all business transactions, because the anxieties and perplexities connected with such persuits, are sometimes inducing causes of insanity. Moreover, I wish you to mark and remember, that for every *single* case of insanity produced by those religious feelings which arise out of evangelical views of Christianity, we may safely calculate upon the preservation of *two* from that affliction, by the salutary and conservative influence of that same religion. By far the greater amount of insanity is among the irreligious and depraved. In so far as they are brought under the influence and power of evangelical religion, are they reformed and preserved from those habits of dissipation, and acts of dishonesty and wild speculations in business, which lead to so many catastrophies, and become the inducing cause of insanity. This subject is beginning to be understood by those who have charge of the insane, who are recommending the exercises and motives of religion, as a means of restoration. The Christian religion is founded on the revealed character of an infinite God, and is therefore adapted and intended to call into exercise the highest powers of the human mind. A religion incapable of interesting the mind, or exciting it to an extent that might, under some circumstances, induce insanity, would, in my humble judgment, be unworthy the attention of intelligent beings." *Rev. D. Holmes.*

But how does it happen that so many who have been deluded by the spirit rappers, become insane and commit some most horrid suicides, when they are assured by the good Universalist and Infidel managers, that the spirits declare that there is no hell? Surely, endless punishment is not the cause of this. Why do Universalists become insane, and why do they commit suicide? Why did A. V. Bassett, a Universalist minister in Dedham, Mass., commit suicide by cutting his throat a few years since? Was Partialism the cause? Why did young Crawford hang himself in the jail at Lowell? Was Partialism the cause of this? Did he believe that an endless hell awaited him in the future? No man with such a belief, possessing as sane a mind as the letters left by Crawford evinced, could have committed suicide. This act was a most cool and deliberate one. We learn from an article published in a Lowell paper at the time, that Crawford had been educated a Universalist, that his parents were of that faith, and that his father was very zealous in the cause. Crawford had connected himself with a gang of counterfeiters, was detected in the business, and confined in jail to await his trial, which would have taken place in June, 1840. Knowing the evidence of his guilt was such that he could not escape the state prison, he resolved on committing suicide. He wrote one letter to a man respecting his business, and another to his mother, assigning the reason for committing the fatal deed, as follows:

"He had got into trouble — and trouble for life — and he thought he would get out of trouble the shortest way." "He bade his friends farewell till they should meet in an unknown world, where parting was not known."

Now, as horrid as it is, we contend that Crawford reasoned like a philosopher, and acted a most consistent part, believing as he did. Why, we ask, should a man suffer in the state prison, and then the ignominy and disgrace all his life of having been there, when heavenly bliss is so near him, that a piece of rope, the razor, or the pistol, will give him a sure transition thither in a few moments? Young Crawford showed that he possessed no slavish fear of his Heavenly Father. He evinced, too, his faith by his works, and this act calls loudly upon those who are of like faith to go and do likewise, and take as many more with them as possible, especially if they are in trouble, and thus show their philanthropy and benevolence.

A few years since a Baptist minister, in Maine, was deluded into a belief of Universalism, and on a day he gave his reasons for renouncing his former belief and embracing his new opinions. This was a great day with the Universalists in that region, and they listened to his story most joyfully. But a short time elapsed, however, before the poor man, availing himself of the privilege of a Universalist, committed suicide by hanging, and thus evinced his faith by his works. A minister of the right stamp for such an occasion was employed for the funeral, and the audience listened to the stale perversion of, "For he that is dead is freed from sin." Rom. 6:7. (Sec. VI.)

Is it said that the man was insane? This act is not to be taken as evidence of it, if Universalism is true. Is it not rational to escape all evil, and secure the greatest amount of permanent good possible? Does not the suicide do this, if Universalism is the truth? Most certainly he does. Is it still contended that he was insane? But how could that have been, when he so firmly believed Universalism? Does Universalism produce insanity? The leaders in the order would do well to be looking into this. This case occurred in Harmony, Maine. For the sake of surviving friends we would say nothing of such cases, were it not to show that modern Universalism, when sincerely embraced, leads directly to suicide, especially when earthly hopes are blasted or comforts destroyed.

The editors in the order are cruelly reckless of the feelings of friends, when they can in any way turn a suicide against future punishment. They iterate and reiterate such cases with all the recklessness of misanthropes. Were other editors equally reckless, they could present an astonishing array of suicides commited by those who had no fear of the future.

The effects of removing all fear from the minds of wicked men, respecting the future, is strikingly illustrated by the French people. We are told by a French writer in the New York Observer, that "it is estimated that there are in France at least three or four thousand suicides a year."

Is it a belief in endless punishment which causes so much suicide among the French? No; for they are as strong in their hatred to this doctrine as American Universalists are. The writer tells us the cause is their belief in Materialism, by which all fear of future retribution is removed. A great portion of the French people look upon man as a machine — to run for a while; and that death is an eternal sleep. The thought of suicide enters into their business calculations, and misfortune in speculation, a little trouble or disgrace, carries them out of the world by their own hands. He gives the case of a comedian, who killed himself because he heard a hiss. To illustrate this position, he presents the following respecting a murderer:

"We have seen the same doctrine advanced before the courts, by an assassin, who was a man of some education. This wretch, named *Lacenaire*, gravely told the court that he had made a sort of *algebraic equation* between the advantages and the dangers of crime. 'I knew well,' said he, 'that by killing others I exposed myself to perish on the scaffold. But what is the punishment of the scaffold? It is a momentary pain, and then comes annihilation. I foresaw what has overtaken me; but meanwhile I have enjoyed the fruit of my assassinations, and I persist in maintaining that I made a good calculation. Since I have fallen into your hands, condemn me, and cut off my head; you are my enemies and I am yours; we shall be even. I do not at all regret having killed several persons to seize what belonged to them; I would do it again if I could.' Thus spoke Lacenaire at his famous trial."

Ungodly men love the doctrine of annihilation in proportion to their love of sin, and as they become wretched by it. It is the good man who can appreciate the value of the soul, and the joys of heaven, who shudders at the idea of annihilation. Now we ask, is there not as much in American Universalism to divest the worst of men of all fear of the future, as there is in French Materialism? Suppose we substitute for these views, so common in France, the idea that unspeakable and eternal bliss awaits every man in the future, irrespective of character in this world, could we expect suicides would be any less frequent among them? The reader can judge.

After all the hatred to evangelical doctrines, and clamor for Universalism, we conclude that there are but few to be found among them who have not their fears, in their thoughtful moments, that punishment awaits the sinner beyond the grave, and that the church, generally, may have been right for eighteen hundred years past, while they have been mistaken. In this way, and this only, can we account for the great desire of life on the part of Universalists, even though some of them are extremely wretched here.

The Christian believes that deliberate suicide would shut his soul out of heaven, and consign it to unutterable woe; and under its influence he never would commit the deed. But Universalism teaches that there is nothing for any to fear beyond this life; that the man who puts an end to his own life, or dies in the act of taking the life of another, shall be immediately crowned with Paul, and enter into bliss; for it says that there is no condition for man in the future, but that in which he will be as the angels of God in heaven. (Sec. CXXXVI.)

One thought more. Such is the disparity of numbers, that for every Universalist minister that becomes insane, there should be at least sixty-one believers in future punishment afflicted in the same way, to make it equal; and so with suicides. What a shout would ring through the Universalist camp, if sixty-one evangelical ministers were to commit suicide on the same day; but this would be no more in proportion than for one Universalist minister to die by his own hands on that day. (Sec. CXXIX.) If there is any argument in the simple fact that believers in future punishment sometimes become insane or commit suicide, that argument lies with equal force against Universalism, since some of its votaries are found in the same condition, and do the same thing. Religious men sometimes become insane, when their religion has nothing to do with producing it, as every well informed man knows.

CXXXIX. Much has been written by Universalists to show that endless punishment cannot be reconciled with the love of God, and much has been written by Atheists to prove that present evil is inconsistent with the idea of an infinitely perfect Being; and the arguments of the last named class are of equal force with those of the first. It by no means follows that because some things appear to us unreasonable, that therefore they are so in themselves or in their relations. Tell a savage of the wonders of the magnetic telegraph, and left simply to his reason he would exclaim, I cannot believe it; for it is unreasonable. But let him become assured of the superior information and strict veracity of his informer, and relying upon his word, he would believe the fact, although his reason could not compass the manner of its existence, or its mode of operations. This faintly illustrates the relation of man's reason to the revelation and ways of God. We say faintly, for while there is a vast difference between an enlightened mind and the mind of a savage, there is, between the greatest mind of man and the mind of the All-wise God, an infinitely greater disparity; hence, what may appear perfectly reasonable to his mind, may appear unreasonable to man. Reason is to be employed in religion to learn what God has revealed, and not to dictate what God must reveal. The sincere believer in the Bible relies upon the superior knowledge and strict veracity of its Author, and therefore admits the existence of facts, when revealed, the mode and relations of which he cannot fully understand. Some things may be far beyond human reason, but not contrary to right reason. God has endued man with only a portion of that reason which he possesses in absolute perfection. The great fault with Universalists is, that while they have professed deference for the Bible, they have ever practised upon Rationalistic principles. (Sec. XCVIII, CXVIII.) They first assume what is reasonable, according to their limited conception of things, in the government of God, and then, not to be considered infidels outright, they bring the Bible twisted into all manner of shapes, to sustain their theories. We believe that endless punishment harmonizes with the love of God, because they are both revealed; and the believer in the Bible need go no further. We believe, also, that sin and present misery harmonize with the love of God. But had we no knowledge of their existence, we could never, by reasoning from the attributes of God, come to the conclusion that they do exist; much less could we harmonize their existence with the love of God. The Bible reveals the love of God, and matter of fact teaches us the sad lesson that human misery is widely extended. To say that this vast amount of human suffering is to secure a greater amount of good to man in the end, does not help the matter, as may be seen Sec. CIV. and CXIV.

CXL. A striking evidence of the antagonism of Universalism to the Bible, is seen in the frequent explanations its advocates are obliged to give of numerous portions of scripture, to keep their people in anything like a believing trim. Common sense often rebels, and the text explained does not remain explained. No class of men are called upon for explanations of scripture so often, according to their own account, as Universalist ministers and editors. It is quite amusing to look over files of the Trumpet, in our possession, for eleven years, and see how often the same text is explained. Some member of a Christian church desires to become a Universalist if he can, and a text must be cleared away for his benefit; or some disciple is in doubt, and something must be done for him; or some believer in eternal punishment has sent a poser to the editor, and that must be attended to. This affords Mr. Whittemore, with some show of reason, an opportunity of publishing his stale stereotyped arguments and perversions again and again. No ministers have so many texts selected for them — none meet with so many inquirers after *truth*. A minister receives a request through the post office; it may be written by himself, to give his views of a certain scripture; and who can blame him now, if he lets go a whole broadside against the Partialists! Who can blame him if he gives the old rigmarole upon *Sheol, Hades,* and *Gehenna?* That some of these letters are written upon the editor's table or in the minister's study, we have no reason to doubt, for priestcraft is not confined to the Romish clergy; but that they have many inquirers who find it impossible to harmonize the views they cherish with the Bible, is also true. It is this difficulty with the Bible, which brings forth such a great amount of doctrinal matter in their periodicals and books. You can seldom take up a number of some of their leading papers, without finding in it a doctrinal essay or sermon, to say nothing of other baseless arguments and clap-trap paragraphs, thrown in by the editor and others. Then look at the great number of their doctrinal books. In proportion to their numbers, they have doubtless ten times more doctrinal matter afloat than any evangelical denomination in our country. Evangelical Christians are not under the necessity of constantly repeating their arguments in proof of their doctrine, or in opposition to Universalism; neither are their editors often catechized concerning troublesome texts. Now why is this? Is it because their people do not study the Bible, or are indifferent to what it teaches? By no means. It is because they confide in the Bible, having no doubt concerning the meaning of those passages used to sustain their doctrine. This great labor of Universalists to prove their doctrines, reminds us of a boy we knew when at school, who was a notorious liar, and seemed to feel obliged to repeat a statement several times, with great vehemence, in order to be believed. Indeed, such is the vast labor required to make Universalism even plausible from the scriptures, that its advocates can find time for but little else save to prove their doctrine, and help the numerous doubting ones.

CXLI. The advocates of Universalism boast much of the superior moral influence of their system, because of the better view it presents of God; and it is assumed that our views of God's penalties are productive of revenge, cruelty, and bloodshed among men; for, say they, if God punishes when it is not for the good of the sufferer, then it is right for man to do the same, as he is certainly at liberty to imitate his God; or, in other words, man may treat an offending fellow man, as God treats an offending creature of his. Now here is a great fallacy, put forth and elaborated by the whole tribe of Universalist advocates, in some form or other. The truth is, we are not at liberty to even attempt to imitate God in everything, for we are to learn our duty, as dependent creatures, not so much from what God *does* as from what he *says*. The fallacy of this argument is seen in the fact that the Supreme does not stand in the same relation to man that one mortal stands in to another; and as the relation differs, so must the conduct differ. God has given us a written revelation to guide us. This points out most clearly our duty to God and man; and if some men have taken vengeance into their own hands with the idea that they have a right to imitate God, it is no proof that the idea of vengeance in the divine administration is false, but only shows that such have mistaken their rule of duty. God demands, and has a right so to do, that his creatures worship him; but has any man a right, in imitation of God, to claim worship from his fellow men? Certainly not. Man-worship has obtained in the Romish Church; but is this to be brought as argument against the doctrine that God is to be worshipped? As well might Universalists do this as to urge the cruelties of wicked men against endless punishment. It will not be contended that the French Atheists were under the influence of this doctrine, for they hated it as ardently as our Universalists do; but the world has witnessed their fierce cruelty and bloodshed, and thousands who clamor against endless punishment in our time, have hearts no better than theirs. The origin of cruelty is found in the depraved nature of man; and under certain circumstances, whatever his doctrinal views, he will be heartless and cruel. The love of God shed abroad in his heart, by the Holy Ghost, can remove the difficulty. But the heart can never be improved by cherishing a hatred to God's penalties. Cruelty and persecution, it is said, grow legitimately out of the doctrine of endless punishment, because men will imitate their God. This is precisely the argument of the French Atheists against the being of a God. He is the Sovereign of the universe. All the sovereignties of the earth grow out of the idea of a sovereign above, and as nature teaches equality, the idea of a king above must be banished from the minds of the people, before earthly thrones can be destroyed. This was their argument, and it is just as forcible against the sovereignty of God as the Universalist argument we are considering is against endless punishment. We are not prepared, however, to deny the doctrine of divine sovereignty, because there is king-craft upon earth.

The scriptures speak of God's executing vengeance, which is the opposite of good. Take the following: "Dearly beloved, avenge not yourselves, but rather give place unto wrath: for it is written, Vengeance is mine; I will repay, saith the Lord. Therefore if thine enemy hunger, feed him; if he thirst, give him drink; for in so doing thou shalt heap coals of fire upon his head. Be not overcome of evil, but overcome evil with good." Rom. 12:19–21. Here man is prohibited the right of taking vengeance on an enemy, and the reason assigned is, that it is God's prerogative. God executes vengeance; but as man does not hold the same relation to his fellow man that God holds to man, as his lawgiver and Judge, he may not imitate God in avenging himself. Man must seek to overcome evil with good; but God, instead of overcoming evil with good, will execute vengeance; and thus we see that vengeance in the passage stands opposed to good, for, "*Vengeance is mine, I will repay, saith the Lord.*" In the light of this, we see the sophistry of that question so often and artfully put by Universalists, namely: "If God requires us to overcome evil with good, will he not do the same for all his creatures?" Is it said that the term vengeance is not to be understood in a harsh sense, but in the sense of a disciplinary punishment for the good of the sufferer? This view reduces the text to a senseless mass of contradiction. It makes the apostle say, "Dearly beloved, do no good unto your enemies; for it is written, good is mine, I will do them good, saith the Lord; therefore, my brethren, overcome evil with good." Attach the sense to "vengeance" that Universalists do, and all must see that this is a correct paraphrase, as absurd as it is. We see that the term must be understood as expressing a positive evil in opposition to good.

Did space admit, it might be shown that the severe punishments recorded in the Bible, such as those upon the Sodomites and others, are liable to the same objection we have been considering; for were these acts of God extensively imitated by his creatures, great cruelty must be the result. Not that God was cruel in destroying the Sodomites, but it would be cruel in men to burn their fellow men with fire and brimstone, because they are not at liberty to imitate God in such a work, for reasons already given.

GENERAL INDEX.

GENERAL INDEX.

SCRIPTURE INDEX.

SCRIPTURE INDEX.

www.ingramcontent.com/pod-product-compliance
Lightning Source LLC
LaVergne TN
LVHW011156110826
845150LV00006B/1236
9781425545642